The Al Qaeda Factor

The Al Qaeda Factor

Plots Against the West

Mitchell D. Silber

PENN

UNIVERSITY OF PENNSYLVANIA PRESS

PHILADELPHIA

Published by
University of Pennsylvania Press
Philadelphia, Pennsylvania 19104–4112
www.upenn.edu/pennpress

Printed in the United States of America on acid-free paper

10 9 8 7 6 5 4 3 2 1

Library of Congress Cataloging-in-Publication Data
Silber, Mitchell D.
    The Al Qaeda factor : plots against the West / Mitchell D. Silber. — 1st ed.
        p.   cm.
    Includes bibliographical references and index.
    ISBN 978-0-8122-4402-1 (hardcover : alk. paper)
    1. Terrorism—United States—Case studies.   2. Terrorism—Europe—Case studies.   3. Qaida (Organization).   I. Title.
HV6431.S474 2012
363.325094—dc23
                                                                2011031901

Contents

Part III. Al Qaeda "Inspired" Plots

Introduction

To What Extent Is Al Qaeda Involved in "Al Qaeda" Plots?

The horrific and devastating nature of the attacks of September 11, 2001, changed the world's perception of al Qaeda. What had been considered a small band of revolutionary terrorists with a capability limited to attacking Western targets in the Middle East and Africa was now something very different. Suddenly the group's threat profile changed drastically and the perception of al Qaeda's capabilities, strength, and ability to project force was boosted to an entirely new level.

Subsequent plots against the West perpetuated this new perception of al Qaeda as an organization that spanned the globe and had a thought-out and precise strategy to defeat the West. In a classic case of mirror imaging—imagining the enemy's characteristics to reflect your own characteristics—the perception grew that al Qaeda was highly organized and rigidly centralized and had deployed recruiters, operatives, and sleeper cells to the West who could be activated on command. These "al Qaeda agents" were also supposedly able to spot recruits, send them to Afghanistan or Pakistan for training, and then launch them back toward the West under precise command and control of al Qaeda central to carry out plots that would fulfill the organization's strategic aims. More than ten years after September 11, 2001, we now know this to be untrue.

Instead, we now know that the role of al Qaeda Core in "global jihadist plots" against the West has varied significantly over time and not all of what have been generally termed "al Qaeda plots" have had equivalent involvement by al Qaeda. This prompted the question that drives this study: How much is al Qaeda (what I call al Qaeda Core) involved in "al Qaeda plots"? Or, what is the "al Qaeda factor" in plots against the West?

This is a fundamental question. If we are to truly understand the nature of the threat posed by the transnational jihad, led in the vanguard by al Qaeda, we must have a greater and more nuanced understanding of the genesis and attempted execution of plots directed against the West (Europe, North America, and Australia). Al Qaeda Core's role should not be overestimated or underestimated, as important resource allocation questions for Western governments derive from the answer to these questions. It affects military, intelligence, and policing activities that are dedicated to preventing the next attack. In a sense, determining "where the action is for the conspiracy" before a plot is launched should drive Western counterterrorism efforts. In military terms, this would be akin to identifying what the Prussian military theorist Carl von Clausewitz called the "center of gravity," or critical element of strength of al Qaeda plots, in order to provide insights on how to thwart them. To date, not enough attention has been focused on this issue.

The importance in assessing the role of al Qaeda Core in plots against the West has been even further magnified with the death this year of al Qaeda's founder and leader, Osama bin Laden. An organization that relied on its top leader for strategy, operational direction, and command and control of its actions abroad will certainly be weakened and less threatening with his demise. However, an organization that had decentralized its operations (whether by design or as a survival mechanism) will continue to pose a threat through its remnants, affiliates, and allies, as well as those whom its message can inspire to action.

What are the criteria by which one will assess the "al Qaeda factor" in any plot? Are there standards or benchmarks for these issues?

The following questions frame the issue.

Was there any al Qaeda role in the formation of the extremist Muslim social networks or "scenes" in Hamburg, Madrid, London, New York, Sydney, Toronto, and other cities that constituted the pool of future conspirators? Did al Qaeda create this pool of recruits through direct efforts—sending emissaries abroad—or, more passively, through the spread of its ideology or through the creation of a heroic narrative that inspires individuals? What was the role of the "al Qaeda preachers" in the West?

In what local context did young men, seeking political and religious answers and who were from varied demographic and economic strata in London, Madrid, Amsterdam, New York, and other major Western cities, begin to adopt al Qaeda's ideology and radicalize? How did the adoption of reactionary interpretations of Islam or the politicization of beliefs radicalize and ultimately mobilize individuals to action?

Was there any al Qaeda role in the formation of the breakaway clusters of men that in many cases formed the embryonic active core of conspirators? Where did the ideologues for these clusters come from? Were they connected to al Qaeda, or were they part of the indigenous local "scene"?

Was there any al Qaeda role in the allocation of responsibilities among the conspirators in the cluster? Was it outside guidance from al Qaeda or organic development that determined who would be in the active core of the conspiracy, who would be a follower, and who would be on the periphery of the plot? What roles did people acquire?

How did these individuals from the cluster link up with al Qaeda? Did a worldwide network of al Qaeda recruiters spot promising recruits and direct them to al Qaeda camps in Afghanistan and Pakistan, or did individuals take the initiative and seek out al Qaeda to carry out their jihadist ambitions? Were there al Qaeda facilitators in certain cities? What was their role and who were they? What role did travel to a "zone of conflict" play?

What type of training did these individuals receive overseas? What skills were acquired? Who provided the training—al Qaeda or another entity? How has this changed over time?

What was al Qaeda's role in the launch of the plot? Just because an individual attended a training camp run by al Qaeda or one of its jihadist allies does not mean that the operation that he subsequently was involved in was suggested or endorsed by al Qaeda. Was the plot "commanded and controlled" by al Qaeda, directed by al Qaeda, or simply inspired by al Qaeda and carried out by an autonomous homegrown group?

Three possible categories for assessing the level of the al Qaeda factor in "al Qaeda plots" can be characterized as follows.

Al Qaeda "Command and Control"

Individuals from the West who traveled to Afghanistan or Pakistan met with someone of rank within in al Qaeda, or their representative, and were given a specific mission to carry out an attack in the West, which was "conceptualized" by al Qaeda Core. The Westerners were provided with specific guidance on means, timing, and targets, although some field control was left to the conspirators. Once the individuals returned to the West, ongoing communication with al Qaeda Core took place though a chain of command that included a "link man," who served as a relay station between the plotters and al Qaeda's Chief of External Operations.

Al Qaeda "Suggested/Endorsed"

Individuals from the West who radicalized in the West and then traveled to Afghanistan or Pakistan, seeking training or to fight in Afghanistan, met someone of rank within al Qaeda, or its representative, and were provided with the suggestion and/or endorsement to carry out some type of attack in the West on behalf of al Qaeda. Other than the city (usually where they were from), the Westerners were not provided with any specific guidance on means, timing, and targets—that was left to the conspirators. Only the idea of carrying out the attack in the West was "conceptualized" by al Qaeda Core. The initiative to carry out the mission resided among the active core of the cluster. Once the individuals returned to the West, there was minimal ongoing communication with al Qaeda Core. In some cases, the conspirators contacted their al Qaeda "link men" for clarification, for example, on how to build an improvised explosive device.

Al Qaeda Inspired

Individuals from the West may or may not have traveled to Afghanistan or Pakistan, and if they did, they may have met with someone of rank within al Qaeda or its representative. However, they were not directed, nor did they receive a suggestion to carry out some type of attack in the West. Rather, members of the cluster took the initiative based on their desire to act on behalf of al Qaeda's ideological and strategic goals to carry out an attack on the West. Al Qaeda Core likely did not know of such a cluster's existence.

Did al Qaeda's Chief of External Operations or an al Qaeda member of similar rank play a role in the plot? For plots that are either al Qaeda "command and control" or "suggested/endorsed," the fulcrum on which these plots, directed at the West, pivot is usually the individual commonly referred to as al Qaeda's Chief of External Operations. Considered the most important position in al Qaeda after Osama bin Laden and Ayman al Zawahiri, there have been since 2001 as many as seven individuals who have held this post in al Qaeda, all of whom have been subsequently caught, killed, or died of natural causes. They include the following: Mohammed Atef (killed in airstrike 2001), Khalid Sheikh Mohammed (caught 2003), Abu Faraj al Libi (caught 2005), Hamza Rabia (killed by drone strike 2005), Muhsin Musa Matwali Atwa, alias Abu Abd al Rahman al Muhajir (killed in April 2006), Abu Ubaidah al Masri (died 2007 from Hepatitis C), Saleh al Somali (killed by drone strike December 2009), and Sheikh Sa'id al Masri (killed by drone strike May 2010). What role did this person have, if any, in the plot?

Was there an al Qaeda "link man"? If so, what was his role? For plots that were al Qaeda "command and control" and even some that were "suggested/ endorsed," there often was a person who played the role of intermediary between the conspirators (once they returned to the West) and al Qaeda's Chief of External Operations. This individual, who was a relay station for communications, served as a layer of protection or buffer between the conspirators and al Qaeda, the organization. This individual would also both issue orders to the operational team in the West and receive status reports from them to relay back to al Qaeda leadership.

What was al Qaeda's role in the operational cycle? Did the group choose the target, direct casing of the target, provide the logistics to deliver the attack, communicate with the conspirators, or assist in the acquiring and/or building weapons to carry out their operation?

The Cases Studied

The preceding set of questions was applied to a sample set of what could be argued were the most important al Qaeda and al Qaeda–like plots against targets in the West between 1993 and 2009 in order to draw conclusions about the role of al Qaeda in "al Qaeda plots." For geographic diversity and to test for consistency, sixteen plots were chosen from Europe, North America, and Australia. Moreover, to test the hypothesis that this phenomenon had resonance over a long time, the cases cover a sixteen-year period. The following cases studied are, in chronological order:

- The 1993 attack on the World Trade Center in New York City
- The 1999 Millennium plot targeting Los Angeles International Airport

- The 9/11 attacks on the World Trade Center in New York City, the Pentagon in Virginia, and targeting the Capitol in Washington, D.C.
- The 2001 "Shoe Bomber" plot targeting a flight from Paris to Miami
- The 2004 March 11 attack on the Madrid Metro system
- The 2004 Operation Crevice plot targeting a shopping mall or nightclub in London
- The 2004 Operation Rhyme plot targeting hotels in London
- The 2004 November 2 assassination of Theo van Gogh and associated plots by the Hofstad Group
- The 2005 Operation Theseus July 7 attack on the London Underground and bus system
- The 2005 Operation Vivace July 21 plot targeting the London Underground and bus system
- The 2005 Operation Pendennis plot targeting a championship rugby game in Melbourne, Australia
- The 2006 Operation Osage plot targeting government buildings, the Toronto Stock Exchange, and a military base in Toronto
- The 2006 Operation Overt plot targeting transatlantic airliners from the United Kingdom to North America
- The 2007 Operation Dagger plot with undetermined targets in Copenhagen
- The 2009 Operation Highrise plot targeting the New York City subway system

In Chapter 16, I examine the 2002 Lackawanna Cluster, which did not involve an actual plot but serves as a point of comparison to the other plots.

Sources of Data

In the research for this book I drew on three different types of source information, recognizing that each has its strengths and weakness. These were legal documents, self-reports, and media reporting.

Legal documents included discovery material presented at trial; trial transcripts when they were available (many countries do not automatically transcribe their court proceedings); notes from such trials when available; and judgments justifying sentences when available. However, not all evidence is presented at trial and this varies from country to country, according to what is viewed as admissible evidence.

A second source of data were terrorist self-reports, either in captured documentary form or deliberately broadcast, and in the form of interviews or court testimony. Certain caveats are associated with this type of data as it often deteriorates into self-aggrandizing propaganda or self-exculpatory statements in court. Furthermore, such retrospective accounts by the terrorists themselves suffer from biased recollections uttered in a specific context, which may not truly reflect what actually took place historically.

The third source of data, media reporting, is a complicated source because often original speculations published shortly after the discovery of a plot have erroneous "facts" that are not eliminated and are carried over into later accounts. This research project used a process of cross-checking media accounts with the other independent sources of data and with later developments in the respective investigations to provide the basis for a higher level of reliability of media reporting.

*   *   *

Sixteen of the most important al Qaeda plots since 1993 have been dissected in the chapters that follow in this precise manner to assess just how much al Qaeda has been involved in "al Qaeda" plots. The dissections themselves as well as the conclusions have important implications for Western police, security, and intelligence services if we are to prevent future terrorist plots and attacks.

PART I

Al Qaeda "Command and Control" Plots

Chapter 1

9/11 (New York, Washington, D.C., and Shanksville, Pennsylvania, 2001)

ON THE MORNING of September 11, 2001, nineteen terrorists, directed by al Qaeda, hijacked four commercial passenger jet airliners. Each team of hijackers included a trained pilot. The hijackers intentionally crashed two of the airliners into the World Trade Center in New York City, resulting in the collapse of both buildings soon afterward and irreparable damage to nearby buildings. The hijackers crashed a third plane into the Pentagon near Washington, D.C. Passengers and members of the flight crew on the fourth aircraft attempted to retake control of their plane from the hijackers; that plane crashed into a field near the town of Shanksville in rural Somerset County, Pennsylvania.

The active core of the cluster of individuals responsible for carrying out the September 11 attacks was radicalized in the West, in Hamburg, Germany. This background construct has been obscured because the plot was hatched in Afghanistan, consisted of the fusion of a Westernized group (from Hamburg) with a Saudi "muscle" group, and was directed against the United States. A variety of other factors in this plot have subsequently reappeared in many of the other major al Qaeda–linked plots targeting the West.

The Hamburg Expatriate Student Scene

The Arab community in the 1990s in Hamburg was relatively small. Consequently, among more fundamentalist elements of the community, almost everyone knew everyone. The younger, more Salafi-inclined individuals, ranging in age from sixteen to thirty, were not in one static group but were distributed among numerous informal and amorphous clusters.[1]

One member of that community, Mohammed Atta, chose to worship at al Quds Mosque, which was known for its harsh jihadi-Salafi rhetoric. Though the mosque was founded by Moroccans, Muslims of all backgrounds attended this location. It frequently featured radical imams, who encouraged the killing of unbelievers along with martyrdom and jihad. By 1996, Atta had not only developed a circle of acquaintances there but was also at the center of a number of student religious study groups.[2] Mohammed Fizazi, an extremist Moroccan imam who traveled Europe, would often spend weeks at a time at al Quds Mosque. He was a forceful advocate of the obligation for all Muslims to participate in jihad and seemed to have a special appreciation for the cluster that included Atta and another Hamburg Arab resident, Ramzi bin al Shibh.[3]

One of the key focal points of the scene was Mohammed Belfas, "a middle-age[d] immigrant from Indonesia, Yemen and Egypt, who had lived in Germany illegally for almost twenty years before being given legal status." He worked for the post office and, more important, conducted a *halaqa* (study group) at the al Quds Mosque. Foreign students that hailed from North Africa, the Persian Gulf, the Levant, and even Indonesia attended the group.[4]

Around 1996, Mohammed Atta, following his religious pilgrimage to Mecca, Saudi Arabia, as well as Moroccan students Mounir el Motassadeq and Abdelghani Mzoudi, began to frequent the study group meetings. At the al Quds Mosque was also "an outspoken, flamboyant Islamist named Mohammed Haydar Zammar": "A well-known figure in the Muslim community (and to German and U.S. intelligence agencies by the late 1990's), Zammar had fought in Afghanistan and relished any opportunity to extol the virtues of violent jihad." Zammar claims to have—and to some degree was witnessed doing so—pushed the core members of the 9/11 plot to participate in jihad and directed them toward receiving training in Afghanistan to fulfill their jihad responsibility.[5]

The members of the Hamburg cell who were directly involved in the September 11 attacks included Mohammed Atta, Ramzi bin al Shibh, Marwan al Shehi, and Ziad Jarrah. However, they were part of a larger and more dynamic group in Hamburg that included other individuals, including Mohammad Belfas, Said Bahaji, Zakariya Essabar, Mounir el Motassadeq, and

Abdelghani Mzoudi. Many of these individuals were students and few, if any, began as radical Muslims. Most were initially apolitical and from unremarkable backgrounds. Moreover, many were fluent in English, Western educated, and accustomed to Western lifestyles. However, as students far from home, this group was vulnerable to radicalization.

Gravitating to Reactionary Islam

Although Mohammed Atta had come from what in Egypt was a relatively secular family, once in the West, his religious commitment intensified. Praying five times a day, strictly observing a halal diet, and avoiding normal student social activities like clubs and sporting events became his pattern.[6] Even this level of religiosity was not sufficient upon his return from hajj in 1995. Atta returned more quiet, introverted, and intense in his level of observance, began to grow a beard as a visual display of his new religious devotion, and spent increasing amounts of time at the mosque.[7]

Atta also began to teach a religious class at a Turkish mosque in Hamburg. However, his class was so strict, most students dropped out. By the time he returned to Egypt in 1998 for a visit, his transformation was obvious—when Atta met up with one of his friends from university, he noted that Atta "had changed a great deal, had grown a beard, and had 'obviously adopted fundamentalism' by that time."[8] Similarly, friends who knew Ramzi bin al Shibh from home in Yemen characterized him as "religious, but not too religious," but by the late 1990s bin al Shibh was advocating that "the highest duty of every Muslim was to pursue jihad, and that the highest honor was to die during the jihad."[9]

For Ziad Jarrah, the catalyst for his change seems to have been a return visit to Lebanon in 1996 during the holiday break. It is unclear what occurred there, but his new, more devout approach upon his return was clearly evident and, in fact, caused friction with his secular girlfriend in Germany. He began to chastise her for not being sufficiently devout.[10] Not long after, he decided to move away and study aeronautical engineering at the University of Applied Science in a suburb outside Hamburg. By 1998, Jarrah began spending time at the al Quds Mosque with bin al Shibh and eventually Atta.[11] In 1997 he began to grow a full beard and started praying on a regular basis. He avoided introducing his girlfriend to his new, more religious friends because she was secular. By 1999 he had become so radicalized that he told his girlfriend "he was planning to wage a jihad because there was no greater honor than to die for Allah."[12]

The catalyst for Marwan al Shehi may have been his father's death. In early 1998 he transferred to school in Hamburg and soon hooked up with Atta's group.[13] By the time al Shehi arrived in Germany in 1996, he was already praying five times a day, but he still wore Western-style clothes. By 1997, following the death of his father, he was avoiding restaurants that served or cooked with alcohol. Soon after his father passed, he also became more pronounced in his faith and stopped wearing Western clothes. When he moved in with Atta and bin al Shibh in 1999, he began to become more Salafi in outlook and, as Shehi noted to a former friend who visited him, he began to emulate the Prophet—a key Salafi signature.[14]

Zakariya Essabar's religious transformation happened rapidly. By 1999, he reportedly "pressured one acquaintance with physical force to become more religious, grow a beard and compel his wife to convert to Islam."[15]

Politicization of Beliefs

An important participant in these sessions and well-known among the Muslims who worshiped at al Quds was Mohammed Haydar Zammar, a three-hundred-pound, Syrian-born, loud-mouthed auto mechanic and jihadi veteran who had fought in Afghanistan and Bosnia. He was promoting the concept of active participation in military jihad to the group and was known as an admirer of bin Laden. Moreover, he ran something of a travel agency for jihadists seeking to go to Afghanistan.[16]

Ramzi bin al Shibh was a key proponent of the idea that "the men were obliged to go to those places where Islam was under attack, to defend it literally as holy warriors." He played jihadi propaganda videos that highlighted Chechnya, Bosnia, and Kosovo. Moreover, he shared Atta's worldview that the real enemies behind all of these conflicts were Jews and America, noting, "One has to do something about America."[17]

Israel and Jews in general animated the men. Atta was known to have said, "How can you laugh when people are dying in Palestine." When Atta interacted with other students in Hamburg, he voiced anti-Semitic and anti-American attitudes, citing a worldwide Jewish conspiracy based in New York City as well as strong antipathy toward secular Arab leaders, like Iraq's Saddam Hussein. Ramzi bin al Shibh shared this conspiratorial worldview.[18]

By the end of 1999, discussions shifted from debates on the legitimacy of jihad to where jihad should be fought—Afghanistan, Bosnia, or Chechnya. The men had reached a consensus on the necessity of their religious-political goal. They wanted to fight; they just had to choose the war. Russian atrocities against the Muslims that they saw in videos about Chechnya motivated the men to originally plan to travel to Chechnya to fight jihad.[19]

The Bait al Ansar Cluster

Mohammed Atta and Ramzi bin al Shibh met in a mosque in 1995 and subsequently became close friends. The Mohammed Belfas study group in the al Quds Mosque provided the forum for the group to expand to include the two students from Morocco, Mounir el Motassadeq and Abdelghani Mzoudi. Subsequently, it was Atta and bin al Shibh who showed up around town at mosques and study groups to serve as mentors and recruiters of foreign students. When, around 1996, Motassadeq moved into an apartment in the student-housing complex, "it became the center where militant Muslim students congregated when on campus, eating meals together from the common kitchen, and discussing religion and politics in the living room."[20]

Ziad Jarrah met bin al Shibh in 1997 at the al Quds Mosque and began attending the study group. In 1998, Atta and bin al Shibh began to share an apartment in the Harbug section of Hamburg with Marwan al Shehi, who "grew very close to Atta." Meanwhile, Zakariya Essabar met Jarrah at the Volkswagen plant, where he had an internship. Motassadeq met Said Bahaji at al Quds and brought him into the group as its last addition. Together, these men spent countless hours thinking, talking, reading, and debating what this reactionary interpretation of Islam required of them.[21]

The group began to coalesce around Atta and bin al Shibh in late 1997. By the summer of 1998, the core of the cluster, Atta, Belfas, al Shehi, and bin al Shibh, were all working together in a computer warehouse, spending time packing boxes. Meanwhile, Belfas was gradually losing influence as Atta perceived him as too "soft" when it came to Islamic matters. By 1998, the private study sessions of the cluster moved out of the mosque and into both a bookstore near the al Quds Mosque and a private flat in Wilhelmsburg.

The group met three to four times a week and hosted sessions that involved extremely anti-American discussions. A year later, Atta, bin al Shibh, and Bahaji and later al Shehi moved and lived together in a flat at 54 Marionstrasse. They called the location Bait al Ansar or "The House of the Supporters of the Prophet." The flat increasingly became "a kind of clubhouse for young Hamburg jihadis who would gather for an evening meal and conversation." By 1999, the cluster became even "more extreme and secretive, speaking only in Arabic to conceal the content of their conversations." Discussions intensified and the focus began to be on fulfilling their duty to fight jihad: "One week, the members were intent on fighting in Kosovo, the next in Chechnya, or Afghanistan or Bosnia. Then men were agreed: they wanted to fight—they just didn't know which war."[22]

Anatomy of the Cluster

Active Core

Mohammed Atta, age thirty-three at the time of the September 11 attacks, grew up in a middle-class, relatively secular family in Kafr el Sheikh, Egypt. His father was an attorney. Atta attended Cairo University, where he earned a degree in architectural engineering and subsequently worked as an urban planner in Cairo for a few years after graduation. In 1992, he went to Germany to continue his studies, first in Stuttgart and then in Hamburg. He attended the Technical University of Hamburg-Harburg through 1999 and received a degree in city engineering and planning. Teachers recall him as a serious and committed student. During his early years in Hamburg, Atta worked part-time as a draftsman for an urban planning firm until he was laid off in 1996.[23]

Marwan al Shehi, age twenty-three at the time of the September 11 attacks, was born in Ras al Khaimah in the United Arab Emirates (UAE). His father had been a local prayer leader. Following his graduation from high school, he joined the UAE military, went through basic training, and then earned a scholarship that would enable him to study in Germany. When he arrived in Bonn in 1996, Shehi was already somewhat religious, praying five times a day. He encountered academic difficulties and requested a leave from his technical, mathematical, and scientific studies in 1997. He ultimately had to repeat the first semester of his studies and subsequently requested to complete his studies in Hamburg. Though it is unclear how he met Atta and bin al Shibh, that association seems to have been part of his motivation to relocate to Hamburg, as he moved in with them. His academic problems followed him to Hamburg; he left his program and began to study shipbuilding in Hamburg at the Technical University in the summer of 1999.[24]

Ziad Jarrah, age twenty-six at the time of the September 11 attacks, was born in Mazraa, Lebanon. He came from a well-to-do family and attended private Christian schools. In April 1996 he moved to Germany to enroll, with a cousin, in a junior college in Greifswald. Jarrah's reputation in Lebanon had been that of a "playboy"; he had been known to frequent discos and drink alcohol. He attended student parties and drank beer. By the end of 1996, after a trip home, Jarrah began to discus the merits of jihad. The next year he changed his academic focus from dentistry to aircraft engineering and enrolled in the University of Applied Sciences. It is unclear if previously established contacts were part of the appeal of moving to Hamburg. Jarrah had a girlfriend who was secular and of Turkish heritage in Greifswald.[25]

Ramzi bin al Shibh, age twenty-nine at the time of the September 11 attacks, was born in Ghayl Bawazir, Yemen, and was known as "religious, but not too religious" during his formative years. After a stint from 1987 to 1995 working for the International Bank of Yemen, he attempted to leave Yemen for the United States but was denied a visa. Subsequently he traveled to Germany and claimed asylum under a false name. Though this enabled him to stay in Hamburg for a period until his application for asylum was denied, he ultimately traveled back to Yemen and then returned to Hamburg under his true name as a student in 1997. His student days were short-lived, however, as he was expelled from school in 1998 due to his poor performance.[26]

Followers

Said Bahaji, age twenty-six at the time of the September 11 attacks, was born in Lower Saxony, Germany, the child of a Moroccan father and a Prussian-Protestant German mother. At age nine, the family moved to Morocco, where his father owned a discotheque. Raised in a secular household, he returned to Germany to study electrical engineering at the Technical University of Hamburg-Harburg in 1996. Bahaji spent five months in the German army before receiving a medical discharge. He had no formal Islamic education and was known to be a fan of video games and Formula One racing. After a bad breakup with a woman at university, he began to explore Islam at the al Quds Mosque and subsequently moved in with Mohammed Atta and Ramzi bin al Shibh in 1998. Atta, bin al Shibh, Mohammed Zammar, Ziad Jarrah, and Marwan al Shehi all attended his wedding to a different woman, which was held at the al Quds Mosque.[27]

Zakariya Essabar, age twenty-four at the time of the September 11 attacks, was a Moroccan citizen and had moved to Germany in 1997 and specifically Hamburg in 1998. He studied medical technology in Hamburg at the University of Applied Sciences. He began to radicalize in 1999 and subsequently went to Afghanistan for paramilitary training.[28]

Mounir el Motassadeq, age twenty-seven at the time of the September 11 attacks, was also of Moroccan descent. He went to Germany in 1993 and then Hamburg in 1995 to study electrical engineering at the Technical University of Hamburg-Harburg. He also traveled to Afghanistan for paramilitary training.[29]

Abdelghani Mzoudi, age twenty-eight at the time of the September 11 attacks, was born in Marrakesh, Morocco, and arrived in Germany in 1993. He had completed university-level courses in physics and chemistry in Morocco before his arrival and subsequently studied in a few German towns before moving to Hamburg in 1995. Though he started his studies at the University of Hamburg-Harburg, he subsequently switched to the University of Applied Sciences. Interestingly, Mzoudi "described himself as a weak Muslim when he was home in Morocco, but much more devout when he was back in Hamburg."[30]

Periphery

Mohammed Haydar Zammar, age forty at the time of the September 11 attacks, was "an outspoken, flamboyant Islamist" who was a regular presence at the al Quds Mosque. Zammar was born in Aleppo, Syria, and raised in a conservative religious family. He moved to Germany at age ten and as a teenager was well-known at local mosques for his piety. In the early 1990s Zammar trained in Afghanistan, spent time in Bosnia, and "relished any opportunity to extol the virtues of violent jihad." He became "a well-known figure in the German Muslim community (and to German and U.S. intelligence agencies by the late 1990s.)" His vocation was that of an unemployed auto mechanic who subsisted on state subsidies and had a wife and six children. Although he was known in the community as somewhat of a loud mouth, his connections in the Islamist and jihadist world enabled him to serve as a pseudo "jihadi travel agent."[31]

Shahid Nickels, age twenty at the time of the September 11 attacks, was a South African who had converted to Islam in high school and spent significant time with the Hamburg cluster between 1997 and 1999. Though he ultimately pulled away from the men as they began to radicalize to violence and Atta became "too strange," he remains one of the most knowledgeable sources of the development of the circle around Atta.[32]

Other Hijackers

Hani Hanjour, age twenty-nine at time of his death (Saudi Arabian)

Waleed al Shehri, age twenty-two at time of his death (Saudi Arabian)

Wail al Shehri, age twenty-eight at the time of his death (Saudi Arabian)

Abdulaziz al Omari, age twenty-two at the time of his death (Saudi Arabian)

Satam al Suqami, age twenty-five at the time of his death (Saudi Arabian)

Fayez Banihammad, age twenty-four at time of his death (United Arab Emirati)

Mohand al Shehri, age twenty-two at the time of his death (Saudi Arabian)

Hamza al Ghamdi, age twenty at time of his death (Saudi Arabian)

Ahmed al Ghamdi, age twenty-two at the time of his death (Saudi Arabian)

Khalid al Mihdhar, age twenty-six at the time of his death (Saudi Arabian)

Majed Moqed, age twenty-four at the time of his death (Saudi Arabian)

Nawaf al Hazmi, age twenty-five at the time of his death (Saudi Arabian)

Salem al Hazmi, age twenty at the time of his death (Saudi Arabian)

Ahmed al Haznawi, age twenty at the time of his death (Saudi Arabian)

Ahmed al Nami, age twenty-three at the time of his death (Saudi Arabian)

Saeed al Ghamdi, age twenty-one at the time of his death (Saudi Arabian)

Overseas Travel and Link Up with Al Qaeda

Originally, the core members of the Bait al Ansar cluster had planned to go to Chechnya to fight the Russians. Russian atrocities against Muslims in Chechnya served as a common motivation for aspiring Muslim militants to join the jihad. However, a chance meeting on a train in Germany with Khalid al Masri in the fall of 1999 discouraged them from going to Grozny and instead put the men in touch with Mohamedou Ould Slahi, an al Qaeda operative who was based in Germany. Subsequently, Slahi explained that many aspiring jihadists were being arrested in Georgia and suggested they train in Afghanistan first via Karachi and Quetta, Pakistan.[33]

In November 1999, the four core members of the Hamburg group, Mohammed Atta, Ramzi bin al Shibh, Marwan al Shehi, and Ziad Jarrah, separately departed Germany for jihad training in Afghanistan. Following the Mohammed Haydar Zammar route, at least two flew via Turkish airways to Karachi, Pakistan, via Istanbul, Turkey. From there it was on to Quetta and then Kandahar, Afghanistan, where the men all met up.[34]

Al Qaeda Recruitment

Although Slahi had directed the men to get training in Afghanistan, it was there that the men were recruited by al Qaeda and selected for the 9/11 operation, which had been under consideration for years. They met Osama bin Laden and Mohammed Atef, pledged their loyalty to al Qaeda, and volunteered for a "martyrdom operation." On their way back to Germany, they met Khalid Sheikh Mohammed in Karachi and ultimately returned to Hamburg in early 2000.[35]

When Mohammed Atta, Ramzi bin al Shibh, Marwan al Shehi, and Ziad Jarrah returned to Germany, the second wave of Abdelghani Mzoudi, Mounir el Motassadeq, Zakariya Essabar, and Said Bahaji went to Afghanistan in the spring of 2000.[36]

Training and Skill Acquisition

The would-be pilots did not receive the necessary flight training in Afghanistan; they would have to return to the West for that. However, the "muscle hijackers" underwent the same type of basic training that any al Qaeda recruit would receive. The basic training course included firearms, heavy weapons, explosives, and topography. According to *The 9/11 Commission Report*, "At least seven of the Saudi muscle hijackers took this basic training regime at the al Farouq camp near Kandahar." Two others trained at al Qaeda's

Khalden Camp.[37] Some special training was given to the "muscle hijackers" at the al Matar complex in Afghanistan. The men were taught "how to conduct hijackings, disarm air marshals, and handle explosives." This included practicing by using knives to butcher a sheep or camel as well as focusing on "storming the cockpit at the earliest opportunity when the doors first opened."[38]

Operational Cycle

Travel to Afghanistan was clearly the catalyst for the men's mobilization to action. Jarrah (January 31), Atta (late February), and bin al Shibh (shortly thereafter) returned to Hamburg in early 2000. Almost immediately they began to research flight schools, determined that training in Germany would not be feasible, and began to pursue training in the United States, which would be less expensive and less time intensive. By March, Atta was e-mailing flight schools in the United States to get further information on the schools. Once they returned to Germany, it was only weeks before they began to take action to move the plot forward.[39]

Logistics

On January 15, 2000, Nawaf al Hazmi and Khalid al Mihdhar arrived in Los Angeles. Two weeks later, they moved to San Diego.[40] On May 29, 2000, Marwan al Shehi arrived in Newark, New Jersey. Mohammed Atta followed on June 3 and Ziad Jarrah arrived on June 27. On December 8, 2000, the fourth pilot, Hani Hanjour, arrived in San Diego.[41]

Funds were provided for their enrollment in flight school by Khalid Sheikh Mohammed's nephew Amman al Baluchi between June 29 and September 17, 2000. In total, $114,500 was provided in five wire transfer transactions from the UAE.[42] The Saudi "muscle hijackers" were selected by bin Laden between mid-2000 and April 2001. Following their specialized training at al Qaeda's al Farouq or Khalden Camp, Khalid Sheikh Mohammed provided each of the men with $10,000 before they departed Pakistan to Saudi Arabia to obtain U.S. visas.

They all arrived in the United States between April and early July 2001. Most settled in Florida in close proximity, opening bank accounts, renting cars, and acquiring mailboxes. Mohammed Atta was likely waiting outside the airport for

Mohamed al Khatani, another Saudi who arrived in Orlando in August, and was to be the final muscle hijacker but was denied entry and sent back to Dubai.[43]

Communications

While Khalid Sheikh Mohammed had a variety of means of communicating with the operatives—one being via Khallad, alias for Tafiq bin Atash (the suspected intermediary between bin Laden and the USS *Cole* bombers), utilizing e-mail to contact Nawaf al Hazmi—the primary conduit was through Ramzi bin al Shibh, who would serve as the al Qaeda "link man" for this plot.[44]

After Ramzi bin al Shibh failed in his third attempt to get a visa to enter the United States, he assumed the role of coordinator between Khalid Sheikh Mohammed and the men in the United States. In July 2001, Mohammed Atta met with Ramzi bin al Shibh outside Madrid in order to inform him of the timing of the attacks, the targets, and how the operation would proceed. The results of this meeting were subsequently reported to Khalid Sheikh Mohammed.[45]

Following the meeting, bin al Shibh purchased two phones—one for contact with Atta, the other for contact with Khalid Sheikh Mohammed. In the following weeks, bin al Shibh would be in frequent contact with Atta via phone, e-mail, and instant messaging. Once the date for the attacks was set, Ramzi bin al Shibh sent Zakariya Essabar and Said Bahaji to Afghanistan. Essabar passed the information to Khalid Sheikh Mohammed once he arrived.[46]

Target Selection/Casing

Potential targets in the United States (World Trade Center, Pentagon, Capitol building, and the White House) had already been identified by al Qaeda leaders in Afghanistan, but late into the plot, there was still some debate as to whether the fourth target would be the Capitol building or the White House.

During the early part of the summer 2001, three men from the Bait al Ansar cluster in Hamburg, Atta, al Shehi, and Jarrah, took the first of their cross-country surveillance flights. They all flew from the East Coast to the West Coast in first class on United Airlines on the types of planes they would be responsible for flying. Hani Hanjour took a similar cross-country type flight in August. Both Ziad Jarrah and Hani Hanjour, separately, took additional practice flights in the early summer with their instructors on the

Hudson Corridor. This would have put them on a flight path that passed the World Trade Center. Hanjour may have also taken additional flights in the Washington, D.C. area. As mentioned, as late as August 2001, there was still some debate between Atta and bin al Shibh as to whether targeting the White House (which bin Laden wanted) was viable.[47]

Skill Acquisition and Weaponization

Ziad Jarrah had arranged to receive flight training at the Florida Flight Training Center in Venice, Florida, and Mohammed Atta and Marwan al Shehi signed up for flight training with Huffman Aviation in Venice. Jarrah obtained a single engine private pilot certificate in August 2000. Hani Hanjour, who already had earned a commercial pilot certificate issued by the FAA as a result of his training in Arizona in 1999, returned to the United States in December 2000 for additional training. He and Nawaf al Hazmi moved to Arizona, and Hanjour took a refresher course before moving on to training on a Boeing 737 simulator at the Pan Am International Flight Academy in Mesa, Arizona.[48]

The September 11 hijackers weaponized with readily available materials. In this case it happened to be knives, which they purchased in mid-August, and planes, which they hijacked.[49]

The Al Qaeda Factor

The September 11 plot was conceived by Khalid Sheikh Mohammed and then discussed with bin Laden in 1996. However, until 1999 it was still missing an important piece. It was the arrival of the first four members of the Hamburg cell in Afghanistan in late 1999, fluent in English, Western educated, and accustomed to the Western lifestyle, that enabled the plot to go forward. There, Khalid Sheikh Mohammed approached the four about participating and they enthusiastically accepted the "martyrdom operation" assignment. A fourth pilot was provided by al Qaeda when Ramzi bin al Shibh was unable to enter the United States. Al Qaeda also provided and trained the fifteen "muscle hijackers."

Al Qaeda was involved in providing training, picking the targets, funding the operation, and providing manpower from start to finish. This was the clearly an al Qaeda Command and Control operation.

Chapter 2

Shoe Bombers' Plot (Paris–Miami, 2001)

ON DECEMBER 22, 2001, British citizen Richard Reid boarded American Airlines Flight 63 from Paris to Miami with the intention of killing himself and all of the other passengers on the flight by igniting an explosive device in the airplane above the Atlantic Ocean. Reid was unable to detonate the explosive device, which had been concealed in his shoes, before passengers onboard were able to subdue him. The ensuing investigation revealed that a second bomber, Saajid Badat, also a British citizen, had withdrawn from the operation one week before Reid boarded his flight to Miami.[1]

The "Londonistan" Scene

The origins of the development of the rejectionist Islamic environment in Britain can be traced back to the fall of the Berlin Wall, the collapse of the "old left" of the communists and socialists, and the burning of Salman Rushdie's book *The Satanic Verses* in the late 1980s. The wider U.K. Muslim community, disillusioned with the left and energized by the Rushdie affair, was seeking new movements through which it could channel its activism driven by a Muslim political identity and consciousness and thus formed the demand side of the equation. Meanwhile, foreign radicals from Africa and the Middle East who immigrated to the U.K. seeking political asylum during the 1980s and 1990s, like Abu Hamza al Masri, Omar Bakri Mohammad, and Abu Qatada, provided the supply side with a radical rejectionist Islamic message in Britain.

While one manifestation of this rejectionist scene primarily appealed to the indigenous British Muslim population who had failed to assimilate into British society and was at the bottom of the socioeconomic ladder—primarily promoted by the Islamist groups Hizb ut Tahrir and al Muhajiroun—another "scene" that overlapped yet had a different core was that of Londonistan. This milieu was dominated by Algerian veterans of the Algerian civil war (which had begun in 1992) who had been on the Groupe Islamique Armé (GIA)/Groupe Salafiste pour la Prédication et le Combat (GSPC) side and, following a stint in France, moved to London in the mid- to late 1990s. Past links to GIA/GSPC veterans provided key ongoing connections with al Qaeda support networks in France and southwest Asia.

Abu Qatada, a Jordanian cleric linked to al Qaeda, and his student, Abu Hamza al Masri, were the key ideologues, dominating this scene and promoting al Qaeda ideology. Both had bona fides in the rejectionist community as Abu Qatada sat on al Qaeda's religious rulings committee and Abu Hamza had been injured in the Darunta al Qaeda training camp in Afghanistan, where he lost an eye and had a hand replaced by a hook and had traveled to Bosnia in the mid 1990s to support the mujahedeen. Because of Abu Hamza's status as a "veteran" of two jihads, he had celebrity status in the community and young men flocked to hear his speeches.[2]

Following an initial period in Luton, Abu Hamza, with the assistance of Algerian veterans, was able to take over the Finsbury Park Mosque. This provided him with a high-profile center of operations from which he could spread his message of support for "jihad" abroad. Any ongoing armed struggles involving Muslims in Bosnia, Chechnya, the Middle East, Afghanistan, and especially Kashmir were discussed and used as evidence to rationalize support for al Qaeda.[3]

Along with Zacarias Moussaoui, Richard Reid and Saajid Badat frequented the Finsbury Park Mosque, where they listened to and were inspired by the sermons of Abu Hamza. Although the two shoe bombers ended up as part of the same operation, their pathway to becoming part of the shoe bomber operation were quite different.

Gravitating to Reactionary Islam

Both the Brixton and Finsbury mosques were key nodes in the U.K. for the proliferation of an interpretation of Islam that promoted military jihad as a means to defend Islam, restore the Caliphate, and fight the West. Though the Brixton Mosque itself may not have been where Richard Reid was first exposed to an extremist interpretation of Islam, he made key connections there that linked him to radical circles around the mosque. The location had a reputation for attracting converts and helping ex-prisoners readjust to life in the outside world and provided a Salafi interpretation of Islam. At Finsbury, Abu Hamza al Masri, as the imam of the mosque and its central figure, promoted a militant interpretation of Islam and wielded a powerful influence over those who passed through its doors. Ultimately, the Finsbury Park Mosque became known as "The Suicide Factory," as many of its alumni went on to perpetrate acts of terror throughout the world. This location was a key hub for making contacts to al Qaeda–linked individuals, and the combination of militant Islam and networking at Finsbury had a significant effect on both Richard Reid and Saajid Badat.[4]

When Richard Reid was sixteen, he left school and drifted into a life of crime. During his second stint in prison, Reid converted to Islam at the behest of his father, who had also converted while in prison.[5]

Upon leaving prison in 1994, Reid gravitated to the Brixton Mosque in South London. According to the chairman of the mosque, "He [Reid] was attempting to learn Arabic and he wanted to learn more about Islam because he was convinced it was the best way of life." Once there, Reid became known for his enthusiasm for the life of the mosque and his eagerness to learn the basic principles of his religion. There is speculation that during this time he attended classes run by Tablighi Jamaat. Subsequently, he began to attend classes outside the mosque run by extremists and to question the peaceful teachings of his original instructors. It is believed that Reid "hero-worshiped" Zacarias Moussaoui, a French Moroccan supporter of militant jihad, who lived nearby, and that Moussaoui had a significant impact on Reid's adoption of extremist ideas.[6]

Abdul Haqq Baker, the chairman of Brixton Mosque, noted, "He [Reid] was asking questions about why we did not share the view of the extremists that this [Britain] is a place of war and Muslims are at war with all of the people here. I explained that this was not a mainstream view and though he was not rude to the administration here, he did have more heated discussions with members of the community. Towards the end I saw a change in him from wearing the beard and the garments towards wearing army jackets." Baker believes that Reid was influenced by classes run in three other centers around Brixton, some of them perhaps run by Moussaoui.[7]

Following his time in Brixton, Reid gravitated to the Finsbury Park Mosque. Between his time at the Brixton and Finsbury Park mosques, Reid became part of the radical Islamist milieu that would come to be known as "Londonistan." In 1998, Reid left the U.K. to study in a Pakistani madrassa, which may have furthered his radicalization.[8]

As a second-generation immigrant, Saajid Badat assimilated into British society while keeping Islam central in his life. Badat attended well-known British schools such as the Crypt Grammar Academy and had memorized the Koran by age twelve. After graduating from secondary school in 1997, Badat moved to London to pursue a secular university degree.[9] In London, Badat began to frequent the Finsbury Park Mosque and soon came under similar radicalizing influences as Reid had. Like Reid, Badat traveled to Pakistan to further his Islamic studies. There, he may have studied at an extremist madrassa in Peshawar.[10]

Politicization of Beliefs

Following his arrest, Richard Reid made a number of comments that demonstrated his rationale for his actions. He expressed significant anger concerning the West and its relations with the Muslim world. The day before Reid's first attempt to bomb American Flight 63, Reid wrote three e-mails and moved them to a drafts folder in his Yahoo account. In a letter to his mother, he wrote:

> what i am doing is part of the ongoing war between islaam and disbelief . . . i didn't do this act out of ignorance nor did i do [it] just because I want to die, but rather i see it as a duty upon me to help remove the oppressive american forces from the muslim lands . . . we do not have other means to fight them . . . we are ready to die defending the true islaam rather to just sit back and allow the american government to dictate to us what we should believe and how we should behave . . . this is a war between islaam and democracy.[11]

During his sentencing hearing, Reid provided more insight into his motivations:

> I further admit my allegiance to Osama bin Laden, to Islam, and to the religion of Allah. With regards to what you said about killing innocent

people, I will say one thing. Your government has killed 2 million children in Iraq. If you want to think about something, against 2 million, I
don't see no comparison. . . . Your government has sponsored the rape
and torture of Muslims in the prisons of Egypt and Turkey and Syria
and Jordan with their money and with their weapons. I don't know, see
what I done as being equal to rape and to torture, or to the deaths of the
two million children in Iraq.[12]

The Embassy Plot Cluster

As previously mentioned, Richard Reid most likely came into contact with
Zacarias Moussaoui in and around the Brixton Mosque. From there, he
moved to the Finsbury Park Mosque, where a number of future terrorists,
including Moussaoui, worshiped. There, Reid is likely to have come into
contact with important individuals in the Londonistan crowd who frequented the location, including the Frenchmen Djamel Beghal and Kamel
Daoudi, both of whom were arrested for their alleged role in targeting the
American embassy in Paris, as well as Nizar Trabelsi, a Tunisian arrested
in Belgium on September 13, 2001, who supposedly had been chosen to
blow himself up in or near the American embassy and had also targeted
an American base in Belgium. These men may have encouraged Reid to
study Islam abroad in Pakistan. Saajid Badat also frequented the Finsbury
Park Mosque and made similar embassy plot connections, such as to Nizar
Trabelsi.[13]

The two airline shoe bombers had a variety of loose affiliations among
the men with al Qaeda links who spent time at Finsbury Park Mosque, including Zacarias Moussaoui, Nizar Trabelsi, Djamel Beghal, and Kamel
Daoudi. According to one account, when Reid would sleep overnight at
Finsbury Park, Beghal would spend time with Reid, telling him of atrocities in the Algerian civil war and of the glories of becoming a mujahedeen.
However, the men never coalesced into a cluster with a specific plan. Rather,
these social relationships were reinitiated in southwest Asia, when both
Richard Reid and Saajid Badat traveled to Afghanistan and received train-
ing at Khalden Camp.[14]

Anatomy of the Cluster

Active Core

Richard Reid, age twenty-eight at the time of his arrest, had been born in Bromley, U.K., in 1973 to an English mother and a Jamaican father. His family was not particularly well-off, and as a child he was repeatedly described as a loner who did not fit in. Reid failed his eleven-year-old examination and, in 1984, was sent to the Thomas Tallis secondary school in Kidbrooke, southeast London. A fellow student noted that "he had this hard-man image that he wanted to portray. But he was soft on the inside. He was quick to follow the crowd if it would give him status." After he dropped out of school, he decided to become a graffiti artist. However, he was convicted of a string of street crimes, including twenty-four robberies and twenty-two thefts. He served sentences in several prisons, including the notorious Feltham Young Offenders' Institution in West London. Reid's father, also a convert to Islam, convinced his son to convert as a means to get out of trouble. In prison his interest in Islam deepened and upon his release, in 1994, Reid began to attend the Brixton Mosque.[15] Reid's aunt noted, "He was so lonely, his life was so empty. . . . He found solace with his Muslim brothers. With him, it became much more than a religion, they became his family." Similarly, according to the chairman of the Brixton Mosque, Salafi Islam provided Richard with the guidance he had never had.[16]

In 1998, Reid left the U.K. to study Islam in Pakistan. He stayed there through 2000 and is thought to have crossed from Pakistan to a training camp in Afghanistan, probably Khalden Camp.[17]

Saajid Badat, age twenty-four at the time of his arrest, was born to immigrant parents (from Malawi) in Britain and grew up in Gloucester. A second-generation immigrant, Badat assimilated into British society while keeping Islam central in his life. By age twelve, Badat had memorized the Koran and simultaneously had done well at St James's Primary School. According to school officials, he had no trouble fitting in at the Church of England school. He was recalled by former classmates and friends as a friendly and popular student. "He was well motivated and hard-working—a credit to his family and to the school," said William Armiger, the headmaster at the time.[18]

Badat was seemingly an excellent example of successful integration as he went on to the well-known British school Crypt Grammar School where he gained four A-levels and ten GCSEs (General Certificate of Secondary

Education). In addition, he enjoyed sports: "An ardent football fan, he supported Liverpool and used to play for a Sunday league team called the Asian Stars." Religion figured prominently in his life as Badat was well-known at the Masjid-e-Noor Mosque in Ryecroft Street in Gloucester. Following his graduation from Crypt Grammar in 1997 and a falling-out with his father, he began a short-lived effort to study optometry in London. It is believed that it was during his time in London that he began to attend Finsbury Park Mosque. It has been said he was moved by accounts of suffering by Muslims in Bosnia.[19] In 1998, he signed up for a trip to Sarajevo to participate in relief efforts for the Muslim community.[20]

According to one account, soon afterward he "suddenly quit his degree course and began a three-year world tour, visiting India, Saudi Arabia, Pakistan and Taliban-controlled Afghanistan." He began this tour with the intention of becoming a religious scholar. He is believed to have received paramilitary training between 1998 and 2001.[21]

Periphery

Zacarias Moussaoui, age thirty-three at the time of his arrest in September 2001, was brought up in the Basque region of southwest France and was of Moroccan extraction. He was raised by his mother after his father left the family. Zacarias was not interested in school or religion and focused most of his efforts on basketball as a youth. Later he was involved with skirmishes with anti-immigrant gangs and came to identify with young Muslims who were affected by the injustices that they perceived to be befalling Muslims in Chechnya and Bosnia. By 1986, he had left France for the U.K. From 1993 to 1995, he earned a master's degree in international business at Southbank University in London. While in the U.K., Moussaoui began spending significant time at first the Brixton Mosque and then the Finsbury Park Mosque, where he was strongly influenced by Abu Hamza al Masri.[22]

Nizar Trabelsi, age thirty-one at the time of his arrest in September 2001, was a Tunisian who had played professional soccer in Germany for Fortuna Dusseldorf. After spending significant time partying and using drugs, his sports career ended and he developed a reputation as a drug dealer with a history of violence. He later became more devout, traveled to Afghanistan, met al Qaeda leader Osama Bin Laden, and asked to become a suicide bomber. He had spent significant time in London at the Finsbury Park

Mosque. Trabelsi claims that he was ordered to go to Belgium, pack a bomb into a lorry, and blow it up—with himself at the wheel—next to the canteen of the Kleine Brogel military base about a hundred miles from Brussels. He was also involved in a plot against the U.S. embassy in Paris, in which he planned to be a suicide bomber. Trabelsi was jailed for ten years in 2003 for his role in the plot against the military base in Belgium.[23]

Overseas Travel and Link Up with Al Qaeda

Both Reid and Badat traveled to southwest Asia in or around 1998 and by 2001 had attended Khalden Camp, where they received training and, it is thought, materiel for their explosive shoe plot.

At some point in 1998, Richard Reid traveled to Pakistan to further his Islamic education. However, there is speculation that based on his relationships at Finsbury Park Mosque, his real motive was to participate in military jihad. This was also the year that Badat quit his degree course in London and began his three-year world tour.[24]

There is incomplete information on the exact whereabouts of both Reid and Badat during this period. However, it is fair to say that some time was spent in southwest Asia and by 2001, both men had trained in al Qaeda camps.

Training and Skill Acquisition

Both Reid and Badat had received training in Afghanistan.[25] Badat reportedly attended both the Khalden and Darunta camps in Afghanistan, first learning the basics of explosives at a camp in Khalden before graduating to the Darunta camp.[26] Reid also attended Khalden Camp. According to some accounts, he was trained by al Qaeda "master bomb maker" Midhat Mursi (aka Abu Khabab al Masri).[27] In addition, a French court document asserts that Reid "took part in combat on the frontlines in support of the Taliban between April 1999 and March 2001."[28]

Reid is reported to have trained at Khalden Camp with Millennium bomber Ahmed Ressam and Zacarias Moussaoui, whom he already knew from Brixton and Finsbury in the U.K.[29] Reid and Badat may have also met up with Nizar Trabelsi in Karachi, as the Pakistani press reported that the three men lived together in Karachi and attended an Islamic seminary in Landhi.[30]

During the summer of 2001, Reid returned to London briefly before he traveled to Amsterdam and Israel. Following his travel to Egypt and Turkey, "on or about November 20, 2001, Badat and Reid traveled to Pakistan." In Karachi they stayed on the same street, though in different hotels.[31]

Al Qaeda Recruitment

Reid was debriefed by al Qaeda–linked individuals about his scouting trips in late fall 2001. In fact, the reports from his reconnaissance mission were discovered on Ayman al Zawahiri's computer in Afghanistan following the U.S. invasion.[32] Also, it seems that the final decision on the targeting of transatlantic passenger jets may have been made by Khalid Sheikh Mohammed. During a March 2007 hearing at Guantanamo Bay, Cuba, he confessed, "I was responsible for the Shoe Bomber Operation to down two American airplanes." All of this is highly suggestive that Reid and Badat were recruited by al Qaeda as a result of their experiences in the camps in Afghanistan.[33]

Operational Cycle

Travel to Pakistan appears to have been the catalyst for the men's mobilization to action. Reid and Badat returned to the U.K. in early December 2001. On December 22, just weeks later, Reid boarded American Airlines Flight 63 from Paris to Miami with his explosive device embedded in his shoes. Badat had booked but not boarded his flight from Manchester, U.K., to Amsterdam in preparation for his flight to the United States. This part of the operational cycle only lasted a few weeks.

Target Selection/Casing

In June 2001, Reid traveled to Amsterdam for ten days, where, it is thought, that he cased out the British embassy and its gardens as a potential target.[34] On July 12, 2001, he flew to Tel Aviv from Amsterdam, observing the security measures on the flight. Reid claims that this is where he got the idea of using explosives hidden in his shoes because it was something that airline security did not check. While in Israel he conducted extensive hostile reconnaissance, visiting train stations, traveling on buses, photographing churches and tall buildings, and noting busy public places and security patterns.[35] However, as previously noted, it seems that the final decision on targeting may have been made by Khalid Sheikh Mohammed.

Logistics

It is likely that al Qaeda Core financed Reid's reconnaissance trips in Israel and Egypt, though no hard evidence other than his subsequent delivery of the detailed reports to al Qaeda exists. It is also likely that al Qaeda Core provided both Badat and Reid with the explosive devices for their shoes.

However, Reid may have also received logistical assistance once he returned from Pakistan in the fall of 2001 in Paris from a group of individuals who were Lashkar-e-Taiba (LeT) supporters. In fact, the French police are convinced that the shoe bomb was made in Paris, implying the existence of an unknown terrorist cell in Paris. Some type of local logistical assistance may be why Reid was unable to explain a number of things to the FBI following his arrest: "He was not able to explain how, since he did not have any funds . . . he had been able to purchase the [explosive] substances and to pay for his travels."[36]

French prosecutors believed that "'this suggests that he . . . benefited from technical and financial support, particularly from the place where he had embarked, namely France.'" French prosecutors charged that Mustafa Ghulam Rama, the owner of a halal butcher shop and a dual British-Pakistani citizen, "served as a compass on French territory" for Reid while he was in Paris. Rama was the president of an organization that French intelligence believes was the French representative for the Pakistani terrorist group, LeT, in Paris. Rama had sent others to train in LeT camps and his butcher shop was long known "as being a place of proselytizing in favor of Jihad in Kashmir." Rama acknowledged meeting with Reid but claimed that others had introduced them.[37]

Communications

Both phone cards and e-mail were important means of communications among Reid, Badat, and Nizar Trabelsi. According to the U.S. Department of Justice,

"Badat and Reid communicated directly and indirectly through . . . electronic mail accounts to coordinate their activities with respect to detonating their shoe bombs to be used to attack American interests."[38] Upon their return from Pakistan in December 2001, Reid and Badat maintained contact with their handler(s). Belgian phone cards, found on Reid, had links to both Badat and Trabelsi.[39] As the launch date for the plot got closer, Badat was in communication with his handlers, and their exchanges reveal his handlers' anxiety about his commitment to the plot. They asked, "What else is wrong" and "what's up?"[40] Immediately before Badat was to launch his attack, he e-mailed his contacts to inform them that he was having "big problems" and was "having trouble playing any sport whatsoever." He added, "you will have to tell Van Damme [Reid] that he could be on his own." Then Badat sent an e-mail on December 14, 2001, "indicating that he might withdraw."[41]

Meanwhile, Reid was sending e-mails to Peshawar, Pakistan, from Paris Internet cafés in the week leading up to the attack ("French sources say many of Reid's e-mails were sent to an address in Peshawar, Pakistan, which they think provides postal-drop and forwarding services for al Qaeda operatives in Europe").[42] After his first attempt to board a flight to the United States failed on December 21, he had an e-mail exchange with an interlocutor in Pakistan who urged Reid to try again the next day, which he did. Information released five years later shed light on who the "link man" was for Reid and Badat.

In September 2006, the Director of National Intelligence (DNI) released information about the role of Ammar al Balucchi, the nephew of Khalid Sheikh Mohammed (KSM): "In late 2001 in Afghanistan, KSM directed Ammar to be the communications intermediary between al-Qa'ida and 'shoe bombers' Richard Reid and Saajid Badat."[43]

Weaponization

The men planned to utilize explosive devices (the shoes) designed to evade airport security and destroy an aircraft in flight. Two explosives were blended together—TATP and PETN.[44] The U.S. indictment asserts that Badat procured his shoe bomb in Afghanistan, most likely from al Qaeda, and brought his device back to the U.K. Subsequently, he separated the fuse and detonator from the explosive and kept it at home. When he was arrested in 2003, Badat reportedly said, "I did not know how to dispose of . . . an Arab gave me these things in Afghanistan."[45] Reid's acquisition of his shoe bomb is less clear. Reid told the FBI that he paid between $1,500 and $2,000 for the explosive device, purchased it in Amsterdam, and wired it into his sneakers himself. Reid claimed to have found the information to make the explosives on the Internet.[46]

While this suggests that the two sets of devices were procured at different locations, the U.S. Department of Justice noted that "the shoe bombs obtained by Badat were substantially similar to the shoe bombs obtained by Reid." The British prosecutor echoed this conclusion, stating they were "essentially identical in chemical composition." In addition, a forensic analysis of both devices showed that "their respective lengths of detonator cord had come from the same batch (indeed the cut mark on Badat's cord matches exactly that of Reid's)."[47] French authorities believed that "Reid did not have the necessary technical knowledge for designing the device."[48]

This suggests two potential scenarios: both men received their explosives in Afghanistan and Reid lied to the FBI, or Reid was given assistance in Europe to create a device that was essentially identical to Badat's device. In fact, the latter is precisely what French officials have asserted is indeed the case—"the explosive device integrated into the shoes was assembled in this country [France]."[49] The fact that the detonator cords were from the same batch and had the same cut marks suggests that Reid was lying and that the two devices originated in Afghanistan, most likely provided by al Qaeda.

The Al Qaeda Factor

With the training and funding provided by al Qaeda, the device and targets provided by al Qaeda, and last-minute e-mail communication with al Qaeda, clearly this was an al Qaeda "command and control" plot.[50]

Chapter 3

Operation Overt (United Kingdom–United States, 2006)

OPERATION OVERT, THE August 2006 transatlantic aircraft plot, was a conspiracy to detonate liquid explosives carried onboard several airliners traveling from the United Kingdom to the United States and Canada. Twenty-five suspects were taken into custody in and around London on the night of August 9, 2006; eleven were charged with terrorism-related offenses.[1]

The Reactionary/Islamist Scene

The origins of the rejectionist Islamic environment in Britain were outlined in Chapter 2. The message created there resonated in the indigenous British Muslim population, which had failed to assimilate into British society, was at the bottom of the socioeconomic ladder, and thus gravitated to these "radicalizers."[2]

One scene in the U.K. that appealed to this population and manifested itself through the growing participation of British residents in "reactionary Islamic and Islamist movements." These included Salafis, Deobandis, Tablighi Jamaat, Hizb ut Tahrir, and Al Muhajiroun, all which nominally seek to re-create the utopia of the Caliphate and stand against the democratic order. These groups appealed to the second- and third-generation British Muslims of Pakistani and Bangladeshi descent who were university students and sought channels through which they could put into practice their activist ideas, redress perceived grievances, and explore their Islamic heritage.

Coupled with the high-profile extremist clerics who had established centers of operation and founded their own radical groups in the U.K., significant numbers of British Muslims were drawn to either actively or passively support jihad abroad. This population, which was dominated by British Muslims of Pakistani heritage (primarily from Kashmir), was sympathetic to the ongoing armed struggles involving Muslims in Bosnia, the Middle East, Afghanistan, and especially Kashmir and thus was vulnerable to polarization. Having relatives in conflict zones enabled travel, further radicalization, and training. Involvement in the extended al Muhajiroun network was a common experience among many of the British Muslims and preceded their ultimate participation in a number of the most serious al Qaeda plots that would emerge from this U.K. rejectionist Islamist scene.[3]

Most of the active and passive core of plotters (Abdulla Ahmed Ali, Assad Sarwar, Tanvir Hussain, Arafat Khan, Waheed Zaman, Ibrahim Savant, and Umar Islam) emerged from overlapping networks of Tablighi Jamaat membership, politically active university students, and an Islamic charity whose offices were across the street (Chatsworth Road) from Mohammed Hamid's bookstore, which was also known as "Osama bin London's book shop." Hamid would be convicted in 2008 of organizing terrorism training camps for British residents in the Lake District of the U.K. Past attendees of these camps included some of the conspirators in Operation Vivace—the July 21, 2005, London bomb plot—including the ringleader, Muktar Ibrahim (see Chapter 8).

Gravitating to Reactionary Islam

Abdulla Ahmed Ali, Assad Sarwar, and Waheed Zaman, among others in the cluster, had been Tabligh Jamaat followers. A number of members of the group regularly attended mosques in their neighborhoods that subscribed to that movement's fundamentalist ideology. Tablighi Jamaat is an Islamic missionary group that rejects secular society and advocates strict adherence to an Islamic dress code and lifestyle. French intelligence has described the group as an "antechamber to terrorism," but it really serves more as a "gateway ideology" for some individuals who may adopt a more militant, violent, and extremist interpretation of Islam.[4] A number of members of the cluster, including Abdulla Ahmed Ali, Assad Sarwar, and Waheed Zaman, regularly visited the same neighborhood mosque on Queen's Road in Walthamstow in East London. This location, Masjid-e-Umer, was regularly visited by members of Tablighi Jamaat and thus this interpretation of Islam had a strong influence there.[5]

Sarwar and Umar Islam (Brian Young) worshiped at the Muslim Education Centre in Totteridge Drive, which was founded when the sternly traditional Markaz ud-Dawa movement moved into town. The center, a charity, proclaims its mission as advancing Islam according to the "interpretation and accepted view of the Ahlus Sunnah wal Jamaa-ah." Web sites linked to this movement emphasize a rejection of Western values and distrust of democracy. Ideologically, this movement is quite close to Salafism and Wahhabism, and the Lashkar-e-Taiba group is a terrorist offshoot from the movement.[6]

Politicization of Beliefs

Disagreement with the wars the U.K. was engaged in Iraq and Afghanistan motivated many of the conspirators. Abdulla Ahmed Ali and Assad Sarwar would meet at lectures at an East London school and discuss the situation in Afghanistan and Iraq. Both were frustrated by the number of refugees created by these conflicts. Ali ultimately came to believe that political activism and aid work were ineffective ways of helping and decided to tackle what they believed was the root cause, Western foreign policy. In his court defense, Ali claimed that there was no plot but that he wanted to create an Internet documentary protesting British foreign policy in Iraq, Afghanistan, and Lebanon.[7] Ali testified that the Iraq war was the critical event that catalyzed his feelings against the United States and the U.K. He called it a "criminal act" and explained during his trial how he came to the conclusion that political protests and relief work were insufficient to change the underlying problems.

> [T]hen you have the whole Iraq situation going on. I think at that time there were reports of a million people being killed already in that war, 80 million refugees there . . . you got all these things going on around you and no doubt it's something that I did care about, especially having been involved in it directly, having seen the suffering and stuff like that, having done—been on demonstrations, protests, constantly

reading the news, human rights reports, stuff like that, seeing both sides of the story, arguments of the story, I became less enthusiastic and confident in things like protests and marches. We had the biggest march ever, 1 million people, and it didn't seem to do anything. We knew now the war was illegal in Iraq and it wasn't a secret no more. It was a lie. It was just deceit. It was a criminal war. In my eyes that made the government criminals because it was a criminal act what they did and obviously they weren't listening to the people and I felt that aid work, as good as it was, is very limited in how far it's going to go. For every two people you help, another 100 are going to be coming into the refugee camps. So to sum it up, basically I though the root problem was not dealing with refugees and protests, these are just dealing with the symptoms. The root problem was the foreign policy and that's something that should be tackled.[8]

Subsequently, Ali's reading of *Signposts* by Sayyid Qutb provided an intellectual framework to legitimize his more militant views. In fact, in his testimony Ali described the book as a "must read."[9]

Waheed Zaman, former head of a student Islamic society at London Metropolitan University, said he had strong political feelings and sought to raise public awareness of the oppression of Muslims. He added: "It was for the government to change its foreign policy and to make the public aware that the problems happening in the U.K. are directly because of foreign policy."[10] A former classmate of Nabeel Hussain, another Metropolitan University student, indicated that Hussain had recently become stricter in his religious practices and had started attending antiwar rallies in Birmingham and Manchester.[11]

According to Abdulla Ahmed Ali and Assad Sarwar, their experiences in 2002 and 2003 traveling to southwest Asia working with wounded Afghan refugees in Pakistan had an important role in the development of their moral outrage against U.K. and U.S. military action in both Afghanistan and Iraq. Ali was shocked by "appalling" conditions in the camps, where he witnessed many people dying. Ali is thought to have been radicalized during this six-month trip. Co-conspirator Umar Islam was also on this trip.[12] In what was believed to be Ali's "suicide" video, he verbalized some of these political grievances and directed them at those he considered the "moral violators." He referred to Osama bin Laden, saying: "Sheikh Osama warned you many times to leave our lands or you will be destroyed and now the time has come for you to be destroyed. And you have nothing to expect other than floods of martyr operations."[13] Umar Islam uttered similar words in his video: "This is revenge for the actions of the U.S. in the Muslim lands and their accomplices such as the British and the Jews."[14]

When officers searched the home Ali shared with his wife and their infant son, they found a document on which he had written the philosophy that inspired his deeds. He wrote: "The psychology of war is that you can defeat your enemy if you take away that which they love the most and strike terror into their hearts. With martyrdom operations they achieve that as the most beloved thing is life and wealth. When your enemy is not scared to die it scares you."[15]

The Walthamstow/High Wycombe Clusters

Twenty-five suspects were taken into custody in and around London on the night of August 9, 2006. Although recorded conversations suggested that the group had even talked of using eighteen suicide bombers with other destinations to be targeted (including Boston, Denver, and Miami), only eleven people (Abdulla Ahmed Ali, Assad Sarwar, Tanvir Hussain, Ibrahim Savant, Arafat Khan, Waheed Zaman, Umar Islam, Adam Khalib, Cosor Ali, Abdul Waheed and Shamin Uddin) were charged in connection with the plot.[16] The cluster was comprised of primarily British-born Muslims of Pakistani or Kashmiri origin, with three converts among the group of twenty-five. Eight of the men had grown up in the vicinity of Walthamstow, in East London, and three in High Wycombe, a town west of London. Their ages ranged from twenty-four to thirty, and they came from a variety of socioeconomic backgrounds. Their professions included students, entrepreneurs, delivery men, and even a Heathrow Airport security official. Their family circumstances ranged from single to newlywed to new fathers, and although a number of the men had some university-level education, none had attended top-tier schools.[17] The names of only twenty-two of the twenty-five were released by British authorities.

The cluster was essentially an autonomous group of young men and women whose motivations, cohesiveness, and radicalization all occurred in the absence of any organized network or formal entry into the transnational jihad. This was a localized, neighborhood phenomenon comprised of a mixture of school friends and acquaintances who had met through charity organizations as well as among the refugee camps of Pakistan. Abdulla

Ahmed Ali was the charismatic ringleader or "emir" of the cell. His preexisting relationships from his youth with some of the other members of this neighborhood cluster were the primary basis for its cohesion. In many ways this cluster was the "Walthamstow Gang." The Islamic Medical Association also played a role in linking members of the group, as a number of the plotters were involved in its activities both in London and abroad.

Abdulla Ahmed Ali and Assad Sarwar initially met when they traveled to the Chaman refugee camp close to Pakistan's border in late 2002 through early 2003 as volunteers for the Midlands-based Islamic Medical Association (IMA). According to their accounts, both were deeply affected by their work tending the injuries of children fatally wounded by U.S. bombs at a refugee camp in early 2003. It was on this trip that they also met fellow defendant Umar Islam, who also worked for IMA in East London. Sarwar and Ali met up again after lectures at an East London school and discussed the situation in Afghanistan and Iraq, as both were frustrated by the numbers of refugees from these conflicts. In fact, they both eventually worked together at the IMA's East London office.[18] Meanwhile, Arafat Khan, who also lived in Walthamstow, went to school with Ali and attended Waltham Forest College, where he met Tanvir Hussain. Umar Islam, Waheed Zaman, and Ibrahim Savant had also taken a martial arts class together.[19]

Anatomy of the Cluster

Active Core

Abdulla Ahmed Ali, age twenty-five at the time of his arrest, was born in London. His parents had moved to the U.K. in the 1960s from Pakistan. However, the family decided to move back to Pakistan for the first seven years of Ali's life. When they returned to the U.K., he grew up in a middle-class household in the Walthamstow area. According to Ali, he had been involved with Tablighi Jamaat since his teens. In fact, even in high school, Ali began to adopt some extremist views; according to one teacher, Ali "thought the Taliban had created a model society in Afghanistan." Ali studied computer systems engineering at City University, where he completed his degree in 2002.[20]

While at university he became politically active, joining demonstrations and handing out leaflets. After graduating, rather than seeking employment in the U.K., Ali instead sought out business opportunities in Pakistan. Subsequently, he worked in the East London office of the IMA, which aimed to aid refugees on the Afghan-Pakistan border. In January 2003, Ali traveled to a refugee camp for Afghans in Pakistan. At the time of his arrest, he was an unemployed former shop worker, yet he and his brother used cash to purchase a $260,000 second-floor flat in Forest Road, Walthamstow, which served as the bomb factory. Ali was married with a two-year-old son.[21]

Assad Sarwar, age twenty-two at the time of his arrest, was born and raised in High Wycombe by his Kashmiri immigrant parents west of London. According to his court testimony, Sarwar turned down a place at university in Chichester because he was homesick. His second attempt, at Brunel University, first in sports science then in earth science, also failed because he found the work too hard. According to his family, Sarwar became a Tabligh Jamaat follower after dropping out of university. His brother noted, "He got actively involved in that and thought that religion [was] more important than study." Sarwar was one of the seven defendants to work for the IMA and also worked out of their East London office. He traveled to a refugee camp in Pakistan in early 2003 to assist refugees. When he returned from the 2003 trip, Sarwar had a number of jobs, including working for Royal Mail and British Telecom, which he left as he said he could not cope with the work. While participating in the plot, he was working as a delivery driver for an Indian restaurant and selling martial arts DVDs on eBay.[22]

Mohammed Gulzar, age twenty-six at the time of his arrest, was originally from Birmingham, England, and was a failed computer studies undergraduate at Portsmouth University. He grew up as a close friend of Rashid Rauf and in 2000 began to attend Tablighi Jamaat sessions and became more religious. According to law enforcement sources, he fled to Pakistan in 2002 when British police sought him for questioning in the murder of a friend's uncle. That friend, Rashid Rauf, also fled to Pakistan around the same time. There is some speculation that the two were both involved in this murder. After Gulzar left the U.K., he spent time in Pakistan, performing missionary work, and then in South Africa from 2004 until September 2005, when he returned to Pakistan.[23]

Tanvir Hussain, age twenty-five at the time of his arrest, was born in Blackburn, Lancashire. He went to Norlington Boys School in Leytonstone, Waltham Forest, in East London before attending City University. Tanvir told the court he did not grow up religious; he regularly used drugs and alcohol during his student years before becoming more observant while working at a NHS sexual health clinic in north London. He had been described as a fashion-conscious person who stayed out with friends and said his life was "just having fun." Hussain noted, "I used to love sports. I used to always play cricket, football, boxing, everything. Any type of sport, I used to love it." He studied business information systems and computer communications at Middlesex University in 2000. Fasting during Ramadan one year, he decided to turn toward religion and subsequently attended an antiwar rally in London.[24]

Followers

Arafat Waheed Khan, age twenty-five at the time of his arrest, was born in Pakistan but was raised in Walthamstow, in northeast London, and knew Ali from school. He failed to complete a business course at Middlesex University and worked at the Link mobile phone shop but resigned in 2006 after his branch came under investigation. Khan described his lifestyle as "going out clubbing, visiting snooker halls, smoking dope and doing hard drugs such as heroin." According to his friend Tanvir Hussain, "Arafat was the life and soul of the party. He was always up for a laugh. Very easy-going guy and he was always joking around, having fun. That sort of sums Arafat up quite well." He was neither political nor religious but was deeply affected by the death of his father in 2005 or 2006.[25]

Waheed Zaman, age twenty-two at the time of his arrest, grew up in Walthamstow and had a very ordinary adolescence, spending hours as a teenager playing computer games and playing soccer. At the time of arrest, he lived opposite the Queen's Road Mosque where at least eight of the suspects are believed to have worshiped. Zaman was a student at London Metropolitan University studying biomedical science. At university he was the president of the school's Islamic society. Like, Assad Sarwar, Zaman was reportedly a Tablighi Jamaat follower and attended study groups at the London headquarters of Tablighi Jamaat in West Ham. He was active politically at university, raising funds and volunteering for Muslim Aid and Islamic Relief charity organizations.[26]

Ibrahim Savant, age twenty-five at the time of his arrest, was born and grew up in Walthamstow, East London, as Oliver Savant. He was raised in a mixed marriage as his father was an Iranian architect and his mother an English accountant. Savant studied at local schools, played the trumpet, and was said to be an accomplished soccer player. According to local accounts, Oliver Savant was a popular boy growing up in the neighborhood. In 1998, the eighteen-year-old Savant converted to Islam and began using the name Ibrahim; soon after his conversion, he began wearing traditional Muslim white gowns (thobes) and grew a long beard. Right around this time, he dropped out of university. Savant, who was by now married, worked as a taxi driver.[27]

Umar Islam, age twenty-eight at the time of his arrest, was born Brian Young in High Wycombe and is of West Indian ancestry. He was born and raised as a Christian. As a youth he adopted Rastafarianism for its "spiritual side." Admittedly a poor student, he smoked a great deal of marijuana and was a big fan of reggae music. His friendship with a man who lived in his building who had just converted to Islam and seemingly had cleaned up his life, as well as a trip to Barbados that revealed the lack of "substance" behind Rastafarianism, prompted Brian Young to convert to Islam in 2000. He later changed his name so that he could enter Saudi Arabia to perform the hajj. Umar Islam was one of the seven defendants who worked for IMA. Umar traveled to Pakistan with Sarwar to help with refugee relief efforts. He worked as a bus ticket inspector, already had children with one woman, and had married a Muslim woman, who was pregnant at the time of his arrest.[28]

Adam Khatib, age nineteen at the time of his arrest, became acquainted with Abdulla Ahmed Ali through Ali's youngest brother and a shared interest in football. His family was originally from Mauritius. "For as long as anyone can remember, Mr. Khatib had dressed like most British teenagers, favoring jeans, T-shirts, sneakers and other Western-style fashion. But last year [2005], he abruptly adopted a new look that apparently reflected a deeper sense of devotion on the part of the British-born Muslim from East London. Mr. Khatib was now seen wearing only traditional Islamic clothing and often talking outside of his family's modest townhouse on Wellington Road with a new set of friends who dressed similarly, some of them with thick beards, Jennifer Phillips, a neighbor, recalled in an interview."[29]

Periphery

British investigators had been monitoring the cluster's activities around the clock in the days leading up to the arrests. The names of twenty-two of the twenty-three individuals arrested were released. In addition to the previously discussed nine members of the the the cluster, the fourteen individuals who were in the periphery of the cluster and most of whom were not charged included Ali's wife, Cosor Ali; Rashid Rauf's brother, Talib Rauf, a university student; Assan Abdullah Khan; Shamin Uddin, a used car salesman; Abdul Muneem Patel, son of Mohammed Patel of the IMA; Mohammed Usman Saddique, a Heathrow airport employee with twenty-four-hour access to the facility; Amin Asmin Tariq, a former body builder; Shazad Khuram Ali, a devout taxi driver; Waseem Kayani; Abdul Waheed, formerly Don Stewart-Whyte, the half brother of a Victoria Secret model; and three brothers, Nabeel Hussain, Mehran Hussain, and Umair Hussain.

Overseas Travel and Link Up with Al Qaeda

Travel to southwest Asia (Pakistan and Afghanistan) provided opportunities for the active core members of the cluster to link up with the transnational jihad and potentially Rashid Rauf and/or al Qaeda. For example, Ali, the alleged airline plot ringleader, made four trips to Pakistan between 2003 and 2006, according to trial testimony.[30]

Three of the men traveled to the IMA's office in Chaman, outside of Quetta, during the fall and winter of 2002–3 as part of an effort to assist refugees from Afghanistan who were in refugee camps in Pakistan. Abdulla Ahmed Ali, Assad Sarwar, and Umar Islam participated in this mission, which involved running an ambulance service at the camps. All three men were deeply affected by the conditions of the Afghans who were refugees from the coalition war effort in Afghanistan.[31]

During the period in 2004 that Ali traveled to Pakistan, the leaders of two other major terrorist plots in Britain made similar trips, according to British court records. Between December 2004 and February 2005, individuals involved in Theseus (the July 7, 2005 plot) and Vivace (the July 21, 2005 plot) all traveled to Pakistan during that three-month window. According to the journalists Janet Stobart and Sebastian Rotella, British anti-terrorism officials assert that the men from all three plots (Theseus, Vivace, and Overt) were trained and directed by Abu Ubaidah al Masri, al Qaeda's Chief of External Operations during this time period. However, this has not been further substantiated.[32]

Abdulla Ahmed Ali traveled to Pakistan between June and December 2005 with Adam Khatib. In October, Assad Sarwar also traveled to Pakistan.

It is unknown whether the men received training during this trip or whether they met up with Arafat Khan, who also traveled to Pakistan during that fall. However, it is likely that Ali, Khatib, and Sarwar met up with Mohammed Gulzar, who was in Pakistan at the same time. Furthermore, this may have been when Rashid Rauf was introduced to Abdulla Ahmed Ali, via Gulzar.[33] Tanvir Hussain traveled to Pakistan in February 2006, where he may have been instructed on how to make HMTD, the high explosive that was to be used in the detonators. Abdulla Ahmed Ali traveled to Pakistan again between April and June 2006, where he is understood to have been selected to head the suicide plot and received training on how to build the devices. Assad Sarwar traveled to Pakistan between June 18 and July 8.[34]

Training and Skill Acquisition

The U.K. Crown Prosecutors asserted that some of the men convicted in this case traveled to the Federally Administered Tribal Areas (FATAs) of Pakistan, where they received explosives training. U.S. officials allege that the training came "from al-Qaida specialists." Some U.K. officials have suggested to media outlets that Abu Ubaidah al Masri may have even trained some of the individuals for the airline plot.[35] Abdulla Ahmed Ali and Assad Sarwar testified that they were in touch with a Kashmiri militant who went by the names "Yusuf" and "Jamil Shah." Sarwar told the court that he received explosives training from this man in Pakistan in the early summer of 2006. However, this most likely referred to Rashid Rauf.[36]

Although Ali had traveled to Pakistan from May to June 2006, at the first trial he claimed that he had researched on the Internet how to make an explosive device using a plastic drink bottle, hydrogen peroxide, and batteries.[37] At the second trial, Ali changed his testimony and explained why travel to Pakistan was essential. He testified that he found online sites to be "a bit wishy washy, and not very detailed." He added that "the whole point of us learning how to do it from someone who's done it before or someone would know about the thing is obviously [it's] quite dangerous dealing with these materials. We don't want to injure ourselves or anything."[38]

U.K. officials noted that "Their bomb design, which has been widely reported, had striking similarities to explosives used in previous terrorist plots. Hydrogen peroxide was the main ingredient in the explosives used in both the July 7 and July 21 plots, while HMTD was also used as the detonator in the July 7 attack."[39] As previously noted, British prosecutors allege that Tanvir Hussain traveled to Pakistan early in 2006, where he was instructed on how to make HMTD.

Al Qaeda Recruitment

Testifying before a Senate committee, the director of the Defense Intelligence Agency, Lt. Gen. Michael D. Maples, described the plotters as "an al Qaeda cell, directed by al Qaeda leadership in Pakistan."[40] Yet U.K. prosecutors did not produce any evidence explicitly linking the plot to al Qaeda. Nonetheless, British and American officials have suggested that al Qaeda's Chief of External Operations, Abu Ubaidah al Masri, may have authorized the alleged airline plot and trained some of the British plotters. Rashid Rauf and Mohammed Gulzar served as intermediate links in the human chain between the network in the U.K. and al Qaeda Core in Pakistan.[41] The plotters also had personal and telephone links to individuals involved in other British al Qaeda–linked plots. Some of these men served as "fixers" who facilitated travel to Pakistan and al Qaeda individuals while others were operatives involved in actual U.K. plots. Two of these included Mohammed Hamid (convicted in 2008 of arranging terrorist training in the British countryside for Operation Vivace) and Muktar Ibrahim, the ringleader of Operation Vivace, who had been in contact via cell phone with Abdulla Ahmed Ali in the spring of 2005, according to British officials.[42]

The significance of links to Mohammed al Ghabra, a U.S.-designated al Qaeda supporter and financier who resides in the U.K, remains less clear. Al Ghabra arranged for the leader of the failed July 21 London suicide attacks to travel to Pakistan for terrorist training and may have had a role in the Operation Overt plot as well. While links between al Ghabra and Abdulla Ahmed Ali have not been confirmed, Mohammed Gulzar, another Operation Overt plotter, went to see al Ghabra as soon as he arrived in the U.K. from South Africa. He picked up a CD and USB stick that contained a video of Nicholas Berg's decapitation as well as Arabic songs.[43]

While the men of the High Wycombe/Walthamstow cluster clearly had numerous connections to al Qaeda–linked individuals, the actual recruitment of the British men to the plot still remains somewhat murky. Nevertheless, repeated travel to Pakistan and links to Rashid Rauf and Mohammed al

Ghabra are clearly the most likely factors connecting them to al Qaeda Core and possibly facilitating their recruitment to the plot.

Operational Cycle

Travel to Pakistan appears to have been the catalyst for the cluster's mobilization to action. A few months after Abdulla Ahmed Ali's return to the U.K. in December 2005, he began initial preparations for a plot by experimenting with hydrogen peroxide in late April 2006. However, additional travel to Pakistan occurred in the spring of 2006 and almost immediately upon Ali's return to the U.K. on June 24, he and the active core members of the cluster began the operational cycle for their "blessed operation" and began to recruit additional participants in the plot. In June an apartment was purchased that would serve as the studio for the filming of the martyrdom videos as well as a bomb factory. The group rapidly reached a peak of activity in its final three weeks before being disrupted in August 2006. The total duration of the operational cycle was six to seven weeks.[44]

Target Selection

The target was transatlantic airliners that would be departing Heathrow Airport and be en route to North American cities in the United States and Canada. Personal improvised explosive devices constructed out of plastic drink bottles and filled with hydrogen peroxide would be detonated by suicide bombers on a number of flights almost simultaneously over the Atlantic and/or as they approached their North American destinations. Prosecutors stated that "at the very least" seven flights were targeted. Given average capacity on these flights (approximately 260 passengers), that would have meant the death of more than 1,700 people.[45]

On August 6, 2006, Abdulla Ahmed Ali sat down in front of a screen at an Internet café, T&I Telecom in Walthamstow, and went to the timetable page of the American Airlines Web site, among others, and began to highlight flight numbers. He selected seven flights on American and Canadian airliners to Chicago, New York, Washington, D.C., San Francisco, Toronto, and Montreal during a two-and-a-half-hour period. They were all heading from Heathrow to North America; round-trip flights were not considered.[46] When police arrested Abdulla Ahmed Ali and searched his jacket pockets, they found a "memory stick containing details of seven flights out of Heathrow to North America along similar lines to the data he had been collating at T&I Telecom shop along with information about hand luggage rules at BAA airports." In the opposite pocket was a diary, which contained such a treasure of information that prosecutors at Woolwich Crown Court described it as a "blueprint" for the attacks.[47]

The flights identified by Ali were all scheduled to depart from Terminal 3 to six cities in North America—San Francisco, Toronto, Montreal, Washington, New York, and Chicago.[48] Police believe they were chosen because they would provide a six-hour window in which all the flights would be airborne and vulnerable to a simultaneous suicide attack. The jets were operated by Air Canada, United Airlines, and American Airlines and involved Boeing 777, 767, and 763 jets capable of carrying an average of 260 people.[49]

Among the notes discovered in Ali's diary were: "select date, five days before jet, all link up"; "calculate exact drops of tang"; "decide on which battery to use for D"; "one drink use, other keep in pocket, maybe will not get through machine"; and "dirty mag to distract." Police said "the plot was drawn up in Pakistan with detailed instructions passed to Ali during frequent trips to its lawless border with Afghanistan." The jury at Woolwich Crown Court was played a surveillance tape in which one member of the gang discussed recruiting as many as eighteen bombers, which, assuming two bombers per plane and 260 passengers per plane, would have emulated the scale of the 9/11 plot that killed almost 3,000.[50]

There was a set of possible "second wave" targets under consideration. Evidence provided at trial suggested that Assad Sarwar had also researched "targets of national and regional significance," including the financial center at Canary Wharf, a gas pipeline between Belgium and the U.K., and various British airports and power stations, including nuclear facilities.[51]

Casing

There seems to be minimal evidence of surveillance conducted on Heathrow Airport by the plotters. However, one member of the cell was supposedly to perform a "dummy run" within seventy-two hours to test airport security.[52]

Communications

In court, Ali, Sarwar, and Gulzar all acknowledged being in frequent communication with men in Pakistan as the plot progressed, although they did not identify Rashid Rauf definitively as their primary point of contact but referred to him as one who went alternately by the names "Yusuf" and "Jamil Shah." Internet cafés, phone calls from kiosks, and untraceable phone cards were the methods of communication.[53] Personal ties clearly played a role as well, as Mohammed Gulzar arrived from South Africa in the final weeks of the plot to act as a "supervisor" for the final stages of the plot. Counterterrorism officials assert that significant communications passed through Gulzar to his old friend from Birmingham, Rashid Rauf, in Pakistan. Consequently, previous links in the U.K. provided a human chain to Pakistan in which Rauf served as the "link man."[54]

Rauf was born in Pakistan but was brought up in the Midlands after his family immigrated to the U.K. from Kashmir in the 1980s. His father was a successful baker from the Ward End area of Birmingham. While living in England, Rauf worked as a deliveryman for his father's bakery. He had enrolled at Portsmouth University in September 1999 but left in the summer of 2002 without graduating. A family friend noted, "He was not particularly religious, though he was a regular at the mosque. He was more into going to the gym or playing football. . . . He was quite a bright kid but he never spoke about politics or 9/11 and Islam or anything."[55]

According to law enforcement sources, Rauf fled to Pakistan in 2002, when British police sought him for questioning in the murder of his uncle, who was stabbed to death on his way home from work in what was described as a "frenzied attack." Following his flight from the U.K., Rauf sought to take part in the fight against the U.S. forces in Afghanistan. There he met Amjad Farooqi, a senior militant in Pakistan, who had a close working relationship with al Qaeda at various levels. Rauf reportedly told intelligence officials that he went into Afghanistan with Farooqi in mid-2002 where he met some of the key al Qaeda leaders.[56] Subsequently, Rauf became a regular visitor to Afghanistan, traveling to various parts of the country to meet al Qaeda figures, though not Osama bin Laden or Ayman al Zawahiri. When Farooqi was killed in 2002, Rauf established direct and regular contact with Abu Faraj al Libi, the Libyan who served as al Qaeda's head of external operations. By the time al Libi was captured in May 2005, Rashid Rauf was already well-known to the first and second line of al Qaeda leaders who maintained some sort of contact with him.[57]

Rauf was arrested in Bhawalpur, Pakistan, a day before some arrests relating to Operation Overt were made in Britain. The Pakistani interior minister, Aftab Ahmed Khan Sherpao, claimed that "he [Rauf] is an al Qaeda operative with linkages in Afghanistan." He was said to be one of the ringleaders of the alleged plot.[58] Rauf's recent travel to Pakistan certainly played a role as a communication mode, as both Ali and Sarwar had been in Pakistan during the May–June 2006 time period.[59]

Communication via these three network pathways had the potential to serve as a medium for command and control. In fact, at the trial sentencing hearing on September 14, 2009, the judge clearly described this plot as an operation run by individuals in Pakistan, a conclusion that appears to based mainly on e-mails Abdulla Ahmed Ali sent to contacts in Pakistan.[60] Referring to the e-mails, the judge stated that "they establish beyond question that the ultimate control of this conspiracy lay in Pakistan." He further noted that "the e-mail correspondence demonstrates that this conspiracy was controlled, monitored carefully and funded by Pakistan, with the defendants Ali and Sarwar high level executives within this country [U.K.]."[61]

For example, Ali received e-mails from Pakistan on both July 31 and August 4 inquiring as to whether British surveillance (the skin infection) was monitoring the conspirators:

How is the skin infection you were telling me about? Has it got worse or is the cream working?

This was probably a reference to the surveillance Ali had detected and reported to Pakistan.

Your skin infection is contagious don't want it spreading. By the way how bad is it do u always get it when you go out or is it only sometimes?? I need as much details as possible so my friend the skin specialist (paps) can help. Do u think u can still open the shop with this skin problem?? Is it only minor??? Or do u think u can still sort an opening time without the skin problem worsening??. . . PS. Have any of the shop assistants with u also got this infection????//.[62]

Weaponization

At the end of April 2006, Sarwar purchased some hydrogen peroxide for
Abdulla Ahmed Ali and Tanvir Hussain to experiment with in the woods
near their home. However, they were unsuccessful. According to the Woolwich Crown Court, following additional travel to Pakistan where the men
received more training, in late July 2006, "Abdulla Ahmed Ali set up shop
in an east London apartment his brother had just purchased as an invest-
ment. Ali testified that he told his brother he would help fix it up for resale."
According to further court testimony, Ali and one of his associates went to
work experimenting with the bomb components. The men planned to inject
a liquid explosive charge into the bottom of empty 500-milliliter bottles of
Lucozade or Oasis drinks.[63] Ali brought key material back from Pakistan—
packets of the sugar-based powdered drink Tang and Toshiba AA batteries:
"Authorities alleged that the Tang would function as fuel for the hydrogen
peroxide-based explosive; the AA batteries would conceal the chemical compound hexamethylene triperoxide diamine (HMTD) for the detonator."[64]
    Gulzar arrived in the U.K. on July 18 and almost immediately began
texting and phoning a number in Pakistan, possibly that of Rashid Rauf. By
July 29, he was in contact with Sarwar as well as Mohammed al Ghabra, the
al Qaeda facilitator who had sent off one of the July 21 bombers to Pakistan
for training in Pakistan.[65] According to court testimony, "Sarwar was essentially the bomb chemist; he purchased and stored the chemicals to make
the liquid explosive and detonator. Their purchases included more than 40
liters of hydrogen peroxide, the main ingredient for the liquid explosive,
which they bought from health food and hydroponics suppliers in Britain."
In fact, Sarwar purchased the key chemicals for that compound both at local
pharmacies in April and July as well as from a hairdressing supply store in
Carmarthen, South Wales, while using the false name of Jona Lewis.[66]
    Another defendant, Tanvir Hussain, was put in charge of making HMTD,
which would be placed in detonators fashioned from hollowed-out Toshiba
batteries that had been bought especially for the purpose in Pakistan. The
hole at the bottom was to be concealed with black foam.[67] The men drilled
holes in the plastic bottles to drain them of fluid. Investigators believe that
"the plan was to refill them with the explosive mixture and reseal the bottles
with superglue. Abdulla Ahmed Ali also figured out how to remove the AA
battery contents in order to insert the HMTD. Beyond that, they were working on the trigger, for which they planned to use a disposable camera wired

to the detonator. . . . While the plotters had not yet assembled a complete device, prosecutors stated that they had acquired all the constituent parts for the three key components: the liquid explosive (40 liters of hydrogen peroxide) from health food and hydroponics suppliers in Britain as well as the detonator, and the trigger—enough to produce at least 20 bombs."[68]

The Al Qaeda Factor

The leading hypothesis of the link to al Qaeda Core is that Rashid Rauf served as a control officer or "link man" for the cluster and was an intermediary between the cluster and al Qaeda Core's Chief of External Operations. American, British, and Pakistani officials have suggested in a variety of venues that the plot was an al Qaeda plot and that al Qaeda's Chief of External Operations, Abu Ubaidah al Masri, conceived of, authorized, orchestrated, and may have even trained some of the individuals for the airline plot. Given that al Masri reportedly died in 2007 of natural causes, we may never know whether this is true.[69]

The official U.S. government position has been that the plot was the work of al Qaeda. Testifying before a Senate committee in February 2007, the director of the Defense Intelligence Agency, Lt. Gen. Michael D. Maples, described the plotters as "an al-Qaida cell, directed by al-Qaida leadership in Pakistan." Moreover, U.S. Secretary of Homeland Security Michael Chertoff noted that "I can't tell you whether operationally it went up to bin Laden, but I think the links to the al-Qaida network are, in my mind, pretty clear."[70]

While British prosecutors did not produce any evidence explicitly linking the plot to al Qaeda, at the trial sentencing hearing on September 14, 2009, the judge clearly described this plot as an operation run by individuals in Pakistan, which, as was noted earlier, he appears to have based mainly on e-mail exchanges Ali had with contacts in Pakistan.

Rashid Rauf's role is probably the key determinant as to what relationship this plot had to al Qaeda Core as he is the key link to it. Was the plot his idea, or was he simply an intermediate conduit between al Qaeda Core and the U.K. plotters?

In 2010, the first legal documents were released that clarified Rauf's exact position within al Qaeda. According to documents relating to Operation Highrise (2009), in 2008 Rauf worked in al Qaeda's external operations section for its chief at the time, Saleh al Somali. This bolstered claims that in the

2005–6 timeframe Rauf was close to Abu Ubaidah al Masri, then al Qaeda's Chief of External Operations.[71] In terms of training, at most, only two or three (Ali, Sarwar, Hussain) of the active members of the cluster may have trained with al Qaeda Core associated personnel. The journalist Sebastian Rotella suggests that they trained with Abu Ubaidah al Masri himself.[72]

Although it does not appear that funding for the operations came from al Qaeda Core, it certainly does seem that training was provided and, most important, as the conspiracy moved into its final weeks, that regular communication occurred between al Qaeda Core in Pakistan and the plotters in the West via Rashid Rauf and Gulzar who had arrived in the U.K. in July to oversee the plot. Rashid Rauf likely provided command and control of the plot on behalf of Abu Ubaidah al Masri and al Qaeda Core. The Woolwich Crown Court judge agreed. In conclusion, Operation Overt was most likely an al Qaeda "command and control" plot.[73]

PART II

Al Qaeda "Suggested/Endorsed" Plots

Chapter 4

Millennium Plot (Los Angeles, 1999)

ON DECEMBER 14, 1999, Algerian citizen Ahmed Ressam took a rented car filled with explosives and attempted to cross the U.S.-Canada border at Port Angeles, Washington, on his way to the Los Angeles International Airport (LAX). An alert customs inspector, who noticed Ressam sweating profusely, had him pull over and his car inspected. This action thwarted an al Qaeda plot against Los Angeles timed for the turn of the millennium on December 31, 1999.

The "Montrealistan" Scene

With the advent of the Algerian civil war in 1992, French-speaking Montreal became a haven for Algerians seeking a respite from the conflict. A loose political asylum policy, generous unemployment benefits, and lax enforcement of immigration regulations all contributed to the growth of a vibrant French-speaking North African diaspora community in Montreal. Along with those simply seeking a better life came mujahedeen veterans from both Afghanistan and Bosnia who also were able to take advantage of the benefits of Montreal and laid the foundation for the development of "Montrealistan" in the mid-1990s. Past links to both GIA and mujahedeen veterans provided key ongoing connections with al Qaeda support networks in London, Paris, and southwest Asia.

Among the North African community in Montreal, one central locus of activity was the Assuna Annabawiyah Mosque, Montreal's largest Salafi mosque. Assuna Annabawiyah attracted more than 1,500 worshipers for Friday jummah prayers. Not only was this a religious hub for the community, but it was also a social center, as young men spent time in and around its adjoining bookstore, where Salafi books and tapes were sold. Ironically, Assuna Annabawiyah Mosque was also the central depot for the North African criminal community to sell their stolen goods, which often included false documents, credit cards, and the spoils from petty theft. Low-level criminality was a common pastime for a number of young men in the North African diaspora community.[1] At the top of the social pyramid among the North African expatriates were the veterans of Afghanistan and Bosnia, whose tales of adventure and heroism intrigued and affected the other members of this larger circle. Once in Montreal, their roles shifted from fighters to facilitators.[2]

Gravitating to Reactionary Islam

The Assuna Annabawiyah Mosque, located in a poor Montreal neighborhood known to locals as Park Extension, served as the primary venue for North Africans in Montreal to be exposed to Wahhabi-Salafi doctrine. Opened in 1993, in a cultural center, the location was funded by Arabs in the Persian Gulf and had a congregation of 2,500 to 3,000. It was a key node in Montreal for the proliferation of an interpretation of Islam that promoted military jihad as a means to defend Islam, restore the Caliphate, and fight the West. At Assuna, recruiting videos that called for martyrdom and for jihad in Afghanistan were distributed regularly. The videos stated, "Come to Afghanistan, come for Jihad. If you are real believers, Allah is expecting you to do an extra job."[3] Ahmed Ressam and Mustapha Labsi first met at the Assuna Annabawiyah Mosque soon after their arrival in Montreal.[4] Abderrauf Hannachi, a forty-something ex-jihadi, was a regular presence there as well.[5]

Politicization of Beliefs

Abderrauf Hannachi was the primary voice of the critique against the West among the men: "he talked about his hatred for the West and, in particular, for the United States: *The American infidels and their culture—immoral dress and music, godless pursuit of wealth—must be stopped. You can help. You can, as I have, join the holy war.*"[6]

The Fateh Kamel Groupe Cluster

The four-room apartment at 6301 Place de la Micorne, in Montreal's Anjou district, became the primary hangout for both the ex-mujahedeen and their wannabe followers. It was rented by Adel Boumezbeur, who worked as a cook and shared with Said Atmani, a veteran of the jihad in Bosnia. In early 1996, both Ahmed Ressam and Mustapha Labsi moved in. Fateh Kamel began to spend more time there as well, hanging out with Atmani, whom he had known in Bosnia. The location began to serve as the "Canadian headquarters of the Algerian jihad network," as well as a sort of den of unemployed petty thieves. It is strongly believed by Canadian authorities that some of the spoils of the criminality, like counterfeit passports, were utilized to aid jihadi enterprises around the world via Kamel's wider network. Not only did telephonic analysis linked the apartment with veterans of the jihad in Bosnia who were in France, Italy, and Turkey, but this location regularly hosted visiting ex-mujahedeen.[7]

When the men were not robbing tourists of luggage, passports, and credit cards, they spent hours on end smoking cigarettes, playing soccer, and criticizing the West and the United States:

CSIS [Canadian Security and Intelligence Service] agents quickly learned of Ressam's frauds and thefts. They also knew Ressam and others were wanted on immigration warrants. But they could barely bring themselves to call Ressam and the Malicorne denizens a "cell." That sort of hyperbole was for [Judge] Bruguière, who referred to the address as the "*appartement de conspiracie.*" The Canadians instead gave the men at the apartment a derisive nickname, the "BOG"—short for "Bunch of Guys." To CSIS, they seemed more pathetic than dangerous—unemployed, no girlfriends, living on welfare and thievery, crammed into a flat reeking of cigarette smoke. When they were overheard recruiting, plotting and spewing anti-Western vitriol, the agents found it nearly comical. An official would later refer to the sessions as "terrorist Tupperware parties."[8]

Time spent in the apartment in Place de la Malicorne, friendships that dated back to Algeria, shared criminal activities, and either participation or interest in jihadi exploits all overlapped, serving to further the stickiness of the Groupe Fateh Kamel Cluster in Montreal. For example, Adel Boumezbeur, Moured Ikhlef, and Fateh Kamel all knew each other from childhood in Algeria and Said Atmani, Abderrauf Hannachi, and Fateh Kamel were fellow travelers and had participated in the al Mujahedeen Brigade in Zenica, Bosnia. Fellow Algerians Mustapha Labsi and Ahmed Ressam rounded out the group. Nevertheless, the men never coalesced into a cluster or bunch of guys with a specific plan directed against the West until Ahmed Ressam and Mustapha Labsi traveled to southwest Asia, where they received training in al Qaeda's Khalden Camp.[9]

Anatomy of the Cluster

Active Core

Ahmed Ressam, age thirty-two at the time of his arrest, was the eldest of seven children who grew up in a small, poor town west of Algiers, Algeria. Ressam's family was relatively well-off, as his father owned a coffee shop and a six-bedroom house. Though his father was a devout Muslim, Ahmed grew up relatively secular, was the first in the family to get a "modern" education, and as a teenager was known for "wearing American clothes like Levi's and Stan Smith sneakers." However, as a sixteen-year-old he developed an ulcer and was sent to Paris for a long course of treatment. This interfered with his studies and he failed an important exam, effectively ending his opportunity to pursue further academic studies at university in Algeria. According to one source, "He applied for jobs with the Algerian police and security forces, but was turned down." Subsequently, he began to work at his father's coffee shop, living a secular life—drinking alcohol, going out with girls, going to clubs, and smoking hashish.[10]

Ressam's time in France laid the foundation for his radicalization. According to his brother, "In France, he read books—banned in Algeria—about how military dictators ruined Algeria's hopes of democracy after it gained independence from France." This had a significant effect on him as it "made him very bitter about his country. He believed that the government was corrupt and began to take up the cause of militant Islamic rebels, to his father's dismay."[11] He worked at the coffee shop for a few years until 1992, when he left Algeria and headed to Marseilles, France, in an attempt to find work and potentially a better life. Civil war had just broken out in Algeria. He subsequently ended up in Corsica, picking grapes, painting houses, and participating in a false documents production ring. After his arrest in Corsica for an immigration violation and before his potential deportation back to Algeria, he flew to Montreal, Canada, in February 1994, seeking political asylum. Though Ressam fabricated a story of imprisonment in Algeria, Canadian authorities allowed him to stay in Canada—releasing him on bond and providing him with welfare benefits, with the caveat that he agree to return for a subsequent hearing.[12]

According to Ressam's trial testimony, during the time he lived in Montreal, he worked for only a week, delivering advertising leaflets. The remainder of the time, he says, he supported himself on welfare payments and by robbing tourists. Although Ressam estimates that he performed this kind of theft thirty to forty times during his stay in Montreal, he says he was arrested for theft only four times and convicted only once. He served no jail time for that conviction but paid a fine. Despite his arrests, he continued to draw welfare benefits of $500 per month, which he was entitled to as a potential refugee. During this time, Ressam says that he and an associate, Mokhtar Haouari, another Algerian refugee claimant, trafficked stolen driver's license numbers, bank cards, and Social Security cards. They also provided Canadian passports and other identity documents to terrorist associates around the world.[13]

Active Core But Arrested Pre-Plot

Fateh (Mustafah) Kamel, age thirty-nine at the time of his arrest, was an Algerian who had immigrated to Canada in 1987 at age twenty-seven. Toward the end of the jihad against the Soviets in Afghanistan, Kamel took part in combat there. Though he returned to Montreal and married a woman from Quebec, he soon left to participate in the next field of jihad, in Bosnia. Over the next few years he would travel among Bosnia, Canada, and Western Europe, serving as a logistics expert, getting recruits and supplies to the battlefield in Bosnia until the Dayton Accords were signed. Between Afghanistan and Bosnia, Kamel made links that ultimately connected him to the GIA and its wave of attacks carried out in 1995–96 in

France. Though he subsequently returned to Montreal and managed the North-South Artisanal boutique, he maintained logistical links to the global jihad. In Montreal, he was considered a leader of the expatriate North African community.[14]

Mustapha Labsi, age thirty at the time of his arrest, also arrived in Montreal in 1994 claiming refugee status. He became Ressam's partner in crime, specializing in robbing tourists' suitcases from hotel lobbies as well as their credit cards, cash, and passports. Though arrested a number of times, he was never deported. In 1996, he, along with Ressam, moved into an apartment with Adel Boumezbeur and Said Atmami.[15]

Rachid Kefflous (Abu Doha), age thirty-four at the time of his arrest, was al Qaeda's operational "field commander" based in London. He was supposed to be a key point man for the Millennium Plot. He was arrested by British authorities in 2001 while attempting to depart the U.K.

Said Atmani, age thirty-three at the time of Ressam's arrest, was a Moroccan who had fought in Afghanistan and then in Bosnia as part of the al Mujahedeen Brigade in Zenica. That was where he had met Fateh Kamel, who subsequently encouraged him to move to Canada. Atmani, who was a stowaway, arrived in Montreal in 1995, rejoined Kamel, and became his top deputy as a talented forger.[16]

Followers

Mokhtar Haouari, age thirty-one at the time of his arrest, was another Algerian refugee claimant who "engaged in the trafficking of stolen driver's license numbers, bank cards, and Social Security cards." With Ressam, he "provided Canadian passports and other identity documents to terrorist associates around the world." At some point, he purchased Mustapha Kamel's trinket shop that sold the stolen goods. He was a childhood friend of Abdel Ghani Meskini and vouched for him to Ressam.[17]

Abdel Majid Dahoumane, age thirty-two at the time of his arrest, was one of the regulars at the apartment and had been a friend of Ressam's since his arrival in Montreal. He had arrived in Canada on a fake French passport in 1995.[18]

Abdel Ghani Meskini, age thirty-one at the time of his arrest, was a childhood friend of Mokhtar Haouari and lived in Brooklyn. Haouari vouched for him and introduced him to Ressam.[19]

Periphery

Moured Ikhlef, age thirty-one at the time of Ressam's arrest, was from the same part of Algiers as Fateh Kamel. He arrived in Canada in 1993 and requested refugee status. He was one of the regulars at the apartment and had been implicated in the 1992 bombing at Algiers airport. Nevertheless, he received Canadian refugee status in 1994.[20]

Adel Boumezbeur, age thirty-one at the time of Ressam's arrest, was born in Algiers but had gained Canadian citizenship. In Montreal he worked as a cook, and the apartment where all the men coalesced was rented in his name.[21]

Abderrauf Hannachi, age thirty-six at the time of Ressam's arrest, was a Tunisian who had a limited educational background. He had gained Canadian citizenship in 1986 and returned to Montreal in 1994 as a veteran of the jihad in Bosnia. He was a regular at the Assuna Annabawiyah Mosque and was known among the circle in Montreal for his stories and jokes as well as his animosity toward the West, particularly the United States. In the summer of 1997 he traveled to Khalden Camp in Afghanistan.[22]

Samir Ait Mohammed, age thirty-two at the time of Ressam's arrest, was an Algerian who had arrived in Germany from Algeria in 1991 to escape the civil unrest there. In Germany, he pursued a law degree and assisted volunteers who were supporting the Bosnian Muslims in the early 1990s. Diabetes is said to have kept him from going to a terrorist training camp. In 1997 he traveled to Canada under a false Belgian passport. His claim to be a refugee was rejected by Canada in 1998. In Montreal, he and Ressam became partners in crime.[23]

Overseas Travel and Link Up with Al Qaeda

In the summer of 1997, a member of the cluster, Abderrauf Hannachi, returned to Montreal from training at al Qaeda's Khalden Camp. He told the other men of the Groupe Fateh Kamel Cluster about what he had learned at the camp and how it had transformed him into a mujahid or warrior. Reinforced by the positive feedback about training from other mujahedeen veterans, Ressam and Labsi began to develop an interest in receiving training themselves. Subsequently, Hannachi reached out to Abu Zubayda, the gatekeeper for al Qaeda's camps in Afghanistan, who secured spots for them in the camps.[24]

On March 17, 1998, Ahmed Ressam departed Montreal for Toronto and ultimately for Pakistan. He arrived in Peshawar, where he stayed for a few weeks before Abu Zubayda set up his travel to Khalden Camp and wrote a letter of introduction. In Khalden, Ressam was grouped with individuals of varied nationalities, including thirty or so Algerians, many from Canada, including two of Ressam's former roommates from the Malicorne apartment, Said Atmani and Mustapha Labsi.[25]

Training and Skill Acquisition

In the six months of basic training, Ressam learned how to use machine guns, handguns, and RPGs and then advanced to bomb making utilizing C4 and TNT. He also had instruction on how to "blow up the infrastructure of a country," urban warfare, assassination techniques, and surveillance. Ressam ultimately moved from Khalden to the Darunta camp and received advanced training in detonator construction and chemical weapons, and even experimented with cyanide and sulfuric acid.[26] Ahmed Ressam is reported to have trained at Khalden Camp with shoe bomber Richard Reid as well as Zacarias Moussaoui, who was subsequently arrested in the United States.[27]

Al Qaeda Recruitment

Although Ressam and the other Canadian Algerians met with Abu Zubayda, he was not responsible for conceptualizing the plot. Rather, it was a self-initiated discussion among the Algerian Canadians, under their emir, Abu Doha aka Amar Mahklulif, an Algerian living in London, that resulted in selecting the date and in identifying an airport in the United States as the potential target. In fact, Ressam told the FBI that he conceived the idea to attack the Los Angeles International Airport himself but that Abu Zubayda encouraged him and helped facilitate the operation.[28] The conspirators were to include Mustapha Labsi, Ahmed Ressam, Fateh Kamel, Said Atmani, and Abu Doha, and the plan was to target the United States from Canada.[29]

In December 1998, when the training for the men was concluding, according to the U.S. complaint, the Algerian Canadians' emir, Abu Doha, traveled to Kandahar to meet Osama bin Laden to "discuss the co-operation and co-ordination between bin Laden's terrorist network . . . and a group of Algerian terrorists whose activities he coordinated and oversaw."[30] This would make sense because in describing the terms of the relationship that existed between Abu Zubayda and Osama bin Laden, Ahmed Ressam stated, "There is no one to who[m] Abu Zubayda must report to in terms of a superior; he is emir." From Ressam's perspective, Abu Zubayda was equal to, not subordinate to, bin Laden. Ressam stated Abu Zubayda was an associate of bin Laden and coordinated and cooperated with him in the training and trainee movements between his (Zubayda's) and bin Laden's camps.[31] Subsequently, in early 1999, Ressam was provided with $12,000 from Abu Doha via Abu Zubayda and most likely originating from Osama bin Laden, as well as hexamine tablets. Ultimately, this was a case of Ressam and his Algerian Canadian associates volunteering for an operation that would be coordinated with bin Laden's network (al Qaeda) rather than their being recruited by al Qaeda.[32]

Operational Cycle

Travel to Afghanistan and Pakistan was clearly the catalyst for the men's mobilization to action. Ressam returned to Los Angeles on February 7, 1999. He then traveled to Vancouver, where he stayed for a month or so before returning to Montreal in April.

Target Selection/Casing

Ressam utilized his return to Canada via Los Angeles from Afghanistan to conduct pre-operational reconnaissance on LAX.[33]

Logistics

Abu Zubayda gave Ressam $12,000, a notebook with instructions on bomb making, and some hexamine tablets and liquid glycol. Ressam was able to bring these materials into Canada through both U.S. and Canadian customs.[34] Ressam's original co-conspirators were all thwarted in their efforts to meet up in Montreal. Said Atmani was arrested in October 1998 in Niagara Falls with fake credit cards. Mustapha Labsi and an Algerian code named Fodail were arrested in the U.K., and Fateh Kamel was arrested in Jordan in March 1999. In the summer of 1999, Abu Doha informed Ressam, from London, that the other members of the Montreal cell had run into problems and that he would be on his own. Ressam decided to continue with the operation without the other members of his cell.[35]

This forced Ressam to recruit a group of North Africans in Canada and the United States who had not trained in Afghanistan. These included: "Abdel Majid Dahoumane, who had been Ressam's friend for much of his time in Montreal and who would help make the bomb; Mokhtar Haouari, a credit-card thief who would finance the plot; and Abdel Ghani Meskini, a con man living in Brooklyn who spoke English and loved American beer and Hollywood movies."[36]

Communications

Before he was arrested, Abu Doha spoke to Ressam via phone and told him that plans had changed and that he would be on his own. He likely would have been the al Qaeda "link man" between Afghanistan and Ressam had he not be arrested in the U.K. Meskini was recruited over the phone by his friend Mokhtar Haouari.[37]

Weaponization

Ressam took his first actions in furtherance of the plot on August 31, 1998, when he entered Active Electronique, the Canadian equivalent of Radio Shack, and purchased wire, solder, circuit boards, capacitors, integrated circuits, 9-volt battery connectors, a soldering gun, and several small, black, plastic boxes. The next day he purchased two Casio electronic alarm watches. He subsequently went to work creating the detonator and timer.[38]

On November 17, 2009, Ressam flew to Vancouver. He and Abdel Majid Dahoumane rented a room in Hotel 2400 through December 14, 1999. The two men began to construct the explosive device.[39] Using Ressam's notes from bomb-training school, the men were brewing a batch of HMTD, an unstable explosive made from hexamine, citric acid, and hydrogen peroxide. It could be inadvertently detonated by a slight jolt. They had stolen some of the chemicals at Evergro Products—the agricultural-supply store. Next, they created the military-grade explosive found in C-4 plastique, this time using hexamine and red nitric acid. The process gave off highly toxic fumes. The men used zinc lozenges and Chloraseptic spray to dull pain in their throats, which were raw from the fumes.[40] Inside Ressam's car were "four timing devices made from Casio watches and 9-volt batteries and 193 pounds of various explosive compounds, among them, RDX."[41]

Then the men rented a Chrysler 300M and hid the components for the explosive device in the space where the spare tire fits. Ressam then began his fateful drive to Port Angeles on the Canada-U.S. border. However, he was stopped by a suspicious U.S. customs official after taking the ferry to Port Angeles on December 14, 1999.[42]

The Al Qaeda Factor

Not only did Ressam receive training and subsequently funds and materiel from Abu Doha and Abu Zubayda in Peshawar before he returned to Canada, he also discussed plans for the Millennium attacks against the United States with Abu Doha while in Afghanistan. Moreover, Abu Doha, who had been sent to London to manage operations in the West from there, was also directly involved in the original versions of the plot. However, once the arrests occurred, Ressam was on his own to carry out the plot. Although both Abu Doha and Abu Zubayda had direct al Qaeda Core links and provided some funding, the plot was essentially conceptualized by the Algerian Canadians and carried out by Ressam with little to no guidance or supervision from abroad. Consequently, this plot is categorized as an al Qaeda Core "suggested/endorsed" plot. There was no al Qaeda command and control.

Interestingly, according to *The 9/11 Commission Report*, in December 1999, just before he attempted the plot, Ressam called "an Afghanistan based facilitator to inquire whether Bin Laden even wanted to take credit for the attack, but he did not get a reply."[43]

Chapter 5

Operation Rhyme (London, 2004)

ON AUGUST 3, 2004, British authorities arrested a group of fourteen men in the Luton area north of London. Two weeks later on August 17, 2004, eight of the men were charged with conspiracy to murder; conspiracy to commit a public nuisance by the use of radioactive materials, toxic gases, chemicals, and/or explosives; and possessing a document or record of information of a kind likely to be useful to a person committing or preparing an act of terrorism.

The group, which was called the "Luton Cell," had no funding, vehicles, or bomb-making equipment, but the incriminating documents included reconnaissance plans, two notebooks containing information on explosives, poisons, chemicals, and related matters, and an extract of *The Terrorist's Handbook*, all classed as "information likely to be useful to a person committing or preparing an act of terrorism" under the U.K.'s Terrorism Act.[20] The four primary plans that the group seems to have considered are the following:

- Attacking several key financial institutions in the United States: the International Monetary Fund and World Bank buildings in Washington, D.C., the New York Stock Exchange and Citigroup buildings in New York City, and the Prudential building in Newark, New Jersey.
- Packing three stretch limousines with commercially available gas canisters and parking them in hotel underground garages (where a truck bomb would not fit) to inflict mass damage and chaos.

- Building a dirty bomb using ten thousand smoke detectors either set on fire or placed on top of an explosive device.
- Blowing up trains under the Thames using set timed explosives on the London Underground in order to cause the river to flood the lines.

Londonistan

Chapter 2 provides an outline of the origins and the development of the rejectionist Islamic environment in Britain. As noted there, one of the "scenes" that developed in Britain was known as "Londonistan," dominated by Algerian veterans of the Algerian civil war, which had begun in 1992.

Abu Qatada, a Jordanian cleric linked to al Qaeda, and his student, Abu Hamza al Masri, were the key ideologues, dominating this scene and promoting al Qaeda ideology. Both had bona fides in the larger British Islamist rejectionist community: Abu Qatada sat on al Qaeda's religious rulings committee and Abu Hamza had been injured in the Darunta al Qaeda training camp in Afghanistan, where he lost an eye and had a hand replaced by a hook. He had then traveled to Bosnia in the mid 1990's to support the mujahedeen. Because of Abu Hamza's status as a "veteran" of two jihads, he had celebrity status in the community and young men flocked to hear his speeches.[2]

Abu Hamza utilized the Finsbury Park Mosque as a high-profile center of operation from which he could proliferate his message of support for "jihad" abroad including Bosnia, Chechnya, the Middle East, Afghanistan, and especially Kashmir.[3] Most of the active and passive core of plotters (Dhiren Barot, Mohammed Naveed Bhatti, Abdul Aziz Jalil, Omar Abdul Rehman, Junade Feroze, Zia Ul Haq, Qaisar Shaffi, and Nadeem Tarmohammed) emerged from overlapping networks of men in and around the Luton area who attended prayer meetings at a variety of locations including Willesden Library, run by the radical cleric Abdullah al Faisal, and at Finsbury Park Mosque, run by Abu Hamza al Masri.[4]

Gravitating to Reactionary Islam

Soon after Dhiren Barot converted to Islam, in 1991–92 he began attending local prayer meetings at Willesden Library and at the Finsbury Park

Mosque. After attending a lecture by Abu Hamza, where he was told of the mujahedeen and the concept of jihad, Barot began to frequently discuss how to help "oppressed" Islamic people abroad.[5] In September 1995, Dhiren Barot told his Air Malta coworkers he was leaving for a trip overseas. He quit his job and traveled to Pakistan that October with a friend known only by the initials "F.C."[6]

Sean O'Neill and Daniel McGrory describe the pathway of a typical young member of the local Islamist scene who attended Finsbury Park and then subsequently joined the Kashmiri jihad:

> Some who ended up at Finsbury Park had previously dabbled with different groups like Hizb-ut-Tahrir . . . and Lashkar-e-Tayyba. Most novices were like Abdullah, possessed of a burning desire to do something, to go somewhere to fight for Allah, but with no clear idea where. Abu Hamza would steer raw recruits like him to adopt an interest in their own roots—in Abdullah's case the ugly, interminable fight between India and Pakistan for control of Kashmir.[7]

Politicization of Beliefs

In his 1999 book *The Army of Madinah in Kashmir*, which portrays the life a typical Kashmiri jihadi and provides advice on fighting Indian soldiers, Barot calls on Muslims to perform their religious duty and commit to "defensive jihad," not only in Kashmir but wherever Muslims are under attack, and concludes by lauding the December 1999 hijacking of an Indian airliner and its diversion to Afghanistan by the Kashmiri militant group Harkat ul Mujahedeen.[8] Though there is some discussion of U.S. policy in the region, in line with al Qaeda grievances, clearly the focus is on Indian and British transgressions.[9]

The Luton Cluster

Out of the eight men charged with terrorism-related offenses, one was a Hindu convert to Islam and the other seven were British citizens of Pakistani descent primarily from the Mirpur region of Kashmir. The men ranged in age from twenty-three to thirty-five and came from a variety of walks of life. They had all grown up attending secular state schools in the greater

London area. Three of the men had completed university degrees, two in engineering and one in architecture, planning, building, and environmental studies. Two others were studying for university degrees, one in graphics information design and the other in business and finance. One man worked as a plasterer and another in a family business that owned garages. The operational leader of the cluster had "worked as an airline ticket and reservation clerk at Air Malta's Regent Street office in Piccadilly from 1991 to 1995" before turning to violent extremism.[10]

Dhiren Barot was clearly the central node among the plotters. According to Mohammed Naveed Bhatti, the postgraduate engineering student, he established a friendship with Dhiren Barot while he (Bhatti) was an undergraduate at Brunel University between 1994 and 1998. He had known and referred to Barot as "Esa." Barot had converted to Islam in 1991, causing a rift with his father, and began attending prayer meetings at Willesden Library Finsbury Park Mosque.[11]

According to Bhatti, although he and Barot had discussed religion, they had not spoken about extreme ideology. It was not until the latter part of 2003 that Barot introduced Bhatti to the plasterer, Abdul Aziz Jalil.[12] Meanwhile, both Nadeem Tarmohammed, the other engineer, and Zia Ul Haq, the architect, seemed to have had preexisting relationships with Barot. Ul Haq had been a friend of Barot's for some time; Tarmohammed and Barot had joint credit card accounts.[13] Bhatti, however, had only met Tarmohammed two or three times and had spoken to him on the telephone.[14]

Although Junade Feroze, who managed garages, was among Barot's most trusted associates, it is unclear how they had met. There is some evidence that they had first met at the Finsbury Park Mosque as Feroze, like Barot, had attended talks and lectures given by the extremist clerics Abdullah al Faisal and Abu Hamza.[15] In terms of the internal dynamics of the cluster, it was Barot who had the rank of "general"; Feroze, Jalil, and Tarmohammed were "lieutenants"; and the others held more junior positions.[16]

Anatomy of the Cluster

Active Core

Dhiren Barot, age thirty-three at the time of his arrest, was born in India's Gujarat province in December 1971. The following year his family relocated to Kenya, his father's native country, but fled to England in 1973 to escape discrimination against Asians.[17] Barot grew up in the working-class neighborhood of Willesden in North London and attended the sought-after Kingsbury High School where he was a studious but average pupil. Consistent with his unremarkable upbringing, "Friends recall that he planned a career in hotel management and had normal teenage interests such as fashion and music. He left school in 1988 and obtained a City and Guilds qualification in tourism before going on to work in various travel agencies and hotels." At the age of twenty, Barot converted to Islam. Between 1991 and 1995, he worked as an airline ticket and reservation clerk at Air Malta's Regent Street office in Piccadilly.[18]

Followers

Nadeem Tarmohammed, age twenty-six at the time of his arrest, was raised in Willesden in north London, just like Dhiren Barot. He graduated in 2002 with a degree in Manufacturing Engineering from Brunel University and subsequently worked as an administrator.[19]

Abdul Aziz Jalil, age thirty-one at the time of his arrest, had studied for a degree in Information Systems at Luton University. However, he worked as a plasterer.[20]

Junade Feroze, age twenty-nine at the time of his arrest, had attended local school and completed his General Certificate of Secondary Education (GCSE) exams (usually taken in year 12, when most pupils are sixteen years old) before going to work at the family business, which involved owning and managing garages.[21]

Qaisar Shaffi, age twenty-six at the time of his arrest, was raised in Willesden in North London and had attended the John Kelly Technology School as a youth. In 2004, he was studying at Hendon College where he was taking a course in business and finance. His occupation was that of a mobile phones sales manager.[22]

Mohammed Naveed Bhatti, age twenty-four at the time of his arrest, had attended school in Harrow and Uxbridge in northwest London. His father was a mechanic at a Jaguar showroom. Bhatti attended Brunel University in 1998 where he obtained a first class degree in systems engineering. In 2002 he began a postgraduate qualification in finite element modeling and analysis, also at Brunel.[23]

Zia Ul Haq, age twenty-six at the time of his arrest, was raised in Wembley in northwest London. He had attended Preston Manor High School (where he was a member of the Air Training Corps) and graduated from University College London with a 2i BSC honors degree in architecture, planning, building, and environmental studies. In 2004, he was working for a chartered surveyor in London.[24]

Omar Abdul Rehman, age twenty-one at the time of his arrest, from Watford, northwest of London, was reading for a degree in graphic information design at the University of Westminster. That summer, he worked at the Ramada Jarvis Hotel, Watford.[25]

Periphery

After weeks of surveillance, British investigators had originally arrested fourteen men in association with this operation. However, six were subsequently released without being charged.

Overseas Travel and Link Up with Al Qaeda

Travel to southwest Asia (Pakistan and Afghanistan) provided opportunities for the active core members of the cluster, especially Barot, to link up with the transnational jihad via Lashkar-e-Taiba (LeT) and al Qaeda, beginning in 1995.

Despite being a Hindu convert to Islam, Barot followed a similar pattern to that of many young British Muslims of Pakistani descent and who passed through the Finsbury Park Mosque before journeying to Kashmir to "investigate the duty of jihad."[26]

Training and Skill Acquisition

In 1995 in northern Pakistan, Barot was exposed to the transnational jihad through his interactions with militant groups such as Lashkar-e-Taiba and by receiving explosive and surveillance training at camps in Pakistan and in Kashmir's Kotti region. There, he learned how to assemble bombs, work with poisons and chemicals, and prepare nitroglycerine. In fact, Barot's notebooks from this period contain information on assembling phosphorous and napalm explosives.[27]

The experience of fighting alongside Kashmiri militants had a catalytic effect on Barot: "After training and spending time with the mujahedeen, he witnessed a side of Islam which cannot be found in the classrooms. It is the Islam that is felt by living and dying in the cause of Allah; loving Muslims and hating the enemies of Allah. Once this lifestyle was instilled in his blood, he began his career as a Mujahid."[28]

Barot was not the only member of his cluster to have traveled to northern Pakistan; three others had also made the trip. Abdul Aziz Jalil made at least one trip to Pakistan. Entry stamps in his passport showed he visited between October and December 1997, and in October 2001 he was issued with a Pakistani entry visa. There is also a reference to a camp in Jalil's will.[29] Junade Feroze traveled to Pakistan between 1999 and 2001. Limited information is available about his movements, but in October 2001 while in Karachi he applied for a new passport, claiming he had lost his other one in Lahore. He is thought to have received terrorist training in Pakistan during 2001.[30] Finally, Zia Ul Haq's passport showed he was a regular visitor to Pakistan, visiting there in 1995, 1997, 1998 (when he stayed for over nine months), 2000, 2002, and 2003.[31]

Al Qaeda Recruitment

Only one individual from Operation Rhyme has been alleged to have been in contact with al Qaeda—Dhiren Barot. The origins of his affiliation with al Qaeda are unclear. This is partially because his life between 1995 and late 1999 remains opaque. While he may have been introduced to the organization through like-minded individuals in London, it is much more likely that the link-up occurred through connections among the Kashmiri militant groups with which he trained.[32] The U.S. Department of Justice's indictment against Barot alleges that in 1998 he was "a lead instructor at a jihad training camp in Afghanistan where recruits were taught to use weapons and received other paramilitary training."[33] Interestingly, the indictment fails to mention at which camp Barot was employed, leaving it unclear as to whether it was one of the camps run by Kashmiri groups or a camp that was directly under al Qaeda's control, such as the Khalden or al Farouq camp in eastern Afghanistan.[34]

The events of 1999–2000 provide mixed evidence of both Barot's Kashmiri focus and his affiliation with al Qaeda. On the Kashmiri side of the ledger, 1999 was the year in which Barot wrote a book titled *The Army of Madinah in Kashmir*, which portrays the life of a typical Kashmiri jihadi and provides advice on fighting Indian soldiers.[35] Barot describes bold nighttime operations in sub-zero temperatures that the mujahedeen conduct and the negligible provisions they bring on their forays into "Occupied Kashmir." Barot calls on Muslims to perform their religious duty and commit to "defensive jihad," not only in Kashmir but wherever Muslims are under attack, and concludes by lauding the December 1999 hijacking of an Indian airliner and its diversion to Afghanistan by the Kashmiri militant group Harkat ul Mujahedeen.[36] Though there is some discussion of U.S. policy in the region, in line with al Qaeda grievances, clearly the focus is on Indian and British transgressions.

Later that same year—1999—Khalid Sheikh Mohammed dispatched Barot to Kuala Lumpur to discuss the status of the jihad in Southeast Asia with Hambali, the Indonesian Islamic terrorist and leader of Jemaah Islamiyah. Authorities believe Barot traveled with Osama bin Laden's former bodyguard, Tawfiq bin Attash, the man who masterminded the 2000 attack on the USS *Cole*.[37] Moreover, according to the 9/11 Commission, at the end of the visit Barot provided Hambali with two addresses, one in the United States and one in South Africa, and told Hambali to reach out to these destinations if he "needed help" from al Qaeda contacts in those countries.[38]

Clearly by late 1999 and early 2000 Barot was interacting and carrying out missions on behalf of top echelon al Qaeda leaders. Regardless of whether he had been recruited by al Qaeda or sworn loyalty via a *bayat* to bin Laden, he was functioning as an "al Qaeda operative." Moreover, the timing of Barot's travel is particularly significant, for it was in January 2000 that 9/11 hijackers Nawaz al Hazmi and Khalid al Mihdar met with Tawfiq bin Attash aka "Khallad," Hambali, and Ramzi Bin al Shibh in Kuala Lumpur to discuss their unfolding plot to attack the United States. There is no evidence that places Barot at this meeting, and Barot is not accused of having foreknowledge of the attacks. However, the fact that he had met with Hambali around this time has led some investigators to speculate that the American address Barot provided Hambali may have been passed on to 9/11 hijackers Hazmi and Mihdar, who arrived in California following the Kuala Lumpur meeting.[39]

Operational Cycle

In 2000 and 2001, Barot and his associates conducted research on U.S. targets in New York and Washington, D.C. Following the successful attacks of 9/11, Barot turned his attention to U.K. targets. Although significant research was conducted even after his 2004 trip to Pakistan, Barot had not begun to acquire any of the components necessary for any of the attacks he had designed when he was arrested in August 2004. The failure to progress in the operational cycle raises the question as to whether Barot ever really intended to carry out the attacks he designed.

Target Selection

Although it is unclear what the catalyst was, in June 2000, Dhiren Barot applied for and won a place at the Mohawk Valley Community College in Rome, New York. Although he was admitted, he never enrolled or attended any classes there. Rather, beginning on August 17, 2000, and continuing through April 8, 2001, different combinations of Barot and either co-conspirators Nadeem Tarmohammed or Qaisar Shaffi entered the United States and conducted surveillance of several buildings in New York, northern New Jersey, and Washington, D.C., as part of a conspiracy to damage and destroy the buildings. These included the International Monetary Fund World Headquarters and the World Bank Headquarters in Washington, D.C., the Prudential Corporate Plaza and World Headquarters Building in Newark, New Jersey, and the New York Stock Exchange Building and the Citigroup Center in Manhattan, New York.[40] According to the 9/11 Commission, in early 2001, he was sent by al Qaeda (by Khalid Sheikh Mohammed, at the behest of Osama bin Laden) to scout potential economic and "Jewish" targets in New York.[41]

Casing

During his trips, Barot produced meticulously detailed casing documents. In New York, Barot and Tarmohammed, the engineering graduate from Brunel University, surveyed targets on Wall Street, including the New York Stock Exchange (NYSE), upon which Barot hoped to launch an arson attack.

The casing documents provide studies of the building's fire security system, ventilation systems, security cameras, X-ray screening systems, and construction materials. He noted nearby fire departments, hospitals, and police stations.[42] As part of a forty-five-page targeting package on the Citigroup Center buildings in Manhattan and Queens, Barot considered exploding car bombs or smashing gasoline trucks into those buildings. As in the case of the NYSE, Barot had studied the building's framework and fire security systems. He noted that the 673-foot-tall Citicorp Building in Queens had a glass frame that "could be devastating in an emergency scenario." In his report he notes, "when shattered, each piece of glass becomes a potential flying piece of cutthroat shrapnel!" Evaluating escape routes, he identified Grand Central Station, the Port Authority bus terminal, the "subway directly next to Citigroup," taxis, buses, "your own personal method," and the "NYC sewer or train tunnel system."[43]

Barot performed similar reconnaissance on the Prudential headquarters on Broad Street in Newark. He took detailed notes on the area and, in an apparent reference to the 1993 World Trade Center bombing, recommended that the building be attacked with a limousine in the parking garage: "The most obvious technique to utilize, that comes to mind—if you do not mind history repeating itself, would be a limousine in the V.I.P. underground car park, with all except the front seats removed in order to facilitate maximum space." The documents are singed "Agent E-a-B," an abbreviation for his alias, Esa al Britani, and an allusion to his view that he was an "agent" acting on behalf of some larger entity.[44] Barot is also reported to have taken helicopter tours over Manhattan as part of his surveillance activities.[45]

Barot and Tarmohammed traveled to Washington, D.C., where they cased the headquarters of the International Monetary Fund (IMF) and the World Bank. Barot sketched plans to explode a car bomb in the underground parking lot of the IMF building and maintained computer files of the building's construction on a computer that was later confiscated by police. He recommended "arson at façade or in underground carpark" as the best plan of attack.[46] In September Tarmohammed returned to the U.K. and Barot followed on November 14.

Following Khalid Sheikh Mohammed's directions in early 2001 to scout potential economic and "Jewish" targets in New York, Barot returned to New York with Qaisar Shaffi, the mobile phones sales manager from Willesden, on March 11, 2001. One month later, Barot conducted video surveillance of targets in New York. Reflecting his level of savvy, authorities discovered surveillance footage of the NYSE, the Citigroup Center, and other buildings in the area of Wall Street and Broad Street in lower Manhattan recorded on a "Die Hard with a Vengeance" tape.[47] Images of synagogues were included in the video footage from the weekend of April 7, 2001. "One clip even contained footage of the World Trade Center, with Barot making an exploding noise as he filmed it. After 9/11, Barot added scrolling text to the bottom of some of the video, noting that security during the time of filming was likely far more lax than after the collapse of the World Trade Center."[48]

While conducting surveillance with Barot, Qaisar Shaffi apparently fell ill and needed to be treated in a New York hospital before returning to London on April 3. The next day, another member of the Luton cluster, Nadeem Tarmohammed, returned to New York ostensibly from the U.K. for a few days before the two returned to England together on April 8. According to the Queen's Counsel (QC) in the U.K., Edmund Lawson, after the attacks on New York and Washington in September, Barot's plans were "shelved by reason of what the terrorists would have regarded as their 'success' in 9/11. They were not, however, forgotten." Lawson added that "the plans were accessed and/or worked on as late as February 2003."[49]

Logistics

After Barot returned to London he took a job as a night watchman in a block of apartments and began plotting different terrorist attacks in London: "Using his fraudulently obtained student identification cards to libraries at Brunel University, Barot conducted research into carrying out a wide variety of chemical and radiological terrorist attacks. He accumulated a personal library of books and documents on chemicals, including one work titled *Hazardous Chemicals Handbook*, discovered at the time of his arrest."[50] Barot's research was consolidated into three documents: "Final Presentation," "Hazards," and the "Gas Limos Project."

"Final Presentation" examines the prospects of using radiological dispersal devices (RDD), or "dirty bombs," in terrorist attacks. In the article's conclusion Barot remarks that just a "few grams of Cobalt 60 with a few explosives are enough to close an area the size of Manhattan" and notes the availability of certain radioactive materials in watches and smoke alarms.[51]

Barot's second paper, "Hazards," treats similar themes, examining the health effects, industrial uses, and security risks of radioactive chemicals. The second portion of the document examines the potential for terrorist attacks with radiological weapons. Although "Final Presentation" and "Hazards" vaguely discuss the potential for terrorist attacks with dirty bombs, they do not appear to have been part of any concrete plan.[52] At the time of his arrest, Barot did not possess any actual chemicals or radioactive material, only studies, the details of which may or may not have provided much new information to al Qaeda's top leaders.

Barot was also creating a plan for coordinated terrorist attacks on hotels in London that, in his mind, had greater potential. Known as the "Gas Limos Project," the plan was drawn up in a thirty-nine-page document. According to British police, Barot's report was found on a laptop during a search of a house in Gujarat, Pakistan.[53] Barot planned to use propane, butane, acetylene, and oxygen to blow up black limousines in underground parking garages at London hotels. He envisioned the attacks would involve six operatives, three drivers, and three armed "decoy" drivers. The plan was designed to be carried out at night, preferably in autumn when the days are short. The attacks were "to be coordinated back to back as they were with 9/11, thus forcing another memorable black day for the enemies of Islam and a victory for the Muslims." The Ritz and the Savoy hotels in London were among those considered as targets.[54]

The "Gas Limos Project" document also included a "rough presentation for [a] radiation (dirty bomb) project." Barot recommended using up to ten thousand smoke detectors placed on explosive devises in a contained area to disperse americium-147. He claimed "to have taken the idea from a 2003 *World Almanac* report that an explosion of 900 smoke detectors harmed forty people. The idea seems to have been a hypothetical one that could have been carried out, according to the document, in London, Spain, or the United States." Barot believed that it would have required roughly ten men and would have taken considerable time to implement.[55]

Finally, with the Madrid attacks of March 2004 in mind, Barot considered attacks on British trains, noting that "I have a friend who is a train driver." He identified the Heathrow Express train line as a possible target and suggested attacks on a Greenwich-bound train that passes under the Thames, noting that the "chaos that would be caused . . . what with all the explosions, flooding, drowning etc. that would occur/result." The Waterloo and King's Cross tube stations were also listed as possible targets.[56]

Communications

In January and February 2004 Barot used a fake passport to travel to Lahore. It is likely that he met al Qaeda–linked individuals on this trip. There is strong speculation that Barot met with Neem Noor Khan, who served as a relay station, or "link man," for communication between the outside world and al Qaeda leadership. When Khan was arrested in July 2004 in Gujarat, Barot's work-ups and targeting packages were found on his computer. According to Queen's Counsel Edmund Lawson, "While there is no direct evidence as to what he did, the obvious inference from the recovery of the Gas Limos Project and other material relating to Barot in Gujarat in July 2004 is that he went to present his proposals for al-Qa'eda approval."[57] Barot had subsequently returned to London, where he remained into the summer until his capture on August 3, 2004.

Weaponization

Interestingly, upon the cluster's arrest, no weapons, chemicals, or radiological materials were found. Nevertheless, Barot was in possession of books and hundreds of pages of documents on hazardous chemicals.[58]

The Al Qaeda Factor

When the bulk of the Operation Rhyme plotters were convicted, Deputy Assistant Commissioner Peter Clarke, head of the Metropolitan Police Counter Terrorism Command, commented,

> Dhiren Barot and his gang were determined terrorists who planned bombings on both sides of the Atlantic. . . . We know Barot was the ringleader of this terrorist cell. However, he needed the help of the seven men who have been jailed today. . . . The seven men jailed today were not the instigators of the planned attacks. They were the planning team and were needed by Barot to contribute expertise in areas that he was lacking. They were the trusted few who researched, carried out reconnaissance and supported Barot. Each had a different role to play. Barot needed minders and drivers—people who could look after him as

he carried out reconnaissance and conducted his meetings. He needed people to carry out research, gain access to specialist libraries, supply vehicles, false identities and travel documents, bank accounts, money and safe houses.[59]

No mention was made of al Qaeda. Among the reasons Peter Clarke may have declined to link Barot to al Qaeda were the following: his exact position within al Qaeda has never been established; no evidence exists that he had pledged *bayat* to Osama bin Laden; and claims that Barot was al Qaeda's highest-ranking official in Britain are unsubstantiated. In fact, it is possible that he never joined the organization but rather was only affiliated with bin Laden through Kashmiri militant groups and was acting more as a terrorism entrepreneur.

Barot's al Qaeda–sponsored trips to Southeast Asia and New York City suggest that at certain times, Barot met and took direction from Khalid Sheikh Mohammed. Not only did he travel to Kuala Lumpur in 2000 with bin Laden's bodyguard to meet Hambali, but he also was dispatched to New York City to scout out targets in 2001. Having been given these assignments would not necessarily mean Barot was an al Qaeda member, but the sensitivity of the missions that he was charged with and his contacts with top al Qaeda members over the years does suggest loyalty to bin Laden and the greater al Qaeda cause. In fact, in the Gas Limos Project document, Barot refers to the al Qaeda bombers of the U.S. embassies in Kenya and Tanzania as "brothers."

Nevertheless, Barot's research in the U.K. seems to have been done on his own initiative rather than as a result of some top-down tasking by al Qaeda Core. Consequently, he composed his documents in the form of proposals, and his trip to Pakistan in early 2004 was likely part of an attempt to gain approval (endorsement) from al Qaeda's leadership for his proposed attacks. The fact that when he was arrested in August 2004 that neither he nor his co-conspirators were in possession of any materials that would be necessary for an attack leads one to the conclusion that Barot had still not received an endorsement from al Qaeda Core for one of his proposals that he had presented in February or Barot was not really a man of action and never really intended to commit an attack but just researched the possibility of attempting one.

As far as an assessment goes, the U.K. "projects" were not designed by al Qaeda Core, nor did Barot receive funding for the operations from al Qaeda

Core. There was some ongoing communication (via Barot's travel) between al Qaeda Core and the plotters, but certainly no command and control effort. While al Qaeda ideology did seem motivate Barot and his cluster, the initiative for the U.K. "projects" seems to have been his own. Finally, because Barot's proposals had been presented to al Qaeda leadership for endorsement, Operation Rhyme is best described as an al Qaeda "suggested/endorsed" plot.

Chapter 6

Operation Crevice (United Kingdom, 2004)

OPERATION CREVICE WAS disrupted by almost simultaneous arrests in the U.K., Canada, and the United States in March 2004. The plot was an attempt to mount a bomb attack in the U.K. to kill and maim as many people as possible and cause unprecedented disruption. The individuals in this cluster had already obtained 1,300 pounds of ammonium nitrate fertilizer, suitable for making bombs, and were storing it in a West London storage unit rented by the cluster. They also had a half-built remote-controlled detonator. The ultimate target had not been fixed, but among the targets seriously considered were the Bluewater shopping mall, the Ministry of Sound nightclub, the U.K.'s 4,200-mile network of underground high-pressure gas pipelines, a twelve-page list of British synagogues, Parliament, and a football stadium. The group had also discussed creating and utilizing a radioisotope bomb; however, at the time of their arrest, these plans had not progressed beyond being aspirational.[1]

The Reactionary/Islamist Scene

The origins and the development of the rejectionist Islamic environment in Britain are discussed in Chapter 2, and the reactionary/Islamist scene was introduced in Chapter 3.

The majority of the active and passive core of plotters (Omar Khyam, Jawad Akbar, Anthony Garcia, Nabeel Hussain, Waheed Mahmood, Shujah

Mahmood, and Salahuddin Amin) emerged from the wider al Muhajiroun network and its links to social and extremist networks in northwest London. Momin Khawaja linked up with this network from Canada, and Mohammed Junaid Babar from the United States. In Luton, Abu Munthir and Mohammed Qayyum Khan were important links between the conspirators and al Qaeda–linked individuals in Afghanistan and Pakistan.

Gravitating to Reactionary Islam

Al Muhajiroun and its extremist interpretation of Islam had a very strong effect on some members of the active core of this conspiracy. Two important nodes for al Muhajiroun activity that drew in members of the Operation Crevice cluster were in Luton, just north of London, and in Crawley, just south of London. While some individuals were attracted to al Muhajiroun as part of their own individual religious awakening, others were attracted to the group by its political message.

The religious appeal of al Muhajiroun was that it presented itself as representing "true Islam" and thus membership could facilitate ultimate personal salvation. Ideologically, though derived from the more political Hizb ut Tahrir, al Muhajiroun framed its message with a much more religious vocabulary and in fact competed with devout Salafi movements for supporters. Both movements shared a belief that literal observance of Islam, as practiced by the Prophet Mohammed and his immediate successors, was the "straight path." Tolerance of other interpretations of Islam were not accepted; they were considered "deviant" and worthy of excommunication or *takfir*. Broad use of *takfir* and intolerance in general toward unbelievers were virtual tenets of al Muhajiroun's ideology. What probably made al Muhajiroun most attractive in the U.K. was its strong link between belief and activism, primarily via political protest activity but also via acts of violence, what the group considered to be legitimate "military jihad" that would facilitate the arrival of the Caliphate.[2]

Omar Khyam, a standout cricket player, planned to study electrical engineering in college but when he was sixteen he began spending time with members of al Muhajiroun in Crawley. He had become more interested in religion in 1998 while he was taking his A-levels at East Surrey College: "I started to pray five times a day and attend mosque more." He also started to attend local classes organized by al Muhajiroun (ALM): "The main theme was to establish an Islamic state. They believed in peaceful means. They wanted to establish it everywhere. In the U.K. as well." Waheed Mahmood met Omar Khyam at the local mosque in either 1998 or 1999.[3]

Politicization of New Beliefs

A significant number of the Operation Crevice conspirators were politically active and aware of international events that affected Muslims worldwide. Thus, al Muhajiroun's political activism appealed to their already awakened political Muslim identities. Nevertheless, ultimately, al Muhajiroun would not be activist enough and the men would move on to political violence: "Both Babar and Khyam aired their criticism of ALM who[m] they thought were all talk and no action; they did no bombing and stuff like that."[4] Soon after Waheed Mahmood met Omar Khyam in Crawley in the late 1990s, he started to attend radical political meetings in Luton. Organized by al Muhajiroun, they were "popular among young men angry with the way they saw Muslims being treated around the world."[5]

Jawad Akbar attended fundamentalist/militant Islamist political circles, both as a student at Brunel University and in the town of Crawley. Subsequently, he started to advocate a violent response to Muslim suffering around the world.[6] Throughout 1998 and 1999 Anthony Garcia and his older brother, Lamine Adam, attended Islamist political meetings and began discussing issues such as the treatment of Muslims in Kashmir.[7]

According to Omar Khyam, by 2002–3 he was more convinced than ever that there was a war against Islam and that the U.S.- and U.K.-led Iraq invasion was the catalyst. He said,

people did not view the U.K. the same as the U.S. The Americans were unjustly in Muslim lands whereas the U.K. had a different view. They were not aggressive like the Americans. The first time I was hearing people saying that the U.K. should be attacked was when the Afghan War started in 2001. But it wasn't a majority. At that time I would make excuses for Britain, saying they had no choice. We were born here so we felt some allegiance to the U.K. But this changed after the Iraq invasion. The Iraq war was the final straw. People really didn't understand why they were attacking Iraq. Was it because there was some oil involvement? It was a war on Islam also. I was in Pakistan at that time.

A lot of people's attitudes changed. Whereas before myself and others made excuses, now they believed the U.K. and America needed to be attacked.[8]

Concerns about events affecting Muslims in Bosnia, Chechnya, Kashmir, and ultimately Afghanistan and Iraq had a significant mobilizing affect on some members of the group. On a visit to Pakistan in 1999, Salahuddin Amin heard an "emotional" speech about the situation in Indian-administered Kashmir, which had a catalytic affect on his life: " I heard a lady making an emotional speech about the atrocities that were happening in Kashmir that was under Indian rule—how women were raped and kidnapped all the time and they had to move from there to Pakistani Kashmir and were in difficulties. . . . She made a very emotional speech and that affected me." Motivated and outraged by what he heard about the alleged suffering of Muslims, he decided on his return to Luton that he would donate part of his wages toward the "cause."[9]

Videos showing the slaughter of Muslims in Chechnya and Bosnia that Salahuddin Amin saw back in Luton further convinced him to help "freedom fighters" in Kashmir buy arms and ammunition: "After seeing the videos he became increasingly angry. He was impressed by the fighters and so he decided, if he got the chance, to join the fighting. He was in his mid-20s by now, and this was 5–6 months before the Twin Towers attack in New York on 11th September." In addition, lectures by Abu Hamza al Masri at the Finsbury Park Mosque in London shortly before 9/11 and the American-led invasion of Afghanistan influenced Amin's decision to join the Afghan fight on the side of the Taliban.[10]

Anthony Garcia asserted that he clearly recalled being shown a video about "atrocities" allegedly perpetrated by Indian forces in Kashmir: "It just showed, like, these atrocities that were taking place in a place called Kashmir, and it was just the worst thing, you know, anyone could have seen. You've got, you know, little children just, you know, sexually abused and women and—you know. I mean, I still remember it quite clear." Garcia remembered crying as he watched the video, which prompted him to do something to help his fellow Muslims in Kashmir and began by fund-raising for the Kashmiri cause. Although by early 2002 he was determined to go to Pakistan and get military training, Garcia insisted he never planned to fight in Kashmir or Afghanistan.[11]

Momin Khawaja, who was from Ottawa, was also strongly affected by events in southwest Asia. According to Canadian court documents, in Khawaja's e-mail communication with a female friend in December 2003 he noted,

lemme tell u sumthin bout me . . . few yrs ago, when the kuffar amreekans invaded Afghanistan, that was . . . the most painful time in my whole life cuz I loved the . . . mujahideen and our bros in Afghanistan so so much that I couldn't . . . stand it. It would tear my heart knowing these filthy kaafir dog . . . Americans were bombing out muslim bros and sisters.[12]

According to a witness for the prosecution, Mohammed Junaid Babar, Omar Khyam wanted to hit British "pubs, trains and nightclubs." Khyam believed that "the UK should be hit because of the UK's support of the US in Afghanistan and Iraq as well as the notion that nothing has ever happened in the UK."[13]

The Crawley/Luton Cluster

This cluster of "all home counties twentysomethings, which had been interested in sport and studying" that came to be the core of Operation Crevice developed around the two greater London al Muhajiroun hubs of activity: Luton and Crawley. Omar Khyam and his brother Shujah Mahmood grew up with Jawad Akbar and subsequently met Waheed Mahmood at political events in Crawley. Jawad Akbar's step-brother, Nabil Hussein, met Khyam in 2003. Meanwhile in Luton, where al Muhajiroun also had a support base, Salahuddin Amin met both Khyam and Waheed Mahmood at the Leagrave Road Luton Center away from the town's central mosque in 2001. This location was already a place where young Islamists met to discuss politics. To many who knew these men growing up, they seemed well integrated into British society. At least four of the men had spent time as university students and all had Westernized, unremarkable backgrounds with secular upbringings. None was educated in Islamic-based schools like madrassas; rather, they attended state schools and pursued modern studies.[14]

In and around the Leagrave Road Luton Center, some of the Operation Crevice conspirators would also meet the mysterious Abu Munthir, a man of Moroccan and Belgian descent who, after 9/11, returned to Afghanistan to fight with the mujahedeen and the Taliban against the coalition forces as well as Mohammed Qayyum Khan, known as "Q," who would ultimately send a number of men including the July 7 (Operation Theseus) bombers to Pakistan for training. Abu Munthir was arrested in Pakistan in 2004, but Q remains at liberty in the U.K.[15]

Friendship, kinship, and worship underpinned the ties among the cluster. Four of the men were of Pakistani heritage, and all had some association with al Muhajiroun. Also, the Crawly crew (Khyam, Shujah Mahmood, and Waheed Mahmood) all prayed together at their local Langley Green Mosque regularly. They met Salahuddin Amin at al Muhajiroun events in Luton in March 2001. Meanwhile, Anthony Garcia hooked up with al Muhajiroun's East London contingent and met Khyam through his brother, Lamine Adam, at an Islamic fair in East London. Mohammed Junaid Babar met both Garcia and Khyam in late 2002. The meeting with Khyam occurred in the Crawley Mosque. Meanwhile, Momin Khawaja met Khyam at that same time as well, at Khyam's house in Hayes.[16]

Anatomy of the Cluster

Active Core

Omar Khyam, age twenty-two at the time of his arrest, was one of the leaders of the Crawley/Luton cluster. He grew up in a largely secular Muslim household in Crawley, south of London. His father had left home when Khyam was eleven years old, and he was thrust into the role of "man of the family," making decisions as to what his younger brother, Shujah Mahmood, could do. Although Khyam became interested in both religion and politics as a teenager, he loved sports and went on to become captain of the school cricket team. Khyam scored well on his GCSEs, and in 1998, while he was taking his A-levels at East Surrey College, he began to pray five times a day and attend ALM classes.[17] However, in late 1999, Khyam left al Muhajiroun because he found the goals and aims of the group unrealistic, such as establishing an Islamic state in Britain.[18]

Instead, he turned his focus to Kashmir. According to Khyam, "Kashmir was a very big issue in my family." In January 2000, following his disen-chantment with ALM, Khyam secretly traveled to Pakistan and attended a mujahedeen training camp. Although his family ultimately found him and sent him home, in 2001, he took out a £16,000 bank loan and flew to Paki-stan again. When he returned from his 2001 trip to Afghanistan, he began a program in computing and mathematics at London Metropolitan Univer-sity in North London before dropping out.[19]

In the U.K., Khyam had a number of short-lived jobs, including one as a telemarketer for AOL but left after less than a week, claiming there was a death in his family. He enrolled in courses at the University of North Lon-don in three successive years but each time dropped out.[20]

Salahuddin Amin, age twenty-nine at the time of his arrest, was another leader of the Crawley/Luton cluster. He had been born in the U.K. but lived in Pakistan from age four through sixteen, speaking only Urdu before re-turning to the U.K. to live in Luton. He quickly mastered English and picked up secular British habits such as drinking and dating. As a youth, Salahud-din was not religious. He rarely prayed and his only trips to the mosque were to celebrate festivals. However, every summer he would return to Pakistan for an extended summer holiday, and one trip in 1999 changed his life.[21] At a resort in the hills above Rawalpindi he heard a woman give an "emotional" speech about the atrocities committed in Indian-administered Kashmir, which had a catalytic affect on his life.[22]

Upon his return to the U.K., Salahuddin Amin became a student at the University of Hertfordshire but took a year off to work as taxi driver to raise funds for Kashmir. Though he ultimately graduated with a degree as a product design engineer, he also began attending al Muhajiroun's militant political meetings, which were held at Leagrave Road Luton Center, as op-posed to Luton's main mosque. These meetings mixed religion and politics to encourage armed support for jihadi fighters. It was in Luton that he met Mohammed Qayyum Khan or "Q."[23]

Followers

Waheed Mahmood, age thirty-two at the time of his arrest, grew up in Craw-ley. Between 1989 and 1995 he worked for British Gas, servicing and repair-ing residential boilers. He later worked in a tile shop, where he ultimately gave a job to Omar Khyam. Around the time of the conspiracy Mahmood worked for a contractor for National Grid Transco. Soon after Mahmood met Khyam in Crawley, he started to attend radical political meetings first in Crawley and then in Luton. Organized by al Muhajiroun, there were "popular among young men angry with the way they saw Muslims being treated around the world."[24]

Jawad Akbar, age twenty-one at the time of his arrest, was born in Pakistan but moved to Italy as a child. At age eight, he moved to Crawley. Akbar worked and studied hard, did well in school, and had a great interest in sports. He was a student at Brunel University, Uxbridge, in northwest London and studied mathematics, technology, and design. While at university Akbar worked part-time at the library and subsequently at Gatwick Airport and had clearance for working airside. At the airport, he worked at Dixons in its "airside" shop and then for the chain of newsstands, Journey's Friend, at its unit inside the Le Meridien hotel. He ultimately met and married a Sikh woman who converted to Islam.[25]

According to his step-cousin, Nabeel Hussain, Akbar became more religious in early 2003, grew a beard, prayed five times a day, and tried to persuade Nabeel to become more religious as well. Much of this transformation occurred after he attended the Malakand camp.[26] At university Akbar began to attend meetings held by a extremist Islamist political group organized by the Islamic Society of Brunel University as well as more fundamentalist study circles in Crawley. Subsequently, he started to advocate a violent response to the problems he saw Muslims suffering around the world. Later, he introduced Khyam to Nabeel Hussain.[27]

Anthony Garcia, age twenty-four at the time of his arrest, had a different upbringing from those of his co-defendants. He was born Rahman Benouis and moved to England at the age of five from Algeria and went to school in Leyton, East London. Garcia grew up with mainly white friends, enjoyed basketball, the music of rapper Tupac Shakur, and dreamed of becoming a male model. Garcia dropped out of school at the age of sixteen. During his teen years, Islam was not an important part of his life. Garcia drifted through a variety of jobs and spent his money on clothes, alcohol, and cigarettes. He adopted the name "Anthony Garcia" for modeling purposes. For regular employment, he worked as a security guard for Group 4 Securicor at sites across London. He also worked in the wine and spirits department of a Tesco branch in Woodford Green, Essex, but was fired after taking too much time off.[28]

During the period from 1998 to 2003, largely under the influence of his older brother, Lamine Adam, he gradually became more religious. Throughout the late 1990s the brothers attended Islamist political meetings and began discussing issues such as the treatment of Muslims in Indian-administered Kashmir. Videos shown at these events had a catalytic affect on him and energized his desire to do something about Kashmir. By the beginning of 2002, Garcia was determined to go to Pakistan and get military training, although he insisted he never planned to fight in Kashmir or Afghanistan.[29]

Mohammed Momin Khawaja, age twenty-four at the time of his arrest, was born and grew up in the suburbs of Ottawa and is said to have enjoyed hockey. He is of Pakistani descent and his father was a university professor. The Khawaja family lived wherever the father taught: in Libya for two years (during the U.S. raids against Tripoli), in Pakistan for two years, and in Saudi Arabia for five years, where his father worked at a technical college. According to Canadian court documents, "After returning to Canada and graduating from high school, Khawaja attended Algonquin College, a local community college where he majored in computer programming. In 2000, he began teaching children the Koran and Islamic history at a local mosque in Cumberland, Ontario. During this time, Khawaja became more religious, grew a beard and began wearing more traditional Pakistani clothing." After graduating from Algonquin College in 2001, Khawaja went to Pakistan, reportedly to look for a wife. Following his unsuccessful effort, he returned to Canada and worked as a contract software developer at Canada's Department of Foreign Affairs.[30]

Mohammed Junaid Babar, age twenty-nine at the time of his arrest, had been born in Pakistan and moved to the United States with his family at age two. He was a naturalized American citizen who spent most of his formative years in Queens. He attended La Salle Military Academy, a boys' military boarding school in Oakdale, Long Island, and graduated with the rank of second lieutenant in 1994. Babar studied pharmacy at St. John's University in New York but dropped out prior to completing the curriculum. Subsequently, he worked as a car valet and a security guard.[31] Babar claims not to have been particularly religious growing up but "held strong political beliefs" that were stirred in the early 1990s when the United States responded to the Iraqi invasion of Kuwait and stationed troops in Saudi Arabia. As part of his exploration of what to do in response to "the Americans invading the Middle East," he read many books and joined activist groups such as Hizb ut Tahrir and al Muhajiroun.[32]

According to Babar, during the 1990s "they [al Muhajiroun] had representatives in New York. I was able to meet them on the internet. We spoke numerous times over the phone and there was also a lot of literature available on the internet I was able to see." As a result of this interaction, he became increasingly politicized and began seeking unity for the Muslim world. Following the attack on 9/11 in which his mother escaped from the World Trade Center, he traveled to the U.K. to meet with Omar Bakri and subsequently to Pakistan. After he arrived in England and made contact with ALM, he was given money and the promise of more when he got to Pakistan. In Pakistan he lived for a time at ALM premises and met people from London and Crawley.[33]

Periphery

Nabeel Hussain, age eighteen at the time of his arrest, was a step-cousin of Jawad Akbar and spent most of his life in Horley, near Crawley. At the time of his arrest he was studying international politics at Brunel University in Uxbridge, West London. Hussain never went to Pakistan for training and appears to have played a relatively minor role in the whole conspiracy. He appeared on the fringe of the alleged plot, and then only in its final months. During the trial he told the court that his interests included "computer games, skateboarding, hanging out with friends, football and going to the movies." His primary link to the conspiracy seems to be that his debit card was used to rent the space to store the ammonium nitrate. According to Hussain, when he discovered that the group was storing fertilizer, he said he mentioned it to a university friend who said that it could be turned into an explosive. "I was scared," said Hussain. "I had never heard of it before."[34]

Shujah Mahmood, age sixteen at the time of his arrest, had been born in Crawley and was Omar Khyam's younger brother. He was not found guilty by the court. Mahmood attended Northgate Primary School and Hazelwick Secondary School in Crawley, both of which were mainly white schools. He struggled educationally and had problems in reading and in math. His older brother, Omar, took on the role of father figure to Shujah when their father left them at an early age. Shujah lived at home with his mother and got a job working at the Debenhams department store on Saturdays and subsequently worked in shelf-stacking at the local Sainsbury's. The prosecution argued that his role was that of a gopher for the cluster, but Mahmood always denied knowing anything about a plot to build a bomb from fertilizer. Nevertheless,

Shujah attended the training camp in Malakand in the summer of 2003 in Pakistan.[35]

Syed Hashmi, age twenty-four at the time of his arrest, was born in Karachi, Pakistan, and immigrated with his family to the United States when he was three years old. His family settled in Flushing, New York, where he was raised and attended school. Hashmi graduated from Robert F. Wagner High School in 1998 and then attended SUNY Stony Brook, where he met Mohammed Junaid Babar and got involved with al Muhajiroun. Hashmi eventually transferred to Brooklyn College, where he earned a bachelor's degree in political science in 2003. He was known to be both a devout Muslim and an activist. Before 9/11 he had organized many al Muhajiroun–related events (lectures and demonstrations) in and around New York City. In 2003, Hashmi enrolled at London Metropolitan University in England to pursue a master's degree in international relations, which he received in 2006.[36]

Kazi Rahman, approximately age twenty-seven at the time of the Operation Crevice arrests, was born in Bangladesh; his family immigrated to Britain while he was a youth. He attended Newham College of Further Education and became a very politically active member of Hizb ut-Tahrir in the mid-1990s, spending significant time on university campuses. Rahman had been arrested with other Hizb ut-Tahrir members in February 1995 in connection with the murder of a Nigerian student who had allegedly made insulting remarks about Islam. Two Hizb ut-Tahrir members were convicted of the murder, but Rahman was acquitted. Subsequently, Rahman joined al Muhajiroun, a more activist splinter group, and associated with a group of individuals of Bengali descent from East London who were interested in doing jihad overseas. Although Rahman ultimately did not participate in the Operation Crevice plot, he was arrested in a police sting operation in 2005 when he attempted to purchase machine guns.[37]

Ahmad Khan, age eighteen at the time of his arrest, is Omar Khyam's cousin. He was a journalism student at Kingston. He was not charged with any terrorist-related offense.

Nadeem Ashraf, age twenty-seven at the time of his arrest, was a graduate in computer studies, training to be a teacher in the U.K. He was not charged with any terrorist-related offense.

Tanzeel Khawaja, age twenty at the time of his arrest, is Mohammed Momin Khawaja's brother. He was not charged with any terrorist-related offense.

Mohsan Khawaja, age eighteen at the time of his arrest, is Mohammed

Momin Khawaja's brother. He was not charged with any terrorist-related offense.

Overseas Travel and Link Up with Al Qaeda

Multiple trips to Afghanistan and Pakistan between 2001 and 2004 by the active core played a critical role in the formation of the conspiracy to attack the U.K. Though the trips began primarily as fund-raisers to provide material support to the Taliban, ultimately these trips provided opportunities for the active and passive core members of the cluster to attend training camps, meet members associated with the Operation Theseus plot (July 7, 2005), link up with the transnational jihad, and meet al Qaeda–associated individuals.

In January 2000, at the age of eighteen, Omar Khyam went to Pakistan, deceiving his mother into believing he was going on a college trip to France, and he stayed in Pakistan for about three months. From Islamabad he was taken to a mujahedeen office and subsequently went to a training camp in Azad Kashmir until the end of March 2000. There he received training in the use of weaponry, rifles, and rocket launchers but had no explosives training.[38]

In 2001, three members of the group moved to Pakistan in the wake of 9/11 and Omar Khyam reestablished his links to Kashmiri militants. In June 2001, Omar Khyam returned to Pakistan to meet up with contacts he had established at the Kashmiri training camp that he had attended in 2000. In addition to ferrying cash raised in the U.K. and army surplus gear into territories where the Taliban and al Qaeda were active, he crossed over into Afghanistan for the first time and met Taliban members before returning to the U.K. in early September.[39] Almost immediately after 9/11, Mohammed Junaid Babar went to the U.K., where he met Omar Bakri in London. Following that meeting he left for Pakistan. Al Muhajiroun member Sajeel Shahid gave him £300 for travel to Pakistan and helped him set up an al Mujahiroun office in Peshawar. Babar ultimately settled in Lahore.[40]

In October 2001, Waheed Mahmood moved to Gujar Khan, Pakistan. He was soon followed by Salahuddin Amin, who moved to Kahuta, Pakistan, in November. Just months before, when was he was in Pakistan for the wedding of his sister, Salahuddin Amin had visited a jihadist training camp in Balakot. However, after 9/11 and a meeting with Khyam at the Crawley Mosque, Amin left the U.K. for Pakistan with the intention of becoming involved in the fight there. After a year in Pakistan, on prompting from Mohammed Qayyum Khan or "Q", he reconnected with Omar Khyam who asked for his help in collecting money and equipment to send to the mujahedeen and other fighters in Afghanistan such as al Qaeda and the Taliban. Amin agreed to do that and became the primary conduit for funds that Khyam raised in the U.K. for Kashmiri and Afghan causes.[41]

Amin was also introduced to Abu Munthir in Pakistan, who received the money and provisions, some of which went to support women and children and some to buy arms. Amin had met Abu Munthir at the mosque he attended in Luton. Ultimately, Amin became the "link man" for Khyam and others relaying funds to Abu Munthir in Pakistan.[42]

In 2002, Momin Khawaja took a three-month trip to Pakistan to supposedly look for a wife. However, according to Khawaja's own e-mail, the purpose of the trip was to support "jihad" in Afghanistan: "So I hooked up wit some bros from UK and else, and we all . . . went over to Pakistan to support Jihad in Afghanistan in 2002. We got there and stayed bout 3 months there, till Allah willed we came . . . back."[43] According to Mohammed Junaid Babar, "He [Khawaja] had come to fight in Afghanistan," recalling a conversation with Khawaja when he picked him up at the airport in Lahore, Pakistan. Khawaja decided against it, however, because the Taliban were on the run from the coalition forces and needed time to regroup.[44]

Omar Khyam also traveled to Pakistan in 2002 (April–June) under the auspices of going to a friend's wedding in April. However, the trip was really as a fact-finding tour to investigate the landscape in Pakistan and Afghanistan following the U.S.-led actions in Afghanistan.[45]

In 2003, the conspirators changed their focus from fighting abroad to carrying out an action inside the U.K. In addition, during this year, almost all of the Operation Crevice conspirators attended at least one of two training camps.[46] In February, Omar Khyam and a number of his associates from Crawley traveled to Pakistan for jihad. Although they used the upcoming marriage of one of their associates, Nadeem Ashraf, in Islamabad as the premise for their trip, the real purpose was to deliver funds to Salahuddin Amin and to get training so that they could fight in Afghanistan. In fact, when Salahuddin Amin was questioned when he returned to the U.K., he noted, "They wanted to get the explosive training because, first of all, their intention was to go and fight in Afghanistan and they asked me to ask Abu Munthir to tell me if they can allow them to go and fight in Afghanistan. But when I asked Abu Munthir he said, *I'll ask my chief and then I'll let you know.*[47]

Later that month a meeting was held at Waheed Mahmood's home in Gujar Khan, attended by Mohammed Junaid Babar, Anthony Garcia, Omar Khyam, Zeeshan Siddique, the rest of Khyam's associates from Crawley, Kazi Rahman and his associates from East London, and Salahuddin Amin, among others. The men were frustrated that they could not get more involved in the fight in neighboring Afghanistan. When Salahuddin Amin arrived, he presented the men with Abu Munthir's response to the request that Khyam had made about fighting in Afghanistan. Amin reported that according to Abu Munthir, "he [Abdul Hadi al Iraqi] wrote me a letter and said that the chief has said that we have enough people here, you know, who are fighting, but what we need is money and equipment. So the best thing would be to go back and keep sending money and equipment, and if they really want to do something, then go back and you can do something there." When Amin was asked about his impression of what the last statement meant, he answered, "You know, like, er, any sort of operation or whatever they're gonna do or like, you know, cause any damage come and do it in the UK."[48]

At this meeting, Waheed Mahmood suggested they carry out attacks in the U.K. He told them that he did not understand why "all these UK brothers were coming to Pakistan to fight when they could easily do; jihad operations in England. Mohammed Junaid Babar said everyone reacted positively to Waheed's suggestions of doing operations in the United Kingdom even though everyone wanted to fight in Afghanistan."[49]

In May, both Omar Khyam and Anthony Garcia traveled back to the region with the hope of getting more involved in the cause. They contacted Mohammed Junaid Babar and asked if they could move in with him at his house in Lahore. Khyam also asked Babar if he could arrange a training camp for him and his associates to conduct physical and weapons training. After Khyam moved into the guest quarters at Babar's residence in Pakistan in June 2003, "Khyam told Babar that he wanted to bomb soft targets, including trains and nightclubs, in England. Khyam also spoke in positive terms about a recent suicide bombing at a restaurant in Israel. In response, Babar said that more needed to be done. This conversation was the first of several that Khyam and Babar had about potential targets for detonating a bomb."[50]

Training and Skill Acquisition

In March 2003, Mohammed Junaid Babar and three associates traveled to Malakand, in northern Pakistan, to arrange with a local *maulana*, or religious teacher, to set up a paramilitary training camp up there for light weapons. They spent four to five days there preparing for it, and they came to an arrangement that Babar and his associates were to provide money and the *maulana* and his son would provide guns, food, tents, ammunition, and everything to train with.[51] In the interim, Salahuddin Amin, Omar Khyam, and "Ayoub" attended a training camp held in the Kohat region of Pakistan in May and June. Here, Khyam, Ayoub, and Amin learned how to create an ammonium nitrate explosive device from a man whom they understood to be an al Qaeda instructor from Tajikistan named Dolat. According to Babar, "The explosives training lasted two days during which they received theoretical training on devices and practical demonstrations." One of these demonstrations included exploding a device in a riverbed.[52]

Omar Khyam described the training in some detail and how they took notes. Nevertheless, he thought "it was not very good training" and that "they did not learn very much at it." They used ammonium nitrate and sulfur and other substances at the camp from Dolat, who mixed the materials and ground the ammonium nitrate into powder. They used aluminum powder to mix with ammonium nitrate and lit it with a fuse that was attached to a detonator.[53]

By July 2003, the main training camp had been set up for the men in Malakand. This camp, in a sense, was an "al Muhajiroun camp" as Babar and Khyam had set it up and funded it. Individuals came and left at different times. Momin Khawaja flew in from Canada, and Jawad Akbar and Shujah Mahmood arrived from the U.K. Two men associated with the July 7, 2005, bombings would also attend the camp briefly—Mohammed Siddique Khan and Mohammed Shakil. Overall, the attendees included Mohammed Juniad Babar, Omar Khyam, Shujah Mahmood, Anthony Garcia, Waseem Gulzar, "Ayoub," Jawad Akbar, Ahmed Ali Khan, Momin Khawaja, Zeeshan Siddique, Mohammed Siddique Khan, and Mohammed Shakil. At this camp, Babar said, they learned how to shoot AK-47s and to assemble and disassemble them and to fire a rocket launcher and a light machine-gun. Everyone participated in the activities except firing the rocket launcher. Ammunition and weapons at the camp were meager, as there were only four or five AK-47s and two rockets for the one RPG. Only Garcia and Zubair, the *maulana*'s son, had a chance to fire the RPGs.[54]

Momin Khawaja described his experience at the camp in an e-mail to a female friend:

> This summer, the foreign mujahideen setup training camp near . . . Afghan-pak border region in NWFP province in Pakistan. We spent sum time there in the summer, and . . . we got even one video of us . . . at the camp, to cover our faces we all wearing sarf . . . lol. it looks . . . like all us wearing niqaabs or something . . . tho it was . . . amazing, the best experience in my whole life, cuz u know the . . . hardship purifies the nafs . . . there was some amazing Ulema . . . there who had spent their whole life in Jihad in Afghan and Kashmir . . . they graduated from Jalaluddin Haqqani's (I'm sure u heard of him . . . from afghan jihad) madressa and were All into Jihad . . . After that, some of the bros were kept in Pakistan for specialized . . . training for guerilla, and sniper training and things like . . . that, and some bros sent to different parts of the world by the arab mujahideen to help out in the jihad worldwide.[55]

Anthony Garcia, who spent a couple of weeks at the camp, was disappointed and noted, "I thought, you know, it would be like the camps I had heard of with monkey bars and stuff. But it was just a field on the side of a mountain with really high grass. It was definitely disappointing."[56] Only Garcia, Ayoub, Khyam, and Zubair took part in the bomb-making experiments that utilized ammonium nitrate, aluminum powder, and urea. Khyam had told his brother Shujah to take those who were not to take part of this group down the mountain. The rest were not aware of any operation planned for the U.K. or that they were testing a bomb. Babar said they tried to do the test twice: the first time it did not go off, and the second attempt was successful and made a U-shaped hole in the ground. It was only a one-kilogram (or less) ammonium nitrate device.[57] Khyam, Garcia, Akbar, and Shujah all returned to the U.K. in August 2003.

As mentioned, two members of the Operation Theseus conspiracy, Mohammed Shakil and Mohammed Siddique Khan, attended this camp. According to court testimony by Shakil, their mission was a fact-finding effort to determine whether foreigners were welcome to fight jihad in Afghanistan and to return to England with the answer. Other accounts assert that Khan traveled to Pakistan in July 2003 with another man to deliver funds raised in the U.K. for jihadi groups, such as Kashmiri fighters or the Taliban.[58]

In fact, Salahuddin Amin testified that he met the two at the airport, "they gave him money amounting to hundreds of pounds for the cause, which he then passed on. Then he bumped into Omar Khyam by chance at the airport and he introduced Khan and Shakil to Khyam and then left and then went off." Khyam confirms the story, noting, "Basically, we were talking at the airport and I said to the guys—three guys that I came to pick up, I said they are going to be going to the camp, and they said they like to come as well. So Amin said, 'Okay, I'll leave them with you.' So I took Ibrahim [Mohammed Siddique Khan] and Zubair [Mohammed Shakil]'s number" and then picked them up two days later.[59]

According to Babar's testimony, it was he who offered Khan and Shakil the opportunity to participate in the camp; however, "they said they had already been through that type of training before in camps in Kashmir before 9/11 and there was no need to go through it again." Babar added, "They wanted to know what the reality was because people were saying in England that al Qaeda and the Taliban said they didn't want any foreign fighters while others were saying they did."[60] Ultimately, according to Babar's testimony, they were persuaded to attend the camp in Malakand, where they both took part in firearms training. Khan and Shakil appeared "confident and experienced" and said they wanted to fight in Afghanistan.[61]

Al Qaeda Recruitment

Before Khyam left Pakistan in August 2003 and following the training camp, he traveled to the northern tribal belt to meet Abu Munthir, the mysterious Belgian of Moroccan descent who had spent time in Luton a couple of years earlier. Khyam's goal was to discuss specific targets in the U.K. and how attacks might be carried out against them. Munthir worked for al Qaeda's field commander in Afghanistan, Abdul Hadi al Iraqi.[62]

Khyam went with Ayoub to meet Abu Munthir in the tribal areas and they were gone for a week to ten days. When Khyam and Ayoub returned from seeing Abu Munthir, they told Babar that "they had discussed the plot with Abu Munthir. Abu Munthir wanted to see everybody that was involved in it. They had informed him they also had someone from America with them too, and he asked specifically if he has an American accent, and that to bring everybody back with him, you know, told Ausman [Khyam] to get everybody up and those who were going to be involved to bring them up to see him." Babar was also told by Khyam that "he wanted to do multiple bombings at the same time . . . pubs, night clubs and train stations." Interestingly, up until that point—when Khyam traveled to visit him and pitch this idea—Babar says that Abu Munthir had not been involved in any plotting directed against the U.K.[63]

Amin testified that "Khyam had been told that, when he was in Pakistan, there was no room for him to fight in Afghanistan and that what he should do is to carry out operations in the U.K." Ostensibly, it was the al Qaeda–linked Abu Munthir who provided this guidance to Khyam. While this guidance did come from an al Qaeda–linked individual, it definitely did not constitute recruitment of the British men by al Qaeda.[64]

Abu Munthir's focus remained on acquiring material needed for the war against coalition forces. For example, in October 2003 Momin Khawaja flew from Ottawa to London and then to Islamabad for a short trip. Babar picked him up at the airport and they subsequently met with Salahuddin Amin. Khawaja had brought funds, a medical kit, invisible ink, and SIM cards. They discussed Abu Munthir's need for night-vision goggles, which Khawaja agreed to try to obtain.[65]

Operational Cycle

Travel to Pakistan appears to have been the catalyst for the cluster's mobilization to action. In Pakistan in February and March 2003, the idea of attacking the U.K. was first floated. By July and August, specific targets were being discussed. On November 4, 2003, the men began purchasing the 1,300 pounds of ammonium nitrate that would be necessary for an explosive device. They began their operational cycle less than four months after they returned from Pakistan. However, once the ammonium nitrate was purchased, the plot seemed to go on hold until February 2004, when Momin Khawaja traveled from Ottawa to London to update the men on the progress he had made constructing a remote detonator. This triggered a conversation between Omar Khyam and Jawad Akbar on February 22, 2004, which focused on discrete targets.[66]

Target Selection/Casing

According to Babar, the concept of simultaneous attacks was Omar Khyam's highest priority: "He wanted to do multiple bombings at the same time, simultaneous or one after the other on the same day."[67] The ultimate target had not been fixed, but among the targets seriously considered were the Bluewater shopping mall, the Ministry of Sound nightclub, the U.K.'s 4,200-mile network of underground high-pressure gas pipelines, a twelve-page list of British synagogues, Parliament, and a football stadium. The group even discussed obtaining a radioisotope bomb; however, these plans seem to have been only aspirational at the time of their arrest.[68] Even as late as February 22, 2004, when a listening device at the Uxbridge home of Jawad Akbar picked up members of the group talking about possible targets, they still had not made a final decision. During this conversation, Akbar referred to attacks on the utilities—gas, water, or electrical—as well as other possible targets: "Alternatively, a big nightclub in central London might be a target. The biggest nightclub in central London, no one can put their hands up and say they are innocent—those slags dancing around. I think the club thing you could do but the gas would be much harder."[69]

Upon the conspirators' arrests in March 2004, Scotland Yard found discs with information relating to the national high-pressure gas and high-voltage electricity network run by National Grid Transco: "The computer discs gave information on 4,200 miles of underground pipelines and 24 compressor stations for natural gas along with 4,500 miles of overhead line and 341 electricity sub-stations. One disc listed oil pipelines and hazardous underground plants. Police believe Waheed Mahmood stole the discs from the subcontractor he worked for."[70] There seems to be little evidence that the group cased any of their targets.

Logistics

Omar Khyam was the primary source on logistics, finances, and training and travel in Pakistan not only for the Operation Crevice cluster but also for the Operation Theseus bombers. Mohammed Junaid Babar helped organize a spring barbecue at the house of a longstanding al Muhajiroun member in April 2003 to raise funds for the training camp in Malakand. While catering staff served lamb kebabs and marinated chicken breasts, approximately $7,000 was raised.[71] When Khyam returned from Pakistan in August 2003, he transported ten bags of aluminum powder as well as approximately $20,000 from Pakistan to the U.K. He buried the aluminum powder in a tin in his family's garden in Crawley.[72] On November 12, 2003, Khyam wired funds from the U.K. to Babar in Pakistan to purchase the materials needed to construct detonators.[73]

In January 2004 Khyam set up a construction firm and tried to set up credit accounts with six different builders' merchants in Grimsby, Crawley, and Slough. He bought torches, nails, and copper piping on the accounts and ran up bills of more than $20,000, some of which he never paid. In February 2004, "Omar Khyam sent a request to Salahuddin Amin, in Pakistan, for information on the ratios of the ingredients needed to construct a bomb. Amin speaks to mujahedin leader Abu Munthir, formerly consulted by members of the conspiracy, and passes the technical information back to the UK."[74]

That same month, Khyam met with members of the Operation Theseus plot and discussed means for raising funds including "scams to rip the country apart economically" like opening fraudulent trade accounts with building merchants and applying for loans under a false name that would never be repaid. Following two additional meetings, the three Operation Theseus co-conspirators opened false building trade accounts. Khyam also discussed the logistical issues of travel to and from Pakistan and the risks that it entailed, ultimately suggesting that Mohammed Siddique Khan plan for "a one way ticket."[75]

Communications

In addition to private meetings, members of the cluster were in regular contact with each other, primarily through cell phone and text messages and unsent e-mail messages left in "save draft" form. Multiple e-mail accounts were accessed from a number of different Internet cafés.[76] In February and March 2004 Omar Khyam was in communication with Salahuddin Amin, who had remained in Pakistan. They used Gulloo e-mail and, in fact, this was the way in which Khyam reached Amin to get the precise ratios necessary for the construction of the ammonium nitrate explosive device he sought to build in London. However, Amin did not know the answer off hand and had to reach out to Abu Munthir for the correct answer. In somewhat broken English, Amin testified that he got the answer for Omar Khyam, noting, "So I said, 'Okay, I'll try to find out for you' [i.e., Omar Khyam]. This is when I went to see Abu Munthir. I went to—I think I went to give him some money or equipment. . . . Then he I think got me the answer."[77] Travel to Pakistan from the U.K. as well as to the tribal regions of Pakistan were also means of communication, specifically with Abu Munthir.[78]

Weaponization

In addition to the bags of aluminum powder obtained by Khyam,[79] Anthony Garcia began to purchase the 1,300 pounds of ammonium nitrate fertilizer from an agricultural merchant on November 4, 2003, which was picked up one week later. Khyam had asked Garcia to do it because he did not look "Asian." Garcia then made the initial visit to the storage facility, Access, in Hanwell to ascertain whether he could hire a unit to store the ammonium nitrate. Later he returned with Khyam and Nabeel Hussain and they paid a deposit to rent the unit. Hussain maintained he was duped by Khyam—the jury agreed and found him not guilty.[80]

As soon as he returned from his 2003 trip to London and Islamabad to Ottawa, Momin Khawaja began to e-mail Khyam that he had begun work on the remote detonating device, which he called the "hifidigimonster." He kept Khyam informed of both progress and delays.[81] On January 25, 2004, Khawaja told Khyam of his technical breakthrough in Ottawa: "nigga praise the most high, we got the devices working done. Nigga praise the most high. Alright bro, I'm going to try and get a booking asap to come over and see you, will try and arrange to come down soon." Khawaja traveled to the U.K. in February and showed Khyam a picture of the device via the Internet. The men had not worked out how to get the device(s) to the U.K.[82] Meanwhile, "in January 2004, Babar traveled again to London in an effort to resolve a dispute among al Qaeda supporters about who was actually working for Abdul Hadi al Iraqi. Shortly after Babar arrived in London, he and Khyam met in Khyam's car. During this meeting, Khyam asked Babar, "Are you with us?" Babar understood Khyam to be asking whether Babar planned to be part of the bomb plot. In response, Babar indicated to Khyam that he planned to work on his own.[83]

When the Khawaja residence was later searched by the Canadian police, principal among the items found were electronic components and devices, electronics instructional literature, an electronic model airplane engine, and military rifles and 640 rounds of ammunition. In Momin Khawaja's brother's bedroom was the "hifidigimonster" itself. It was noncommercial and had been built from commercially available parts. The basic circuitry had been printed out and, using an acid etching process, turned into copper circuits with other components added in a customized assembly fashion. It consisted of two primary modules, a transmitter and receiver, which would only activate upon receiving a coded signal. Tests indicated that it had the ability to receive signals effectively from a remote distance, two hundred meters away in the open and one hundred meters in an urban environment.[84]

In late February or early March, Omar Khyam reached out to Salahuddin Amin, who was still in Pakistan. He needed the precise ratios of ammonium nitrate to construct the device, telling Amin, "I forget already, you know." Amin subsequently obtained the information from Abu Munthir and he passed it on to Khyam.[85]

The Al Qaeda Factor

The Operation Crevice conspirators established a link to al Qaeda Core via Abu Munthir and Abdul Hadi al Iraqi. Hadi al Iraqi, a former major in Saddam Hussein's army, was al Qaeda's field commander of the Afghanistan theater of operations and was in contact with the Crevice group primarily as part of their logistics support effort to him and his fighters. In fact, another New York ALM member, Syed Hashmi, allowed his London flat to be used to store supplies and money that Mohammed Junaid Babar was shipping out to Abdul Hadi al Iraqi in Afghanistan. The supplies included ponchos, torches and boots, night-vision goggles, and money. According to former New York City ALM member, Mohammed Junaid Babar, Khyam openly boasted he was working for Abdul Hadi al Iraqi, calling him his "Emir." Nevertheless, the chain of command from Abdul Hadi al Iraqi to the U.K. support network was not particularly straightforward.[86]

For example, Khyam had indicated to Babar that he was working for Abdul Hadi al Iraqi, who was "number 3" in al Qaeda. That terminology has always been problematic and in no circumstance referred to al Qaeda's Chief of External Operations. Moreover, there had been some disagreements among the brothers in London and in Crawley, and even Omar Khyam had a conversation with Salahuddin Amin as late as October 2003 and asked Amin whom he was working for. Amin told him that he, too, was working for Abdul Hadi al Iraqi.[87]

As a result of the confusion and conflict, Mohammed Junaid Babar made contact with Abdul Hadi al Iraqi in late 2003 or early 2004 and met with him four times over a six-week period. Babar testified that he wanted to meet him,

initially because I wanted to make contact and (b) because—we didn't go through with it in my initial testimony, but there was a lot of confusion going on, who was working for Abdul Hadi. So the first meeting was just to clear up who was—certain people who and which people were working for Abdul Hadi and who were not working for Abdul Hadi. The second meeting was also not arranged—the second meeting was because we were still having the disagreements. So we needed to go back to Abdul Hadi and clear up the picture. And the reason for the third and fourth meeting[s] was not because of me. I had no intention of seeing him again.[88]

The discussions with the theater al Qaeda commander, Abdul Hadi al Iraqi, also covered the provision of material for his fighters: "During the first meeting at a mosque in North Waziristan, Pakistan, Hadi al Iraqi confirmed that he had received the gear that Babar had sent him a few months earlier, specifically boots, sleeping bags, and clothing, which Babar had received from Amin. In addition, Babar and another individual gave Hadi al Iraqi 10,000 Pakistani rupees to support jihad activities. Approximately one week later, Babar traveled to meet with Hadi al Iraqi again. During this meeting, Hadi al Iraqi asked Babar to provide him with materials to support al Qaeda's jihad activities in Afghanistan. Specifically, Hadi al Iraqi asked Babar to provide him with money and gear, namely, ponchos, shoes, socks, and sleeping bags. Babar agreed to this request."[89]

The last two meetings were to deliver the goods collected in the U.K. and to introduce Hadi al Iraqi to a few British men who wanted to join the fight in Afghanistan. On those trips, Babar delivered ponchos, waterproof socks, raincoats, sleeping bags, one set of night vision goggles, and one set of binoculars with night vision capability.[90]

Mohammed Junaid Babar described his understanding of the organizational relationships between individuals he was dealing with and al Qaeda–associated individuals.

Omar Khyam worked for a man named Q who lived in Luton, near London. Q and Abdul Waheed had ties to al Qaeda. Salahuddin Amin also worked under Q so far as U.K. matters were concerned, but under Abu Munthir as concerned Pakistani operations. Munthir was a leader in Pakistan, who responded to al Qaeda higher up, Shekh Abdul Hadi.[91]

Clearly there was not a straightforward chain of command for the support and supply network.

As far as the Operation Crevice plot was concerned, Abu Munthir, Abdul Hadi al Iraqi's aide de camp, though tantalizingly close, never provided the Crevice conspirators with a clear plan of action. When Khyam and Ayoub returned from seeing Abu Munthir in September 2003, they told Babar that "they had discussed the plot with Abu Munthir." Although Abu Munthir said he was interested in meeting all those who would be involved with the plot, the meeting never happened. The individuals had dispersed by the time Abu Munthir made that request.[92]

At the meeting with Abu Munthir, Salahuddin Amin testified that "Khyam had been told that, when he was in Pakistan, there was no room for him to fight in Afghanistan and that what he should do is to carry out operations in the U.K., and now he was e-mailing him to ask how to detonate 600 kilograms of ammonium nitrate, which was in Khyam's possession in the UK." Ostensibly it was the al Qaeda–linked Abu Munthir who provided this general guidance or suggestion to Khyam.[93]

Clearly the Crevice group, as Mohammed Junaid Babar and Salahuddin Amin's testimony in U.K. court makes clear, had made contact with individuals (Abu Munthir and Abdul Hadi al Iraqi) with high-level al Qaeda Core links. However, the Crevice conspirators were neither commanded nor controlled by al Qaeda; rather they received endorsement and general direction from Abu Munthir. The group was never able to meet with Abu Munthir, as he had requested after Khyam's visit in August/September 2003—the security situation changed almost immediately after the Khyam-Abu Munthir meeting when "Q" visited Pakistan and Pakistani authorities were following him.[94]

Given that that Abu Munthir, who was clearly linked to al Qaeda, said that "you can't get to the front and you should return to the U.K. and conduct operations there," the Operation Crevice plot should be considered an al Qaeda "suggested/endorsed" plot.

Chapter 7

Operation Theseus (London, July 7, 2005)

THE JULY 7, 2005, London transit bombings were a series of coordinated bomb blasts that hit London's public transport system during the morning rush hour. At 8:50 A.M., three bombs exploded within fifty seconds of each other on three London Underground trains. A fourth bomb exploded on a bus nearly an hour later in Tavistock Square. The bombings killed fifty-two commuters and the four suicide bombers, injured seven hundred, and caused a severe day-long disruption of the city's transport infrastructure countrywide.

The Beeston/Dewsbury (Leeds) Scene

The South Asian (Pakistani) community in Northern England is dominated by individuals of Kashmiri descent. As a result, from a social and political perspective, this diaspora community has a keen interest in events occurring in the Indian subcontinent. As Mohammed Siddique Khan's associate, Wahid Ali, noted, "In the area that we live in Beeston is all Kashmiri really and, I don't know, I can always remember when I used to go the Jum'ah prayer they were always doing collection and everything for the Kashmiri people, the Kashmiri cause and people talking about it." It is not surprising then that significant numbers of British Muslims were drawn to either actively or passively endorse jihad abroad in Kashmir: supporting the Kashmiri fighters was an "Islamic obligation" as well as a heroic, romantic cause.[1]

Moreover, for this community in northern England, supporting "resistance to occupied Kashmir" dovetailed with other ongoing armed struggles involving Muslims in Bosnia, Chechnya, the Middle East, and Afghanistan, and thus young men in the community were vulnerable to polarization. Furthermore, familial links to relatives in conflict zones enabled travel, further radicalization, and training. As Wahid Ali testified, there was nothing uncommon in the community about going to train in Pakistan: "Islamically and morally I think it's 100 per cent, if you want help your Muslim brothers, correct. . . . A lot of brothers used to go to Kashmir training camps. It's just the whole romantic idea of going there, training, helping your brothers, because we all used to just come back. Out of a hundred per cent, I reckon or ninety per cent would come back."[2]

In and around the Beeston/Dewsbury scene, Mohammed Siddique Khan was leading and participating in Outward Bound–type activities, such as paintball outings and hiking and camping trips to Wales and the Lake District with youth groups from the Leeds area. These events served as bonding and vetting opportunities and were often preceded by Islamist-themed lectures. The paintball sessions were preceded by meetings at participants' homes during which the group would gather to watch graphic videos before engaging in the physically rigorous and warlike action games.[3] It is believed that through one of these outings, Khan met Germaine Lindsay.[4] Wahid Ali testified that he had participated in a number of these outings.[5]

Local younger men of South Asian descent also spent time at the local community center, the Hamara Healthy Living Centre, in Beeston, playing pool, boxing, and "hanging out." Extremists often used the club as a venue to proliferate their radical messages to the more susceptible youth. Violent jihad was a frequent topic of discussion at the club. In fact, one of the gyms in the area was known as "the al Qaeda gym" because of its significant extremist membership.[6]

The seven men associated with this plot (Mohammed Siddique Khan, Shehzad Tanweer, Hasib Hussain, Germaine Lindsay, Wahid Ali, Sadeer Saleem, and Mohammed Shakil) emerged from three overlapping social networks: a community-based vigilante group, the Mullah Boys; experiences at militant Kashmiri training camps in Pakistan; and links to extremist networks in London, including members of the Operation Crevice plot. Mohammed Siddique Khan was the most deeply involved with these networks as he had friendships with a variety of al Muhajiroun and Crevice individuals such as the al Qaeda facilitator—Mohammed Qayyum Khan (aka "Q"), Crevice plotters—Mohammed Junaid Babar, Omar Khyam, Sala-huddin Amin—and future British suicide bombers Omar Sharif and Asif Hanif, who traveled to Israel to attack the Mike's Place bar in Tel Aviv. An important node in the London-based Islamist scene that Mohammed Siddique Khan, Shehzad Tanweer, and Germaine Lindsay had had visited occasionally was the Finsbury Park Mosque in London, where Abu Hamza spoke.[7]

Gravitating to Reactionary Islam

Some reports identify both Mohammed Siddique Khan and Shehzad Tanweer as having been members of the Mullah Boys. This fluid group of fifteen- to twenty-year-old, second-generation Pakistanis decided to act against a wave of community-wide drug usage. Khan was a leading member. The group was known to kidnap young Pakistani drug addicts and, with the consent of their families, hold them in a flat near the Wahhabi-inclined mosque on Stratford Street. There they would forcibly cleanse them of their drug habits. More important, at some point in the mid-1990s, when Khan first got involved with the Mullah Boys, he became interested in Wahhabi fundamentalism; this pitted him against his family's traditional approach to Islam.[8] According to an account of an interview with Mohammed Siddique Khan's brother, Gultasab, "Siddique had found that the traditional, community-run mosque on Hardy Street [Kashmir Muslim Community Center and Mosque] had nothing to offer him; it was run by Kashmiri Muslims, who had no idea how to connect with the second generation. They spoke and wrote in Urdu, and the only time they interacted with the younger Muslims was when they taught them to recite the Koran by rote—in Arabic."[9]

Meanwhile, the Stratford Street Mosque was run by Pakistani Tablighi Jamaat members and the Bengali mosque on Tunstall Road was run by primarily Bangladeshis. Although Khan tried all of the mosques, he ultimately chose the Stratford Street Mosque, which followed the more rigid, orthodox, Deobandi school of Islam, with a heavy Tablighi Jamaat presence.[10] However, by 2001, the two leading members of the Operation Theseus group, Mohammed Siddique Khan and Shehzad Tanweer, left the local Deobandi mosque in Beeston, saying its approach to outreach was too narrow, its focus too apolitical. The young zealots felt contempt for the mosque's imams, who were from the Indian subcontinent, spoke minimal English, and knew little of the challenges British Muslims faced. Moreover, the Deobandi mosque did not address the issues of concern to the members of the Theseus group and instead abided by an injunction by mosque elders that politics or current events involving Muslims should stay outside the mosque.[11]

The local Salafi/Wahhabi mosques did things differently. They delivered sermons and printed publications in English. Khan's Urdu was poor, so the only things on Islam he could read were Wahhabi-approved English-language publications. Khan's progression to Wahhabism was reinforced by the fact that some of his friends, and future Mullah Boys, were converting too.[12] Khan began to pray regularly at school and attend mosque on Fridays. He gave up fighting, bouts of drinking, and using drugs. He began volunteering as a teaching assistant at an elementary school. Shehzad Tanweer changed as well, giving casinos a rest and growing a beard. Hasib Hussain appeared to become more religious—he began wearing traditional clothing and a prayer cap after a trip on hajj to Saudi Arabia in 2002.[13]

Germaine Lindsay had been strongly influenced by the extremist preacher Sheikh Abdullah al Faisal (also of Jamaican origin), who had served a prison sentence in the U.K. for soliciting murder, incitement to murder, incitement to racial hatred, and distributing material promoting racial hatred. Lindsay is believed to have attended at least one lecture given by al Faisal and to have listened to tapes of other lectures by him.[14]

Politicization of New Beliefs

After Khan, Tanweer, and their friends left the mosques, they gravitated to the Iqra Learning Center, a bookstore in Beeston, just blocks away from the youth center. It seems clear that Iqra was a pivotal site in the course of their radicalization. The location was a "dawah center" and hosted a variety of religious classes. This was part of the process of gradually separating themselves from secular society and radicalizing toward violence. They were soon joined by Hasib Hussain.

Here they were free from their parents' Islam as well as from scrutiny. They had political discussions about Iraq, Kashmir, and Chechnya, organized study groups, accessed the Internet, and produced jihad DVDs depicting crimes by the West on the Muslim world. This local bookshop was a central node in the community for radical Islam. Not only did it sell Islamic books, tapes, and DVDs, but it also hosted lectures and discussion groups on

Islam. Iqra became known in the community for selling "under-the-counter-stuff," such as videos of what was taking place in Bosnia, Chechnya, and Iraq, including extremely graphic footage and narration aimed at inciting rage. Among other things, Iqra had audio tapes of Maulana Masood Azhar, the leader of Jaish-e-Mohammed.[15] According to Wahid Ali, he and Tanweer spent a significant amount of time watching the Chechen videos: "We watched the brothers fighting in Chechnya against the Russians and it was really inspirational watching." Moreover, these videos, coupled with audio cassettes and books about the massacre of Muslims in Bosnia from the Iqra bookstore, transformed Wahid Ali into "a committed brother." He had a religious revival and within two months of his first exposure to this material expressed a desire to attend a training camp so that he could "help liberate Muslim lands."[16]

Both Mohammed Siddique Khan and Shehzad Tanweer recorded video statements explaining the rationale behind their actions.[17] Their clearly politicized message included the following:

Your democratically elected governments continuously perpetuate atrocities against my people all over the world. And your support of them makes you directly responsible, just as I am directly responsible for protecting and avenging my Muslim brothers and sisters. Until we feel security you will be our targets and until you stop the bombing, gassing, imprisonment and torture of my people we will not stop this fight. We are at war and I am a soldier. Now you too will taste the reality of this situation.[18]

Shehzad Tanweer added to this political message, noting, "What have you witnessed now is only the beginning of a string of attacks that will continue and become stronger until you pull your forces out of Afghanistan and Iraq. And until you stop your financial and military support to America and Israel." Tanweer argued that the non-Muslims of Britain deserved such attacks because they voted for a government that "continues to oppress our mothers, children, brothers and sisters in Palestine, Afghanistan, Iraq and Chechnya."[19] These views had been underpinned by a general belief among the cluster members that Muslims were being oppressed worldwide. Their associate, Mohammed Shakil, commented on the effect that videos available at the Iqra bookstore about the treatment of Muslims in the Balkans in the 1990s had on him.

I remember back in the early—back when I started practicing is when I first saw actual footage of what had happened in Bosnia and places like Kosovo and Albania and these sorts of countries, I mean these are sorts of things I had never been exposed to before and when I see this [*sic*] videos, especially the Bosnia video which is nearby here, I think that really had an effect on me and when I seen the massacre and the mass killing I mean I could not believe that one human being could do this to another—do you understand—and it was like happening everywhere in Bosnia, Kosovo and many, many countries and it was so close that it made me feel that its [*sic*] Muslims that are getting slaughtered by disbelievers in them countries so that was about the first part of this question.[20]

The Beeston/Dewsbury Cluster

This offshoot cluster was one driven by preexisting friendships of young men who had grown up together in the greater Leeds area in the towns of Beeston and Dewsbury. Three of the four bombers—Mohammed Siddique Khan, Shehzad Tanweer, and Hasib Hussain—were second-generation British citizens of Pakistani descent from Beeston and Dewsbury. Germaine Lindsay, a fourth bomber, was a first-generation Jamaican who lived in Buckinghamshire, a county adjacent to the county of West Yorkshire, and had links to ALM and the Beeston cluster via the extremist cleric Abdullah al Faisal. To many who knew them, all four were described as being well integrated into British society. All four had Westernized, unremarkable backgrounds with secular upbringings. None had been educated in Islamic-based schools like madrassas; they had attended state schools and pursued modern studies. Three of the bombers came from well-to-do families.

In March 2007, three other men were arrested in connection with the July 7 bombings. Two of the men were arrested at Manchester Airport attempting to board a plane due to depart for Pakistan that afternoon. The other man was arrested in the Beeston area of Leeds, West Yorkshire, at an address on the street where one of the suicide bombers had lived before the attacks. Wahid Ali, Sadeer Saleem, and Mohammed Shakil also grew up in the Beeston area, were members of the Beeston/Dewsbury Cluster, and were associates of the bombers. They were charged in the U.K. with conspiring with the four bombers to cause explosions in London between November 2004 and July 2005.[21]

The four London bombers and their three co-conspirators were essentially an autonomous cluster of young men whose motivations, cohesiveness, and radicalization all occurred in the absence of any organized network or formal entry into the transnational jihad. This was a localized, neighborhood phenomenon as Mohammed Siddique Khan, Shehzad Tanweer, Hasib Hussain, Wahid Ali, Sadeer Saleem, and Mohammed Shakil all grew up together in the Beeston area and attended the same mosques, gyms, and community organizations, and hung out at the Iqra bookshop. Khan, as one of the oldest of the cluster, was clearly its leader.

Not surprisingly, it was the association between Khan and Tanweer that was the closest. They are thought to have known each other since childhood. In addition, Hasib Hussain's brother played cricket with Tanweer when they were children. It is not known how Hussain met Khan, but after 2001, Hussain was involved in local youth work projects and by late 2004 was a frequent associate of the two, attending the jujitsu class with Khan at the Hamara Center. Subsequently, Khan was a regular visitor to the Hussain family home.[22] Co-conspirator Mohammed Shakil testified in court that he used to drink alcohol and smoke marijuana with Mohammed Siddique Khan before he (Khan) became devout. Meanwhile, Wahid Ali noted that he had grown up across the street from Tanweer and that the pair had become good friends playing football and cricket together as well as lifting weights at the local gym (the Hamara Healthy Living Centre) with all the "local lads."[23]

Germaine Lindsay, who was born in Jamaica and brought up in Huddersfield, was the only July 7 bomber who was not from Leeds area. He began traveling to Dewsbury and Beeston regularly to attend Arabic and martial arts classes in 2003. The Arabic-language classes were taught at the Iqra bookstore and jujitsu classes were held at the Hamara Centre. His sister, who had not converted to Islam, lived in the area near Leeds and was another reason that he was a frequent visitor to the area. He likely met Mohammed Siddique Khan and the other men of the cluster during those trips. Subsequently, his wife, Samantha, and Khan's wife, Hasina, became "good friends."[24] In fact, based on an account given by one of Mohammed Siddique Khan's neighbors in the immediate aftermath of the attack, she confirmed that "men often visited their home wearing the flowing robes of the devoutly Muslim. She remembers a man whose accent sounded Jamaican visited recently."[25]

Anatomy of the Cluster

Active Core

Mohammed Siddique Khan, age thirty at the time of his death, was raised in a lenient, not strictly religious household. Some accounts describe Khan as a teenager who tried in almost every way to "shed his ethnic skin," who often went by the nickname "Sid," and "who had been remembered as wearing a leather jacket and cowboy boots, praising the virtues of American life after a brief trip there at age 15."[26] A school friend noted that growing up, Khan "seemed to have more white friends than Asian friends [and] . . . used to hang around with white lads playing football. . . . He was very English. Some of the other Pakistani guys used to talk about Muslim suffering around the world but with Siddique you'd never really know what religion he was from."[27]

Khan studied business at the local Leeds Metropolitan University. Following graduation, in 2002, he worked for the Benefits Agency and the Department of Trade and Industry. After obtaining his university degree he had secured a job as a teaching assistant at Hillside Primary School. According to some accounts, he won the affection of his workers and the parents of his students, but the job paid a modest salary, one upon which it proved difficult to support his wife and young child.[28] After marrying Hasina—a Deobandi Muslim woman whose family was from India and whom he had met at university in 1997—Khan was ostracized by his family and "wanted nothing to do with him." Shortly before the attacks, Khan's wife announced she was pregnant with their second child and, according to friends, Khan was overjoyed and claimed that it was "Allah's will."[29]

Shehzad Tanweer, age twenty-two at the time of his death, was economically the most well-off of the four, coming from a hardworking and prosperous family. His father was a successful merchant who owned several restaurants. Tanweer had also been known as hardworking; he helped out in his family's restaurant, among other jobs. In his youth, he had a pattern of involvement in scuffles that formed along racial lines but no criminal history. According to his associate, Wahid Ali, Tanweer became religious at age fifteen or sixteen and grew a beard. Tanweer had been close to earning a two-year degree at Leeds Metropolitan University, majoring in sports science with a specialization in cricket and jujitsu before dropping out in 2003. Tanweer was said to be working in his father's fish and chips store up until July 2005. Tanweer was said to have an estate worth $200,000.[30]

Followers

Hasib Hussain, age eighteen at the time of his death, grew up in the same neighborhood as Khan and Tanweer. The youngest of four children, he was said to be an introvert. Although he had a good secondary school attendance record, he dropped out in 2003. Hussain was involved in sports, playing both football and cricket for local teams. According to people from the neighborhood, "He had been a chubby child—'dorky' by some accounts and peers testified to the fact that he was often picked on and mocked at school. He had gotten into trouble for drug use as a teen and eventually his parents sent him to Pakistan in hopes of reacquainting him with traditional Islamic values." At the time of the July 2005 bombing, Hussain, just eighteen, was awaiting results from a series of academic tests that he had taken at Thomas Danby College in Leeds.[31]

Germaine Lindsay, age nineteen at the time of his death, was a Jamaican-born British resident who converted to Islam at age fifteen, in 2000, and married a white convert. He was described as a bright child, successful academically at school, artistic, musically inclined, and good at sports. Lindsay spent his teenage years close to Leeds, in Huddersfield, West Yorkshire.[32]

Periphery

Wahid Ali, age twenty-two at the time of the attacks, arrived in the U.K. from Bangladesh as a three-year-old. His parents died within a month of each other about a year later. He was brought up by foster parents, whom he claimed used to beat him, and ended up dropping out of school with failing grades. According to his court testimony, he was "looked after" by his best friend, Shehzad Tanweer, nicknamed Kaki, who lived only yards from his house in Beeston: "We used to do normal kiddie stuff, play football and cricket with all the local lads. I was quite childish back then, I think, I probably still am now, and Kaki was more mature." As a result of the time that he spent at the Iqra bookstore, Waheed began to turn his focus from sport to the plight of Muslims around the world, specifically Muslim brothers in

Afghanistan and Kashmir. Nevertheless, Ali stated during the trial that up until the attack in 2005, he and Tanweer played "football" and cricket and weight lifted together.[33]

Sadeer Saleem, age twenty-five at the time of the attacks, was from Beeston. His family immigrated to the U.K. from the Mirpur region of Pakistani Kashmir in the 1970s and settled in Middlesbrough. During his youth, he drank alcohol and "went clubbing." He had attended Leeds College of Technology and took a spray painting course, which he could not continue due to his asthma. Saleem was married and had a young daughter. Mohammed Shakil was his brother-in-law. Saleem "found religion in 2000" and served as a trustee at the Iqra bookshop in Leeds. Although he and Wahid Ali did not grow up together, by 2001 they were close friends. He also was a caretaker at the Hamara Centre and held odd jobs at various fast food restaurants between 2002 and 2004.[34]

Mohammed Shakil, age thirty-one at the time of the attacks, was born in Karachi, Pakistan, but immigrated with his family to the U.K. in 1981. His family came from the Mirpur region of Pakistani Kashmir. As a youth he had been into "hip hop dancing." At the time of his arrest, Shakil lived in a house in Firth Mount, one of the more affluent neighborhoods of Beeston. He worked as a taxi driver for Gee Gee cars in Beeston. Shakil had three sons, aged eleven (approximately), five, and an infant. Neighbors described Shakil as a pleasant and talkative man who walked with a limp, wore Western clothes, and played cricket in the street with his sons. Shakil had attended a Kashmiri militant training camp for three days in 1999 while he was on a family trip to Kashmir, where he had family. According to Shakil, attending the camp was a spontaneous decision. He was a longtime friend of Mohammed Siddique Khan before their friendship dissolved in 2003–4.[35]

Hasina Patel, age twenty-nine at the time of the attacks, grew up in a prominent Muslim Indian family from the state of Gujarat. She married Khan in 2001 after meeting at university. She worked with disabled children and helped get Khan a job at Hillside as a mentor to counsel troubled students and help immigrant children settle into the British school system. After the bombings, Hasina was arrested on suspicion of being an accomplice to the bomb plot, and was accused of knowing that her husband was planning to bomb London and of failing to alert police. However, she was not charged and was released.[36] British investigators based in West Yorkshire consider the core members of the cluster to be part of a wider local group that may have had some awareness of the pre-attack activities that the active core had participated in. In fact, Khan's wife, Hasina, Hasina's brother, Arshad Patel, and her cousin Imran Motala were also initially arrested and then released. Moreover, Khalid Khaliq, who was also arrested in the sweep, was accused of possessing an al Qaeda "training manual."[37] In total, the cluster may have been made up of as many as eighteen people, including two individuals not publicly identified to date. It remains to be seen as to whether charges can or will be brought against these individuals.

Overseas Travel and Link Up with Al Qaeda

The three trips that Mohammed Siddique Khan took to Pakistan and Afghanistan between 2001 and 2004, coupled with travel by Shehzad Tanweer, Wahid Ali, and Sadeer Saleem provided opportunities for the active and passive core members of the cluster to attend training camps, meet members associated with the Operation Crevice plot, link up with the transnational jihad, and potentially even meet al Qaeda–associated individuals.

Mohammed Siddique Khan was plugged into the wider Islamist and jihadi network prior to 9/11. In the wake of the trial of the three July 7 co-conspirators, it was revealed that Khan and Wahid Ali had traveled to Pakistan and Afghanistan earlier than previously known. Sadeer Saleem had originally planned to accompany Khan on this trip, but he bowed out at the last minute. In June 2001, just months before 9/11, Ali and Khan traveled to Pakistan to take part in a training camp run by Harkat ul Mujahedeen (HuM), a Pakistani extremist group proscribed in the U.K. as a terrorist organization. Khan's uncle, who lived in Pakistan, was able to connect the men to HuM—in fact, they were picked up at the Islamabad airport by a HuM van. Both men stayed in a mountain camp in Mansehra, in the North West Frontier Province of Pakistan, and learned how to fire Kalashnikovs and rocket-propelled grenade launchers, among other activities.[38]

At the camp they met two Arabs from the UAE who planned on traveling to Afghanistan. On a whim, Khan and Ali decided to "go with the flow" and via HuM contacts traveled to Afghanistan to see the Taliban on the front lines. By the time they reached their destination, Ali and Khan were both suffering from serious diarrhea and were told by the fighters they were too inexperienced to go to the front line. Ali stayed at base camp helping with the cooking, but Khan recovered enough to make trips to the front line but did not get involved in the fighting. The two returned to the U.K. on September 5, 2001.[39]

Following this firsthand experience with jihad overseas, according to one account, back in the U.K. Khan worked with ALM members Omar Sharif and Asif Hanif and traveled to Manchester multiple times to recruit other youngsters for training in Afghanistan. In 2003, both Sharif and Hanif would travel to Israel in to commit suicide attacks at Mike's Place in Tel Aviv.[40]

The Operation Crevice trial revealed that in 2003 Mohammed Siddique Khan had been in contact with Mohammed Qayyum Khan (called "Q"), a suspected al Qaeda contact based in Luton. In fact, in July 2003, Qayyum would send Khan and July 7 co-conspirator Mohammed Shakil to Pakistan. According to court testimony by Shakil, their mission was a fact-finding effort to determine whether foreigners were welcome to fight jihad in Afghanistan and to return to England with the answer. Mohammed Siddique Khan likely met "Q" through Mohammed Shakil, who had known "Q" from his brief time as a student at the University of Bedfordshire in Luton between 1997 and 1999, before he moved back to Leeds. Mohammed Siddique Khan traveled to Pakistan in July 2003 with another man (Shakil) to deliver funds raised in the U.K. for jihadi groups, such as Kashmiri fighters or the Taliban via Operation Crevice conspirator Salahuddin Amin, an important link in the mujahedeen supply network. Their trip to Pakistan in 2003 lasted from July 24 to August 7.[41] In fact, Salahuddin Amin testified that he met the two at the airport and "they gave him money amounting to hundreds of pounds for the cause, which he then passed on. Then he bumped into Omar Khyam by chance at the airport and he introduced Khan and Shakil to Khyam and then left and then went off."[42]

Operation Crevice leader Omar Khyam confirmed the story, noting, "Basically, we were talking at the airport and I said the guys—three guys that I came to pick up, I said they are going to be going to the camp, and they said they like to come as well. So Amin said, 'Okay, I'll leave them with you.' So I took Ibrahim [aka Mohammed Siddique Khan] and Zubair [aka Mohammed Shakil]'s number" and then picked them up two days later.[43]

According to the Crown prosecutor's witness, Mohammed Junaid Babar, it was he who offered Khan and Shakil the opportunity to participate in the camp. However, "they [Khan and Shakil] said they had already been through that type of training before in camps in Kashmir before 9/11 and there was no need to go through it again." Babar added, "They wanted to know what the reality was because people were saying in England that al Qaeda and the Taliban said they didn't want any foreign fighters while others were saying they did."[44] Ultimately, according to Babar's testimony, they were persuaded to attend the camp in Malakand, where they both took part in the firearms training. Khan and Shakil appeared "confident and experienced" and said they wanted to fight in Afghanistan.[45]

On November 18, 2004, Khan and Tanweer departed the U.K. for Pakistan. Video footage presented at the trial of the July 7 co-conspirators showed Khan's farewell speech to his wife and daughter, which was made just prior to his departure. Khan notes in the video to his infant daughter, "Sweetheart, not long to go now. And I am going to really, really miss you a lot . . . I just wish I could have been part of your life . . . but I have to do this thing . . . I am doing what I am doing for the sake of Islam." Queen's Council Neil Flewitt commented, "It is clear from the passage that Khan did not expect to see his daughter again. Put bluntly, he knew he was going to his death."[46]

The Queen's Council prosecution asserted that Khan and Tanweer had planned for martyrdom abroad, but shortly after arriving in Pakistan to fight, their plans changed and they chose to return to Britain to launch the first suicide attacks within the U.K.[47] In the Home Office's official assessment of the July 7 attacks, it acknowledges that Khan and Tanweer's visit to Pakistan from November 2004 to February 8, 2005, could have been a key point in the development of the notion to attack the United Kingdom, but it offers no evidence that either Khan or Tanweer trained in any formal camps or that they met with any known terrorists during their time there; the report only goes so far as to say "it seems likely that they had some contact with Al Qaeda figures."[48]

The diary of Khan's wife, which was presented as evidence at the spring 2008 trial, notes that Khan changed his plans as of November 26, 2004: Khan would be returning from Pakistan, not going to his death there. As the Crown prosecution noted, her diary said, "If we look to 26th "S [Mohammed Siddique Khan] rang, good news, back by Feb? So it looks as if by 26th November Hasina Patel knew that Sid was coming back?" This is a critical piece of information as it suggests that at this point, the purpose of Khan and Tanweer's trip to Pakistan changed—it was no longer to fight abroad and now, in retrospect, signaled that they had a new mission—in the U.K.[49] Interestingly, on December 26, 2004, a little more than a month after Khan and Tanweer departed for Pakistan from the U.K., Wahid Ali and Sadeer Saleem traveled to Islamabad from Manchester. On their visa applications, they noted that they wanted to see Saleem's grandfather; however, that same grandfather left for the U.K. from Pakistan only two weeks after the pair arrived, thus calling into question the validity of the reason for the trip.[50] Rather, it seems that the pair's intent was to join Khan and Tanweer at a training camp in Pakistan. In fact, according to Wahid Ali's testimony, Khan had told the two, "'What's going to happen is me [Khan] and Kaki [Tanweer] are going to go out first, we're going to sort out the contacts and then we'll give you a call. Be ready to move out any time soon, yeah, and then just come over.' I said, 'Sweet, no problem.'"[51]

Training and Skill Acquisition

After Tanweer picked up Wahid Ali and Sadeer Saleem in Islamabad at the airport and had a brief stay in Faisalbad, Tanweer drove them to Peshawar, where they were met by some Afghans who took the three men to a training camp. According to Wahid Ali's court testimony, the next day Tanweer told his two friends from the U.K., "We've already done what you've done, you can catch up to us in a bit, in about five/six weeks. So just ride it out here and we'll see you soon." After approximately three weeks during which Ali and Saleem participated in weapons and physical training with men from the "tribal belt" at the compound to which they had brought to by the Afghans, Khan and Tanweer returned. At that point Khan told the two men that plans had changed and that rather than stay in Pakistan, Khan and Tanweer were going back (to the U.K.) to "do something for the brothers." Ali and Saleem subsequently left the camp, toured around Pakistan, and returned to the U.K. on February 26, 2005.[52] It is unknown if either Khan or Tanweer received explosives training during this trip.

Al Qaeda Recruitment

Whether this occurred or not is unknown and remains one of the greatest mysteries surrounding this plot. As previously noted, Khan and Tanweer had planned for martyrdom abroad, but shortly after arriving in Pakistan to fight their plans changed and they chose to return to Britain. Recruitment of the men by al Qaeda to be part of a plot against the U.K. would certainly explain the change in direction. However, the Home Office's official assessment of the July 7 attacks offers no evidence that either Khan or Tanweer trained in any formal camps or that they met with any known terrorists during their time there.

Operational Cycle

Travel to Pakistan appears to have been the catalyst for the cluster's mobilization to action. Khan and Tanweer returned to the U.K. on February 8, 2005. As a result of previous fallings-out that Mohammed Siddique Khan had with Mohammed Shakil and Sadeer Saleem, they were not included in the plotting; Hasib Hussain and Germaine Lindsay were included instead. The first acts in furtherance of the plan were the purchase of materials for the bombs on March 31, 2005, about seven weeks after their return to the U.K. On July 7, 2005, they launched their attack. The total duration of the operational cycle was approximately five months.

Target Selection/Casing

During a two-day visit to London on December 16–17, 2004, Wahid Ali, Sadeer Saleem, Mohammed Shakil Khan, Germaine Lindsay, and Hasib Hussain visited the London Eye and the Natural History Museum. The Crown prosecution alleged that this was a "reconnaissance mission." Queen's Counsel Neil Flewitt said that the trip was "an essential preparatory step in the revised plan to bring death and destruction to the heart of the United Kingdom and there were striking similarities between the sites visited by the group and the locations of the July 7 explosions." All the defendants admitted traveling to London but said that it was to enable Wahid Ali to meet his sister for purely social reasons.[53] This trip occurred after Khan and Tanweer had arrived in Pakistan and potentially after they had been redirected or redirected themselves toward an attack against the U.K.. According to Flewitt, this was not coincidental.[54]

There most certainly was a later reconnaissance/dry run visit to London on June 28, 2005, by Khan, Tanweer, and Lindsay: "The three journeyed from Beeston to Luton and then to King's Cross station before traveling on the underground. They were picked up on CCTV near Baker Street tube station later in the morning and [returned] to Luton at lunchtime. Train tickets found at 18 Alexandra Grove after the attack suggest there had been additional visits to London in mid-March."[55]

Logistics

In early 2004, before the decision was made to attack the U.K., Khan and the cluster were in regular communication with Omar Khyam, the ringleader of Operation Crevice and one of the individuals who had met Khan and Shakil at the Islamabad airport in 2003 before attending a training camp in Malakand. He was a source of advice on logistics for al Qaeda supporters in the U.K.

In February 2004, Khan, Tanweer, and Ali traveled from Yorkshire to the south of England for a five-minute meeting with Khyam. Another meeting three weeks later was recorded by authorities in Khyam's car. Among the subjects discussed were means for raising funds, including "scams to rip the country apart economically" like opening fraudulent trade accounts with building merchants and applying for loans in a false name that would never be repaid. Following two additional meetings, the three July 7 co-conspirators opened false building trade accounts.[56]

At this meeting Khyam also discussed the logistical issues of travel to and from Pakistan and the risks that it entailed, ultimately suggesting that Khan plan for "a one way ticket":

> There was a time when you just land and go in to Afghanistan as a tourist like, training camp and come back, obviously you know that time is finished . . . because every time you come back you're going to make yourself hotter—your youth, travelling into Pakistan and out of Pakistan, and they watch that yeah so when you come back and meet up with the brothers yeah you make the brothers here hotter as well. . . . This is a one-way ticket bruv and you agree with that yeah and you're happy with this.[57]

Khyam also suggested cover stories to explain why Khan was traveling to Pakistan and that he would have to wait until it was clear before getting involved in operations there.

> you will be enrolling in colleges, doing electronic courses, computer

courses, whatever you want to do and you will be given a normal life-style. You're a British guy come to study in Pakistan, it's a lot cheaper here and that's all that will happen for the first few months up to four or five months, we need to get intelligence that they are following us, want them to follow us, until they think that these guys are nothing. When we feel the time is right (unclear) emir operations start (unclear) it all depends on the situation everybody wants to go to the front everybody wants to fight.[58]

Communications

Beyond the private meetings with Khyam, members of the cluster were in regular contact with each other primarily through cell phone and text messages. For example, in December 2004, when the group allegedly conducted surveillance in London, mobile phone calls were made among the three July 7 co-conspirators and Hasib Hussain as well as Germaine Lindsay.[59] At least twenty calls from Haroon Rashid Aswat's mobile telephone were made to the bombers in the days before the attacks, although it is still unclear if he had any direct role in the plot.[60]

Evidence presented at the coroner's inquest into the July 7 bombings in February 2011 has shown that Mohammed Siddique Khan was on the receiving end of a number of phone calls from different landlines (possibly public call boxes) in Rawalpindi, Pakistan, that began on April 23, 2005. Khan was the only bomber to receive calls and it appears that he did not call Pakistan himself. The calls increased in frequency in mid-May through June, when the explosive devices were being built. The final call was on July 2, just five days before the attack. Consequently, one of the investigators assigned to the July 7 case agreed that these calls were "probably connected to some guidance or some means of communicating information concerned with the manufacture of the bombs and then, ultimately, their detonation."[61]

The men also utilized text messages. In fact, text messages referencing the 1980s television show *The A-Team* "began a week before the bombings and continued until July 6, when the tone of the messages became more sober as Khan disclosed that he was having problems meeting the other three bombers at the pre-arranged time due to a family health emergency.[62]

Weaponization

The rucksack bombs used in the attacks were homemade using relatively inexpensive, commercially available ingredients. Although these explosive devices could be manufactured solely using publicly available information, it is likely that the group obtained specific instruction, tips, or advice from bomb experts during their travel to Pakistan.[63] The first purchase of material to build 2–5 kilograms of homemade peroxide-based explosive was on March 31, 2005. Materials consistent with these processes (black pepper, hydrogen peroxide, HMTD high explosives) as well as DNA linking the three co-conspirators were discovered at the apartment in Alexandra Grove in Leeds, which was believed to be the "bomb factory."[64]

As previously noted, Mohammed Siddique Khan received several phone calls from Rawalpindi beginning April 23, 2005. Since the calls increased in frequency in mid-May through June, when the explosive devices were being built, there is reason to believe that Khan was receiving guidance from Pakistan on their construction.[65]

The Al Qaeda Factor

Mohammed Siddique Khan and Shehzad Tanweer made videotapes in which they described their reasons for becoming what they called "soldiers." The tapes, which had been edited as "As Sahaab productions" produced by al Qaeda's official media wing, featured al Qaeda's second in command, Ayman al Zawahiri, in a way intended to suggest a direct link between Khan and al Qaeda. However, Khan did not say anything that linked the bombing to al Qaeda, and it would not have been particularly difficult for editors to splice al Zawahiri into a previously taped video. In fact, an official inquiry by the British government reported that the tape claiming responsibility had been edited after the attacks and that the bombers had no direct support from al Qaeda. Nevertheless, these tapes have been cited as evidence that the July attacks were linked to al Qaeda Core.[66]

British prosecutors did not produce any evidence in the trial of the July 7 co-conspirators explicitly linking the plot to al Qaeda. Yet American, British, and Pakistani officials and journalists have suggested in a variety of venues that the plot was an al Qaeda–directed plot from Pakistan. A variety of potential intermediate links to al Qaeda Core are tantalizingly possible. There are three leading hypotheses as to the nature of these links.

The first is the link to Abu Munthir and Abdul Hadi al Iraqi. This hypothesis is based on the connectivity that the July 7 bombers may have established via these two men to al Qaeda Core via the Operation Crevice plotters.

During their summer 2003 trip to Malakand, Khan and Shakil clearly attended a training camp with other British wannabe jihadists, including Khyam and other members of the Operation Crevice cluster. This group, according to Mohammed Junaid Babar's testimony, had made contact with two individuals with high-level al Qaeda Core contacts. One was a former Luton man known as Abu Munthir, which was almost certainly a nom-de-guerre. Munthir was described as a "senior Mujahedeen figure" who received material and financial support from the U.K. The other was Abdul Hadi al Iraqi, a former major in Saddam Hussein's army and al Qaeda's commander of the Afghanistan theater of operations.[67] Abdul Hadi al Iraqi had contact with the group as part of their effort to funnel funds and supplies (night vision goggles) to him. According to Mohammed Junaid Babar, Khyam openly boasted he was working for Abdul Hadi, calling him his "Emir."[68] Moreover, another New York ALM member, Syed Hashmi, "allowed his London flat to be used to store supplies and money that Babar was shipping out to Abdul Hadi al Iraqi, then head of al Qaeda's operations in Afghanistan. The supplies included ponchos, torches and boots, useful for recruits fighting US troops in remote parts of Afghanistan."[69] However, regardless of this al Qaeda link and the training that occurred at the camp, clearly no direction or coordination was provided to Khan and Shakil from this trip as they continued to seek out more general advice from Khyam later that winter of 2004, as recorded by MI-5.

British court records reveal an intriguing coincidence in the timing of trips to Pakistan made by leaders of four major terrorist plots in Britain between December 2004 and February 2005. The ringleaders involved in four major U.K., al Qaeda–linked cases (Operation Crevice, Operation Theseus, Operation Vivace, and Operation Overt) all traveled to Pakistan during that three-month window.[70] According to one theory, it was during this trip, in late November 2004, that Hadi al Iraqi re-tasked both Khan and Tanweer to attack the U.K. Khan and Tanweer allegedly traveled to Karachi and met Hadi al Iraqi, who recognized the potential for redirecting already radicalized British Muslims who had traveled to the region with the desire to become mujahedeen in Afghanistan or Iraq. Again, this would be inconsistent with Hadi al Iraqi's focus on establishing a supply network that would support his fighters in Afghanistan.[71]

The second possible link is Abu Ubaidah al Masri. Some British antiterrorism officials have asserted that members of all four plots who traveled to Pakistan between November 2004 and February 2005 were trained and directed by Abu Ubaidah al Masri, al Qaeda's Chief of External Operations at the time. However, to date, there has been little corroboration of this hypothesis.[72]

The third link possible is Haroon Rashid Aswat. For a period of time, Aswat, a Briton of Indian descent, was considered the "possible mastermind" of the attacks. He became a person of interest because at least twenty calls from Aswat's mobile telephone were made to the bombers in the days before the attacks.[73] Aswat had grown up in a town near Leeds and in the ten years since he had left was believed to have traveled to various terrorist camps in Afghanistan and Pakistan. As the investigation proceeded, public reports slowly ceased to identify Aswat as a key player in the events, suggesting that the evidence of his connection must have been lacking or altogether absent.[74] Aswat was arrested in Zambia on July 20, 2005, and deported to the U.K. on August 7, 2005 and arrested on his arrival. However, despite being in British custody for more than three years, during the trial of the trial of the July 7 co-conspirators his name was not raised nor was his potential role as the intermediate link to al Qaeda discussed.[75]

While Khan and Tanweer likely received some operational instruction during their stay in camps in the winter of 2004–5 and knew individuals that had varying levels of connectivity to al Qaeda, it is still unclear whether the bombers were specifically directed to attack the U.K. by al Qaeda. While phone records have provided evidence of ongoing communication between the U.K. plotters and Pakistan, it is unclear if this was for technical information relating to the device or for direction for Pakistan. Moreover, even non-public information remains ambiguous about this issue. The final word on this issue may be the UK Home Office's assessment, which was released in 2006.

In the Home Office's official assessment of the July 7 attacks it acknowledges that Khan and Tanweer's visit to Pakistan from November 2004 to February 8, 2005, could have been a key point in the development of the notion to attack the U.K, but it offers no evidence that either Khan or Tanweer trained in any formal camps or that they met with any known terrorists during their time there; the report only goes so far as to say "it seems likely that they had some contact with Al Qaeda figures."[76] The new evidence presented at the coroner's inquest in February 2011 of ongoing communication between Pakistan and Khan from April 23 to July 2, 2005, is certainly suggestive of some overseas guidance but still not decisive in determining an al Qaeda role. In the final analysis, unless further evidence becomes available, Operation Theseus cannot be considered an al Qaeda Core "command and control" plot but rather an al Qaeda "suggested/endorsed" plot.

Chapter 8

Operation Vivace (London, July 21, 2005)

ON JULY 21, 2005, four attempted bomb attacks paralyzed London's mass transportation system. The failed events occurred midday at Shepherds Bush, Warren Street, and Oval stations of London's Underground and on a bus in Shoreditch. A fifth bomber, after having a change of heart, abandoned his device without attempting to set it off. Only the detonators of the bombs exploded, causing only one minor injury. All the suspects fled the scenes after their bombs failed to explode. Twelve additional individuals were arrested for their roles in supporting the bombers prior to or immediately following the attempted attack.[1]

Londonistan

See Chapter 2 for background on the formation of this "scene."

Gravitating to Reactionary Islam

As previously noted, the Finsbury Park Mosque was a key node in the U.K. for the proliferation of an interpretation of Islam that promoted military jihad as a means to defend Islam, restore the Caliphate, and fight the West. This was the primary radicalization node for the members of the Operation Vivace cluster, who almost unanimously all arrived in the U.K. as immigrants seeking asylum and with little if any knowledge of Islam. Most members of the cluster had spent their teen years as average secular members of society, drinking alcohol, clubbing, and chasing girls. Many had even been involved in low-level criminality and had manipulated the social welfare system to collect unemployment benefits, live in public housing, and qualify for financial aid to attend university. Following exposure to extremist sermons at the Speakers Corner at Hyde Park in London, many gravitated to the Finsbury Park Mosque around 2000, began to regularly attend religious services there, and were captivated by the imam Abu Hamza al Masri.[2]

Here the men were exposed to an extremist interpretation of Islam and key connections were made to radical circles. As noted earlier, the mosque had a reputation for attracting converts, helping ex-offenders readjust to life in the outside world, and providing a Salafi interpretation of Islam. The combination of message and networking at Finsbury had a significant effect on the men of the Vivace cluster.[3] Muktar Said Ibrahim, Yassin Omar, Adel Yahya, and Ramzi Mohammed had all frequented the Finsbury Park Mosque and were dedicated followers of Abu Hamza. In addition, Yassin Omar and Muktar Said Ibrahim had been in possession of taped Abu Hamza sermons. The group members had a large collection of radical religious sermons, extremist literature, and violence-laced videos stored on audio, video, and computer disk. Several of these espoused the rhetoric of Osama Bin Laden, Abu Hamza al Masri, and Sheikh Abdullah al Faisal.[4]

According to their friend Stephen Bentley, "Both Ibrahim and Omar had extremist views against the U.K. and America and would often discuss Jihad in Iraq, Afghanistan and Chechnya." Both Ibrahim and Omar seemed keen and willing to go fight there, including fighting the British and American troops in Iraq. According to a Saudi student who knew the men of the July 21 cluster and testified in court, Yassin Omar's religious views were "fanatic and radical as well. . . . He was trying many times to convince me for Jihad and also he was trying to convince me those people who's doing suicide bombing, they are right—when we have seen the 9/11 speech and the 19 hijackers, he was trying to convince me they are right." These conclusions were based on the scholars whom Omar followed—Abu Hamza and Sheikh Faisal.[5]

Partly as a result of his exposure to radical Islam at Finsbury Park, Muktar Ibrahim began to distribute Islamic literature on the streets of London. Yassin Omar and Ramzi Mohammed began to wear more traditional Islamic clothing; they were often seen in robes and traditional head covering.

Several cluster members attempted to take over a South London mosque after accusing the imam of being too moderate.[6]

The private home of two individuals who spent a great deal of time at Finsbury Park—Mohammed Hamid (Osama bin London) and Attila Ahmet (Abu Abdullah) —was another venue where the members of the July 21 cluster were encouraged to adhere to an extreme version of Islam whereby the murder of non-believers is permissible. Mohammed Hamid and Attila Ahmet played the role of local ideologues for the group members.[7] During the sessions at Hamid's apartment, both Hamid and Ahmet utilized religious justifications to encourage the men to turn to violence:

"Allah made it obligatory to fight. When you understand the deen [faith or religious path] you have to fight, yeah?"

"Allah said he loves those that fight with their lives and their wealth and their family's wealth as well in his cause."

"Allah says they are cowards. It's an obligation for Allah to fulfill[l] jihad. Allah says it is quite easy for him to punish the kuffar."[8]

Politicization of New Beliefs

Muktar Ibrahim's religious beliefs were politicized as he spent significant time listening to the sermons of both Abu Hamza and Sheikh Faisal. According to his roommate, the Saudi student, they influenced Ibrahim's interpretation of jihad so that he came to understand it as "Fighting those people who's killing Muslim people"—specifically Americans, British, and Russians. Ibrahim cited Americans because American soldiers were killing Muslim people in Afghanistan, in Iraq, and "also in Somalia, long time ago," British because "also the British Army are killing also Muslim people," and Russians "because they are killing people in Chechnya."[9]

Various members of the group were remembered by those who knew them as exhibiting "aggressive rhetoric rooted in anger against Britain's support of U.S. policy in Iraq." In addition to talking out against U.K. and U.S. foreign policy at the Speakers Corner, Mohammed Hamid participated in protest demonstrations against Western foreign policy in places like Iraq and Afghanistan. Some of his younger acolytes would meet at a gym in West London to discuss the injustices being dealt to the Muslim world and the ways in which they could respond. One option was military force, and, as a result, many of the men would eventually attend jihadi paramilitary training camps in rural England and Wales run by Mohammed Hamid and Atilla Ahmet. The worldview they promoted was, "You are attacking our people in Muslim countries, in Iraq, in Afghanistan," Mr. Ahmet said, referring to the British and American governments. "So it's legitimate to attack British soldiers and policemen, government officials, and even the White House."[10]

The Speakers Corner Cluster

This cluster was primarily made up of first-generation immigrants from the Horn of Africa. A number of the men had come to the U.K. as refugees from conflicts in this region involving Somalia, Ethiopia, and what is now Eritrea. Although they lived in various parts of London, they were linked through their attendance at the Finsbury Park Mosque and at private prayer circles taking place in private residences in London. Eventually members of the cluster would bond further in training camps and Outward Bound–type activities in rural regions of the U.K. The group was primarily influenced by Mohammed Hamid, who was also a private prayer circle leader, and its operational leader, (Emir) Muktar Said Ibrahim.[11]

This group of primarily African refugees bonded as a cluster via a number of different venues. While Yassin Omar and Adel Yahya had met as teenagers in the mid-1990s, Muktar Ibrahim met Adel Yahya when they both lived at the Curtis House apartment building sometime in 2000. According to the Saudi student who was a roommate of both Muktar Ibrahim and Adel Yahya at different times, Ibrahim, Yasin Omar, and Yahya were very close friends: "They spend most of the time together. They trust each other also." It is likely that a few of the men, including Ramzi Mohammed and Hussain Osman, first came into contact at Speakers Corner at Hyde Park in London in 2003. However, the Finsbury Park Mosque was by far the most important locus of activity for almost all of the members of the active core (Muktar Ibrahim, Yassin Omar, Hussain Osman, Ramzi Mohammed, and Adel Yahya). In 2003, at Speakers Corner, a number of the men met Mohammed Hamid. Subsequently, the men began to attend late-night sessions at Hamid's East London flat as well as at training camps that he conducted, including one in May 2004 in the Lake District in which Muktar Ibrahim, Yassin Omar, Adel Yahya, Ramzi Mohammed, and Hussein Osman all participated. In total, more than twenty people went on the trip, which included sessions of group prayer and military-like formation maneuvers, according to the police officer who observed its final day.[12]

When Ibrahim, Omar, Manfo Asiedu, and Yahya came back from the May training outing, they all had positive reactions to it. Ibrahim often asked his roommate, the Saudi student, about taking Omar, Yahya, and him to training camps in Yemen so that they could learn to use military weapons. However, according to the Saudi student, he refused.[13]

The Ideologues

Mohammed Hamid, aka "Osama Bin London," age forty-eight at the time of the attack, was born in Tanzania to ethnic Indian Muslim parents. When he was five, his family immigrated to the U.K. and at age twelve he moved to London. Hamid had a troubled youth and turned to crime and drug use. He would eventually be convicted of robbery, burglary, and possession of drugs at age nineteen. Hamid was incarcerated and spent time in and out of young offenders' prisons. He eventually became a crack cocaine addict. Later, however, Hamid claimed that he "found salvation" during a chance trip to a mosque with his brother. Following a trip to India, where he met his second wife, he moved back to London and became a community activist, promoting a militant Islamic message.[14] In early 1997, Hamid purchased the Al Quran bookshop at 22 Chatsworth Road in Hackney. This location, as well as a number of stalls he oversaw at mosques, would serve as platforms for him to spread his anti-Western worldview that focused on war zones involving Muslims such as Bosnia, Afghanistan, Chechnya, and Kashmir. After 9/11, Hamid began to preach on topics related to Islam at the Speakers Corner in Hyde Park. He made a point to reiterate that he believed that Muslims had nothing to do with the attacks of 9/11. In 2002 he traveled to Pakistan ostensibly to bring medical supplies to refugees in the North-West frontier. In 2003 Hamid met a number of the Operation Vivace cluster members at Speakers Corner and invited them to meetings and prayers at his home in East London. Hamid also organized jihadi training camps in Lake Country, north of London. These camps and meetings were regularly attended by the Operation Vivace plotters.[15]

Attila Ahmet aka "Abu Abdullah," age forty-one at the time of the attack, was born in London to Turkish Cypriot parents. He was a former soccer coach who converted to Islam. Ahmet served as the right-hand man for Abu

Hamza al Masri at the Finsbury Park Mosque. When control of the mosque was finally taken away from al Masri and his acolytes, Ahmet began preaching on the street outside the mosque. He claimed to be the number one al Qaeda individual in Europe (but in reality had no direct connections to al Qaeda). Ahmet frequented the private meetings that took place at Mohammed Hamid's home in East London. During these sessions, Ahmet would rant that his purpose in life was to sacrifice one's self. He urged the attendees, "you have to fight. It is better to fight and let them kill you, than let them put you in prison."[16]

Anatomy of the Cluster

Active Core

Muktar Said Ibrahim, age twenty-seven at the time of the attack, had immigrated to London in 1990 at the age of twelve from what was the war zone that was formerly Ethiopia and is now Eritrea. Ibrahim went to college and studied leisure and tourism but subsequently dropped out and began using marijuana heavily. By June 1993 he had been convicted of the indecent assault of a fifteen-year-old and by 1995 he had been involved in two gang-related robberies. For these crimes, Ibrahim was sentenced to five years in the Feltham Young Offender's Institute. Some have suggested that it was at Feltham where Ibrahim became more devout. Regardless of where this spiritual awakening occurred, upon his release in 1998 Muktar gravitated toward the Islamist political scene in London and began to attend Finsbury Park Mosque, where he became an acolyte of Abu Hamza al Masri.[17] In 2003 Ibrahim left the U.K. to "do jihad" in Sudan. In 2004 he attended a training camp in Lake Country, organized by Mohammed Hamid and attended by other members of the cluster. Ibrahim received paramilitary training there, and in 2005 he was arrested in London for attempting to distribute Islamic literature.[18]

Followers

Yassin Omar, age twenty-four at the time of the attack, was born in Somalia where he had attended a Koranic school. Omar immigrated to the

U.K. in 1992 at the age of twelve with his sisters. Shortly after his arrival in the U.K. he was placed in foster care and moved among a variety of homes until his eighteenth birthday, when he was given his own apartment at Curtis House in the Southgate suburb of London. Although he began to study science at university, he subsequently dropped out and spent time "playing video games and hanging out with his friends." However, by the late 1990s Omar had begun to explore militant Islam and started to spend time at Finsbury Park Mosque. This continued, and "during 2000 and 2001 Omar became increasingly attracted to Islam." He began to dress in traditional robe and hat, spent more time at the Finsbury Park Mosque to hear Abu Hamza, and began to cut himself off from his old friends. In 2003 Omar participated in paramilitary training in Scotland, and in 2004 he participated in a paramilitary/jihad training camp in Cumbria, Wales. Also in 2004 he attended a training camp in Lake Country, organized by Mohammed Hamid and attended by other members of the cluster.[19]

Ramzi Mohammed, age twenty-four at the time of the attack, was born in Somalia and was raised in a refugee camp. His father had been forced to join one of the militias and his mother, fearing for his safety, sent Mohammed and his brother to the U.K. via Kenya in 1998. Upon his arrival as a seventeen-year-old in the U.K., he was placed into the care of social services and one year later was given a government-sponsored apartment in West London. Mohammed, originally a non-practicing Muslim, worked at a local bar in the Waterloo Train Station. According to some accounts, Mohammed was fond of drinking alcohol, dance clubs, and socializing with women of many religions.[20] By 2003, he began to show more interest in his Islamic heritage and began to frequent Speakers Corner, where different speakers would harangue the crowds about Islam. To avoid interacting with alcohol, which was forbidden by his newfound religiosity, he left his job at the bar and became a manager at the American Bagel Factory but eventually gave up that job as well, as it involved cutting bacon. By January 2004, Mohammed had begun associating with Muktar Ibrahim and Yassin Omar, regularly attending sermons by Abu Hamza at Finsbury Park Mosque. He also began attending the private weekly meeting at Mohammed Hamid's home in East London. In 2004, he attended a training camp in Lake Country, organized by Mohammed Hamid and attended by other members of the cluster. Ramzi was the father of two children with his Swedish girlfriend of Eritrean origin.[21]

Hussain Osman, age twenty-seven at the time of the attack, was born in Ethiopia, immigrated to Italy in 1992, and arrived in the U.K. in 1996 at age eighteen. Upon his arrival, Osman claimed to be Somali and requested asylum. According to Osman's Ethiopian girlfriend, who knew him from Italy, Osman liked to consider himself a gangster, but in the U.K. he became more involved in Islam. Osman was also frequently in attendance at Speakers Corner, where it is believed that he may have met the other plotters. In 2004 he attended the training camp in Lake Country organized by Hamid. At the time of the bombings, Osman was living with his wife and three children in a block of flats in Stockwell.[22]

Manfo Kwaku Asiedu, age thirty-two at the time of the attack, was born in Ghana. He was raised in a middle-class family and worked in the family's agriculture business. Using false documents, Asiedu immigrated to the U.K. in 2003 at the age of thirty. Upon his arrival, he sought out a mosque where he could worship and found the Finchley Mosque, which was also frequented by Yassin Omar. Before the July 21 attacks, Asiedu worked at odd jobs, including as a handyman, painter, and decorator. After a fire devastated his apartment in June 2005, he moved in with Yassin Omar.[23]

Adel Yahya, age twenty-three at the time of the attack, was born in Ethiopia and spent a significant amount of time during his youth in Yemen. He immigrated to the U.K. in 1991 at the age of nine. Yahya attended a local community school and was remembered as a well-adjusted child who enjoyed football, games, and computers. He became friends with Yassin Omar at school, and by 2000 or 2001 Yahya and Omar began to frequent the Finsbury Park Mosque to hear Abu Hamza's lectures. Yahya began to withdraw from mainstream society and was frequently attendance in various private study groups with some of his fellow cluster members. Nevertheless, he was enrolled in London Metropolitan University and was studying for a degree in computer networking. In 2004 he attended the training camp in Lake Country organized by Hamid. Yahya was married. In November 2007, he pleaded guilty to collecting information of a kind likely to be useful to a person preparing an act of terrorism.[24]

Shakeel Ishmail, approximately age twenty-three at the time of his death in 2004, was born in the U.K. and lived in Hackney. He was one of Mohammed Hamid's primary assistants at the al Quran bookstore. It is believed that he died on his trip to Pakistan with Muktar Ibrahim in 2004–5.[25]

Rizwan Majid, approximately age twenty-two at the time of his death in 2004, was born in the U.K. and lived in Walthamstow. He had gone on some of Mohammed Hamid's training trips and spent time at the al Quran bookstore. It is believed that he died on his trip to Pakistan with Muktar Ibrahim in 2004–5.[26]

Periphery

Wahbi Mohammed was born in Somalia and is the older brother of Ramzi Mohammed. Although he was not in the active core of the cluster, he met with the bombers on the morning of July 21, 2005, before they set off to carry out their attack. It is widely believed that he was in possession of the plotters' martyrdom videos and was tasked with distributing them and his brother's suicide note to his family upon the successful completion of the terror attack. After the failed bombing attempt, Wahbi provided his brother, who was in hiding, with food and supplies including a cell phone. As a result of information collected it is asserted that Wahbi had knowledge of the impending attack and failed to disclose said information to the authorities. He was convicted in February 2008 for his role as an accomplice.[27]

Siraj Yassin Abdullah Ali, age thirty at the time of the attack, was raised by the same foster family as Yassin Omar and was a childhood friend of his. In 2005, Ali shared the apartment one floor above Yassin Omar's with Muktar Said Ibrahim. A police search of the residence revealed that Ali had knowledge of the impending attack and failed to disclose said information to the authorities. He was convicted in February 2008 for his role as an accomplice.[28]

Abdul Sharif, age twenty-eight at the time of the attack, is the older brother of Hussain Osman. Abdul provided his brother with a passport so that he could escape to Italy. Sharif also helped his brother secure a safe house in Rome. He was convicted in February 2008 for his role as an accomplice.[29]

Muhedin Ali, age twenty-seven at the time of the attack, was a friend of Hussain Osman, Osman's wife, Ramzi Mohammed, and Wahbi Mohammed. Ali had offered to provide Osman with a safe house in London while he was being sought by police. Police tracked multiple calls between Ali and the other failed plotters while they were on the run. Ali possessed Ramzi's suicide note on the morning of July 21, 2005. He was convicted in February 2008 for his role as an accomplice.[30]

Ismail Abdulrahman, age twenty-three at the time of the attack, provided Hussain Osman with a safe house after the failed attacks. Abdulrahman acted as a runner retrieving a passport and video camera (believed to have been used to film the martyrdom videos) to facilitate the alteration and destruction of evidence as well as provide cover for Osman's escape. He was convicted in February 2008 for his role as an accomplice.[31]

Yeshi Girma, age twenty-nine at the time of the attack, was the wife and mother of three children with Hussain Osman. Girma had prior knowledge of the intended attack and assisted Osman evade authorities. She was accused of providing false information to police, arranging transportation, and providing access to medical treatment for her injured husband. She was convicted in June 2008 for her role as an accomplice.[32]

Esayas Girma, age twenty at the time of the attack, was Yeshi Girma's brother and Hussain Osman's brother in-law. He provided Hussain with a "clean" cell phone and helped him evade authorities immediately following the attempted bombing. He was convicted in June 2008 for his role as an accomplice.[33]

Mulumebet Girma, age twenty-one at the time of the attack, was Yeshi Girma's sister and Hussain Osman's sister in-law. She provided Hussain with medical treatment for his injuries, assisted in moving him to a secondary safe house, and attempted to destroy evidence (clothing worn by Hussain). She was convicted in June 2008 for her role as an accomplice.[34]

Mohammed Kabashi, age twenty-three at the time of the attack, was Mulumebet Girma's fiancée and assisted Osman by providing safe houses and helping dispose of evidence. He pled guilty in February 2008 to assisting an offender and failing to disclose information about acts of terrorism in relation to Osman.[35]

Fardosa Abdullahi, age seventeen at the time of the attack, was Yassin Omar's fiancée. Following the failed bombing attempt, Omar fled to Fardosa's family home were he spent the night. Fardosa helped Omar disguise himself as a woman by providing him with a burka and handbag and gave him a cell phone. She later accompanied him to the train station. She pled guilty in July 2008 to assisting an offender and failing to disclose information about acts of terrorism.[36]

Overseas Travel and Link Up with Al Qaeda

Muktar Ibrahim, the emir of the cluster, was the only person to travel abroad to zones of conflict involving Muslims and to receive paramilitary training overseas. His trips consisted of a trip to Sudan in 2003 and a trip to Pakistan in 2004–5. It is believed that his trip to Pakistan enabled him to participate in training camps, link up with the transnational jihad, and even meet al Qaeda–associated individuals.

Not much is known about Muktar Ibrahim's trip to Sudan. However, when he returned from Sudan, he bragged that he received jihadi training and learned to fire rocket-propelled grenades. According to a key witness at the trial (the Saudi student), Ibrahim told him he was going to "do jihad" and added: "He told me that maybe I wouldn't see him again, maybe we are going to see each other in heaven."[37]

Ibrahim and two U.K. citizens of Pakistani descent, Rizwan Majid and Shakeel Ishmail, were followed to Heathrow Airport by MI5 agents before departing for Pakistan in December 2004. Both of his traveling companions hung out at the Al Quran bookstore and had participated in paramilitary training trips with Mohammed Hamid and Muktar Ibrahim. Ibrahim said that they were traveling to Pakistan via Bahrain and Abu Dhabi to attend Majid's marriage ceremony. However, according to British press accounts, "MI5 judged they were going to take part in holy war activities in Pakistan. It was thought this might include going to terrorist training camps." According to Ibrahim's Saudi roommate, "actually they told me very clear: they are going go for Jihad."[38] The three men were questioned by Scotland Yard's Special Branch before they boarded their flight and were found to be carrying thousands of pounds in cash, a military first-aid kit, and a ballistics manual. Nonetheless, MI5 allowed them to travel to Pakistan.[39]

Training and Skill Acquisition

Muktar Ibrahim claimed he received jihadi training and instruction on firing grenades in Sudan. It is likely that he received some training in the production of improvised explosive devices out of hydrogen peroxide when he visited Pakistan as well as saw military action. No other information is available on his training experience overseas.

Ibrahim returned from Pakistan alone. According to the testimony of his Saudi roommate, Ibrahim said that the two men Ibrahim had traveled to Pakistan with had died on the trip: "I asked him what had happened. He didn't tell me much, but he did tell me that he had come back to the UK but he didn't say why. . . . . It was later when I heard that the two Pakistani males and Hakim all died while fighting Jihad."⁴⁰

Al Qaeda Recruitment

This is unknown. Given that Muktar Ibrahim knew al Qaeda—linked individuals in the U.K., it is likely that Ibrahim met al Qaeda–linked individuals in Pakistan and Afghanistan. Furthermore, it is possible that an al Qaeda–linked individual provided general guidance to Muktar Ibrahim to do something in the U.K., but no definitive evidence exists.

Unlike many of the British citizens of Pakistani descent, who had familial connections to Pakistan, Ibrahim was from East Africa and is unlikely to have had similar links to southwest Asia. As a result, it is likely that he relied upon British "jihadi networks" to enable his 2004 trip. Mohammed al Ghabra, a known al Qaeda–linked individual who resides in the U.K., was likely the "fixer" for this trip. Al Ghabra is a U.S.-designated al Qaeda supporter and financier. According to the British press, "Mohammed al Ghabra, a 27-year-old Syrian who has been given British citizenship, is said by British security sources to have arranged for the leader of the failed 7/21 London suicide attacks to travel to Pakistan for terrorist training. The sources said al Ghabra instructed a second terrorist suspect to facilitate a four-month trip to Pakistan by Muktar Said Ibrahim, the leader of the July 21 gang."⁴¹

Al Ghabra's al Qaeda résumé is impressive, as the U.S. Treasury Department notes:

Mohammed Al Ghabra has backed al Qaida and other violent jihadist groups, facilitating travel for recruits seeking to meet with al Qaida leaders and take part in terrorist training. . . .

Al Ghabra has organized travel to Pakistan for individuals seeking to meet with senior al Qaida individuals and to undertake jihad training. Several of these individuals have returned to the UK to engage in covert activity on behalf of al Qaida. . . .

In addition, Al Ghabra has also provided material and logistical support to other terrorist organizations based in Pakistan, such as Harakat ul-Jihad-I-Islami (HUJI). While in Pakistan, Al Ghabra met with Haroon Rashid Aswat, who is currently detained in the U.K. and subject to a U.S. extradition request on terrorism charges. . . .

Al Ghabra maintains contact with a significant number of terrorists, including senior al Qaida officials in Pakistan. In 2002, Al Ghabra met with and stayed at the home of Faraj Al-Libi, who, until he was detained by Pakistani authorities in 2005, served as al Qaida's Director of Operations. Al Ghabra is also in regular contact with UK-based Islamist extremists and has been involved in the radicalizing of individuals in the UK through the distribution of extremist media.[42]

The link between Muktar Ibrahim and Mohammed al Ghabra is as follows: in December 2004, when Ibrahim was preparing to depart the U.K. for Pakistan, he was followed to Heathrow airport by MI5 undercover agents: "The MI5 team was tailing the man driving him, Rauf Mohammed, an Iraqi taxi driver who was suspected of working with al Ghabra in helping radical British Muslims travel to Iraq to fight against British and American troops. According to a British security service source, MI5 knew that the trip to Pakistan was arranged by Rauf Mohammed, acting on the instructions of Mohammed al Ghabra."[43]

Based on an analysis of travel records, it is clear that Muktar Ibrahim was in Pakistan at the same as the July 7 bombers Mohammed Siddique Khan and Shehzad Tanweer as well as their associates, Wahid Ali and Sadeer Saleem. However, Ibrahim denied ever meeting them and no definitive evidence or intelligence has been able to link the two groups conclusively. Nevertheless, the similarity of the hydrogen peroxide explosives used in both bombings remains a tantalizing and unexplained coincidence.

Based on an analysis of phone records, it is clear that Muktar Ibrahim was in Pakistan at the same as a number of the Operation Overt conspirators. Both preceding his departure from the U.K. to Pakistan (December 2004) and following his return (May 2005), calls were made from Ibrahim's phone to Abdulla Ahmed Ali, the ringleader of Operation Overt; there were also calls made to a phone registered to Ali's wife. Ibrahim claimed not to know Ali, and his only explanation for these suspicious phone linkages was that one of the individuals who traveled to Pakistan with Ibrahim in December 2004 was from Walthamstow and may have used his phone to call Abdulla Ahmed Ali, who was from the same hometown.[44]

Muktar Said Ibrahim was also in contact with Rashid Rauf, who served as a facilitator for travel and communications in Operation Overt.[45] Despite this suggestive information, no definitive evidence or intelligence has been able to link the two groups operationally. Nevertheless, the shared contacts remain an unexplained coincidence.

Operational Cycle

Travel to Pakistan by Muktar Ibrahim appears to have been the catalyst for the cluster's mobilization to action. Ibrahim returned to the U.K. in March 2005. The first acts in furtherance of the plan were the purchase of materials for the bombs in April 2005, only weeks after Ibrahim's return. They launched their attack on July 21, 2005. The total duration of the operational cycle was less than five months.

In 2004 and 2005 members of the cluster all attended paramilitary training camps established by Mohammed Hamid aka "Osama bin London" in Cumbria in the Lake District of the U.K., five hours north of London. These camps taught jihadist ideology as well as military tactics and exercises.[46] In 2004, Muktar Ibrahim, Yassin Omar and Adel Yahya traveled to Scotland to conduct unarmed paramilitary training in preparation for jihad in Afghanistan or Iraq. In April 2005, Muktar Ibrahim began to conduct Internet research into the creation of explosive devices composed of hydrogen peroxide and TATP.[47]

Target Selection/Casing

British authorities were able to obtain little information regarding the selection of the targets or any surveillance of the targets prior to the attack. During the trial, Manfo Kwaku Asiedu was asked, "Did you think of any symbolism in the name of the stations?" His reply was negative. Muktar Said Ibrahim also stated at trial that there was "no plan" behind the specific targets. Certainly there is speculation that the July 21 plotters attempted to emulate the July 7 attack by targeting mass transit, specifically the London Underground.[48]

Communications

There is no definitive evidence that the July 21 plotters were in ongoing communication and receiving instructions from persons in Pakistan.

Nevertheless, after his return from Pakistan in the spring of 2005, Muktar Ibrahim was in extended phone contact with phones linked to Abdulla Ahmed Ali as well as Rashid Rauf.[49] One other July 21 plotter was in contact with an al Qaeda–associated individual in the U.K. that spring. In March 2005, Yassin Omar had called Rangzieb Ahmed, a Pakistani man living in Manchester who was subsequently convicted of being a member of al Qaeda.[50]

Weaponization

Between May 9 and July 5, 2005, the plotters purchased 443 liters of hydrogen peroxide from local London businesses. Manfo Kwaku Asiedu bought bottles of hydrogen peroxide for the improvised explosive devices that the group constructed. A total of 443 liters of hydrogen peroxide were purchased from three different businesses. Using a discount card, he purchased the peroxide on at least four visits to a shop (Sally's Hair and Beauty Supplies) in London where he acquired nearly all the peroxide stock available at the store. He had the store place additional orders for peroxide, saying it was for stripping wallpaper. Another shop from which Asiedu purchased stock from was Hairways in Tottenham. The final shop was Pak Cosmetics. When the conspirators were again asked what they were using the peroxide for, they said that they were carpenters and used it for "washing wood and stuff" and for building work.[51]

Yassin Omar's apartment served as a bomb factory, and the group used the stove to boil the hydrogen peroxide to a 70 percent concentration. They purchased Chapatti flour to use as an accelerant and flashlight bulbs powered by 9-volt batteries to ignite the devices.[52] The men used cardboard tubes filled with TATP to act as detonators and purchased 1.6-gallon plastic tubs to house the devices, and various metal objects (screws, nails, washers, and tacks) were added to the mix to ensure maximum casualties from fragmentation.[53] On July 15, 2005, Muktar Ibrahim conducted a small test of the explosives.[54]

However, because the backpack devices utilized by Muktar Ibrahim, Yassin Omar, Ramzi Mohammed, and Hussain Osman utilized hydrogen peroxide that never reached the necessary 70 percent concentration, the devices failed to explode when the attempt to detonate them in the London mass transit system was made on July 21, 2005. Manfo Asiedu decided not to carry out his attack and abandoned his device.

The Al Qaeda Factor

British prosecutors did not produce any evidence in the trial of the July 21 conspirators explicitly linking the plot to al Qaeda Core. The members of this cluster clearly radicalized in the U.K. If there had been a link to al Qaeda, operationally, it most likely ran through Muktar Ibrahim, the emir of the group and the only individual who had traveled to Pakistan and had the widest network of extremist links (e.g., al Ghabra). Nevertheless, despite tantalizing linkages and travel overlap in Pakistan among both the July 7 bombers and some of the Operation Overt plotters with Muktar Ibrahim, there is little in the way of hard facts that can conclusively show any direct links between the July 21 plotters and al Qaeda Core. Also, this was not a copycat plot, as the July 21 plotters were clearly engaged in procuring dual-purpose materials prior to the July 7 attack.

Nevertheless, the overlap of travel dates of Ibrahim and two of the July 7 bombers as well as the similarity in their explosive devices suggests a link between the plots. Ibrahim was in Pakistan from December 2004 through March 2005 and these dates overlap with the dates that Mohammed Siddique Khan and Shehzad Tanweer were in Pakistan. It is unclear whether the two met while in Pakistan, but the bomb-making techniques used by both groups were nearly identical and no other device of its kind had been used in the U.K.[55]

Based on his links to al Qaeda–associated individuals like Mohammed al Ghabra and some of the Operation Overt plotters, it seems likely that Muktar Ibrahim could have trained in an al Qaeda camp or have been trained by an al Qaeda trainer and may have received general direction to carry out an attack in London. However, according to the testimony of the conspirators, the targets were not chosen by al Qaeda and there was little, if any, ongoing communication between Muktar Ibrahim and Pakistan in the lead-up to the plot. As a result, the lack of information about Ibrahim's Pakistan trip and connections he made there certainly prohibit Operation Vivace from being called an al Qaeda "command and control" plot. Rather, the body of evidence points, much like the Operation Theseus plot, to an al Qaeda "suggested/endorsed" plot.

Chapter 9

Operation Dagger (Copenhagen, 2007)

OPERATION DAGGER INVOLVED two men: Hammad Khurshid and his accomplice, Abdolghani Tohki, who planned to detonate explosives at unknown targets in Denmark. Danish authorities initially arrested eight individuals in September 2007, disrupting the plot after a period of surveillance. However, charges against six of the eight were later dropped. The two men who were tried in court had produced TATP in an apartment and detonated a small amount as a test. They also possessed bomb-making manuals and martyrdom videos, and, according to Danish prosecutors, the main plotter, Khurshid, had attended an al Qaeda training camp. The Danish intelligence service (PET) has described the duo as "militant Islamists with international contacts, including leading members of Al Qaeda." Khurshid—a Danish citizen of Pakistani origin—was sentenced to twelve years in prison, while Tohki—an Afghan national—was sentenced to seven years in prison, after which he will be deported. Both men were sentenced in October 2008.[1]

The Danish Scene

The foundation of the radical Islamic environment in Denmark is almost unequivocally linked to the establishment of a small diaspora Egyptian community in Copenhagen during the early 1990s by Egyptian Islamic Group (Al Gama'a al Islamiyya) refugees who sought asylum in Denmark. Although this group of Egyptians was always quite small, it had direct and ongoing links with Egyptian Islamic Group members worldwide, including Omar Abdel Rahman in New York City. Moreover, some members of this tight community had traveled to Afghanistan to participate in the anti-Soviet jihad and train in camps. Most prominent among these Egyptian Afghan veterans were Talaat Fouad Qassem and seven of his group who settled there. Abu Laban, who would later gain notoriety for creating the "Cartoon Crisis," was among Qassem's followers. This Denmark-based radical milieu was gradually enlarged during the 1990s by the emergence of a population of militant Islamist North Africans who, though they backed the transnational jihad, also had a North African focus and directed their support toward groups such as the GIA, GSPC, GICM, and Salafia Jihadia. From here, direct lines can be drawn to the development of critical hubs, such as the Norrebro residential district of Copenhagen, which underpinned the growth of radicalization and extremist Islamic social networks in Denmark and enabled the development of the 2005 Glostrup Plot and 2006 Odense Plot clusters, comprised primarily of either first- or second-generation Muslims living in Denmark.[2]

The eight individuals arrested (Hammad Khurshid, Abdolghani Tohki, J. Khurshid, S. A., and four other individuals who were not named) were part of a larger circle of Islamist radicals in Copenhagen. Although there is limited unclassified information on their wider circle, the two were friends and among a group of eight men, aged nineteen to twenty-eight, who were initially arrested. The two convicted plotters went to the same mosque in Norrebro that had been frequented by others who had been part of the rejectionist scene in Copenhagen and connected to terrorism. The mosque, which is known for a very radical interpretation of Islam, has acted as meeting place for young terrorist sympathizers involved in other Danish terrorism cases. For example, all the individuals involved in the so-called 2005 Glostrup case met each other in the mosque on Heimdalsgade. Several of those who were involved in that case were later convicted of planning terrorist acts.[3]

Gravitating to Reactionary Islam

Little has been published on Khurshid and Tokhi's backgrounds, but there is some evidence that Tokhi was influenced by a group of Salafis in Copenhagen. In 2005, Tohki was part of a lecture circle of four or five young men led by "S. A." S. A. would preach once a week to the young men on a bench in the neighborhood where Tohki was going to school. S. A. urged the men to follow the Salafi form of Islam.[4] Subsequently, Tohki joined the Salafi circle, which met in a basement in Norrebro and Salafis appeared to play an increasingly important role in Tohki's life. In 2006 Tohki expressed a desire to go to Yemen for forty days to attend a religious school but was unable to get a visa. Soon after, he changed his appearance and began wearing traditional Islamic clothing.[5]

Both Khurshid brothers and Tohki attended the Taiba Mosque on Heimdalsgade in Norrebro. Taiba is known as a location for a very radical interpretation of Islam and has served as a meeting place for young terrorist sympathizers. The mosque is infamous as the mosque of choice for individuals tied to three of Denmark's recent terrorism cases dating back to 2005.[6] Hammad Khurshid, his brother, and Abdolghani Tohki apparently went to the Taiba Mosque. It is believed that is where they met S. A. As previously discussed, S. A. had met Tohki in 2005.[7] However, they may have also met via links to members of the 2005 Glostrup case. Both Hammad Khurshid and Tohki were in telephone contact with Abdulkadir Cesur, one of the main plotters in the case, as well as two of the five others arrested in the case. Police also recorded Tohki talking to Abdul Basit Al Lifa, who was convicted in the case.[8] Al Lifa was known to have been influenced by S. A. as well.[9]

From a historical standpoint, Abu Ahmed, a well-known Salafi in Copenhagen extremist circles, was a self-appointed imam at Taiba Mosque, led study groups of fifty to sixty people, and was known to defend al Qaeda before he was ejected from the location in 2005.[10] Taiba Mosque was also where the North African extremist Said Mansour acted as a mentor to young people. In 2007, Mansour was sentenced to over three years in prison for promoting terrorism. He was a distributor of jihadi videos and made speeches calling for jihad against the West.[11]

Nevertheless, there is little evidence that Hammad Kurshid's radicalization necessarily took place in Copenhagen. His upbringing in Pakistan and frequent travel between that country and Denmark may be more relevant to his radicalization to violence. Although he attended the Taiba Mosque, there is no public evidence clarifying whether he was radicalized before this or if his attendance there triggered his radicalization.

The "Glasvej cluster" was composed of eight men who were initially arrested and associated with Hammad Khurshid, Abdolghani Tohki, and J. Khurshid near the Khurshid flat on Glasvej Street. The group was heterogeneous; members of the group originated from Afghanistan, Pakistan, Somalia, and Turkey. However, six of them held Danish citizenship. According to one account, the men looked to a twenty-nine-year-old spiritual sanctioner publically identified as "S. A." for guidance.[12]

Anatomy of the Cluster

Active Core

Hammad Khurshid, age twenty-one at the time of his arrest, is a Danish national of Pakistani origin. He was born in Denmark, but he and his parents moved back to Pakistan in 1987 when he was two years old. According to his brother, when they were older, the two often traveled back and forth between Pakistan and Denmark. Khurshid lived in an apartment with his brother in Copenhagen. Khurshid was a trained painter and worked in a textile outlet in Jysk.[13]

Followers

Abdolghani Tohki, age twenty-one at the time of his arrest, is an Afghan national who arrived in Denmark when he was approximately seven years old. A close friend of Tohki noted, "He was a very quiet guy who often went home after school and read religious books. On Muslim holidays he put on traditional Afghan dress, but on a daily basis, he wore ordinary clothes, like jeans."[14] Tohki attended a local secondary school but dropped out in his second year after having problems. Around this time he was in contact with circle of Copenhagen Salafists including the above-mentioned S. A., who had a significant influence on him.[15]

Periphery

"J" Khurshid, age twenty-four at the time of his arrest, is a Danish national of Pakistani origin and the older brother of Hammad. He was born in Denmark, but his parents moved back to Pakistan and, according to him, the two often traveled back and forth to Pakistan to visit them. Both brothers

worked as taxi drivers. Although initially arrested with Hammad, "J" was subsequently released.[16]

"S.A.," age twenty-nine at the time of his arrest, was eldest of the eight arrested in the case and is suspected as acting as a local spiritual leader. It is believed that he provided instruction on the Koran and put Tohki in touch with militant Islamic groups in Copenhagen. This was not the first time S. A. was accused of playing this role as he is suspected of having had contact with several persons involved in the 2005 Danish Glostrup terrorism case. In 2004, S. A. was part of a study group on a trip to London that met the noted al Muhajiroun extremist Omar Bakri Mohammad. Though S. A.'s day job was in the computer sector, he was better known for running a Koran school in Brondby Strand and held weekly meetings in 2005. It is during those meetings that he first encountered Tohki, who was nineteen years old.[17]

Overseas Travel and Link Up with Al Qaeda

As previously discussed, both Hammad Khurshid and Tohki were in telephone contact with members of the 2005 Glostrup group.[18] It is certainly possible that it was through these relationships with local militant Islamists as well as others at the Taiba Mosque and through S.A.'s network that Hammad Khurshid and Tohki linked up with the elements of the transnational jihad. However, alternatively, the connections may have been overseas links in Pakistan.

According to Hammad Khurshid's brother, the brothers traveled regularly to Pakistan to see their parents. Their most recent trip to Pakistan had been in 2007, returning to Copenhagen on May 30. The most important and direct connection between Khurshid and the transnational jihad runs through a lower-level al Qaeda–linked individual, Abu Nasir al Qahtani. According to the Danish Prosecutor's Office, the covert videotapings of Khurshid's apartment in Copenhagen revealed that at one point, when Hammad Khurshid was watching videos of a 2005 escape from Bagram Prison and al Qahtani's face appeared on the computer screen, Khurshid told his spouse about his acquaintance with al Qahtani. Khurshid noted, "He was my best friend, who was just under him."[19]

Training and Skill Acquisition

PET and the Prosecutor's Office believe that Khurshid underwent military training at a camp in Pakistan at some time during the years leading up to 2007, receiving training in reconnaissance, combat techniques, and the use of explosives in Pakistan or Afghanistan. In fact, PET has nearly fifty pictures of Khurshid that were allegedly taken in a training camp in Pakistan or Afghanistan.[20] It is highly likely that it was during a trip to southwest Asia that he became acquainted with al Qahtani. The Prosecutor's Office account is consistent with an account published by the journalist Sebastian Rotella on the most recent activities of al Qaeda's Chief of External Operations, Abu Ubaidah al Masri. Rotella's account seems to describe Khurshid quite accurately:

> Last spring, he [Abu Ubaidah al Masri] taught bomb-making in compounds in North Waziristan to aspiring suicide attackers, including a 21-year-old Pakistani living in Denmark and a 45-year-old Pakistani-German, according to U.S. and European officials. . . . Aided by U.S. intercepts of communications to Pakistan, Danish police put the 21-year-old under surveillance along with his associates, one of whom had been in Pakistan at the same time. . . . Police installed clandestine cameras and microphones in the 21-year-old's apartment in a scruffy area that mixes immigrant families and young Danes. In early September, the cameras filmed the 21-year-old and an Afghan suspect as they sang militant songs and mixed TATP, the explosive used in the London attacks. The two even conducted tests of detonators in a vestibule, officials say.[21]

When Khurshid returned to Denmark from his trip to Pakistan, he possessed a bomb-training manual that he had copied during his visit to the Red Mosque in Islamabad. The Red Mosque is a known haven for radical Muslims and was the site of a clash between Pakistani authorities and Islamist hardliners in the summer of 2007.[22]

Al Qaeda Recruitment

This is unknown. It is possible that Abu Ubaidah al Masri or another al Qaeda-linked individual recruited Khurshid or provided general guidance for

Khurshid to undertake something in Denmark. As previously mentioned, Khurshid traveled frequently to Pakistan.

Operational Cycle

Travel to Pakistan appears to have been the catalyst for Khurshid's mobilization to action. He returned to Denmark on May 30, 2007. Upon his return he and Tohki began to procure the components necessary to build explosive devices. Khurshid and Tokhi then spent the next four months in the operational cycle preparing for a terrorist attack.

Authorities began monitoring Khurshid upon his return to Denmark. Danish intelligence was informed by a foreign service that Khurshid had attended a terrorist training camp in Pakistan.[23]

Target Selection/Casing

Authorities were able to obtain little information regarding the pair's target. They did find a drawing by Khurshid of what looked like a bus or train car and calculations of what type of a pressure wave would develop from an explosion, leading to the assumption that mass transit would be the target. However, both men denied the terrorism charges and claimed the TATP was to be used for fireworks.[24]

Logistics

At the airport, a search of Khurshid's luggage revealed a manual on how to build explosives, among other items. He also returned with approximately $5,000 in funds.[25] Khurshid and Tohki were searching for 3-volt light bulbs for possible use as detonators. They procured enough chemicals to produce a small amount of TATP, the same type of explosive used in the 2005 London bombings. They also searched online for remote control toy cars that could carry a load of up to 20 kilograms.[26] In addition, Khurshid and Tohki searched the Internet for information on TATP and how to become a holy warrior.[27]

Communications

Telephone monitoring revealed that Khurshid often spoke with an unnamed person in Pakistan who was designated by the U.S. government as a terrorist recruiter.[28] Strangely, "Khurshid also had e-mail correspondence with several people in Pakistan to identify popular tourist destinations and obtain the addresses of various hotels and embassies, including the Danish mission [in Pakistan]." The Danish prosecutor alleged that Khurshid may also have been "looking into the possibility of planning a terrorist attack in Pakistan."[29]

Weaponization

Authorities had bugged Hammad Khurshid's apartment and observed him experimenting with TATP. In August 2007, Khurshid was observed making TATP and chanting, "Accept my last greeting, because I am on my way to a martyr attack. Perhaps I cannot return." Later Khurshid successfully manufactured a small amount of TATP, which he and Tohki detonated in the stairwell of Khurshid's apartment building. On the surveillance video, Khurshid tells Tohki they have enough to blow off a head or arm.[30] Both men filmed the production, referring to the video as "The Preparation." They were recorded saying, "This is some of the explosives. We'll see you in a week."[31]

The Al Qaeda Factor

Based on the unclassified evidence, it appears that al Qaeda involvement in this plot was most likely confined to training in Pakistan and any continuing contact that Khurshid had with individuals there did not seem to be of a "command and control" nature. Khurshid does not appear to have discussed operational issues relating to Denmark with his contacts in Pakistan. As mentioned above, he spoke frequently with an unnamed person in Pakistan who was designated by the U.S. government as a terrorist recruiter.[32] Khurshid's communications with Pakistan, following his return to Copenhagen, regarding the location of the Danish embassy are puzzling, however. It would seem unlikely that he was planning an attack there from Denmark.

Given the scant amount of information about any possible target, it seems likely that Khurshid and Tohki's main concern might have been developing an operational explosive first and worrying about a target later. This suggests that any guidance from al Qaeda was mainly instructional and the details of an attack were to be left to Khurshid and Tohki. While it seems like Khurshid trained in an al Qaeda camp and/or was trained by an al Qaeda trainer, the targets were not chosen by al Qaeda and there was no evidence of any ongoing "command and control" by al Qaeda in Pakistan. The most likely case was that Khurshid was trained and encouraged by al Qaeda to do something in Denmark. Therefore this plot falls into the al Qaeda "suggested/endorsed" category.

Chapter 10

Operation Highrise (New York, 2009)

ON SEPTEMBER 9, 2009, Najibullah Zazi drove from his home in the Denver, Colorado, area to New York City. He drove to the city with the intention of detonating explosives, with two associates, on the New York City subway during rush hour as one of three coordinated suicide "martyrdom" bombings on September 14, 15, and 16, named Operation Highrise.[1] Spooked by a car stop at the George Washington Bridge and subsequent surveillance, he abruptly flew back to Denver and was arrested days later. Both Zazi and his high school friend, Zarein Ahmedzay, have pled guilty to conspiring to use weapons of mass destruction, to conspiring to commit murder in a foreign country, and to providing material support to a terrorist organization. A third co-conspirator and high school friend, Adis Medunjanin, has pleaded not guilty to similar charges. Zazi said he was recruited by al Qaeda in Pakistan for a suicide "martyrdom" attack against the United States and that his bombing target was the New York City subway system

The New York City Scene

The nature of the environment in which Najibullah Zazi and his associates, Zarein Ahmedzay and Adis Medunjanin, radicalized is still unclear. New York City's diverse Muslim communities encompass diaspora populations from South Asia (Pakistan, Afghanistan, India, Bangladesh), the Middle East (Egypt, Palestinian, Lebanon), West Africa, Yemen, and the Balkans. The nature of the city as a melting pot coupled with its easy mass transit system forces these varied ethnic groups to interact and is a counterweight to the development of homogenous ethnic enclaves in the city. In fact, in Flushing, Queens, where Najibullah Zazi, Zarein Ahmedzay, and Adis Medunjanin all attended high school, there are a few blocks (Parson's Boulevard) where Afghans generally settle, but this area is in fact surrounded by a much larger ethnic Chinese population. There are three mosques in the general neighborhood where Afghans and Pakistanis worship, but none is noted for political or extremist rhetoric.

A few provocative anti-democratic, anti-Western, pro–al Qaeda groups—the Islamic Thinkers Society and Revolution Muslim—have a significant presence in New York City, providing street *dawah* and sponsoring rallies in midtown Manhattan, which serve to attract politicized Muslims to their cause. However, neither Najibullah Zazi nor his associates seem to have had any linkages or interactions with these American Al Muhajiroun spin-off organizations.

The men were part of two overlapping scenes. One "scene" that Najibullah Zazi, Zarein Ahmedzay, and Adis Medunjanin were a part of was a basketball scene that included friends from the neighborhood, primarily of Afghan descent, who played pickup basketball in parks in Flushing, Queens.[3] Probably more important, the other "scene" involved a group of men who, from the beginning of 2008 until July of that year, attended the al Badr Mosque on Bath Avenue in Brooklyn to hear the lectures of Sheikh Mostafa Elazabawy on Saturday nights where, according to Medunjanin, the discussions covered religion and politics.[4]

Gravitating to Reactionary Islam

Little is known about the three men's radicalization processes. In fact, Abdulrahman Jalili, president of the Zazi family's Queens mosque, noted, "I never saw any wrong acts. . . . He wasn't acting strangely or anything. I never suspected him of doing anything like that." But there are unknowns, Jalili admitted, things he wouldn't see in those like Zazi who worshiped alongside him or others he wouldn't know who may have influenced Zazi.[5]

What is known is that Zazi had volunteered his time as a janitor at a local mosque, the Masjid Abu Bakr Siddique. The mosque's imam, Sherzad, remembers Zazi joining a protest against the imam's anti-Taliban rhetoric. This is the first indicator of any support for a radical organization; it was early 2005. After the protest, friends grew concerned about Zazi's appreciation for a radical Indian physician and speaker on Islam, Dr. Zakir Khan. In YouTube clips, Dr. Khan states, "If [bin Laden] is fighting enemies of Islam, I am for him . . . if he is terrorizing America—the terrorist, biggest terrorist—I am with him. Every Muslim should be a terrorist." It is certainly possible that Zazi appreciated these sentiments expressed on the Internet and that they helped shape his worldview. Zazi's friends also said that at approximately the same time, Zazi grew serious and was "chastising them for their interest in popular music and began expressing other fundamentalist views." They also noticed that he started wearing a tunic and grew a beard. A local from the neighborhood said that "Najib is completely different. . . . He looks like a Taliban. He has a big beard. He's talking different." Not only did his appearance changed but so did his demeanor. Patrons of his Wall Street coffee cart claim that he became more fervent and spoke out against the West, saying that his customers were materialistic and unhappy because they were not devout Muslims.[6]

According to Medunjanin, he only became more religious during ninth grade when he was playing football. Before one game, he prayed and subsequently threw a touchdown. However, when he did not pray before a subsequent game, he broke his left arm. When he tore his anterior cruciate ligament the next week, also after failing to pray, he concluded that Islam should "take a higher priority in his life." However, it was not really until Medunjanin began to attend college when he really felt that he became religious and subsequently grew his beard, spent more time in mosque, and began to spend more time with Najibullah Zazi.[7]

During the winter of 2006, Adis Medunjanin traveled to Dubai and then to Mecca, Saudi Arabia, as part of an effort to deepen his knowledge of Islam by attending an Islamic academy. However, he was unsuccessful in this effort and was not accepted to the school. Medunjanin returned to Saudi Arabia in 2007 with a friend from the Abu Bakr Mosque in Queens, Nadr Hasanoff, as part of a hajj trip as well as an effort to gain admittance into the University of Medina, but they were not accepted.[8] Medunjanin admitted listening to Anwar al Awlaki lectures but claimed to be unaware that Awlaki had made statements emphasizing that undertaking violent jihad was incumbent upon all Muslims.[9]

Politicization of Beliefs

There is limited information on what triggered the political radicalization of the men. Adis Medunjanin noted that from the beginning of 2008 until July of that year, he, Zazi, and Ahmedzay all attended the al Badr Mosque on Bath Avenue in Brooklyn to hear the lectures of Sheikh Mostafa Elazabawy on Saturday nights. According to Medunjanin, there they would discuss current affairs and politics.[10]

Adis Medunjanin noted in an interview that when he returned from his hajj trip to Saudi Arabia, he "saw the reporting regarding the way Muslims were being treated at the Abu Ghraib prison (new images had been released at around this time). This angered him and caused him to promote jihad at the mosque and after the basketball game with friends, but no one *had the balls*. Adis felt that he had to do something to join the fight that his fellow Muslims were in. There was so much that the U.S. was doing that was not right, that he had to do something to help his fellow Muslims. . . . Adis decided that he would go to Afghanistan and join the Taliban. There he would fight and kill U.S. soldiers that were stationed there."[11]

Moreover, with the United States and coalition forces at war in Afghanistan, occasional reports of accidental killings of Afghans by coalition forces, and the escalating use of drones, there was a ready-made set of political grievances that existed for an Afghan community that was likely torn between its loyalty to the United States and family and relatives under fire in Afghanistan. Young men in the community, searching for identity, would be especially vulnerable to politicized accusations of crimes committed by the West in Muslim lands, particularly if they could be viewed on the Internet. These dynamics may have contributed to Zazi and Ahmedzay's decision to travel to Pakistan to fight on behalf of the Taliban against coalition forces.

The Flushing High Cluster

Najibullah Zazi, Zarein Ahmedzay, and Adis Medunjanin all spent time together in Flushing and attended Flushing High School together. These neighborhood and school ties were the factors that underpinned their development into a break-away cluster that would travel to Pakistan together in an attempt to get into the fight against coalition forces in Afghanistan. The Operation Highrise conspirators were essentially an autonomous cluster of young men whose motivations, cohesiveness, and radicalization all occurred in the absence of any organized network or formal entry into the transnational jihad. This was a localized, neighborhood phenomenon. The young men bonded while playing billiards and video games with friends as well as basketball with other Afghan boys in the yard at Public School 214.[12]

Anatomy of the Cluster

Active Core

Najibullah Zazi, age twenty-four at the time of his arrest, was born in Paktia, Afghanistan. In 1991 or 1992 his family left the war-torn Jaji district and moved about a hundred miles to Hayatabad, Pakistan, which was on the outskirts of Peshawar. In 1999, at age fourteen, Zazi immigrated to Queens with his father. He attended school while his father drove taxi cabs for a living. Zazi grew up as a practicing Muslim. In fact, "as a teenager, he often carried two things, his basketball and a prayer mat." He attended Flushing High School, but he dropped out at the age of sixteen. He said that he did not want an education; he would rather work and earn money. He was materialistic and liked "nice clothes, nice shoes, everything." He first worked at a bodega in Flushing; the owner noted that he was very consistent with his daily prayer. Zazi later quit and took a job manning a coffee cart near Wall Street from 2005 through 2008. Sometime in 2006, Zazi flew to Pakistan and married, by arrangement, his nineteen-year-old cousin. She lives with their two children in Pakistan.[13]

    Zarein Ahmedzay, age twenty-four at the time of his arrest, was born in Afghanistan but was raised in Flushing. He attended high school with Najibullah Zazi. Ahmedzay took the civil service test to become a New York City firefighter in 2007, but worked driving a yellow taxi cab.[14]

    Adis Medunjanin, age twenty-five at the time of his arrest, was a Bosnian immigrant who came to the United States in 1994, grew up in Flushing, and was naturalized in 2002. According to friends, "Medunjanin played running back and wide receiver for the Flushing High School Red Devils." When told of his potential involvement in the plot, his football coach for two years noted, "This pretty much is a shock, what I'm hearing here. . . . He was just like your average regular kid—he was a really nice kid, pretty much a student, too." Medunjanin graduated from Queens College in June 2009 with a degree in economics. According to members of the Queens College Muslim Student Association, Medunjanin "was a well-known and respected figure in the group's prayer room, where he came to worship two or three times a week." He had "a long beard, was humble, quiet and highly regarded for his knowledge of Islam." However, Medunjanin was considered so religious that some members of the Muslim Student Association considered him "intimidating." At the time of his arrest, he was working as a security guard for Stellar Management.[15]

Periphery

Abdul Hameed Shehadeh, age twenty at the time of the plot, was a U.S. citizen, born and raised in New York, who was a regular attendee at the al Badr Mosque on Bath Avenue in Brooklyn during the first half of 2008. According to Adis Medunjanin, Shehadeh, referred to as "Abdul Hamid Filistiny" in court documents, would discuss politics and current events with Medunjanin and others at Sheikh Mostafa Elazabawy's Saturday night lectures at the mosque and gave his phone number to Medunjanin. Although Medunjanin notes that Shehadeh did not know of his plans to travel to Pakistan and Afghanistan, during the summer of 2008 Shehadeh himself departed New York City for Islamabad, Pakistan, and had told a few individuals that "he intended to travel to Pakistan to join the jihad there." Pakistani officials refused to admit him and he returned to New York City on June 15, 2008. He was subsequently arrested on October 23, 2010.[16]

Nadr and Sabir Hasanoff, two brothers ages unknown and thirty-three, respectively, at the time of the plot, were dual citizens of the United States and Australia who had lived in Brooklyn. Sabir Hasanoff was a senior manager at Pricewaterhouse Coopers who graduated from Baruch College in Manhattan. Pricewaterhouse employed Hasanoff from 2003 to 2006. Medunjanin traveled with Nadr, a friend from the Abu Bakr Mosque in Queens, to Saudi Arabia on hajj and to gain admittance into the University of Medina in 2007, but they were not accepted. Nadr and Sabir also were regular attendees of the al Badr Mosque on Bath Avenue in Brooklyn to hear Sheikh Mostafa Elazabawy's Saturday night lectures during the first half of 2008. Sabir was subsequently charged in April 2010 with conspiring to give computer advice, buy wristwatches, and do other tasks to help al Qaeda "modernize." According to Medunjanin, the Hasanoffs did not have any knowledge of the fact that Zazi, Ahmedzay, and Medunjanin had received training from al Qaeda.[17]

Overseas Travel and Link Up with Al Qaeda

Najibullah Zazi took four trips to Pakistan between 2004 and 2008. The second trip led to his marriage in 2006 to his cousin, the third was a visit to his wife and child in 2007 (little else is known about this trip), and the fourth was with Zarein Ahmedzay and Adis Medunjanin in 2008. It was on the fourth trip that Zazi and his associates linked up with the transnational jihad and trained and met with al Qaeda–associated individuals.

According to Adis Medunjanin, in April 2008 Najibullah Zazi, Zarein Ahmedzay, and Adis Medunjanin collectively decided to travel to Afghanistan to join the fight with the Taliban against U.S. troops stationed there. "They did not wish to join al-Qaeda because they conduct suicide missions; they did not want to perform a suicide mission." In fact, Adis Medunjanin wanted to eventually "become a great general that would lead the Taliban troops in battle" like a Muslim warrior from Islamic history. Furthermore, according to Medunjanin, the men devised a plan to travel to Pakistan under the guise that Adis would be looking for a wife there. Once in Pakistan, the men knew they could stay with relatives of both Zazi and Ahmedzay, who lived there.[18] The men flew from Newark Liberty International Airport in Newark, New Jersey, via Doha, Qatar, to Peshawar, Pakistan, at the end of August 2008. They were met at the airport by Zazi's family and taken to Zazi's family house, which was fifteen minutes from the airport and in which a number of members of his extended family lived. In Peshwar, they attended mosque five times a day, went to restaurants, and went to a bazaar to purchase local clothing.[19]

The men made an initial attempt to cross into Afghanistan via the Torkham border crossing, which ultimately failed. The taxi they took from Zazi's house was stopped at a checkpoint by the Pakistani army. When the troops noticed Adis Medunjanin's light skin and long beard, the men were ordered out of the taxi and subsequently questioned before being released by army personnel. However, the cab had driven off and they had to take another taxi back to Peshawar.[20] According to Zarein Ahmedzay's plea, he substantiated that he, Zazi, and Medunjanin initially attempted to enter Afghanistan but were turned back at the border and returned to Peshawar. During the next few days, the men attended a number of local mosques in the vicinity of Zazi's uncle's house and inquired in the mosques as to how to get assistance so that they could get training in Afghanistan and conduct jihad. At one of the mosques, they were told that they should return to Zazi's uncle's house and wait for someone to pick them up the next day. At five A.M. the next day, two men (one of them "Ahmad"; last name unknown) appeared at the house with a gray Toyota and told them that they were there to take them to training. Over the course of two days, the five individuals traveled over back roads with fewer checkpoints before arriving in Miram Shah, Pakistan, where Zazi and his associates were dropped off at the house of a local Pashtun man.[21]

The next day, Zazi, Ahmedzay, and Medunjanin were met at a newspaper shop by a caravan of vehicles including three or four sedans and pickup trucks. "Abdul Hafeeze," aka Saleh al Somali, and "Ibrahim," aka Rashid Rauf, who spoke English with a British accent, introduced themselves to the men and told them that they "would be presented with a serious decision" and wanted to know if they were willing to be martyrs and accept a suicide mission. Zazi, Ahmedzay, and Medunjanin responded that they wanted to attend a training camp but were unsure about conducting suicide missions. The three Americans then entered one of the vehicles and drove with "Abdul Hafeeze" and traveled for the better part of two days before being dropped off at the house of a man, introduced as "Yusuf," aka Ferid Imam, a Canadian who spoke Arabic, Pashtu, and English with an American accent. During the next two weeks, the men received daily military weapons training and religious indoctrination on the rewards of fighting and dying in jihad from "Yusuf" and his assistant.[22]

Essentially at this point, the men from Flushing had met senior al Qaeda Core members: Saleh al Somali, the head of international operations for al Qaeda, and Rashid Rauf, a key al Qaeda operative. Based on the fact that none of the men was of Pakistani or Afghan descent and that they were being shown al Qaeda videos at the house, Adis Medunjanin deduced that they were being trained by al Qaeda and not the Taliban.[23]

According to Canadian authorities, Ferid Imam, aka "Yusuf," was a former student at the University of Manitoba, who departed Canada for Pakistan in 2007 to train for and carry out terrorist acts against NATO forces in Afghanistan. Clearly, by 2008, he was in a position to train Zazi, Ahmedzay, and Medunjanin on the use of small arms.[24]

It is also likely that the men met Abid Naseer, a twenty-four-year-old Pakistani who had lived in the U.K. since 2006, as well as Mikael Davud, a thirty-nine-year-old ethnic Uygher with Norwegian citizenship, both of whom were in Peshawar at the same time as Zazi and Ahmedzay. These two individuals were involved in plots in Manchester, U.K., and Oslo, Norway, respectively, that also seem to be linked to the mysterious "Ahmad."[25]

Training and Skill Acquisition

According to Adis Medunjanin, at this first "camp," which they attended between August and October 2008, the men from Flushing received training on a variety of weapons including the AK-47, the PK machine gun, and the rocket-propelled grenade launcher. There was classroom training in which the men learned how to assemble and disassemble the weapons. This culminated in a trip up into the more mountainous terrain where the men were able to fire some of the weapons.[26]

Following the two-week training session, Medunjanin was asked by "Abdul Hafeeze" to participate in a suicide mission against either the Pakistani Inter Services Intelligence Directorate or the Pakistani army. When he turned this opportunity down, he suggested that it might be best for him to return to the United States and just provide financial support to "Abdul Hafeeze." Subsequently, he was driven from the training "camp" back to Kohat, Pakistan, returned to Zazi's uncle's house, and began to prepare to return to New York in September 2008.[27]

Although Adis Medunjanin departed Pakistan from Newark in late September, Zazi stayed to receive further training—in explosives. In November 2008, the mysterious "Ahmad" transported Zazi back to Waziristan from Peshawar for explosives training. Ahmedzay had decided against the additional training. It is likely that Zazi received instruction in creating hydrogen peroxide explosives, as this was the content of the notes that he e-mailed back to himself and showed Ahmedzay.[28]

Al Qaeda Recruitment

Ahmedzay's guilty plea decisively answers this question. Saleh al Somali, likely the head of al Qaeda's external operations, as well Rashid Rauf
and Adnan el Shukrijumah, two important Western al Qaeda members, all
played critical roles in recruiting and redirecting the men from Flushing:

> Upon arriving [at the first training camp], they met with two al Qa-
> eda leaders, but did not learn their true identities . . . the leaders were
> Saleh al Somali, the head of international operations for al Qaeda,
> and Rashid Rauf, a key al Qaeda operative. The three Americans said
> that they wanted to fight in Afghanistan, but the al Qaeda leaders
> explained that they would be more useful to al Qaeda and the *jihad* if
> they returned to New York and conducted attacks there. During the
> training, al Qaeda leaders continued to encourage them to return to
> the United States and conduct suicide operations. They agreed, and
> had further conversations with al Qaeda about the timing of the at-
> tacks and possible target locations in Manhattan. Al Qaeda leadership
> emphasized the need to hit well-known structures and maximize the
> number of casualties.[29]

Operational Cycle

Travel to Pakistan was clearly the catalyst for the cluster's decision to
target the United States directly. Zazi and Ahmedzay returned to the
United States in January 2009. Beginning in June 2009, Zazi began re-
viewing the bomb-making notes from his training and conducted research on where to buy the ingredients for the explosives. Later that summer, Zazi, Ahmedzay, and Medunjanin met in New York City and agreed
to conduct a coordinated suicide bombing in the New York City subway
system in the coming September. However, it was not until August 2009
when Najibullah Zazi initiated contact with the group's al Qaeda point
of contact or "link man" named "Ahmad" that the plot actually began to
move forward.[30]

Target Selection/Casing

According to Ahmedzay's guilty plea, the men had agreed with al Qaeda during their time at the training camp in Waziristan about the timing of the attacks and possible target locations in Manhattan. Although al Qaeda leadership gave general instructions about hitting well-known targets and maximizing casualties, they left the specifics to the conspirators. Ultimately, the decision to attack the New York City subways was based on Zazi's creation of only relatively small amounts of TATP—the men thought it would still be effective in subway attacks. No casing of targets was known to have occurred.[31]

Logistics

The plot was self-funded. Zazi took detailed notes during his training and e-mailed a summary of the notes to himself in December 2008 so that he could access them when he returned to the United States.[32]

Communications

During the summer of 2009, Zazi, Ahmedzay, and Medunjanin met in person in New York City and agreed to conduct a coordinated suicide bombing in the New York City subway system in the coming September. However, it was not until August 2009 when Najibullah Zazi self-initiated contact with the group's al Qaeda point of contact or "link man" named "Ahmad" via email, that the plot actually began to move forward. When "Ahmad" replied via e-mail, Zazi informed him in coded terms that the suicide operation was ready to proceed and asked for the precise instructions for constructing one of the devices that he had been trained to build while in Pakistan.[33]

   Zazi e-mailed "Ahmad" to let him know that "the wedding" was about to occur. According to the indictment and court filings, "Saleh al-Somali communicated with Zazi through 'Ahmad,' an al Qaeda facilitator in Peshawar, Pakistan. In early September 2009, after Zazi constructed the detonator explosives for the attack, he emailed with 'Ahmad' in Pakistan about the proper ingredients for the flour-based main charge explosive."[34] "Ahmad" was the same individual whom Abid Naseer, a member of the Operation

Pathway conspiracy (Manchester Easter plot 2009) had reached out to via e-mail as a middleman between the men in the U.K. and Salah al Somali. Clearly "Ahmad" had played the role of "link man" for another al Qaeda–linked cluster.[35]

Weaponization

In July and August 2009, Zazi purchased large quantities of the components necessary to produce TATP and twice checked into a hotel room near Denver, where bomb-making residue was later found. By the first week of September, he had already constructed a sufficient quantity of detonator explosive that could be used in multiple improvised explosive devices. On September 8, 2009, Zazi rented a car and drove from Denver to New York, taking with him the explosives and other materials necessary to build the bombs. Zazi arrived in New York City on Thursday, September 10. Zazi and others intended to obtain and assemble the remaining components of the bombs over the weekend and conduct the attack on Manhattan subway lines on September 14, 15, or 16, 2009. However, shortly after arriving in New York, Zazi suspected that law enforcement was investigating his activities. Zazi and the others discarded the explosives and other bomb-making materials, and Zazi traveled back to Denver.[36]

The Al Qaeda Factor

After Ahmedzay, Zazi, and Medunjanin were forced to return to Peshawar after they had been turned back at the Afghanistan border, they met with "Ahmad," who took them to Waziristan to attend a training camp. There they met al Qaeda members Salah al Somali, Rashid Rauf, and Adnan el Shukrijumah.[37]

While the men from Flushing had agreed to conduct an operation on behalf of al Qaeda and even discussed the timing of the attacks and possible target locations in Manhattan with senior al Qaeda members, once the men from Flushing returned to the United States, there seems to have been limited communication between them and al Qaeda.[38] Only in the final weeks before the planned attack did Zazi attempt to contact "Ahmad" and others overseas to finalize the specifications of the weapon and to inform al Qaeda that the date of the "wedding" was approaching.[39]

Clearly this is a plot with direct links to al Qaeda Core. It was conceived of and presented to the men of Flushing to carry out by individuals who represented al Qaeda's external operations effort. Although there was some communication between the men in the West and al Qaeda Core through the mysterious "Ahmad" via Zazi's reaching out to him with last-minute questions about the explosive mix and desire to alert al Qaeda of the imminency of the plot, this does not constitute command and control by al Qaeda Core. Ultimately it was up to Zazi, Ahmedzay, and Medunjanin to pick not only the time but the targets. As a result, Operation Highrise is categorized as an al Qaeda "suggested/endorsed" plot.

PART III

Al Qaeda "Inspired" Plots

Chapter 11

Tradebom Plot (World Trade Center, New York, 1993)

THE 1993 WORLD TRADE CENTER bombing occurred on February 26, 1993, when a car bomb was detonated below Tower One of the World Trade Center in New York City. The 1,500-pound urea nitrate-hydrogen gas-enhanced device was intended to knock the North Tower (Tower One) into the South Tower (Tower Two), bringing both towers down and killing thousands of people. It failed to do so, but it did kill six people and injure 1,042.

The attack was planned by a group of conspirators including Ramzi Yousef, Mahmoud Abouhalima, Mohammed Salameh, Nidal Ayyad, Abdul Rahman Yasin, and Ahmad Ajaj. They received financing from Khalid Sheikh Mohammed, Yousef's uncle. In March 1994, four men were convicted of carrying out the bombing: Abouhalima, Ajaj, Ayyad, and Salameh. The charges included conspiracy, explosive destruction of property, and interstate transportation of explosives. In November 1997, two more were convicted: Yousef, the mastermind behind the bombings, and Eyad Ismoil, who drove the truck carrying the bomb.[1]

The al Kifah Scene

The origins of the development of the rejectionist Islamic environment in New York can be traced back to the establishment of the al Kifah Brooklyn refugee center, which was a branch of the Office of Services, the Pakistan-based organization that Osama bin Laden helped finance and lead and would later become al Qaeda. In fact, it was Mustafa Shalabi, an Egyptian who founded and ran the center, whom bin Laden called in 1991 when he needed help moving to Sudan. Shalabi was murdered in 1991 in a case that remains unsolved but took place at a time when the "Blind Sheikh," Omar Abdel Rahman, and Shalabi were quarreling over how funds were raised and spent.[2]

The al Kifah Center, on Atlantic Avenue in Brooklyn, began in the late 1980s as a desk in the al Farouq Mosque and subsequently moved into a "small apartment in a building a few doors away at 566 Atlantic Avenue, above what is now a perfume factory, with just enough room for a desk, a few chairs, a phone and a fax machine." Its location placed it right in the middle of "a strip of Arab restaurants and Islamic bookstores on Atlantic Avenue, between Third and Fourth Streets," which was a neighborhood that comprising immigrants from the Middle East and North Africa.[3]

The center's stated purpose was to raise money and recruit fighters to help the U.S.-backed Afghan mujahedeen, who rebelled against the communist government in Afghanistan after an invasion by the Soviet Union in 1979, and during the late 1980s it served as a conduit to Afghanistan for local volunteers who wanted to fight alongside the Afghan mujahedeen as well as a fund-raising network and propaganda arm. However, following the Soviet withdrawal from Afghanistan in 1989, it changed its focus from Afghanistan and instead became a local hub of radical Islamic activity directed against the West and was a primary node linked to individuals convicted in connection with the 1990 murder of Rabbi Meir Kahane, the 1993 World Trade Center attack, and the 1993 "Landmarks Plot."[4]

The arrival in Brooklyn in 1990 of Sheikh Omar Abdel Rahman, the blind Egyptian cleric who had been a leading member of al Jemaah Islamiyah, or the Egyptian Islamic Group, and was accused of issuing the fatwa that authorized the assassination of Anwar Sadat, figured prominently in the redirection of al Kifah against the West. At al Kifah, Rahman "preached the message of Sayyid Qutb's *Milestones*, characterizing the United States as the oppressor of Muslims worldwide and asserting that it was their religious duty to fight against God's enemies." This rejectionist message had a powerful impact among those who were regulars at al Kifah and al Farouq. Among the convicted members of the Tradebom cluster who frequented and were radicalized at al Kifah and al Farouq were Mohammed Salameh, Mahmoud Abouhalima, and Nidal Ayyad. By the time Ramzi Yousef arrived with his plot in 1992, these men were prepared to strike out against the power that they viewed as a primary moral violator of Muslims worldwide—the United States.[5]

Gravitating to Reactionary Islam

Sayyid Qutb's *Milestones* and the religious/political ideology promoted by al Jemaah Islamiyah had a powerful influence on the conspirators in the Tradebom plot. The "Blind Sheikh" advocated a religious interpretation that rejected the West, and this was ingrained into the regulars at both the al Farouq and al Salam mosques in Brooklyn and New Jersey, respectively.

According to his speeches and writings, Rahman perceives the United States as the primary oppressor of Muslims worldwide, as active in assisting Israel to gain power in the Middle East, and largely under the control of the Jewish lobby. Rahman also considers the secular Egyptian government of Mubarak to be an oppressor because it has abided Jewish migration to Israel while seeking to decrease Muslim births. Rahman believes that jihad against Egypt and the United States is mandated by the Koran. Formation of a jihad army made up of small "divisions" and "battalions" to carry out this jihad was therefore necessary, according to Rahman, to beat back the oppressors of Islam, including the United States.[6]

While Omar Abdel Rahman was the leading figure in this group, others from Egypt and the Palestinian territories had similar religiously informed worldviews. For example, Egyptian, Mahmoud Abouhalima had been active in al Jemaah Islamiyah growing up and while attending university in Alexandria, Egypt, before seeking asylum in Germany. In addition, according to his brother, Mohammed Salameh, in his final years in high school on the West Bank, "became religious, started to pray and read the Koran with other friends in high school. He stopped most of his past activities and hobbies. . . . He was not a fundamentalist. He was interested in Islamic teachings." Salameh earned a degree in Islamic studies from the University of Jordan.[7]

Politicization of Beliefs

Participation in al Jemaah Islamiyah in Egypt was the most relevant manifestation of political activism for some of the members of the Tradebom cluster. The "Blind Sheikh" had a leadership role in the group and was a virulent opponent of the secular Egyptian government. According to some accounts, it was Israel's dramatic victory in the Six-Day War over Egypt that triggered his radicalization against the state, "almost overnight," according to one source.[8] Mahmoud Abouhalima, as a teenager, "developed a deep and growing hatred for Egypt because he felt his country offered little hope for his generation's future." Subsequently, he started to hang around with members of the outlawed al Jemaah Islamiyah.[9]

The Tradebom Cluster

Several of those convicted in the World Trade Center case and the subsequent "Landmarks Plot" were associated with the al Kifah Center and al Farouq Mosque, as well as the al Salam Mosque in Jersey City, where they discussed politics and religion even before the "Blind Sheikh" and Ramzi Yousef arrived in New York.

Following his arrival in New York from Germany in 1986, Mahmoud Abouhalima spent significant time at both al Kifah and al Farouq. It was through his interactions at these locations that he met Mohammed Salameh, and they subsequently participated in weekend paramilitary camps in upstate New York, day trips to gun ranges in Connecticut and Long Island, and even survival and surveillance courses with an Army Special Forces instruction guide, provided by Ali Mohammed, who had been in the Egyptian army, as early as 1987. Other participants in these weekend events were El Sayyid Nosair, the future Rabbi Meir Kahane assassin, and Nosair's accomplice in the Kahane shooting, Bilal Alkaisi. Participation in these events gave the group a sense of mission.[10]

Alkaisi was considered a protégé of El Sayyid Nosair and sought to be the emir of the group once Nosair was arrested. Both men were at the hotel when El Sayyid Nosair assassinated Rabbi Meir Kahane in 1990. Nidal Ayyad was also a close friend of Mohammed Salameh.[11]

Although Rahman did not arrive in the United States until 1990, a group of his followers began to organize a jihad army in New York in 1989. At that time, law enforcement had several of the members of the group under surveillance. In July 1989, on three successive weekends, FBI agents observed and photographed members of the jihad organization, including (at different times) Nosair, Clement, Hampton-El, Mahmoud Abouhalima, Mohammed Salameh, and Nidal Ayyad, shooting weapons, including AK-47s, at a public rifle range on Long Island. Although Rahman was in Egypt at the time, Nosair and Abouhalima called him there to discuss various issues, including the progress of their military training, and tape recorded these conversations for distribution among Rahman's followers. Nosair told Rahman, "we have organized an encampment, we are concentrating here."[12]

When the "Blind Sheikh" arrived in New York City in 1990, it was the leader of the al Kifah center, Mustafa Shalabi, who brought the sheikh to the al Farouq Mosque and into the Tradebom cluster. Mahmoud Abouhalima worshiped at both the Abu Bakr Mosque in Brooklyn and the al Salam Mosque in Jersey City. Upon Sheikh Omar Abdul Rahman's arrival in New York, Abouhalima became his part-time bodyguard and driver.[13]

When Ramzi Yousef arrived in 1992, he took command of the emerging cluster as its emir. Mohammed Salameh became his deputy and Mahmoud Abouhalima and Nidal Ayyad served as logistics coordinators.[14] "Once in New York, Yousef assembled a team of trusted criminal associates, including Mohammed Salameh, Nidal Ayyad, Mahmoud Abouhalima and Abdul Rahman Yasin. Together, the conspirators implemented the bombing plot that Ajaj and Yousef had hatched overseas."[15]

Sheikh Omar Abdul Rahman was born in Egypt and had been blinded by diabetes as an infant. He studied at Cairo's famed al Azhar University and subsequently became a critic of Egypt's government for not adhering sufficiently to Islamic principles. Rahman became a leading member of al Jemaah Islamiyah. He was accused of issuing the fatwa that authorized the assassination of Anwar Sadat but was acquitted due to ambiguities surrounding his precise role.[16]

Following Sadat's death, Sheikh Rahman traveled the world recruiting and encouraging volunteers to join the battle against the Soviets in Afghanistan. In 1990, Rahman succeeded in obtaining a tourist visa to the United States from the U.S. embassy in Sudan. After a falling out at al Farouq in Brooklyn, he became the leader of the al Salam Mosque in Jersey City. Nevertheless, in the New York City scene, he became the chief ideologue and proponent for military jihad.[17]

The U.S. government asserted in the "Landmarks Plot" trial that

Rahman, a blind Islamic scholar and cleric, was the leader of the seditious conspiracy, the purpose of which was "*jihad*," in the sense of a struggle against the enemies of Islam. Indicative of this purpose, in a speech to his followers Rahman instructed that they were to "do *jihad* with the sword, with the cannon, with the grenades, with the missile . . . against God's enemies." Rahman's role in the conspiracy was

generally limited to overall supervision and direction of the membership, as he made efforts to remain a level above the details of individual
operations. However, as a cleric and the group's leader, Rahman was
entitled to dispense "*fatwas*," religious opinions on the holiness of an
act, to members of the group sanctioning proposed courses of conduct
and advising them whether the acts would be in furtherance of *jihad*.[18]

Anatomy of the Cluster

Active Core

Ramzi Yousef, age twenty-five at the time of the attack, was born in Kuwait
as Amit Basit Mahmud Abdul Karim, where his father, an engineer of Pakistani descent, worked for Kuwaiti airlines. Since his mother was Palestinian,
he grew up in the Palestinian community outside of Kuwait City. As a youth
he excelled in math and science and was quite popular among his schoolmates. According to some accounts, when he was a teenager, Yousef's father
"embraced fundamentalism and moved the family to the rural Baluchistan
part of Pakistan."[19] Yousef went for further schooling abroad in Wales at
the West Glamorgan Institute of Higher Learning, where he specialized in
computer-aided electronics and earned a degree in 1989. According to one
account, while at school he became associated with a "local chapter of the
Egyptian Muslim Brotherhood."[20]

Some time following the Iraqi invasion of Kuwait in 1990, Ramzi Yousef
traveled to Afghanistan and attended Khalden Camp. There he met Ahmed
Ajaj and together they learned how to construct homemade explosive devices
sometime between 1991 and 1992. In addition, during this time at the camp
near Peshawar it is possible that Yousef met both Omar Abdel Rahman and
Mahmoud Abouhalima, the Egyptian cabdriver he would later meet up with
in Brooklyn.[21] In 1991 Yousef went to the Philippines and trained members
of the Abu Sayyaf Group in explosives. This violent Islamist group had been
funded by Osama bin Laden's brother-in-law as early as 1998.[22]

Mohammed Salameh, age twenty-five at the time of his arrest, and of
Palestinian heritage, was born near Nablus, an Arab town on the West Bank.
In his final years of high school, Salameh, according to his brother, "became religious, started to pray and read the Koran with other friends in high
school. He stopped most of his past activities and hobbies. . . . He was not a

fundamentalist. He was interested in Islamic teachings." Salameh earned a degree in Islamic studies from the University of Jordan. He arrived in the United States in 1988 on a six-month tourist visa with the intention of earning an MBA but did not follow through with it. Salameh settled in Jersey City and lived there illegally for the next five years. He attended the al Salam Mosque in Jersey City.[23]

Mahmoud Abouhalima, age thirty-three at the time of the attack, was born in Kafr al Dawar, a poor village fifteen miles south of Alexandria, Egypt. In spite of the meager surroundings, his father was a mill foreman and the family was relatively well-off. As a teenager, according to his friends, "Abouhalima developed a deep and growing hatred for Egypt because he felt his country offered little hope for his generation's future." Subsequently, he started to hang around with members of the outlawed al Jemaah Islamiyah, which considered Sheikh Omar Abdel Rahman as its spiritual guide. Abouhalima studied education at Alexandria University but ultimately quit school and, following a number of crackdowns and arrests of his friends in the movement, fled Egypt and traveled to Germany as a tourist in 1981 where he sought political asylum.[24]

Although his application for asylum was rejected, he married a German citizen, enabling him to remain in Munich, and pursued a teaching degree. Abouhalima learned German and worked menial jobs as a dishwasher and behind the meat counter of a grocery store. He never assimilated into German society. Rather, "Abouhalima's social life revolved around the Egyptian immigrant community in Munich, especially the orthodox Muslims he met while praying in makeshift mosques. He invited several Muslim friends who needed housing to live temporarily with him and his wife. Abouhalima conducted many smoky gatherings in their home, where groups of Egyptians would sit and discuss politics in Arabic."[25] Abouhalima condemned the governments of Egypt (Sadat and later Mubarak), along with their supporters like the United States. Abouhalima had little regard for Germans. When his first wife refused to convert to Islam and later had an abortion, Abouhalima divorced her and married a German woman who would convert to Islam.[26]

In 1985 Abouhalima and his new wife traveled to the United States for a three-week visit. They settled in Brooklyn and did not return to Germany. Abouhalima took advantage of a 1986 amnesty program for migrant farmers and ultimately became a legal permanent resident. He subsequently got a chauffeur's license, drove cabs in New York City for the next five years, and was known as the Blind Sheikh's driver. In New York, Abouhalima spent significant time at the al Kifah Center. After obtaining his green card in late 1988, Abouhalima took several trips to Pakistan during the next twenty months, most likely facilitated by the al Kifah center, where he received paramilitary training.[27]

Nidal Ayyad, age twenty-five at the time of the attack, was born in Kuwait to a Palestinian family. In 1985 he immigrated legally to the United States and began to study biochemical engineering in Rutgers University in New Jersey, from which he graduated in early 1991. After his graduation he was employed as a research engineer for Allied Signal in Morristown, New Jersey. He primarily worked with chemicals used in pharmaceuticals and paints.[28] In his free time Nidal Ayyad volunteered at al Kifah. He was filmed by FBI agents shooting weapons at the Calverton Shooting Range in 1989 with Mahmoud Abouhalima, El Sayyid Nosair, and Mohammed Salameh.[29]

Followers

Abdul Rahman Yasin, age thirty-three at the time of the attack, and of Iraqi heritage, was born in Bloomington, Indiana, where his father came to study for a Ph.D. Shortly after his birth, Yasin's family moved back to Iraq and for the most part, he grew up in Baghdad. In 1992, Yasin was able to use his American citizenship to obtain a U.S. passport from the U.S. embassy in Amman, Jordan, and thus enter the United States. Yasin was a student at City College and lived in the same building as Mohammed Salameh and Ramzi Yousef, who had also arrived in the fall of 1992.[30]

Eyad Ismoil, age twenty-two at the time of the attack, was born in Kuwait and attended high school in Jordan. He entered the United States in 1989 on a student visa to study engineering at Wichita State University, where he enrolled at the Intensive English Language Center to study English as a second language. Ismoil overstayed his visa and moved to Dallas, Texas. In December 1992, he was contacted by Ramzi Yousef, with whom he relocated to New York City on February 22, 1993, to begin preparing for the attack. Ismoil would drive the Ryder truck into the World Trade Center garage.[31]

Ahmed Ajaj, age twenty-seven at the time of the attack, and of Palestinian heritage, was born in the West Bank and immigrated to Houston, Texas, where he sought asylum and worked as a pizza delivery driver. He returned to the United States on September 1, 1992, after having received training on how to construct homemade explosive devices at al Qaeda's Khalden Camp in Afghanistan with Ramzi Yousef. When he went through customs at JFK upon his arrival, Ajaj was found to be carrying a "terrorist kit" that he and Yousef had assembled in Pakistan: "The kit included, among other things, handwritten notes Ajaj had taken while attending explosives courses, manuals containing formulae and instructions for manufacturing bombs, materials describing how to carry-off a successful terrorist operation, videotapes advocating terrorist action against the United States, and fraudulent identification documents." After becoming "belligerent" with INS inspectors who noticed his altered passport and found his "terrorist kit," Ajaj was subsequently detained pending a hearing. Ajaj later pleaded guilty to using an altered passport and served six months in prison.[32]

Periphery

El Sayyid Nosair, age thirty-five at the time of his assassination of Rabbi Meir Kahane in 1990, was born in Port Said, Egypt, but was forced to move to Cairo in his adolescence after Israel's victory over Egypt in the 1967 Six-Day War. He had arrived in the United States in 1981 after studying industrial design and engineering at the Helwan University Faculty of Applied Arts. Three years after his graduation, in 1981, he immigrated to the United States. He settled in Pittsburgh and worked as a diamond cutter. During his early years there, he embraced American society—from nightclubs and fast food to museums and dating.[33] Sometime in 1982 he began to re-embrace a fundamentalist interpretation of his faith, lost his job, and, after two accusations of rape, moved from Pittsburgh to Jersey City in 1983. After a serious electrical accident that he received as an electrician's assistant, Nosair found work as a maintenance man in the basement of the Manhattan Civil Court Building. During this time, he became a "fixture" at al Kifah.[34]

Ibrahim el Gabrowny, age forty-three at the time of the attack, was Nosair's older cousin. In advance of Nosair's trial for the murder of Rabbi Meir Kahane, el Gabrowny traveled to Saudi Arabia, met with Osama bin Laden, and raised $20,000 for his defense. In 1992, before Ramzi Yousef's arrival in the United States, el Gabrowny was involved with an aspirational plot to bomb twelve Jewish targets in and around New York City. However, this never got past the stage of discussion. According to one investigator, his role was that of a "group elder" who dispensed advice, mediated conflicts, and provided a private meeting place for the group in Brooklyn (most of the men lived in Jersey City). He was linked to al Kifah, the "Blind Sheikh," Nosair, and Clement Hampton-El. Ultimately he would be convicted of participating in a "seditious conspiracy; assault of a Federal agent and city police detective seeking to search his home after the World Trade Center bombing and possession of false identification documents and false passports" as a result of the 1994 Landmarks Plot.[35]

Clement Rodney Hampton-El, age fifty-five at the time of the attack, was a black convert to Islam who had fought in Afghanistan and worked as a medical technician. He was known as Dr. Rashid and was a leading member of a group of African American converts to Islam who had access to weapons, knew the participants of the al Kifah scene, and would later be convicted for his participation in a seditious conspiracy, bombing conspiracy, and attempted bombing as part of the 1993 "Landmarks Plot." According to the prosecutors, he was the weapons supplier for the "Landmarks Plot" group, "having sought detonators for bombs, arranging for an informer to obtain a pistol and organizing military-style training."[36]

Ali Mohammed, age forty at the time of the attack, was an ex-officer in the Egyptian army and a member of Egyptian Islamic Jihad. He attended the U.S. Army's Special Operations Warfare School at Fort Bragg and worked as a contract agent for the CIA until he was dismissed due to the suspicion that he had Hezbollah ties. He reentered the United States in 1986 and was able to enlist in the U.S. Army as a supply sergeant and was posted back at the same Special Forces base that he had been at in the early 1980s.[37] In 1987 he took a leave of absence and fought against the Soviets in Afghanistan. After he returned to the United States he spent weekends in Brooklyn and New Jersey, having reestablished his links with both Mustafa Shalabi and Omar Abdel Rahman, whom he had known in Egypt. In 1990 he moved to Sacramento with his wife, staying in the U.S. Army as a reservist.[38]

Bilal Alkaisi, age twenty-six at the time of the attack, had studied explosives and served as a trainer at an al Qaeda camp. In 1987 he participated in the shooting range outings in Calverton. In 1990 he accompanied Nosair to the Marriott Hotel where he was supposed to be the "getaway driver" after the Kahane shooting. However, he shirked his responsibility after the shooting (some say because he was in the process of receiving a parking ticket), leaving Nosair to fend for himself. During the summer of 1992, after a squabble with Mohammed Salameh in which Salameh pulled a gun on him, Alkaisi left the group.[39]

Overseas Travel and Link Up with Al Qaeda

Many of the men who would be involved with the Tradebom plot were fellow travelers and spent time in Afghanistan either for training or to fight against the Soviets during the late 1980s and early 1990s. Relationships made during these trips persisted and ultimately provided the underlying links that connected the conspirators involved in the plot.

In 1985, Omar Abdel Rahman visited the front lines in Afghanistan and developed relationships with the Afghan warlord Gulbuddin Hekmatyar, the jihad theoretician Abdullah Azzam, and Osama bin Laden. He is believed to have made subsequent trips as well.[40]

After obtaining his green card in late 1988, Mahmoud Abouhalima took several trips to Pakistan during the next twenty months, where he received paramilitary training. These trips were almost certainly facilitated through the al Kifah center in Brooklyn.[41]

Some time following the Iraqi invasion of Kuwait in 1990, Ramzi Yousef traveled to Afghanistan and attended Khaldan Camp. There he met Ahmed Ajaj and together they learned how to construct homemade explosive devices sometime between 1991 and 1992.[42] In addition, it is possible that Yousef met both Omar Abdel Rahman and Mahmoud Abouhalima during this time.[43]

In 1991–92 Ramzi Yousef began to plan a bombing attack within the United States. He is believed to have discussed his plans with his uncle, Khalid Sheikh Mohammed.[44]

In 1992 Ahmad Ajaj and an associate, who was a San Antonio cabdriver and a fund-raiser for al Kifah, flew together from Texas to Pakistan. Subsequently, Ajaj received explosives training at an Afghanistan training camp with Ramzi Yousef. Ajaj spent four months in Pakistan before returning to the United States with Yousef and a bomb manual later seized by the U.S. government.[45]

Al Qaeda Recruitment

When Ramzi Yousef was in Afghanistan during 1990–92, through his own initiative, he began to plan a bombing attack within the United States. It is believed he discussed his plans with his uncle, Khalid Sheikh Mohammed.[46] However, this was before Khalid Sheikh Mohammed had taken an oath of loyalty to Osama bin Laden and al Qaeda, so Yousef cannot be said to have been recruited by al Qaeda.

Operational Cycle

Ramzi Yousef arrived in the United States on September 1, 1992, traveling with Ahmed Ajaj from Pakistan. Both men were on the same flight but sat apart and acted as if they were traveling separately. Ajaj was ultimately detained following his inspection at JFK Airport after it was discovered that he was carrying bomb-making instructions in his luggage. Yousef's arrival catalyzed the men in the Tradebom cluster, who had been considering targeting twelve Jewish locations in New York City, to plan to attack the World Trade Center. On February 26, 1993, just less than six months since Yousef's arrival in the United States, the Tradebom cluster carried out the attack against the World Trade Center. The operational cycle lasted less than six months.[47]

Logistics

In October 1992 Mohammed Salameh and Nidal Ayyad opened a series of bank accounts together in the United States. According to trial documents, "Some of that money was later used by Salameh to rent a storage shed in Jersey City, New Jersey, where the conspirators stored chemicals for making explosives. Yousef also drew on that account to pay for materials described in Ajaj's manuals as ingredients for bomb making."[48] Khalid Sheikh Mohammed funded Yousef's efforts with a wire transfer of $660 on November 3, 1992, from Qatar to this bank account of Yousef's co-conspirator, Mohammed Salameh.[49] The bomb-making manual was an al Qaeda document—two separate translations of the bomb-making manual that Ajaj brought with him from Pakistan to New York in September 1992 have a heading on the document says, "Al Qaeda" or "The Base." In addition, the document lists a publication date of 1989, a year after bin Laden founded the organization, and the place of publication is Afghanistan.[50] Some investigators believe that a portion of the $20,000 that el Gabrowny raised from bin Laden for Nosair's defense was utilized to purchase material for the World Trade Center bomb.[51]

Communications

According to *The 9/11 Commission Report*, "During the fall of 1992, while Yousef was building the bomb that he used against the World Trade Center, KSM [Khalid Sheikh Mohammed] and Yousef had numerous telephone conversations during which Yousef discussed his progress and sought additional funding."[52] In December 1992 Yousef reached out to Ajaj, who was still in detention, via his lawyer:

Ajaj stayed abreast of the conspiracy's progress through telephone conversations with Yousef. Ajaj never contacted Yousef directly but telephoned a friend, Mohammad Abukhdeir in Texas, who then, as an intermediary, either relayed messages or patched three-way calls to Yousef. According to the government, Ajaj, Abukhdeir, and Yousef discussed the bombing conspiracy in code, referring to Yousef as "Rashed," the bomb plot as the "study" and the terrorist materials as "university papers." During one such conversation on December 29, 1992, Ajaj agreed to convey the terrorist materials to Yousef. Specifically, Ajaj informed Yousef that the United States District Court for the Eastern District of New York had ordered the government to return Ajaj's belongings, including the terrorist materials. When Yousef, who wanted to take advantage of this surprising opportunity, asked Ajaj if he could take possession of Ajaj's belongings, Ajaj at first agreed but then opined that its shipment to Yousef would jeopardize Yousef's "business" which would be "a pity!"[53]

While building the World Trade Center bomb, the builders kept in close phone contact with el Gabrowny and the "Blind Sheikh." Salameh and Yousef repeatedly called el Gabrowny at home and at the Abu Bakr Mosque and the "Blind Sheikh" at home. Abouhalima also obtained a telephone calling card, which the conspirators used to contact each other and to call various chemical companies for information about bomb ingredients.[54]

Casing

On February 15, 1993, Nidal Ayyad rented a car for Mohammed Salameh and himself to use to scout the World Trade Center bomb location: "He

[Mohammed] entered the B-2 level of the parking garage in the early afternoon, checked out his surroundings for about a half hour, then headed back to New Jersey. Then, on February 24, Salameh conducted his final reconnaissance of the World Trade Center."[55]

Weaponization

During the summer of 1992, Mohammed Salameh, Nidal Ayyad, and Bilal Alkaisi had accumulated $8,500 from a fraudulent check-cashing scheme—some of these funds would later be used to purchase the chemicals for the World Trade Center bomb. In mid-November 1992 Salameh and Yousef began to call chemical companies to get information on bomb-making materials. By the end of the month, utilizing a pseudonym, Salameh had rented a shed at the Space Station storage facility on Mallory Avenue in Jersey City. It cost $4,400.[56]

Ayyad used his position as an engineer at Allied Signal to order the necessary chemical ingredients for bomb making and to order hydrogen tanks from ALG Welding Company that would enhance the bomb's destructive force. Abouhalima obtained "smokeless powder," which the conspirators used to make explosives. Smokeless powder and all the other chemicals procured by the conspirators for the bomb were stored in the shed rented by Salameh.[57] On December 1, the men took delivery of 1,000 pounds of urea and 1,500 pounds of nitric acid from City Chemicals in Jersey City. By December 19, Yousef and Salameh began to investigate where they could acquire initiators, necessary for the explosives, and called a variety of chemical companies.[58] In early January, Yousef and Salameh moved into a new apartment on 40 Pamrapo Avenue in Jersey City, near Bayonne. By the end of the month, Yousef had arranged for chemical companies to deliver aluminum, magnesium, ferric oxide, and more nitric acid to their storage shed.[59]

On February 23, 1993, Salameh rented a yellow van at DIB Leasing, a Ryder dealership in Jersey City, with a cash deposit of $400.[60] On February 25, Salameh "took delivery of three tanks of compressed hydrogen—to be used as an accelerant in the explosion—at the Malory Avenue storage shed." These tanks were then subsequently assembled as part of the bomb later that afternoon at the apartment that he shared with Yousef. The next day the truck bomb would be driven into the World Trade Center parking lot in the Ryder truck.[61]

The Al Qaeda Factor

Materials taken from Ahmed Ajaj when he entered the country in 1992 with Ramzi Yousef indicated that "the plot or plots were hatched at or near the Khalden camp" in Afghanistan.[62] At the camp Ajaj and Yousef learned how to make bombs, discussed "bombing targets in the Untied States and assembled a 'terrorist kit' that included bomb-making manuals, operations guidance, videotapes advocating terrorist action against the United States, and false identification documents."[63] According to Khalid Sheikh Mohammed, he learned of Yousef's intention to launch an attack inside the United States in 1991 or 1992 when Yousef was receiving explosives training in Afghanistan.[64]

During the fall of 1992, while Yousef was building the bomb he would use in that attack, Khalid Sheikh Mohammed and Yousef had numerous telephone conversations during which Yousef discussed his progress. Khalid Sheikh Mohammed funded Yousef's efforts with a wire transfer of $660 on November 3, 1992, from Qatar to Salameh's bank account.[65] The bomb-making manual was an al Qaeda document. Two translations of the bomb-making manual that Ajaj brought with him from Pakistan to New York in September 1992 have a heading of "Al Qaeda." In addition, the document lists a publication date of 1989, a year after bin Laden founded al Qaeda, and the place of publication is Afghanistan.[66] Some investigators believe that a portion of the $20,000 that el Gabrowny raised from bin Laden for Nosair's defense was used to purchase material for the World Trade Center bomb.[67]

It would be inaccurate to claim that this was al Qaeda Core plot because neither Khalid Sheikh Mohammed nor Ramzi Yousef had sworn a formal oath of loyalty to bin Laden and al Qaeda. Nevertheless, the affinity of the Tradebom plotters' ideology and inspiration—jihad against the far enemy—which would become a core al Qaeda doctrine, provides an ideological linkage. Thus the plot be can classified as an al Qaeda "inspired" plot.

As an interesting postscript, the "Blind Sheikh" and his imprisonment in the United States has become a cause célèbre for al Qaeda, and Osama bin Laden, before his death, did declare that the death of the "Blind Sheikh," whenever it happens, should be avenged.

Chapter 12

Madrid Train System (March 11, 2004)

ON MARCH 11, 2004, between 7:37 and 7:42 A.M., a series of ten coordinated bomb explosions devastated the Cercanias (commuter train) system of Madrid, killing 191 people and wounding 1,841. All of the trains had been coming from Madrid's eastern suburbs toward the city center and Atocha train station. Although more than 100 people have been investigated in connection with the bombings, 29 were charged with participating in the terrorist attack, and of the 29, six were charged with 191 counts of murder and 1,755 counts of attempted murder. The active core of the cluster of individuals responsible for carrying out the March 11 attacks was primarily radicalized in Madrid.

The Salafi Jihadi Scene in Madrid

The Arab community in the 1990s in Madrid was led by individuals who had Muslim Brotherhood backgrounds and originated from Syria, seeking refuge after the Assad regime's crackdown. However, by nationality, the scene was dominated by Magrehbi Arabs from North Africa who came to Spain for economic opportunities. While some of these Moroccans, Algerians, and Tunisians worked at or owned small shops in Madrid, some were university students and others were involved in a trans-Mediterranean drug enterprise based on the import of hashish to Europe from Morocco and ecstasy to northern Europe.

One of the Syrians who played a leadership in the jihadist support scene in Madrid until his arrest in 2001 was Imad Eddin Barakat Yarkas, also known as Abu Dahdah. During the 1990s, Abu Dahdah organized a militant Salafi support network for jihadis fighting in or returning to Spain from Bosnia, Chechnya, and Afghanistan. Dahdah prayed at the M-30 Mosque in Madrid until approximately 1995, when he was expelled from the location for preaching violence. (The mosque was named "M-30" because of its proximity to Madrid's M-30 motorway.) His vocal support of jihadi causes as well as his international links to al Qaeda–associated individuals made him a central figure among those recruiting and indoctrinating for al Qaeda in Spain. The core members of this scene would play a critical role in the further radicalization of the Madrid bombers. Abu Dahdah had sent both funds and young men from Spain to al Qaeda training camps in Afghanistan. He was arrested after 9/11, accused of setting up the July 2001 meeting between Mohammed Atta and Ramzi bin al Shibh in Spain.[1]

A contingent of first-generation North African Muslim men in their late teens and early twenties, who generally had low levels of both formal education and occupational standing, gravitated into the orbit of Abu Dahdah. Some of these young men owned or managed small businesses while others were part-time workers there. Also in the mix were university students, who appeared to have promising futures, as well as a cluster who had criminal records in Spain for drug trafficking and other petty crimes. Regardless of their background, these men were provided with both tapes and books justifying jihad and romanticizing the cause of the mujahedeen overseas. Many of them led somewhat of a double life, having experimented with becoming "Westernized" (drinking alcohol, selling drugs, and womanizing) but at the same time gravitating to a mosque that hosted al Qaeda–linked individuals and promoted al Qaeda jihadist ideology.[2]

The network that developed around Abu Dahdah also had a social aspect. One witness noted that a regular part of this social scene was picnic outings at the Alberche River: "Since 2000 approximately, the witness has attended the meetings at the river; in 2001 he and fifteen more individuals gathered in one of those meetings. There, the witness realized that Amer Azizi was the most radical and respected of all. Azizi was the one who spoke to the people, encouraged them to join the Jihad in Afghanistan. Abu Dahdah was the other one who used to express his radical thoughts; he used to say 'instead of spending an euro in a coffee, you should give it for helping the Taliban regime.'" Not surprisingly, Amer Azizi, who had returned from training in Afghanistan in the summer of 2001, was a strong proponent of the jihad in Afghanistan and used these settings to tell "war stories" romanticizing jihad.[3]

After the arrest of Abu Dahdah and the flight of Amer Aziz, the scene moved to several neighborhood mosques in and around Madrid, including the Villaverde neighborhood on the outskirts of the city. At this point, Mustapha al Maymouni stepped into a leadership role.[4]

Gravitating to Reactionary Islam

Abu Dahdah's followers met in a variety of locations. "It was in mosques, worship sites, countryside gatherings and private residences where most of the members of the Madrid bombing network adopted extremist views." Furthermore, according to one witness, "It seems to be very clear that the meetings at the river were an important key in terms of recruiting and proselytism for the cause of the Jihad in Afghanistan. The leaders of the meetings were Imad Eddin Barakat Yarkas alias Abu Dahdah, and Amer Azizi alias Uthman al Andalusi. Other individuals, who attended the meetings, participated in the March 11th attacks: Serhane Ben Abdelmajid Fakhet, Basel Ghalyoun, Asrih Rifaat Anouar, Abdelnnabi Kounjaa, Mohamed Ouldad Akcha and Rachid Ouldad Akcha." Dahdah supplied tapes and books that provided religious legitimacy for jihad and thus reinforced the righteousness of the cause to the young men of immigrant neighborhood of Lavapies in Madrid. This contributed to the radicalization of a number of the men.[5]

One of the young men who was influenced by Abu Dahdah and Amer Aziz was Serhane Fakhet, a Tunisian university student. One witness noted that he started to radicalize once he came in contact with Amer Azizi in 2001 before the September 11 attacks. "The other individual who expressed his radical thoughts to the witness was Serhane [Fakhet], who agreed with all that Amer Azizi and Abu Dahdah said. Serhane attended the same meeting at the river."[6]

What preceded this radicalization was a combination of personal religious revival as well as circumstance that brought Serhane Ben Abdelmajid Fakhet to the M-30 Mosque and exposed him to Salafi Islam. When he was a university student in Madrid, Fakhet worked in the restaurant that is attached to the mosque and, as a result, sometimes went to the weekly religion class taught by the imam. His visits to the mosque increased after his religious pilgrimage to Mecca, Saudi Arabia, in 1998. According to Moneir Mahmoud Aly al Messery, the primary imam at the M-30 Mosque, "Then, for three or four years, I sensed that he [Fakhet] had some extremist thoughts. . . . He would ask telling questions, such as whether the imam believed that the leaders of the Arab countries were true believers, or if Islam authorized the use of force to spread the religion." In 2003 he married a sixteen-year-old Moroccan girl who, in true fundamentalist Wahhabi style, "veiled her face and dressed entirely in black, including gloves."[7]

Over time Fakhet evolved from student to teacher and ran some of the small group *halaqa* prayer/discussion sessions. This was noted by one of the protected witnesses: "The witness stated that at every meeting, Mustapha Maymouni was who sang the verses of the Jihad, and who decided that Mohamed Ouazzani should memorize the verses. Serhane [Fakhet] used to follow Maymouni in the talking, inviting the others to join the Jihad. He was serious, emotional and enthusiastic, to the point that he could make you cry. He mentioned the women who at the time of the prophet did the Jihad: if women did it, what kind of men they were if they didn't do at least the same. Then he talked with rage and strength: Algeria, Tunesia [*sic*], Morocco governed by infidels, there was no difference between them and the Christian and Jewish infidels, they were perhaps worse."[8]

Another young man who turned to Salafi Islam as part of his radicalization pathway was Jamal Zougam, who ran a profitable cell phone store in Madrid and had seemed to enjoy the pleasures of secular life in Madrid. A key catalyst for him was that his ties to Tangiers, Morocco, persisted (primarily to visit his father) and provided an introduction to fundamentalist Islam via local radicals in Tangiers. There he was exposed not only to Mohammed Fizazi, an extremist Moroccan imam who played a significant role in Zougam's radicalization to violence, but also to the three local Beniyach brothers, who were from Tangiers and all had direct links to overseas jihad and potentially al Qaeda. One Benaiyach brother died in Afghanistan fighting American forces in Tora Bora, another, who was a veteran of Bosnia and Chechnya, was arrested after the Casablanca bombings, and a third, who also was in Chechnya, was also arrested in Morocco.[9] In addition, Jamal Zougam and Abu Dahdah were very close, given that they both had commercial activities in the Lavapies neighborhood.[10]

Incarceration provided Jamal Ahmidan, a somewhat non-observant Moroccan who had been incarcerated for knifing someone almost ten years earlier, his full-fledged adoption of militant Islam. While he was in a Moroccan jail over the course of about two and a half years, he became fascinated by some of the inmates who were veterans of the Afghan jihad: "These jihadists used the prisons—a haven of disaffected men who are ripe for radicalization—for attracting future recruits." Ahmidan also became fascinated by their radical views.[11]

Ahmidan was released in 2000 and was wholly transformed—he had adopted jihadi-Salafi Islam. Upon his return to Spain, Ahmidan not only prayed the required five times a day but spoke incessantly about jihad and his desire to fight the Americans in Iraq. Although Ahmidan stopped drinking and using drugs following his transformation, he continued to sell drugs to non-Muslims, or unbelievers. His childhood friend Said Berraj may have introduced him to the Abu Dahdah circle.[12]

Politicization of New Beliefs

A protected witness for the Spanish prosecution underscored in his/her testimony the importance of the political element of the men's new beliefs, noting that

> during the meetings, Serhane [Fakhet], Mustapha Maymouni and Moutaz talked about the JIHAD as well as about the brothers in Palestine, Afghanistan and Iraq . . . as he was able to hear them talking about those issues given that the whole group was asking the Spaniard about the killings of their brothers in Palestina, Chechnya and Iraq. . . . The witness states that Serhane used to talk all the time about helping their brothers, using always the expression "brothers of the martyrs." They talked about themselves as brothers of the martyrs, referring to those who were dying in Chechnya, Afghanistan.[13]

The arrest of Imad Eddin Barakat Yarkas (Abu Dahdah) in 2001 by Spanish authorities, based on his links to the 9/11 attack, "inspired and infuriated the Tunisian [Fakhet]," noted a Spanish official familiar with the Madrid cluster. "He was the only one who kept insisting that the group had to do something in Spain. Why go to Afghanistan if you can fight jihad here?"[14]

Following Spain's participation in the 2003 Iraq War Coalition, Fakhet's activities became more radical, according to Spanish court documents: "During 2003, Fakhet spent considerable time cruising jihadi websites for ideas on terrorist attacks. Based on analysis of his computer's hard drive, Fakhet was specifically interested in the explosives used in both Bali and Casablanca."[15] Fakhet frequently watched politically themed graphic jihadi videos that highlighted supposed atrocities against Muslims worldwide and the righteousness of the mujahedeen's cause: "The scenes showed different places, and also a man with Chechnian clothes who dies as a martyr and is taken through some caves to be buried at night. At the beginning of the video, she could see three photos, one of Osama Bin Laden, another one of Ayman al Zawahiri, and a third one of an individual who was about to die and get buried as a martyr later. This third individual was wearing a red beard. Most of the people in the burial wore Afghan clothes."[16]

Another trial witness also cited the political videos, noting that a young Moroccan, "Mustapha Maymouni was attracted to the Jihad by Amer Azizi in collaboration with Imad Eddin Barakat Yarkas alias Abu Dahdah; the three of them were even watching videos related with Chechnya (and other places where the Jihad could possibly take place) at the residence of Amer Azizi. Abu Dahdah with Amer Azizi incited Mustapha Maymouni to join the Jihad." According to one witness, among the Lavapies cluster, it was Spain's participation in the war in Iraq that provided the justification to attack Spain. The witness noted that "given the perspectives of the conflict in Iraq, Spain had become an enemy of Islam, and then, it would be necessary to attack Spain."[17]

The Abu Dahdah Remnant Cluster

Following the arrest of Abu Dahdah by Spanish authorities and the flight from Spain by Amer Azizi in the wake of the 9/11 attacks, the new leaders who stepped into the void in this scene were the Moroccan, Mustapha al Maymouni, the Tunisian, Serhane Fakhet, and the Egyptian, Rabei Osman el Sayed Ahmed. This cluster of young men who originated from the Lavapies neighborhood of Madrid comprised primarily North African immigrants who had come to Europe seeking economic opportunity. The men were an odd mix of students and small business owners. Jamal Zougam and two other Moroccans, Mohammed Boutaliha and Zougam's half-brother Mohammed Chaoui, worked in a cell phone shop in the neighborhood. Lavapies was also where Serhane Fakhet and many Moroccans met at Abdelhouahid Berraj's barbershop to talk, drink holy water, and eat at the

Alhambra restaurant. However, by 2002, most of the action involving the major characters had moved out to the southern suburbs of Madrid.[18]

In addition to the Abu Dahdah Remnant Cluster,

> a group of delinquents led by Jamal Ahmidan appeared directly related with the March 11th attacks. . . . This group was completely new to the radical Islamic investigations, but well known for its delinquent activities, over which the UDYCO [Spanish authorities] from Madrid had an investigation running in reference to the band of Jamal Ahmidan. Lavapies was where Jamal Ahmidan reconnected with his childhood friends from Tetouan, Rachid and Mohammed Ouldad Akcha and Abdelnabbi Kounjaa. Together, they were part of a drug gang and network that was based in Madrid and linked Tetouan, Morocco, to Europe. Hashish was imported from Morocco and sold in Europe and brought ecstasy from northern Europe to southern Europe. Though the gang became devout in their religious observance, they justified their criminal activities as a means to an end—helping Islam.[19]

Based on a retrospective analysis of bills, shared apartments, cars, and telephones, by the fall of 2003 the Abu Dahdah Remnant Cluster and the Lavapies drug gang had merged. Nevertheless, there is one question that remains unanswered: How and when did Serhane Fakhet, Jamal Ahmidan, and their respective clusters meet?

Following the arrest of Abu Dahdah in the fall of 2001, the group began to coalesce around Rabei Osman El Sayed Ahmed, known to all as "Mohammed the Egyptian." He filled the void in Dahdah's absence and provided jihadi books and tapes to followers, including Serhane Fakhet, Basel Ghalyoun, and Fouad Amghar. This cluster, a splinter group from the M-30 Mosque, spent significant amounts of time watching jihadi videos.[20] The radicalization of the active core of conspirators in the Madrid attacks moved out of the mosque and into a variety of non-mosque locations in and around Lavapies, including Berraj's barbershop, Serhane Fakhet's apartment, and an unidentified store located in Lavapies where they "watched videos containing images of exercises in training camps, as well as images that exalted the value of the Jihad." They also began to spend more time in Villaverde, on the southern outskirts of Madrid. Mohammed Maymouni and Serhane Fakhet served as leaders among the group.[21]

Videos were also utilized to imbue in the men a shared sense of moral outrage against the West. For example, Muhannad Dabas's wife testified that they watched a video "in which several 'infidel' soldiers, from a foreigner country, could be seen; these Western soldiers were at a Muslim family house, the woman was veiled, and one could see how the soldiers forced members of this family to carry out horrible acts such as forcing the father to have intercourse with his daughter, and so on. In the videos, one could also see whole families lying on the ground and how a tank passed over them; in still another video one could see how they were buried in the desert sand, with just the head out and soldiers shooting at the heads. The voices in the video were inaudible and one could only hear the voice of a narrator. The witness affirms that it was not an old video judging by the uniforms they wore. The witness was very uneasy with those images."[22]

Mustapha al Maymouni was a Moroccan who had lived in Madrid and was a close associate of the Lavapies cluster, in particular Serhane Fakhet. In fact, Fakhet married his sixteen year-old sister. Maymouni was a known associate of Abu Dahdah and Amer Azizi before the November 2001 arrest of Abu Dahdah. According to one source, "After he disappearance of Abu Dahdah from the scene, al Maymouni maintained relations with other Moroccan jihadists in Madrid and Morocco who[m] he visited frequently." He intended to travel and fight in Afghanistan in 2002, but was unsuccessful in these efforts. In April 2003, Spanish police alerted judge Baltasar Garzon to the existence of an Islamist militant cell in Madrid led by Maymouni—this was the remnants of the Abu Dahdah group in Madrid and was composed mostly of Moroccans. However, he was arrested in the wake of the 2003 Casablanca attacks in Morocco and, as a result, was out of the picture significantly before the Madrid group went operational.[23]

Rabei Osman el Sayed Ahmed, age thirty-three at the time of the attack, was born in Egypt and was known as "Mohamed the Egyptian" to the men in Madrid. He had served in the Egyptian army and may have had some exposure to explosives during his service. He also had a degree in electronics from a technical school in Egypt. Though some have alleged that he was a member of Egyptian Islamic Jihad, was imprisoned in Egypt, and was a veteran jihadi who had fought in both Bosnia and Afghanistan, this has not been verified. In 1999, he came to Europe seeking asylum (claiming to be Palestinian) and, after passing through France and Germany, where he was detained, disappeared mysteriously and ended up in Madrid. He began attending Friday prayers at the M-30 Mosque in 2001, where he came in contact with many of the Madrid bombers. Following the arrest of Yarkas, for a brief period of time he took a leading role in the cluster among Serhane Fakhet, Basel Ghalyoun, and Fouad Amghar. However, he ultimately moved back to Italy and, as a result, was out of the picture before the Madrid group went operational.[24]

Anatomy of the Cluster

Active Core

Serhane ben Abdelmajid Fakhet, age thirty-five at the time of the attack, had been a promising Tunisian scholarship student who had come to Spain to study economics at Autonomous University of Madrid and who ultimately was considered an ideological leader of the cell. After growing up in a middle-class family in Tunis, Fakhet moved to Madrid in 1994, armed with €29,500 in Spanish-government scholarships to study economics. However, over the next few years Fakhet withdrew from school and the world in general. He was described as having become "incommunicative." (The exact nature of this personal crisis has not been disclosed.) As a consequence, Fakhet spent more and more time in the Salafi mosques and was only interested in talking about Islam and the misery of the world.[25] Nevertheless, Fakhet lived somewhat of a double life as a real-estate agent whose boss told the Spanish press that he was a "wonderful salesman," and held the record for the number of apartments sold in a month. However, he was solitary, avoiding his coworkers and "remained sequestered in his Muslim world."[26]

Fakhet had tried out the evangelical Islamic group Tablighi Jamaat before he switched to Salafi Islam and began to be a regular among Abu Dahdah's group at the M-30 Mosque. Over time, Fakhet took a leadership role in the group. This position solidified after the arrest of Mustapha Maymouni in Morocco after the Casablanca attacks in 2003.[27]

Jamal Ahmidan, age thirty-four at the time of the attack, was born in Tetouan, Morocco, a poor town in northern Morocco. He had departed from Tetouan in 1993 for Madrid as part of an attempt to evade arrest after killing an associate in an attempted robbery. He followed his brother, who owned a small shop in the immigrant neighborhood of Lavapies, and subsequently became heavily involved in drugs, specifically heroin.[28]

In 1995, while running a small-time heroin gang in and around Madrid, Ahmidan decided to "kick his drug habit." A religious awakening helped him beat his addiction and, subsequently, he helped brothers from his hometown of Tetouan who were similarly addicted overcome their addiction. The Oulad Akcha brothers would forever be in his debt. In spite of his religious awakening, he continued running his drug business with the mind-set that selling drugs to infidels was acceptable. In 2000, Ahmidan was arrested for selling false documents in Madrid but soon escaped from the detention center.[29] On a trip to Morocco to visit family, he was re-arrested and had to serve two and a half years in jail for the murder he had committed in 1993. There he was further exposed to radical Islam by veterans of the jihad in Afghanistan that the Moroccan government had detained for subversive activities. Ahmidan emerged from prison as a changed man in 2003 and subsequently returned to Madrid.[30]

Back in Spain, Ahmidan led a double life. Though he had adopted jihadi ideology, Ahmidan returned to his drug-dealing ways and seemed well integrated in secular Spanish society as his Spanish friends included women who sported crop tops, tattoos, and piercings. At the same time he began to socialize with childhood friends from Tetouan, including Rachid and Mohammed Ouldad and Abdennabi Kounjaa and began to attend services at the M-30 Mosque. He became the head of an ecstasy and hashish network that was run by close family members based in both Morocco and Spain. He was given the nickname "El Chino" (the Chinese).[31]

Followers

Jamal Zougam, age thirty-one at the time of the attack, was born in Tangiers, Morocco, and had lived in Spain since 1983. According to one source, "He and his half-brother Mohammed Chaoui had opened up their own mobile phone shop. Jamal Zougam was described as handsome, likable and one of the more popular youths among the Moroccan community living in Madrid. He enjoyed alcohol, women, and discos and seemed to be perfectly integrated into Spanish society." In 2001 he stabbed a man for ostensibly religious reasons—attempting to bring a dog into the Alhambra restaurant in Lavapies.[32]

Within the cluster, Zougam had some of the most extensive ties to militant Islamists in Europe and Morocco. Not only was he close to Imad Eddin Barakat Yarkas, but Zougam had also offered financial aid to Mohamed Fizazi, a fiery militant Moroccan imam who was known to travel throughout Europe delivering sermons supporting violent jihad against the West.[33]

Allekema Lamari, age thirty-nine at the time of the attack, was born in Algeria and trained as an architect's assistant/engineer. He came to Spain and worked for five years picking vegetables in a small rural village in Navarre. Lamari was arrested in Spain in 1997 and sent to prison for belonging to the Algerian GIA (Armed Islamic Group). He spent six years in prison (two in Alcalá-Meco) and was set free in July 2002. "After coming out of prison, Allekema Lamari—already cold and very religious—presented a more fanatic profil [sic]. He was solitary, cautious, ideologically uncontrolled and dangerous. . . . . This radicalization and resentment towards Spain have made that since his coming out of prison his only objective is— as he declared to his closest circles—to carry out, on the national territory, terrorist attacks of great magnitude with the purpose of causing the largest number of victims possible. He also commented the possibility of materializing this threat with train derailments or big fires." He had been released in 2002 from jail in a case of mistaken identity and returned in October 2003 to Madrid, where he knew Mohammed Afalah.[34]

Youssef Belhadj, age twenty-seven at the time of the attack, was born in Tousine, Morocco, and had radicalized and in lived in Molenbeek near Brussels and adopted the GICM (Moroccan Islamic Combat Group) ideology. He had frequent phone connections with another individual involved in the Madrid plot, Abdelmajid Bouchar, a year prior to the Madrid attack. He fled the Leganés safe house in Madrid before Spanish authorities surrounded it; he was arrested in Belgium in February 2005. The authorities believe he is Abu Dujana al Afghani—the "al Qaeda leader in Europe's" purported spokesman who claimed responsibility for the Madrid attacks on a videotape days after the attacks.[35]

Said Berraj, age twenty-one at the time of the attack, was born in Tangiers and ran a barbershop in the Lavapies neighborhood in Madrid. In 2000, Beraj was detained in Turkey with Amer Azizi on their way to Afghanistan to train with al Qaeda. The men were subsequently released without being charged. Following Berraj's trip to Saudi Arabia on hajj, Moroccans in the Lavapies neighborhood frequented his location to drink holy water, making his shop a locus of activity in the community. Berraj was said to be involved with men who had links to GICM and was also in close contact with Serhane Farkhet and Basel Ghalyoun in Madrid.[36]

Mohammed Chaoui, age thirty-three at the time of the attack, was born in Tangiers and was Jamal Zougam's half-brother. He had immigrated to Spain with Zougam's mother in 1983. Chaoui opened up a mobile phone equipment shop in Lavapies with Zougam and another Moroccan in 2000.[37]

Basel Ghalyoun, age twenty-four at the time of the attack, was born in Homs, Syria, and came to Spain in the late 1990s for engineering studies. He lived in Madrid in the Lavapies suburb in the same flat with Mohannad Almallah Dabas and another student, a Moroccan, Fouad el Morabit Anghar. Ghalyoun had been involved in Abu Dahdah's cell for some time. He was supposedly well-known to Spanish authorities. Following Dahdah's arrest, he gravitated to Rabei Osman el Sayed Ahmed. Ghalyoun worked at a cell phone company. His apartment served as a locus for the group meetings prior to the March 11 attack. Ghalyoun testified that Fakhet began to "talk of carrying out an attack in Spain, making jihad," at these meetings.[38]

Abdelmajid Bouchar, age thirty-one at the time of the attack, was born in Ait Lahcen Oualla, Morocco, and was a local track champion. Witnesses claimed to have seen him leaving one of the bombed trains. Bouchar fled on foot when Spanish authorities approached the Leganés safe house. He was arrested in Belgrade in August 2005.[39]

Mohannad Almallah Dabas, age thirty at the time of the attack, was born in Damascus, Syria. Dabas had obtained Spanish citizenship, resided in Madrid, and hosted meetings in his house for the purpose of assisting members of al Maymouni's group. Cluster members Basel Ghalyoum and Fouad el Morabit lived at his house.[40]

Fouad el Morabit Anghar, age thirty-one at the time of the attack, was born in Nador-Mar, Morocco, and came to Spain to study aeronautical engineering. He became a follower of "Mohammed the Egyptian" and lived with fellow student Basel Ghalyoun on Calle Virgen.[41]

Mohammed Larbi ben Sellam, age twenty-seven at the time of the attack, was born in Tangiers. He attended the meetings at Ghalyoun's apartment, which served as a locus for the group meetings prior to the March 11 attack.

Hassan el-Haski, age forty-two at the time of the attack, was born in Geuelmin, Morocco, and was considered a leader of the GICM in Europe even before the attacks of March 11, 2004. He had lived in Belgium before he moved to Spain. El-Haski saved e-mails as drafts on accounts he shared with other members of the cluster: "They all knew the password and so they could access the accounts to read his comments and post replies."[42]

Mohammed Belhadj, age twenty-eight at the time of the attack, was born in Tousine, Morocco. He rented the apartment in Leganés where the seven terrorists blew themselves up. He fled to Syria, where he was arrested in 2007.[43]

Mohammed Afalah, age thirty-four at the time of the attack, was from Ighmiren, Morocco. He was not at the Leganés apartment when it was raided, and there is strong evidence that Mohammed Afalah became a suicide bomber in Iraq. He is believed to have driven a car packed with explosives into an Iraqi army checkpoint in Baghdad's Doura neighborhood on May 19, 2005, killing one soldier and injuring another eight.[44]

Abdelilah Hriz, age twenty-six at the time of the attack, was from Morocco. He was charged with engaging in activities relating to facilitating travel for extremists who sought to go to Iraq to fight coalition forces.[45]

Saed El Harrak, age twenty-nine at the time of the attack, was born in Beni Guerfet, Morocco.[46]

Hicham Temsamani Jad, who was in his thirties at the time of the March 11 attack, was a Moroccan from Tetouan who served as an imam in Toledo, Spain, who spent time with the men in Toledo, outside of Madrid, and in Lavapies. He also served as a religious authority, officiating at the water rites and prayers held at Berraj's barbershop, as well as a mentor to Serhane Fakhet. He was arrested after the 2003 Casablanca attacks and for his potential involvement in a plot to blow up a refinery in France.[47]

Rachid Ouldad Akcha, age thirty-four at the time of attack, was born in Tetouan, Morocco, came from a secular family, and was a childhood friend of Jamal Ahmidan, who helped him overcome his addiction to heroin through a religious awakening. Rachid was involved in Ahmidan's drug business in Madrid.[48]

Mohammed Ouldad Akcha, age twenty-eight at the time of attack, was born in Tetouan, Morocco, came from a secular family, and was a key Ahmidan deputy as well as a childhood friend of Jamal Ahmidan, who helped him overcome his addiction to heroin through a religious awakening. Mohammed was involved in Ahmidan's drug business in Madrid.[49]

Abdennabi Kounjaa, age twenty-four at the time of the attack, and originally from Tetouan, Morocco, had grown up secular in Morocco but was attracted to both Tablighi Jamaat and Salafi Islam before leaving Morocco. Following his arrival in Madrid in 2002, he became involved in the Oulad Akchas drug gang while Ahmidan was in prison in Morocco.[50]

Periphery

Hamid Ahmidan, age twenty-seven at the time of the attack, was born in Tetouan, Morocco, and was arrested two weeks after the attacks with 20 kilograms of drugs. He was Jamal Ahmidan's cousin.[51]

Rachid Aglif, age twenty-five at the time of the attack, was born in Khouribga, Morocco, but had come to Spain with his father as a ten-year-old and attended local schools in Madrid. He radicalized after the invasion of Iraq and was a member of Ahmidan's gang. Aglif worked in his family's halal butcher shop in the Lavapies neighborhood.[52]

Otman El Gnaoui, age twenty-eight at the time of the attack, was born in Tetouan, Morocco, and radicalized after the invasion of Iraq in 2003. According to some, he was a close associate of Jamal Ahmidan and was involved in the transportation of the Goma-2 dynamite for the attack.[53]

Abdelilah El Fadoual El Takil, age twenty-four at the time of the attack, was born in Tetouan, Morocco.

Rafa Zouheir, age twenty-four at the time of the attack, was born in Casablanca and was an associate of Jamal Ahmidan. He had been arrested and imprisoned for jewelry theft in September 2001. In prison he met Antonio Castro Toro and Jose Emilio Suarez Trashorras, who were miners but had been arrested for dealing drugs. The relationship between Zouheir and Suarez and Toro ultimately was the linkage that enabled the Ahmidan group to acquire the Goma-2 dynamite for the attack. Zouheir had worked for the Spanish authorities as an informant for a period of time.[54]

Asri Rifaat Anouar, age twenty-four at the time of the attack, was born in Tetouan, Morocco. His mother passed away when he was young; he was raised by his father and stepmother. When he arrived in Madrid in 2002 he initially worked as a candy vendor. When he began to explore religion, he met Basel Ghalyoun, an associate of Serhane Fakhet. This may have been the link between Fakhet's group and Ahmidan's group. Anouar, a member of Ahmidan's gang, was suspected of placing the explosive device on the AVE high-speed rail tracks.[55]

Mohamed Bouharrat, age twenty-four at the time of the attack, was born in Tangiers, Morocco, and was allegedly responsible for recruitment and gathering information on targets.[56]

Nasreddine Bousbaa, age thirty-two at the time of the attack, was born in Constantine, Algeria. He was allegedly involved in document forgery.[57]

Mahmoud Slimane Aoun, age forty at the time of the attack, was born in Beirut, Lebanon. He was allegedly involved in document forgery.[58]

Mohamed Moussaten, age twenty-three at the time of the attack, was born in Khababa, Morocco, and had been suspected of helping fugitives (his uncle Mohamed Belhadj and Mohammed Afalah) to flee Spain after the attacks.[59]

Jose Emilio Suarez Trashorras, age twenty-seven at the time of the attack, of Spain, was responsible for leading the miner/drug gang that exchanged dynamite stolen from the Conchita mine for hasish.[60]

Overseas Travel and Link Up with Al Qaeda

Before 9/11, Abu Dahdah's network facilitated travel for young men in Spain who sought to train or fight in Afghanistan. Nevertheless, none of the men directly associated with the March 11 attack traveled there or to Chechnya for training. However, one of the most well-known individuals who had traveled between Afghanistan and Madrid before 9/11 was Amer Azizi, who had fought in the jihad in Bosnia in 1995 and subsequently settled in Madrid and married a Spanish woman. Azizi knew both Jamal Zougam and Serhane Fakhet; his cell phone number was found on both of their phones. In the fall of 2001, following the attacks of 9/11, Azizi escaped from Spain to Afghanistan as he was about to be arrested. He reportedly left Spain dressed as a woman with the passport of Mohannad Almallah (but with a different photo); he went to London first and then to Afghanistan.[61]

Al Qaeda Recruitment

There is no hard evidence to support an operational link or recruitment among the Madrid cluster by the al Qaeda organization. Most hypotheses that have sought to link the attack to al Qaeda operationally cite Amer Azizi as the potential link. Though he left Spain in November 2001, some researchers and officials believe that he is the missing link between the Madrid perpetrators and al Qaeda Core. This theory cites a report claiming that Azizi's fingerprints were found at the house in Chincon, where the bombs were assembled, and speculates that he snuck in and out of Spain just before the attacks to manage the operation. However, this report has not been substantiated.[62]

The *Los Angeles Times* reported that a senior Spanish official said, "There are people who have seen Azizi in Spain after the attacks. It looks like he came back and may have directed the others. If he was here, his background would make it likely that he was the top guy. We have reliable witness accounts that he was here in significant places connected to the plot. The idea of Azizi as a leader has become more solid."[63] Adding additional support to this hypothesis was a Reuters story citing a FBI report that Abu Musab al Suri had dispatched Azizi in December 2003 to play the role of operational supervisor.[64]

The Spanish professor Fernando Reinares cites the deaths of Amer Azizi and Hamza Rabia, al Qaeda's Chief of External Operations, together in a Hellfire strike from a Predator drone in December 2005 in Pakistan as further proof of Azizi's likely links to al Qaeda Core and thus direction of the plot in Madrid by al Qaeda Core. Intriguingly, he notes that according to a court witness, "Azizi and 'The Tunisian' had 'frequent contacts' and communicated by e-mail in 2002 and 2003," thus raising the possibility that Azizi tasked Fakhet with carrying out the Madrid plot via e-mail.[65] Nevertheless, in spite of all of these theories and circumstantial data, the findings of the Spanish High Court was that there was no operational link to al Qaeda.

Operational Cycle

Rather than direction from al Qaeda, the primary catalyst that pushed the Madrid group to commit violence seems to have been the anonymous posting on December 10, 2003, of a document called *Jihadi Iraq: Hopes and Dangers: Practical Steps for the Blessed Jihad* on the Global Islamic Media, a popular jihadi Web site. The forty-two-page document discusses ways to defeat the U.S. occupation of Iraq. Its strategy was to leave the United States with the complete financial burden for the occupation, which eventually would result in its withdrawal. The way to accomplish this goal was to politically force U.S. allies to withdraw from Iraq.

Once the Madrid group committed to violence in December 2003, they scrambled to acquire the capability to launch the attack.[66] *Jihadi Iraq* was also found in Serhane Fakhet's computer and is believed to have influenced the timing of the attack. The document called for a campaign of bombings, shortly before the March 14, 2004, general elections. The bombings would bring about a change of government, which would then order the withdrawal of Spanish troops from Iraq.[67]

Therefore we say that in order to force the Spanish government to withdraw from Iraq, the resistance should deal painful blows to its forces. This should be accompanied by an information campaign clarifying the truth of the matter inside Iraq. It is necessary to make utmost use of the upcoming general election in Spain in March next year. We think that the Spanish government could not tolerate more than two, maximum three blows, after which it will have to withdraw as a result of popular pressure.[68]

Logistics

Rafa Zouheir introduced the Ahmidan gang to a group of drug-dealing miners (Antonio Toro, Emilio Trashorras, and Carmen Toro-Trashorras) who had access to Goma-2 dynamite from the Conchita mine. This first meeting, also attended by Jamal Ahmidan, Mohamed Oulad Akcha, and Rached Aglif, in September 2003 in a McDonald's restaurant in Madrid would ultimately lead to the acquisition of the dynamite used for the attacks. At this meeting, the concept of trading hashish for dynamite was discussed.[69]

It is believed that after the posting on December 10, 2003, of *Jihadi Iraq* the plot began to coalesce and Ahmidan accelerated the exchange of hashish for Goma-2 dynamite with the miners.[70] At his legal hearing on June 15, 2004, sixteen-year-old Gabriel Montoya Vidal, who worked for the miner/drug gang, testified that the first shipment of Goma-2 dynamite took place during the first week of January 2004. Sergio Alvarez Sanchez traveled from Aviles to Madrid on a commercial bus with a suitcase containing about 15 to 20 kilograms of dynamite in exchange for 400 grams of hashish (street value of a little more than $1,600). The second shipment was done by "Jimmy," another youth from Aviles, using the same method, a few weeks later.[71]

On January 28, Jamal Ahmidan rented a house near Chinchon to store hashish and the dynamite and to build the bombs. It is unclear who came to the house besides Ahmidan, his cousin Hamid, the Oulad Akcha brothers, Zougam, Gnaout, Morabit, Ghalyoun, Fakhet, Kounjaa, and Anouar. Gabriel Montoya Vidal carried the third shipment at the beginning of February. He got the fifteen- to twenty-kilogram bag from Trashorras's home. In Madrid, Montoya went to a bar opposite the bus stop, called a number, identified himself as the "Asturian," and was told to wait there. Half an hour later, Jamal Ahmidan called him from across the street and took the shipment in his car.[72] On February 27, 2004, the same individuals who had attended the initial fall 2003 meeting met at a McDonald's in Madrid. At this meeting, they agreed to accelerate the shipments, which would total 200 kilograms of dynamite for approximately 35 kilograms of hashish (30 kilograms and 7,000 euros). On the same day, Ahmidan and his gang stole a Renault Kangoo minivan for the operation.[73]

On February 28, Jamal Ahmidan, Mohamed Oulad Akcha, and Abdennabi Kounjaa all traveled to the Conchita mine to acquire the final shipments of Goma-2 dynamite. Between midnight and noon the next day, the men brought two rucksacks each out of the mine. Gabriel Montoya Vidal served as the facilitator for the Moroccans.[74] On March 3 and 4, Jamal Zougam bought twenty "hot" cell phones from two Indian merchants in Madrid, and two days later Abdelnabbi Kounjaa and Rifaat Anouar Asrih rented a safehouse in Granada. On March 6, they rented an apartment in Leganés. The cost of this Madrid operation was $54,000 to $71,000, funded completely by the sale of illegal drugs.[75]

Communications

According to the wife of Muhannad Dabas, an associate of the men from the Lavapies cluster, the men utilized a variety of techniques to mask their communications. For example, they did not "use their own telephones, but public telephones such as telephone booths or restaurant phones. She knows this because she heard them many times telling an interlocutor that they were going to call again from outside, and then they would go to a telephone booth in the neighborhood and call again; those were called 'green telephones' and they would use many phone cards."[76]

Text messaging was also a very important mode of communication among the men. Telephone records analyzed retrospectively confirm this.[77] Hassan el Haski also saved e-mails as drafts on accounts he shared with other members of the cluster.[78]

Target Selection/Casing

There is little evidence that the men cased their targets before they attacked the Madrid rail system. However, they had lived in Madrid for some time and likely knew the system quite well. When the police went through the debris from the destroyed apartment in Leganés, they found indication of future targets, which included the Madrid Lerida high-speed train line, a bilingual primary school, a Jewish recreational center outside Madrid, a Jewish hostel in Avila, and a marketplace, to be hit during the Easter holidays.[79]

Weaponization

As discussed earlier, Jamal Ahmidan, Mohamed Oulad Akcha, and Abdennabi Kounjaa acquired the final shipments of Goma-2 dynamite during February 28–29. On March 3 and 4, Jamal Zougam purchased twenty stolen Mitsubishi Trium T-110 cell phones to serve as detonators.[80]

It is possible that Rabei Osman el Sayed Ahmed had provided training to the men in Madrid on how to create the phone-activated triggers for the explosive devices.[81] In Milan, where he took on other disciples after he left Madrid in early 2004, he trained one of them on how to activate mobile phones via computer, "focusing specifically on software with which a user can send the same text message to a number of previously selected mobile phones." In fact, the Egyptian introduced his disciple to "Oxygen Phone Manager 2," a program specifically designed to control the functions of a Nokia phone. The phones used in Madrid to detonate the bombs were Nokia phones.[82]

There are a few other theories on how the devices may have been built. One theory is that Serhane Fakhet built the devices, just as he had downloaded tactical information on how to make bombs and how to use cell phones as detonators. Another argues that Jamal Zougam, as an individual familiar with cell phones, may also have been able to build the devices. Finally, the miner/drug gang members who were familiar with explosives may have taught the conspirators how to build the devices.

Thirteen bombs were made consisting of ten kilograms of Goma-2 dynamite surrounded by nails and screws. The detonators were connected to cell phones. Two did not explode. Basel Ghalyoun Abdennabi Kounjaa and Jamal Zougam put bombs in the trains. Another bomb was created with twenty-six pounds of Goma-2 dynamite that was placed on the high speed AVE train line, but it was wired incorrectly and discovered on April 2, 2004.[83]

The Al Qaeda Factor

As the Spanish researcher Javier Jordan notes, "The revised question then becomes whether Serhane's group devised the plan and sought comment, or asked permission from members of al Qaeda's European network, or conversely al Qaeda suggested it to him and his group." While the bombers may have been inspired by Osama bin Laden, a two-year investigation into the attacks by Spanish authorities has found no evidence that al Qaeda helped plan, finance, or carry out the bombings, or even knew about them in advance, according to state prosecutor Olga Sanchez. Furthermore, Spanish judge Juan del Olmo believed that "local cells of Islamic extremists inspired through the Internet" were guilty of perpetrating the March 11 attacks.[84] Nevertheless, a number of hypotheses exist surrounding just who was responsible for the attacks.

A number of claims of responsibility were made in the aftermath of the March 11 attacks: on the evening of March 11, the London office of the well-known Arabic daily newspaper *Al Quds al Arabi* received an e-mail from the Abu Hafs al Masri Brigades, a group claiming affiliation with al Qaeda, claiming responsibility for the attack: "The squadron of death has managed to penetrate the heart of Crusader Europe, striking one of the pillars of the Crusaders and their allies, Spain, with a painful blow. This is part of an old game with Crusader Spain, ally of America in its war against Islam."[85] The e-mail mimicked the way messages had previously been sent by al Qaeda to the newspaper and as a result, it was seen as a legitimate al Qaeda communiqué and was made public immediately.[86]

On the Saturday night after the attack, March 13, a television station in Madrid received a call from a man speaking Spanish with a Moroccan accent who said that a videotape had been placed in a trash bin near the M-30 Mosque. In the video, a man wearing a hood and dressed in white holding a Sterling assault rifle read a statement: "We declare our responsibility for what has occurred in Madrid, exactly two and a half years after the attacks on New York and Washington." The speaker identified himself as Abu Dujan al Afghani, "the military spokesman for Al Qaeda in Europe." He continued, "It is a response to your collaboration with the criminal Bush and his allies. You love

life and we love death, which gives an example of what the Prophet Muham-
mad said. If you don't stop your injustices, more and more blood will flow."[87]

At six o'clock in the evening on April 3, three hours after the start of
the Leganés siege, a handwritten fax in Arabic, signed by Abu Dujan al
Afghani, arrived at *ABC*, a conservative daily in Madrid. Referring to the
bomb found beside the AVE tracks the day before, the author argues that it
failed to explode because "our objective was only to warn you and show you
that we have the power and capacity, with the permission of Allah, to attack
you when and how we want." The letter demanded that Spain withdraw its
troops from both Iraq and Afghanistan by the following Sunday. Otherwise,
"we will turn Spain into an inferno and make your blood flow like rivers."[88]

These claims of responsibility did not clarify the origins of the plot.
Though Amer Azizi left Spain in November 2001, some researchers and officials believe that he is the missing link between the Madrid perpetrators
and al Qaeda Core. He was a veteran of the jihad in Bosnia, had trained in al
Qaeda's camps in Afghanistan, and had been indicted in Spain for helping
plan the September 11 attacks and for being a senior member of al Qaeda.
Up until he left Spain he had been very involved with the Lavapies cluster,
frequenting the M-30 Mosque, Alhambra restaurant, and Berraj's barbershop and knew Eddin Barakat Yarkas, Jamal Zougam, and Serhane Fakhet.

This theory cites a report that Azizi's fingerprints were found at the
house in Chincon, where the bombs were assembled, and speculates that he
snuck in and out of Spain just before the attacks to manage the operation.[89]
Reports from the *Los Angeles Times* and Reuters also presented evidence
that support this theory.[90]

Aziz's death alongside al Qaeda's Chief of External Operations, Hamza
Rabia, in Pakistan in December 2005 was cited as further circumstantial
proof of Azizi's likely links to al Qaeda Core.[91] However, al Qaeda's leaders
did not rush to take credit for the Madrid bombings; Osama bin Laden first
mentioned them a month later in an audio recording. It took until November 2005 before Ayman al Zawahiri alluded to the March 11 attacks in a
video praising the suicide bombings of July 7, 2005, in London.[92] Ultimately,
"evidence from the pretrial hearings, the trial itself, interviews with the perpetrators, as well as police and intelligence agents strongly suggest that al
Qaeda Core had nothing to do with the plot at any time."[93]

In the ruins of the apartment building in Leganés, police found the
shredded remains of a videotape. It was the final statement of Fakhet and
two other members of the cell, which called itself "the brigade situated in

Al Andalus." Unless Spanish troops left Iraq within a week, the men had declared, "we will continue our jihad until martyrdom in the land of Tariq ibn Ziyad." In addition, Fakhet referred to the Spanish occupation of Al Andalus (Spain), which began in 1492 with Ferdinand and Isabella's reconquest of Spain from the Moors: "You know of the Spanish crusade against Muslims, and that not much time has passed since the expulsion from Al Andalus and the tribunals of the Inquisition. Blood for blood. Destruction for destruction!"[94]

According to Spanish intelligence reports, "Given his height, corpulence, voice tone, expressions and emphasis put in the reading of the communiqué, the person in the center of the video image has been identified, with a high probability, as Allekema Lamari."[95] Further supporting the hypothesis that this was an autonomous attack planned to affect the Spanish elections was Jamal Zougam's first question when he emerged at court after being held incommunicado for five days: "Who won the elections?"[96]

On the one-year anniversary of the attacks a senior Spanish counterterrorism official told the *New York Times*, "There are many questions that remain unclear. The most important is: Who masterminded March 11?"[97] Nevertheless, based on the evidence available to this researcher, the most likely scenario is that, as the Spanish High Court judge Juan del Olmo noted, it was "local cells of Islamic extremists inspired through the Internet" who were guilty of carrying out the March 11 attacks, and thus it was an al Qaeda "inspired" plot.

Chapter 13

Hofstad Group Plots (Netherlands, 2004–5)

DURING A TWO-YEAR period between October 2003 and October 2005, police and security services in the Netherlands conducted a series of arrests of second-generation young men and women, primarily of Moroccan heritage and Dutch citizenship, on terrorist charges. The most notorious arrests were in the direct aftermath of the assassination of Theo van Gogh in central Amsterdam on the morning of November 2, 2004, by Mohammad Bouyeri. Bouyeri shot van Gogh several times, slit his throat, and attempted to decapitate him before he impaled letters into van Gogh's body explaining his actions, calling for jihad and the fall of the United States, Europe, and the Netherlands. However, there were at least three other inchoate plots involving political assassinations as well as potential attacks on Schiphol Airport, a nuclear power plant, the Dutch police, and the headquarters of the Dutch General Intelligence and Security Service (AIVD) that were disrupted by arrests. The loose cluster of men and women who were responsible for these plots targeting the Netherlands were called the Hofstad Group.

The Salafi Scene in the Netherlands

The Dutch Muslim community primarily comprises two major nationalities: approximately 350,000 individuals of Turkish origin and 300,000 individuals of Moroccan descent. The Moroccan community resides primarily in major Dutch cities and has had some difficulty integrating into Dutch society and culture. This community traces its roots in the Netherlands to the 1960s when many emigrated from Morocco for economic reasons, arriving as temporary guest workers. More than 90 percent of the Moroccan population is of Berber heritage. Most of the emigrants came from the Rif region of Morocco and were not well educated. According to Dutch police officials, second-generation Moroccans are five to six times more likely to be involved in crime than other Dutch citizens.[1]

Transnational Saudi Arabian efforts to propagate literalist Wahhabi Islam has played a significant role in the Netherlands in providing a religious infrastructure for the growing Moroccan population. Beginning in the 1980s, the Saudis, via non-governmental organizations (NGOs), established Wahhabi-oriented mosques in the major cities of the Netherlands, including the el Tawheed Mosque (Amsterdam), the al Fourkan Mosque (Eindhoven), and the As-Soennah Mosque (The Hague). Moreover, the imams who preached at these locations promoted a hard-line Wahhabi/Salafi message that rejected secular Dutch society. While this message had limited appeal to first-generation Moroccans, who brought their own traditions with them to the Netherlands, the marginalized second-generation of Moroccan Dutch youth was vulnerable to this message of "pure Islam."[2]

Gravitating to Reactionary Islam

The individual members of the Hofstad cluster relied heavily on their own personal research as the early drivers for their initial adoption of a militant Islamic world view. Nevertheless, there were a few primary locations where individuals in the cluster solidified these religious views, including the three mosques mentioned above that promoted the austere Wahhabi/Salafi interpretation of Islam. The imams at some of these locations praised suicide bombers and sold literature that advocated killing homosexuals. Later on, the cell phone shop in Schiedam and then Mohammed Bouyeri's apartment in Amsterdam became sites of regular religious "living room meetings." There, young men deepened their knowledge of radical Islam and discussed the concept of jihad.[3]

Following Bouyeri's seven months in prison in 2001 and his mother's death, he became more devout in his religious observance. He began frequenting the el Tawheed Mosque and changed his dress from jeans and sneakers to a jelabiya and skull cap. Moreover, while his earlier writings in the *Over the Field* journal emphasized "tolerance and respect," his newer writings noted that devotion to Islam was the ultimate ideal—more important than racial, political, national, ideological, and material matters.[4] By the end of 2001, Bouyeri was displaying signs that he had adopted a fundamentalist interpretation of Islam: he grew a beard, began to wear traditional Islamic clothing, and was engrossed in studying Islamic scripture. By the spring of 2002, Bouyeri began to distribute his own anti-Semitic and anti-Dutch pamphlets outside the el Tawheed Mosque.[5]

During the sessions in Bouyeri's apartment, Ridouan al Issar was frequently the speaker. The AIVD noted in the spring of 2003 "that within this network [Hofstad] a leader [Ridouan al Issar] is making himself known." The AIVD further noted that in locations in and outside Amsterdam the network frequently met "to listen to radical sermons of a preacher. He has a charismatic appearance and has a lot of influence on youngsters in the network who are looking for identity and meaning. They are given answers in the form of religious interpretation and leadership. This way the participants reinforce their radical Islamic ideas. In this context the subject of violent 'jihad' is often brought up."[6] However, over time, when al Issar was not available, Bouyeri often led the sessions, and he would ultimately surpass al Issar in stature among the group.

In July 2004, Bouyeri translated and posted work from the fourteenth-century author Ibn Taymiyyah on the Internet on Web sites where others would see it. He used this text as the ideological legitimization to kill people who "fight Islam in the Netherlands" and who insult the prophet Mohammed. On the basis of this document Bouyeri considered the murder of van Gogh a religious duty.[7] The adoption of this set of beliefs was not limited by any means to just Bouyeri. Other witnesses at the main Hofstad trial noted that a leading member of the Hofstad Group, Nourredine el Fatmi, often talked about the religious doctrines that underpinned jihadist issues. This included *takfir,* the act of excommunicating and denouncing moderate Muslims as apostates who should be killed. In addition, Sara Pastoors testified that the men talked a lot about "Tawheed" (unity of G-d), "Takfir," "Taghut" (following idols), and jihad.[8]

Politicization of New Beliefs

Activism on behalf of the Palestinian cause was an important initial activity for a number of the men and women who would come to be involved in the Hofstad Group. Later, as the group jelled and the prayer and discussion circles came to be held in Bouyeri's apartment, they took on more overt political overtones as the men watched videos about mujahedeen in Iraq and Chechnya and listened to tapes of speeches promoting the legitimacy of killing non-Muslims. Bouyeri also promoted highly politicized views of Islam on the Internet and in his writings.[9]

Samir Azzouz, his wife, Abida Kabaj, and Martine van den Oever were all initially involved in the activist Muslim scene in the Netherlands via their pro-Palestinian activism. For Samir Azzouz and Abida Kabaj, it was in response to the Second Intifada, which began in 2000, and for Martine van den Oever, it was via humanitarian groups such as the Al Aqsa Foundation and the Jerusalem Foundation.[10] The articles that Bouyeri would write for the community center, where he volunteered, became increasingly more radical as his religious and political views became intertwined. In early 2002, Bouyeri was writing about tolerance and mutual respect, but by April 2003 he was comparing the Dutch police to Nazis and calling for American soldiers in Iraq to be beheaded. By mid-2003 his writings became even more radical: "the Netherlands is now our enemy, because they participate in the occupation of Iraq. We shall not attack our neighbors but we will those who are apostates and those who are behaving like our enemy."[11]

According to the Norwegian researcher Petter Nesser, "There are indications that Bouyeri was the 'communications coordinator' of the Hofstad Network. He was very active on the Internet and hosted a very politicized MSN group called *Muwahhidin* (groups.msn.com/MuwahhidinDeWare-Moslims). Using his alias, Abu Zubair, he wrote articles about Islam and translated texts of influential radical Islamist thinkers, such as Abu Ala Mawdudi and Sayyid Qutb in March 2004. Investigations of the Internet lives of Bouyeri and other members of the Hofstad Network revealed the existence of a radical and Iraq-focused discourse on seemingly harmless chat-rooms for young North African immigrants to Holland."[12] Bouyeri also referred to Abu Hamza al Masri's *Allah's Governance on Earth* to argue that democracy is the same as disbelief and that Muslims who participate in elections or operate as representatives in democratic institutions are disbelievers.[13]

Nesser suggests with good cause that domestic politics in the Netherlands provided a driving force behind the Hofstad Group's moral outrage and Bouyeri's politicized mobilization to action.

The notes pinned to the body of the victim indicated that the murder was mainly motivated by events in Holland, and that it was part of a broader conspiracy aimed at killing several Dutch politicians who have criticized Muslims living in the Netherlands and called for tougher immigration laws. The document lashed out against Dutch policies towards Muslims and Islam in general, as well as a concrete proposal by Hirsi Ali's party VVD, to "screen" Muslim immigrants to make sure they did not sympathize with radical ideologies. The author(s) of the letter voiced strong anti-Semitism, and argued Dutch politics is "dominated by Jews". The claim was exemplified with reference to the Jewish mayor of Amsterdam, Job Cohen. The letter accused Hirsi Ali of being part of a Jewish conspiracy aimed at *"terrorizing Muslims and Islam"*, leading a *"crusade against Islam"*, on the *"political arena of Holland."*[14]

When another member of the Hofstad cluster who had been under surveillance by Dutch police and intelligence, Jason Walters, was arrested in 2003 and before being subsequently released, the authorities confiscated his computer and found chat logs where he had specifically sought out religious sanction for attacks that had political motivations, clearly demonstrating his rationale. During a chat on September 19, 2003, Walters sought sanction (via a friend: Galas03) from Imam Abdul-Jabbar van de Ven for jihad. Abdul-Jabbar was a Dutch convert who was a traveling imam. Walters's screen name was "Mujaheed":

Mujaheed: "you have to go to jabbar"
Galas03:   "I will see him today InshaAllah at the lesson"
Mujaheed: "Go and ask him if it is here allowed to slaughter the unbelievers and/or to steal their possessions"
Galas03:   "He has said about it, see it this way: the government, ministries, police etc., their blood and possessions is halal [we can take], because they openly declared war to the islam, but before you do something you have to think twice about what will happen with the islamic community."
Mujaheed: "OK djazaak Allah. This is the fatwa needed. Now I can slaughter every police, minister, soldier, officer etc. And robe [*sic*] them."[15]

The Hofstad Cluster

The Hofstad Group was a cluster of mostly young Dutch Muslims of Moroccan ancestry. The group was made up of ten to twenty young Muslim men and women between the ages of eighteen and twenty-eight, typically but not necessarily of the second generation, as well as a small group of converts. Beyond the Saudi-sponsored mosques in the Netherlands, the phone shop in Schiedam, outside Rotterdam, was the key initial meeting place for many of the core members of the cluster. It was a place where young Muslim men watched videos and discussed the appropriateness of jihad. Nourredine el Fatmi, an illegal Moroccan immigrant, worked in the phone shop, and Samir Azzouz met Jason Walters there sometime in 2002. Ridouan al Issar, a Syrian in his mid-forties who was a self-proclaimed Islamic expert (without any real religious credentials) and claimed to have been a mujahedeen veteran, lived above the shop. Despite al Issar's limited knowledge of Islam, it exceeded that of the youths and, coupled with his charisma, he attracted young male followers.[16]

It is likely that Mohammed Bouyeri came into contact with Samir Azzouz once he moved to Amsterdam. The two were "observed together in five different apartments in Western Amsterdam that were frequented by members of the group." By December 2002 they had invited al Issar to lecture at Bouyeri's apartment in Amsterdam for "living room meetings." Zine Labidine, who became a regular visitor at the meetings at Bouyeri's apartment, worked in the phone center in Schiedam in 2004, where he came into contact with Ridouan al Issar and attended the el Tawheed Mosque. In addition, most of the core members of the group (Bouyeri, Hamdi and Rachid Belkacem, Youssef Ettoumi, Nourredine el Fatmi), as well as a group of young women, were active members of the *Muwahhidin* Internet group.[17]

A group of ten to twenty young Muslims, primarily of Moroccan ancestry, met in Bouyeri's apartment in Amsterdam a couple of times a week. The meetings were somewhat exclusive and considered mysterious—in order to attend, one would have to be introduced by an existing member in good standing. During these prayer and discussion circles (*halaqas*), the men watched videos about mujahedeen in Iraq and Chechnya and listened to tapes of speeches promoting the legitimacy of killing non-Muslims. By the summer of 2003, a core group of fifteen to twenty members including Bouyeri, Azzouz, el Fatmi, Jason Walters, Akhnikh, and al Issar had solidified.[18]

Ridouan al Issar (aka Abu Khaled), who was somewhere between forty-three and forty-five at the time of the assassination, was called the "the spiritual leader of the Hofstad network" by the AIVD, though that interpretation changed over time. Al Issar, a trained geologist, settled in Germany in 1995 as a secular individual, living off welfare payments after his request for asylum was rejected by Germany. In 1996 he was arrested in Aachen with small amounts of heroin and hashish. By 1998 he had moved to the Netherlands and filed an application for asylum. While this was pending, it seems he began to turn to self-taught Islam, adopting a militant interpretation of the religion. After some time he began to give lectures about the Koran in mosques in the Netherlands. Ultimately his application for asylum in the Netherlands was rejected as well and he went underground traveling back and forth between Germany and the Netherlands. He was arrested in Frankfurt in January 2003 for using a false passport as well as in the Netherlands in November 2003 for suspicion of planning bomb attacks. He was transferred back to Germany but seems to have found a way back to the Netherlands. There is some speculation that he utilized the identity of a member of the Syrian Muslim Brotherhood who was imprisoned in Syria.[19]

Al Issar lived in an apartment above the phone shop in Schiedam and this was where he first took a leadership role, promoting his militant views on Islam to an ignorant cluster of young males comprising illegal Moroccan immigrants, second-generation Dutch of Moroccan heritage, and converts. Though al Issar's knowledge of Islam was limited, for a certain period, the combination of his charisma and his audience's relative ignorance enabled him to serve as a local ideologue and hold sway over them and draw in others.[20]

Anatomy of the Cluster

Active Core

Mohammed Bouyeri, age twenty-six at the time of the assassination, was born in West Amsterdam, the son of Moroccan immigrants. He was raised in Slotervaart, a lower-income suburb of Amsterdam in a community with a heavy concentration of Moroccans. The abundance of satellite dishes underscored the community's ongoing ties to Morocco and the Arab world. Bouyeri was described as a cooperative and promising example of the second generation in Holland by some people knew him in at this stage. His father and he attended a local mosque "known for its moderation." He attended a top secondary school, Mondrian College, where he graduated as a "B-level student." He attended a local polytechnic school to study accounting and information technology but reportedly spent a lot of his time "on the streets." He had a reputation for having a quick temper, and he was arrested for an assault involving a knife and another Moroccan youth. Bouyeri served several months in jail for attacking Dutch police and was released in September 2001. Some friends suggest that it was in prison that he began to radicalize. Others suggest it was the death of his mother from breast cancer during that same time period that served as the catalyst.[21]

After being released from prison, Bouyeri switched his academic pursuits from accounting to social work and began volunteering at the Eigenwijks community center. His friends say he began to wear "traditional" clothing and grew a beard. He was also more sensitive to political issues such as the Arab-Israeli conflict. Community workers recall his efforts to bring together Dutch politicians and the Moroccan immigrant community for discussions, to organize a neighborhood clean-up campaign, to tutor local youths in computers, and to organize soccer matches that sometimes pitted local youths against the police. At one time he sought funding for a new youth center but failed to secure funding from the Dutch government.[22]

The failure to get funding for a new youth center may have influenced Bouyeri's transformation as subsequently he dropped out of school and began to collect unemployment benefits. Meanwhile, his religious convictions deepened, and his views on social issues became more conservative. Bouyeri ultimately disassociated himself from the community center and left his part-time job there in August 2003. Bouyeri objected to the serving of alcohol at functions at the center and to women's attendance at events, both of which the community center's management found unacceptable. Ultimately he left the neighborhood and began living in a small apartment in central Amsterdam where he could sit behind his computer for hours on end and read radical Islamic texts, translate them, write articles, and distribute them via the Internet under a pseudonym.[23]

Samir Azzouz, age eighteen at the time of the assassination, was born in Amsterdam to Moroccan immigrants. While he was not raised in a religiously observant household, he was taught about Islam, learned Arabic in his youth, and attended el Tawheed Mosque. Azzouz attended an Islamic primary school called As-Siddieq, which promotes a very strict interpretation of Islam. Its curriculum has been described as having anti-Western and anti-Jewish tendencies, and teaching about the "holocaust" is forbidden. It is possible that "the young Samir Azzouz developed some of his early radical ideas in the school benches of the As-Siddieq school."[24]

In fourth grade he began to do poorly and started skipping school. He subsequently enrolled in an Islamic comprehensive school in Rotterdam. In 2002, as a seventeen-year-old, he married a twenty-three-year-old woman, Abida Kabaj. Azzouz, who was energized by the Palestinian cause, further radicalized in high school. In early 2003, he was detained in Ukraine with a friend while attempting to go to Chechnya for jihad and was sent back the Netherlands. Following his return to the Netherlands, he settled in Rotterdam and began to spend time at the nearby Schiedam phone center and befriended Jason Walters. Later that year, he was arrested on possession of chemicals appropriate for bomb making but was released. In June 2004, he was arrested in connection with a supermarket robbery and found in possession of bomb-making materials, night-vision goggles, a silencer, ammunition, and maps and floor plans of Borssele nuclear power station, Schiphol Airport, the Dutch Parliament, the Dutch Ministry of Defense, and other public buildings in The Hague.[25]

Nourredine el Fatmi, age twenty-two at the time of the assassination, was born in the poor Moroccan village of Midar and, following his parents' divorce, immigrated illegally to Spain at age fifteen before coming to the Netherlands in either 1998 or 1999. He worked in the phone shop in Schiedam where he met Jason Walters and Samir Azzouz as well as Ridouan al Issar. He was considered one of the leaders of the group and was admired by many of the Hofstad women for his ideological knowledge. In 2004, he was arrested in Portugal for his alleged role in an assassination attempt of the Portuguese prime minister at the European Football Championship. However, the evidence was not sufficient for a conviction. When the Hofstad Group was arrested in the wake of the assassination, el Fatmi fled to Morocco before returning in 2005.[26]

Jason Walters, age nineteen at the time of the assassination, was the son of an American soldier and a Dutch woman. His parents divorced at an early age and his father was treated for alcoholism. Although Jason attended a local Baptist church as a youngster with his father, ultimately both Jason and his younger brother converted to Islam as teenagers in 2000. He quickly seemed to take a radical turn and both he and his younger brother, Jermaine, were expelled from the Amsterdam el Fath Mosque for voicing radical views. He spent a great deal of time on the Internet and adopted a militant interpretation of Islam, calling himself Abu Mjahid al Amerikie and contacted other like-minded individuals online. According to friends, "In secondary school, Jason manifested himself as a fervent defender of the United States. He would tolerate no criticism of America. After his conversion to Islam, he completely turned to the other extreme. He now considered his father's country to be the 'army of disbelief.'" Nevertheless, Jason finished his secondary education and read Arabic languages and Islamic studies at the University of Leiden. The two brothers imposed strict religious rules in the home of their divorced mother, who decided to move out of the house with her daughter. His father, who had separated from the family, was not in contact with his sons. As a result of the conflicts at home, the brothers moved from Amsterdam to The Hague.[27]

Ismail Akhnikh, age twenty-one at the time of the assassination, was born in Amsterdam to a Moroccan family of eleven children. "According to his neighbors, "he had been a difficult boy from childhood. Although he was a good student, he was so unmanageable that he was expelled from his school for vocational training in Amsterdam." He was subsequently was sent to Syria by his family for religious education before he found employment in the Netherlands in the hi-tech industry. He attended the el Tawheed Mosque, where he met members of the Hofstad Group.[28]

Followers

Ahmed Hamdi, age twenty-six at the time of the assassination, was born in Beni Said, Morocco. He was a housemate of Bouyeri, and the Dutch prosecutors and police believe that he was probably the group's "treasurer," administering their finances which included paying rent for apartments and fees for communication devices, as well as wiring money to members who traveled abroad. Hamdi also served as the group's computer expert and may have worked with Bouyeri as an assistant webmaster on the MSN-group *Muwahhidin.* He worked in the duty-free zone of Schiphol Plaza and for the cable company UPC. According to his wife, Hamdi moved in with Bouyeri after frequent fights with his wife over his relationship with a girlfriend. She also noted that it was Hamdi's relationship with Ismail Akhnikh that catalyzed his radicalization. Hamdi was a member of the discussion circle around al Issar.[29]

Soumaya Sahla, age twenty-one at the time of the assassination, grew up in a traditional Moroccan family in The Hague. It seems that a trip to Mecca with her father was the catalyst for her radicalization. Following her trip, she began to wear a burqa and attended the Salafi As-Soennah Mosque. Soumaya was very active on the Internet as early as 2000, when she discussed the call to fight in Chechnya: "Oh brothers who sympathise with our brothers and sisters in chechenia please go and commit jihad when you are up to it physically and mentally." Following a short-lived marriage, she returned to her parents' house in 2004. Through her Internet postings she met Nourredine el Fatmi, whom she married in April 2005. In June 2005 she was arrested on a train platform in the Netherlands with el Fatmi and was found to be carrying automatic weapons and addresses of Dutch politicians.[30]

Mohammed Chentouf, age twenty-nine at the time of the assassination, was raised in The Hague. He was the son-in-law of Ridouan al Issar and befriended Samir Azzouz at the phone center in Schiedam. He was a conspirator in the "Piranha" investigation to attack the AIVD headquarters.[31]

Saleh Bouali, age twenty-seven at the time of the assassination, was born in Morocco and lived in Rotterdam running a stand in a market in The Hague. He was active on the Internet and had enough connectivity in Pakistan to set up Jason Walters's first trip to Pakistan.[32]

Abid Kabaj, age thirty-four at the time of the assassination, was born in The Hague. She was a convert to Islam and had a university education. She met her husband, Samir Azzouz, online and was very active in anti-Israel activism in the Netherlands.[33]

Periphery

Bilal Bakaja, age nineteen at time of the assassination, had been involved in several major criminal acts, including armed robberies and a series of violent incidents beginning at age thirteen. He was allegedly part of a criminal gang. He became well acquainted with Mohammed Bouyeri. Bakaja was diagnosed with mental illness in 2003 and in 2007 entered the police station of Slotervaart and stabbed two police officers with a knife. Although one of the officers sustained serious injuries, she shot and killed Bakaja.[34]

Abdullah Bakaja, age seventeen at time of the assassination, had been involved in several major criminal incidents with his older brother.[35]

Zine Labidine Aourghe, age twenty-six at the time of the assassination, was an illegal immigrant from Nador Province, Morocco. He was a regular visitor at the meetings at Mohammed Bouyeri's apartment and worked in the phone center in Schiedam in 2004, where he came into contact with Ridouan al Issar and attended the el Tawheed Mosque. Labidine temporarily lived with Jason Walters in his house in The Hague and regularly visited the Internet café in the Willem Nakkenstraat in Amsterdam.[36]

Jermaine Walters, age seventeen at the time of the assassination, was the son of an American soldier based in the Netherlands and a Dutch woman. His parents divorced at an early age and his father was treated for alcoholism. Although Jermaine was raised in a local Baptist church, both he and his older brother, Jason, converted to Islam as teenagers in 2000. Jermaine and Jason were expelled from the Amsterdam el Fath Mosque for voicing radical views. The two brothers imposed strict religious rules in the home of their divorced mother, who decided to move out of the house with her daughter. His father separated from the family and was not in contact with his sons, and they decided to move from Amsterdam to The Hague.[37]

Outhman Ben Ali, age thirty-four at the time of the assassination, was a Dutch-born citizen of Moroccan descent who worked as a translator for AIVD and leaked transcripts of telephone taps to the Hofstad Group.[38]

Mohammed Fahmi Boughabe, age twenty-three at the time of the assassination, was born in al Hoceima, Morocco, but came to the Netherlands with his mother under the terms of the Netherlands's family-reunification policy. His father had worked in the Netherlands for more than twenty years. Boughabe was a friend of Samir Azzouz and Mohammed Bouyeri. He met Bouyeri in the el Tawheed Mosque and attended the meetings that were organized at his house, where he also met Ridouan al Issar. He worked in construction.[39]

Nadir Adaraff, age twenty-three at the time of the assassination, was born in Ait Tznachte Tchouket, Morocco. He "was a regular visitor of Mohammed B.'s house and was friends with Fahmi B [Boughabe]. He was one of the visitors of the living-room meetings in Mohammed B.'s home. In his view, these meetings were very professional." He served a minimal sentence for his association with the group.[40]

Rachid Belkacem, age thirty-one at the time of the assassination, was a Dutch-born Muslim from Zierikzee and a regular visitor of the phone center in Schiedam, where he may have met Ridouan al Issar. Accounts suggest that he helped smuggle al Issar out of the country following van Gogh's killing, taking him to Zaventem Airport near Brussels by car. From there al

Issar flew via Greece to Turkey and then Syria. Belkacem was eventually arrested in London in June 2005, when weapons, ammunition, videotapes, and radical Islamic recruitment material were found in his apartment. He was extradited to the Netherlands and was found dead in his home in 2006, foaming from the mouth. This death is still being investigated.[41]

Mohamed el Morabit, age twenty-three at the time of the assassination, was born in al Hoceima, Morocco, and came to the Netherlands in 1998. He met a number of members of the cluster at el Tawheed Mosque, including Samir Azzouz. He was arrested in 2004 "at the same time as Nourredine el Fatmi in Portugal during the European Football Championships. He was then handed over to the Dutch AIVD intelligence service."[42]

Rachid Bousana, age twenty-six at the time of the assassination, grew up in Beni Said, Morocco, but was raised in the same neighborhood of Amsterdam as Mohammed Bouyeri. The two worked together as teenagers in Amsterdam. Mohammed Bouyeri left an envelope with him in case "anything should happen to him." He worked as a service engineer for Geotronix.[43]

Mohamed el Bousklaoui, age twenty at the time of the assassination, was born in Amsterdam and was a childhood friend of Mohammed Bouyeri. Some accounts suggest that he looked up to Bouyeri and was considered a Bouyeri follower. In 2004, he traveled with one of the main suspects, Nourredine el Fatmi, to Portugal where he was arrested and subsequently released.[44]

Zakaria Taybi, age twenty at the time of the assassination, was born in Amsterdam. He had attempted to work as a cleaner at Schiphol Airport but was unable to get a security clearance. He traveled with Jason Walters twice to Pakistan in 2003.[45]

Youssef Ettoumi, age twenty-seven at the time of the assassination, was born in Amsterdam and at age fifteen served time in jail for burglary. He knew members of the Hofstad Group from the neighborhood. His computer was found to have files on how to build explosives.[46]

Bilal Lamarni, age nineteen at the time of the assassination, was born in Amsterdam. He was a friend of Bouyeri and worked in the neighborhood as a pizza delivery man. He was also very active in the online forums. While in prison for intimidating the Dutch politician Gert Wilders online, "Bilal spoke with fellow detainees about training camps in Afghanistan and about wanting to die as a martyr."[47]

Brahim Harhour, age twenty-one at the time of the assassination, was born in Amsterdam. He was a close friend of Mohammed Hamdi.

Hannan Sarrokh, age twenty-three at the time of the assassination, was born in the Netherlands and was married to *Lahbib Bachar,* who was twenty-six at the time of the assassination. Sarrokh and Bachar knew Samir Azzouz and allowed Nourredine el Fatmi to hide in their home in the year after the van Gogh assassination. In addition, "Bachar and Sarrokh admitted that they made all kinds of preparations for attacks, on the orders of Azzouz and el Fatmi, including hiding them from authorities in a Brussels apartment and trafficking automatic weapons to that apartment." She and her husband subsequently became witnesses for the state against Azzouz and el Fatmi.[48]

Malika Chaabi, age sixteen at the time of the assassination, was born in Amsterdam and was known by a number of the young men in the Hofstad Group. She ran away from home and was sought after by Mohammed el Morabit as a wife. However, in October 2004, Mohammed Bouyeri officiated at her marriage ceremony to Nourredine el Fatmi in his apartment. Witness accounts say that there were about ten young men in Bouyeri's house and on the night of the marriage, el Fatmi talked about the need to kill the infidels. Later that night, supposedly, el Fatmi showed her jihadist videos.[49]

Martine van den Oever, age twenty-five at the time of the assassination, was raised as a Christian in a small town outside The Hague. She converted at age eighteen as a result of interactions with some classmates who were Muslim and attended the As-Soehnnah Mosque. She dabbled in a variety of careers, including as a Dutch police officer and as a social worker. She was an activist for Palestinian political causes, traveling to the region and working for both the Al Aqsa Foundation and the Jerusalem Foundation. Subsequently, she became significantly more devout and began to wear a burqa. Through these political activities she met Samir Azzouz's wife and by 2005 was hosting Hofstad events in her house.[50]

Overseas Travel and Link Up with Al Qaeda

Members of the Hofstad Group attempted to travel to Chechnya and Pakistan to receive military training and/or fight jihad; however, no one linked up with al Qaeda.

In January 2003 Samir Azzouz and a childhood friend from the Netherlands attempted to reach Chechnya via Ukraine in an effort to join the fight against the Russians. Both were arrested in the Ukraine and sent back to the Netherlands. During the summer of 2003, Jason Walters and Ismail Akhnikh traveled to Pakistan. Akhnikh left after about three weeks; Walters stayed for about a month. Zakaria Taybi, a friend from the Netherlands, joined them for only a week. According to Walters, he received basic training in Pakistan, learning how to use all types of weapons. He suggests that the training camp he attended belonged to the Kashmiri extremist movement Jaish-e-Mohammed run by Maulana Masood Azhar.[51]

Training and Skill Acquisition

After Walters returned, he tried to convince his Internet friend Galas03 that he had to go with him to a training camp in Pakistan and described his training. In an Internet chat Walters said, "come to pakistan with me there they will train you, how to use guns, how to make weapons, just everything after that you can return." Jason boasted about his proficiency with weapons: "I can assemble and disassemble a kalashnikov blindfolded, also a seminov and all the other pistols and rifles." Walters also discussed the types of weapons he had trained on, including "seminov, kalashnikov, MMG, zakayev, TT pistol, Makarov, hand grenades en rpg those I all learned."[52] In December 2003, Jason Walters and Zakaria Taybi returned to Pakistan, but it was only for nine days.

Al Qaeda Recruitment

Although Walter's training occurred at a Jaish-e-Mohammed camp, he was not recruited to carry out any operation in the West on any organization's behalf.

Operational Cycle

Arrests of several members of the Hofstad Group (Walters, Azzouz, al Issar, and Akhnikh) began in October 2003, suggesting that the group was gradually moving toward an operational phase. A combination of events overseas (Dutch participation in the Iraq war), perceived "insults against Islam" (the summer 2004 release of *Submission* by Theo van Gogh and Ayan Hirsi Ali), and a rising anti-Muslim discourse within Dutch domestic politics seemed to be the catalysts for the turn to violence among the members of the Hofstad Group.

Although those arrests seemed to interrupt a few inchoate operations, the group continued in its general trajectory toward violence. On November 2, 2004, Bouyeri, ostensibly on his own, assassinated van Gogh in Amsterdam in broad daylight. In 2005 and 2006, members of the Hofstad Group who were targeting the Dutch police and the AIVD headquarters in two separate plots were arrested.

Logistics

Ahmed Hamdi most likely handled the group's finances and served as the group's computer expert.[53]

Communications

According to Dutch officials, the men utilized a variety of ways to communicate with each other and exchange information, including Internet cafés and USB memory sticks.[54] By the summer of 2004, Bouyeri, Hamdi, Rachid Belkacem, Youssef Ettoumi, and Nourredine el Fatmi were all active members of the *Muwahhidin* Internet forum.[55]

Target Selection/Casing

Dutch authorities declared that after the van Gogh assassination, the group was "planning follow-up operations targeting Ayan Hirsi Ali and other preeminent Dutch political figures" as well as potentially targeting the Dutch police, AIVD, and even an El Al airlines flight while it was arriving or departing from Schiphol Airport.[56] Dutch authorities arrested Nourredine el Fatmi in June 2005 (he had managed to escape from the Netherlands during the major post–van Gogh assassination sweep) at Lelylaan Station in Amsterdam, together with two women: his wife, Soumaya Sahla, and her friend Martine van den Oever, a Dutch convert to Islam. El Fatmi had a fully loaded machine gun, silencer, and ammunition and was believed to be preparing to attack Dutch politicians.[57] On October 14, 2005, the Dutch police arrested Samir Azzouz, Ismail Akhnikh, Jason Walters, Mohammed Chentouf, Abdullah Bakaja, and Brahim Harhour for plotting to attack the AIVD headquarters. This case was called the "Piranha Plot."[58]

Weaponization

According to Petter Nesser, on "October 14, 2003, group members, Samir Azzouz, Ismail Akhnikh, Jason Walters and Ridouan al Issar were arrested for planning an attack in the Netherlands. While the others were released for lack of evidence, Azzouz was tried but acquitted because he had assembled the wrong mix of fertilizer for explosives. It is unknown where he acquired the materials."[59] In June 2004, Azzouz was arrested again, this time on charges relating to a supermarket robbery. He was found in possession of bomb-making materials, night vision goggles, a silencer, ammunition, and maps and floor plans. Though he would stay incarcerated through April 2005, he ultimately was acquitted as the court decided that there was not sufficient evidence to convict him of preparing to conduct a terrorist act as a "concrete threat."[60]

By October 2004, Mohammed Bouyeri had purchased his own gun and was practicing his shooting. He used a semi-automatic pistol made in Croatia—an HS (9mm) of the year 2000: "It is still unknown how Bouyeri got hold of this weapon. However, it can be easily found on the internet and on the black markets it costs between 1000 and 1500 euro."[61] A witness testifying against Nourredine el Fatmi in the Piranha Plot told the court that he rented accommodations in Brussels, was involved in gun smuggling, and practiced with firearms in an Amsterdam park.[62]

The Al Qaeda Factor

With its absence of overseas links, Hofstad Group is seen as the paradigm of a homegrown, al Qaeda–inspired terrorist group driven by al Qaeda's ideology. There were no direct contacts or links between the members of the network and al Qaeda Core. Moreover, Mohammed Bouyeri's "Open Letter to Hirshi Ali" identifies the same set of enemies that al Qaeda Core would identify as its enemies and predicts their defeat and demise.

And like a great prophet once said: "I deem thee lost, O Pharaoh."

(17:102) And so we want to use similar words and send these before us, so that the heavens and the stars will gather this news and spread it over the corners of the universe like a tidal wave. "I deem thee lost, O America." "I deem thee lost, O Europe." "I deem thee lost, O Holland." "I deem thee lost, O Hirshi Ali." "I deem thee lost, O unbelieving fundamentalist."[63]

Chapter 14

Operation Pendennis (Australia, 2005)

ON NOVEMBER 9, 2005, Australian police and security services raided properties in Melbourne and Sydney, arrested eighteen men, and seized bomb-making materials as well as maps of Casselden Place, the Melbourne headquarters of the Departments of Foreign Affairs and Trade and Immigration. Although the target set for this group was never definitively determined, the Melbourne suspects had filmed the Australian Stock Exchange and Flinders Street Station, Melbourne's landmark central train exchange. In addition, members of the Sydney cluster had been arrested in 2004 while casing out the Lucas Heights nuclear power plant and reportedly had targeted the Sydney Opera House and the Sydney Harbour Bridge.[1] According to the judge who presided over the trial of the Sydney cluster, "Benbrika's [the emir of the group] aim was to stage terrorist attacks so shocking to destroy buildings and kill people in the cause of jihad that the Australian government would be forced to withdraw troops from Iraq and break off its alliance with the U.S."[2]

The Ahlus Sunnah Wal Jamaah Association (ASJA) Scene

The Ahlus Sunnah Wal Jamaah Association is the preeminent Sunni fundamentalist organization in Australia. From the late 1990s up until the last few years, it has supported and promoted an extremist ideology that has attracted individuals who ultimately became involved in politically motivated violence in Australia and abroad. With locations around the country, it has served to underpin Australia's Islamic scene. In 1988, a connection was established between Sheikh Mohammed Omran, a Jordanian-born asylum seeker who arrived in Australia in the 1980s, and Abu Bakr Bashir, the spiritual leader of the Indonesian terror group Jemaah Islamyiah (JI). This link would underpin much of the development of the scene in Australia in the years to come.[3]

Australia's Muslim community of approximately 340,000 is relatively new. Australia's policy of absorbing significant numbers of refugees from war-torn regions of the world played a role in the establishment of this community as significant numbers of Sunni Lebanese refugees, escaping the civil war that ravaged Lebanon during the 1970s and 1980s, settled in Australia, primarily in Sydney and Melbourne. Many second-generation Australian citizens from this Lebanese diaspora work as tradesmen and continue to live in the larger cities.

In the 1980s throughout Australia, Sheikh Mohammed Omran established Ahlus Sunnah Wal Jamaah Association (ASJA), a strict Salafi organization. There were prayer centers set up in Melbourne and Sydney, where concentrations of Sunni Lebanese immigrants were the highest. These two major cities were the two most important nodes in the Australian Islamic scene. In Melbourne, Omran oversaw the Michael Street Mosque in the suburb of Brunswick. In Sydney, another Salafi cleric, the Lebanese-born Sheikh Abdul Salam Mohammed Zoud, headed the Haldon Street Prayer Hall in the heavily Muslim district of Lakemba and played a role in setting up a related extremist offshoot organization geared toward a younger demographic, the Islamic Youth Movement (IYM).

Many of the children of the Lebanese immigrants adopted Omran and Zoud's fundamental brand of Islam and joined IYM and ASJA. Further fueling the rejectionist element in Sydney was the fact that under the direction of Abu Bakr Bashir, twin brothers, Abdul Rahim and Abdul Rahman Ayub, were appointed the co-heads of JI in Australia and were regular attendees at the Lakemba mosque. Their presence enabled a fusion between Asian and Arab Muslim communities.[4]

In addition to those arrested as a result of Operation Pendennis and the Ayub brothers, other radical individuals, who would come to be associated with al Qaeda–affiliated terrorism, were familiar faces at the Haldon Street Prayer Hall and interacted with the Pendennis group. Bilal Khazal, who was identified as having trained with al Qaeda and was associated with the ASJA and IYM, was a prominent sheikh in Australia and may have fostered an extremist environment. The Lashkar-e-Taiba trained terrorists Willie Brigitte, Faheem Khalid Lodhi, and Jamal all spent significant time in and around the Haldon Street prayer room in Lakemba. This dynamic was not restricted to males, as an entire cohort of female Caucasian converts embraced al Qaeda–inspired Islam in Sydney, led by matriarch Rabiah Hutchinson, who was at the time married to one of the Ayub brothers.[5]

While men like Sheikhs Omran and Zoud first attracted those who would come to be arrested in Operation Pendennis, ultimately the two sheiks were insufficiently radical for the conspirators. Instead, it was Abdul Nacer Benbrika who inspired the men to turn to violence against Australia. The loosely knit group from Melbourne and Sydney looked to Benbrika as their spiritual leader. In fact, Benbrika had worked as a teacher at ASJA before he broke from the group in 2001 because Sheikh Omran's brand of Islam was not radical enough. Many arrested as a result of Operation Pendennis had followed Benbrika away from Omran and Zoud's rejectionist ASJA/IYM network. Some, utilizing international connections to groups such as Jemaah Islamiyah were able to travel to Pakistan and Afghanistan to participate in terrorist training camps.[6]

Gravitating to Reactionary Islam

ASJA had been founded in the 1980s and had affiliated organizations in Melbourne, Sydney, and Perth. It was a hardline Salafi organization that promoted a Wahhabi worldview and an austere, literal interpretation of the Koran that rejected Australian democracy. Sheikhs Omran in Melbourne and Zoud in Sydney were its most charismatic and influential leaders. With little competition, this organization was able to dominate the supply side of providing the interpretation of what "real Islam" should be and gained significant traction with the recently established Lebanese populations in those cities. Moreover, Omran had significant credibility because he was well connected in international Salafi circles. One of his childhood friends was the British-based al Qaeda proponent Abu Qatada, whom Omran brought to Australia in 1994 for a speaking tour.[7]

While the Islam that Omran preached was anti-Western, it did not explicitly call for violence. However, it did provide an intellectual framework that supported the military defense of Islam under certain circumstances.

Consequently, those who left Omran's orbit did so because they sought out a less restrictive and more militant jihadi-Salafi ideology.[8]

Abdul Nacer Benbrika, a native Algerian and leader of both the Sydney and Melbourne clusters, appears to have begun his radicalization journey once he arrived in Australia in 1989 through an apprenticeship to Sheikh Omran. However, he ultimately broke away, potentially inspired by Abu Qatada. In fact it is Abu Qatada's visit to Australia in 1994 that some consider the "pivotal event in the emergence of the jihadist movement in Australia and the radicalization of [Abdul Nacer] Benbrika." The interpretation of Islam that Benbrika promoted focused particularly on the central concept of monotheism or "*tawheed.*" More important, however, he regarded violent jihad as an integral part of a Muslim's religious obligations—a belief he constantly reinforced though his teachings and his ordinary discourse with his offshoot group.[9]

Outside the classes that Benbrika taught, he associated, informally and socially, with some of the same young men so that, at some indeterminate time, they, with him, formed a group, or, in Arabic, a "jemaah," of which he was the leader. The jemaah existed, under Benbrika's direction, for the purpose of engaging in violent jihad. Benbrika regarded the destruction of the "kuffar"—Arabic for "unbelievers"—as an essential aspect of the Islamic religion. "The jemaah would achieve this by acts of terrible violence in this country, or, perhaps elsewhere. In Australia, such terrorism would be directed towards coercing the Australian Government into withdrawing Australian forces from Iraq, as the presence of such troops in that country was seen as oppressive to Muslims and the Islamic religion."[10] At least six out of the ten members of the Melbourne cluster had attended Omran's classes at the Brunswick mosque before leaving to join Benbrika's splinter group.[11]

Politicization of New Beliefs

Based on information that came to light at the trial of the Melbourne cell, much of the group's frame was shaped by Benbrika's discussion and interpretation of international current events and his belief that the Islamic community was under attack from the non-Islamic community of infidels. Benbrika rejected Australian democratic society, noting, "I don't believe in this country. I don't believe in this law." He said that Muslims were committed to engage in violent jihad to persuade the government to withdraw Australian troops from Afghanistan and Iraq. He told one of his acolytes, "We don't want to just kill one, two or three, if we kill a thousand then they will sit up and listen and then they will bring the troops back from Iraq." Benbrika preached that there was no difference between the government and the people who elected the government officials.[12] Benbrika called Osama bin Laden a "great man" and endorsed the goals and actions of Algeria's Salafist Group for Call and Combat (GSPC).[13]

The Sydney Cluster

The Sydney Cluster was one of two led by Benbrika. It was group of about fifteen men who had been considered individuals of concern by Australian intelligence for some time. Virtually all were male Muslims between the ages of twenty-one and forty who were either citizens or longtime residents of Australia. Nine men from this cluster were arrested on November 8, 2005, and charged with planning a terrorist attack linked to Operation Pendennis. The men were Khaled Cheikho, Moustafa Cheikho, Mohammed Ali Elomar, Abdul Rakib Hasan, Khaled Sharrouf, Omer Jamal, Omar Baladjam, Mirsad Mulahalilovic, and Mazen Touma. Saleh Jamal (who was serving five years in jail in Lebanon on weapons charges), Willie Brigitte (who has been detained in France on suspicion of planning a terrorist attack in Sydney), and Faheem Khalid Lodhi (the Sydney architect who was arrested as part of his involvement in a plot against Sydney directed by Lashkar-e-Taiba [LeT]) had all been associated with this cluster.[14]

Almost all the men in the cluster were members of ASJA and followed Abdul Salam Mohammed Zoud in Sydney at the Haldon Street mosque. This location, in the Sydney neighborhood of Lakemba, was a hub of activity for transplanted Lebanese Australians. Sheikh Zoud taught an offshoot of the fundamentalist Wahhabi form of Islam. Moreover, two brothers from Indonesia's JI were regular attendees at the prayer room in Haldon Street as they utilized the location as a base from which they sought to start up and run a branch of JI in Australia.[15]

The active core of the Pendennis Sydney cluster revolved around men who were trained by LeT or had been connected with suspected terrorist operatives in the past. These individuals included Khaled Cheikho, his nephew Moustafa Cheikho, Khaled Sharrouf, and their associates. Khaled had married the daughter of Australian female convert Rabiah Hutchinson, the matriarch of the radical Islamist community in Australia. Khaled Cheikho and Abdul Rakib Hasan attended an LeT training camp in 1999–2000 and subsequently, Khaled's nephew, Moustafa, attended an LeT camp in November 2001, where he met a future convicted terrorist, Willie Brigitte.[16]

The Sydney men also attended at least two makeshift training camps in Australia, where they practiced at shooting ranges, which they had set up themselves. The first was the Curranyalpa trip, which occurred during March 16–18, 2005. This camp was booked under a false name using a fraudulent phone service. In attendance were Abdul Rakib Hasan, Mohammed Elomar, Khaled Cheikho, Khaled Sharrouf, and three men from the Melbourne cluster, Aimen Joud, Fadal Sayadi, and Ahmed Raad. The second trip occurred during April 12–14, 2005, and was booked in the same manner as the first trip had been. Present at the camp were Mohammed Elomar, his son, Abdul Rakib Hasan, Khaled Cheikho, Moustafa Cheikho, and Mazen Touma.[17]

The Melbourne Cluster

This second cluster formed when Benbrika broke away from Omran's Michael Street Mosque in Brunswick, taking the most violent, radical elements of the congregation with him. Benbrika had found that the message there was not radical enough, so he formed his own group with a handful of young men he called his students, though most were friends and relatives. Some he had met when he had taught at various mosques and at Islamic organizations such as the Islamic Information and Support Centre of Australia (IISCA). Virtually all were male Muslims between the ages of twenty and twenty-eight who were either citizens or longtime residents of Australia. At least six of the ten members of this cluster had originally attended Omran's lectures before joining Benbrika's breakaway group.[18]

The men from this cluster arrested on charges linked to Operation Pendennis included Abdul Nacer Benbrika, Shane Kent, Aiman Joud, Ahmed Raad, Ezzit Raad, Abdulla Merhi, Fadal Sayadi, Izzydeen Atik, Amer Haddara, Hany Taha, Bassam Raad, Majeed Raad, and Shoue Hammoud. Approximately seven of the Melbourne suspects were second-generation Australians, the children of Lebanese immigrants who had grown up somewhat secular and had began practicing Islam only eighteen months before their arrest. According to court testimony, "Though a few were students, most were tradesmen and laborers, including plumbers and painters. Several had minor criminal records."[19]

Two other men who had links to the cluster but were not part of the Operation Pendennis arrests were Jack Thomas and a twenty-year-old Canberra-born convert to Islam named Ahmad Kalek. Both were associates of fellow convert Shane Kent. All three are believed to have trained abroad potentially at al Qaeda's al Farouq camp.[20]

As mentioned previously, most of Benbrika's followers were friends and/or relatives of one another (e.g., Ahmed Raad had attended high school with his brother Ezzit Raad and Fadal Sayadi before dropping out in eleventh grade).[21] Although the men in this cluster had originally followed Sheikh Mohammed Omran and his group, ASJA, Benbrika preached a more militant form of Islam. Benbrika said, "According to my religion, jihad is part of my religion and what you have to understand is that anyone who fights for the sake of Allah, when he dies, the first drop of blood that comes from him out all his sin will be forgiven." The Melbourne suspects also participated in outdoor bonding activities, including paramilitary-like training at a rural Kinglake property and at various commercial hunting properties. For example, in March 2005, Aiman Joud, Fadal Sayadi, and Ahmed Raad went to a property at Louth, a remote location in far western New South Wales, where they camped with some other young men. The evidence before the court showed that firearms were discharged and a curious device consisting of a battery connected to a number of spark plugs was found after they left.[22] Furthermore, as the Crown argued, "The evidence also shows that the common interest of each of the accused in the pursuit of violent jihad was the glue that bound them together as a close knit, secretive organisation, supportive of each other and of the common cause of the organisation, the fostering or preparing the doing of a terrorist act. . . . They treated one another as trusted brothers; they referred to each other as brothers. In contrast, they treated outsiders and even newcomers with suspicion."[23] Since the majority of Muslims in Melbourne were of Turkish or Albanian descent, this group, by its very composition, primarily Australians of Lebanese descent, stood apart from the rest of the local community. In fact, the Islamic Council of Victoria called Benbrika's group "a splinter of a splinter of a splinter" and compared him to a cult leader with no standing in the wider community.[24]

Benbrika, who was forty-five at the time of his arrest, had arrived in Australia in 1990 from Algeria. He had been an Algerian Airlines electrical technician. He settled in the northern suburbs of Melbourne, an area with a large Muslim population, and married a Lebanese woman who was an Australian citizen with whom he had six children. He received Australian citizenship in 1998. For a time he attended, prayed at, and studied at the Melbourne religious center run by Sheikh Mohamed Omran in Brunswick. After rising to serve as Omran's deputy, Benbrika subsequently broke off from Omran because his group was not radical enough. Some say that Benbrika was inspired by Abu Qatada, whom Omran brought to Australia on a speaking tour in 1994. Rather than studying jurisprudence at a recognized Islamic university, Benbrika taught himself Islam and largely cut himself off from the wider community. Beyond having a spiritual and ideological influence, the Crown prosecution argued that, "Benbrika, was at the hub of the organization and he was its director and its leader" and that "Benbrika constantly invoked he purported to be religious authority to reassure his co-accused that they should feel comfortable about, and committed to, pursuing a cause that embraced indiscriminate murder of innocent citizens." Benbrika was found guilty of "knowingly belonging to a terrorist organization."[25]

Anatomy of the Cluster

Active Core (Sydney Cluster)

Mohammed Ali Elomar, age forty at the time of his arrest, came to Australia from Tripoli, Lebanon, in 1977. His eleven brothers and sisters reside in Australia, most of whom have their own businesses. His father died in 1994 and his mother passed away while he was in custody in 2008. Elomar attended school at Bankstown but left after completing Year 10. Considered intelligent and ambitious, "Elomar successfully undertook a Metal Fabrication apprenticeship with the Water Board. He has been part of and worked in a family construction business for approximately fifteen years. This business entailed working with structural steel on building sites." Elomar has been married to his wife for twenty-two years and has six children. He has operated his own drafting business but on occasions has also worked with his brothers in the family businesses. Elomar was well respected by the other members of the cluster who appear to have treated him with some degree of deference and considered him the leader of the Sydney cluster.[26]

Abdul Rakib Hasan, age thirty-four at the time of his arrest, came to

Australia from Bangladesh at age eighteen. He had grown up in a large, poor family and attended school from the age of eight until sixteen before going to work sporadically in his brother's garment factory. His education was basic and he had no particular vocational skills. Nevertheless, Hasan came to Australia to study business computing but gave up the course after a couple of weeks because his English was not good enough. Hasan then worked for a while at the Intercontinental Hotel in the housecleaning section but did not pursue any further studies. According to court testimony, "Shortly before his arrest, [Hasan] had been working at the Halal Indo-Malay butcher's shop in Lakemba." This was in the same building as the Haldon Street prayer room and served as a hub of extremist activity in Sydney. Hasan was a primary point of contact with Benbrika in Melbourne. Hasan had been investigated for helping the convicted terrorist Willie Brigitte arrange three safe houses while the he and Faheem Khalid Lodhi were plotting a LeT-directed attack in Australia. Furthermore, "Hasan was also named as a key player in a series of alleged terrorist training camps in the Blue Mountains. These were run by [a] Malaysian man, Asman Hashim, who also set up training camps for Jemaah Islamiyah in the Southern Philippines."[27]

Khaled Cheikho, age thirty-two at the time of his arrest, is the uncle of Moustafa Cheikho. Khaled Cheikho was born in Lebanon in March 1973 and has ten siblings, all of whom reside in Australia. Khaled Cheikho's family immigrated to Australia when he was three years of age. He was educated at Punchbowl Primary School and Bankstown Boys' High School but left before the end of his eleventh year: "Cheikho was an average student who tended to enjoy sport more than his academic pursuits." His employment record was fairly sporadic, and he told the psychologist he met with after his arrest that during his late teenage years and up until his twenties he experimented with "sex, drugs and rock 'n' roll." Cheikho became disenchanted with his lifestyle in his early twenties and he started to practice Islam. He reported that he became concerned about a lack of substance in his life. As he became more devout he adopted the strict Salafi interpretation of Islam. Khaled is believed to have trained in a paramilitary camp run by LeT in 1999–2000. Following his arrest, Khaled Cheikho described Allah's law as the "only law worthy of ruling mankind" and said that democracy was "full of shit . . . so you tell Howard this and pass it on to Bush the motherfucker tell him [I'm] gonna come and chop him up."[28]

Followers (Sydney Cluster)

Moustafa Cheikho, age twenty-eight at the time of his arrest, is the nephew of Khaled Cheikho. He grew up in a broken home and attended four primary schools before completing a high school vocational degree, which was essentially trade focused. Upon leaving school, he secured an apprenticeship as a mechanic but subsequently sustained an injury to his back and worked in the security industry until about 2003 and obtained a license to use firearms. According to the psychologist who interviewed him after his arrest, "from 1995 onwards, Cheikho's interest in the Koran developed and intensified until he ultimately made a full commitment to the devout observation of his religion in 1999 and attended the Prayer Hall at Lakemba twice a day during the past ten years, where he came more under the influence of his uncle Khaled Cheikho." Moustafa acknowledged that he had a continuing and strong bond with his uncle "to this day." Like his uncle, Moustafa trained in a paramilitary camp run by LeT in 2001–2. French terror suspect Willie Brigitte allegedly trained with him.[29]

Mohamed Omar Jamal, age twenty-one at the time of his arrest, is the younger brother of Saleh Jamal, who was convicted in Lebanon on terrorism charges. Born in Australia, Jamal came from a broken family, went to school, but was expelled from school as a result of conflict with teachers in year 9. According to court testimony, "He then went on to TAFE and completed the equivalent of a Year 10 Certificate. He had an interest in computers and developed considerable skills in this area. Shortly afterwards he began his own business of building and fixing computers. This was his job until the time when he was arrested." While in high school, Jamal had experimented with drugs and alcohol, and he remained friendly with a substance-abusing group even after he left school. When Jamal decided to get away from drugs and alcohol and left that group of friends, his brother introduced him to the mosque: "He insisted that Jamal should pray five times a day. By degrees, Jamal became religious and devout. He started going to lessons about Islam. Through this, he was introduced to some of his brother's friends. This group, as it happened, included some of the co-offenders. The introduction led to his early relationship with some of the co-offenders."[30]

Khaled Sharrouf, age twenty-four at the time of his arrest, is linked to Willie Brigitte via his brother-in-law, Mohammed Ndaw, who, based on his network of associates, was deported to his native Senegal due to Australian security concerns.[31]

Omar Baladjam, age twenty-eight at the time of his arrest, was a former child actor from a popular television show who had starred in ABC's *Wildside* and *Home and Away* and ran a painting business. When authorities tried to arrest him, he shot at them. He was married with two children.

Mirsad Mulahalilovic, age twenty-nine at the time of his arrest, was a Bosnian who arrived in Australia as a refugee from the conflict in the Balkans and worked as a painter.

Mazen Touma, age twenty-five at the time of his arrest, had juvenile convictions for assault and drug possession.

Periphery (Sydney Cluster)

Rabiah Hutchinson, age fifty-one at the time of the arrests of the Sydney cluster (she was not charged), was considered the matriarch of the local Islamic scene in Sydney. As a nineteen-year-old, she backpacked throughout Indonesia, converted to Islam, and joined an Islamic resistance group opposed to Indonesian president Suharto. Eventually "Hutchinson became a supporter of Islamic clerics Abu Bakar Bashir and Abdullah Sungkar, who two decades later formed the al Qaeda–linked group, Jemaah Islamiyah (JI), which orchestrated the 2002 Bali bombings." After her marriage to JI's leader in Sydney, Abdul Rahim Ayub, ended in 1989, she traveled with her six children to Pakistan to support the Islamic forces fighting to oust the Moscow-installed regime in Afghanistan's capital, Kabul. Subsequently, "she became well regarded within the Taliban government as a single woman living with her children under Islamic code." After the U.S. invasion following the September 11 attacks, she fled to Iran until the Australia Security and Intelligence Organization (ASIO) located her and brought her back to Sydney in 2003.

Bilal Khazal, age thirty-four at the time of his arrest, was one of four children and came to Australia as a three-year-old. He returned to Lebanon to live with relatives after a few years in Australia, not returning until he was about eighteen. He is married with two children. Although Khazal had worked as a baggage handler for Qantas Airlines for more than twelve years, his prominence in the Lakemba extremist community, history of links to al Qaeda–affiliated individuals, and both travel and training experiences suggest that he may have played a significant role in the radicalization of some of the men among the Sydney cluster. That said, Khazal was arrested in 2004, more than a year before the Pendennis arrests.[32]

Khazal lived in Lakemba and was a leading figure in two Australian Sunni extremist Islamic organizations, IYM and ASJA, as well as the prayer center in Haldon Street. Khazal played a role in the publishing of their magazine, *Nida'ul Islam* (Call of Islam), and the maintenance of their Web site. He also compiled a book, *Provisions on the Rules of Jihad*, which is basically a terrorist training manual. Khazal's first known contact with ASIO was on November 17, 1994, after he was stabbed as part of a factional struggle in Lakemba.[33]

According to a CIA report, Khazal trained in a military camp in Afghanistan in 1998. During his time there, Khazal supposedly was a confidant of Osama bin Laden and his deputy, Ayman al Zawahiri. Moreover, Spanish court documents described conversations between Abu Dahdah, a leading al Qaeda–linked sheikh in Madrid, and Khazal, including one in which Khazal requests Dahdah's help in moving an associate secretly around Europe. The documents also claim that Khazal met another alleged terrorist in London. Khazal was the subject of ASIO investigation at the time of the Sydney Olympics in 2000.[34]

The CIA report notes, "Al Qaeda has reportedly become very active in Australia and there are rank and file and leadership elements heading to Australia with forged passports. The al Qaeda leadership has allegedly delegated responsibility to Bilal Khazal. Khazal is reportedly planning an explosives attack against some US embassies . . . the current target is in Venezuela . . . Khazal also has plans to attack with explosives US interests in the Philippines."[35]

Khazal was arrested in May 2004 and charged with collecting or making documents likely to facilitate terrorist acts, an offense for which he was found guilty in September 2008. He was sentenced to twelve years in jail.[36]

Active Core (Melbourne Cluster)

Aiman Joud, age twenty-one at time of his arrest, had been born in Australia to Lebanese parents. His parents emigrated from Lebanon in 1980. He was two when his mother died giving birth to a fourth child. Joud attended a Catholic school and an Islamic college before dropping out of school at age sixteen. He was unmarried. While attending school he worked at a fruit shop, a computer shop, and in his parents' café in Flemington. After leaving school, Joud traveled to Egypt and Lebanon with family members.

When he returned to Australia in early 2003, he began his first full-time job as a tiler. In the year leading up to his arrest, he worked as a construction supervisor for his father's company, which was developing a shopping complex. Joud was a devout Muslim and attended Islamic classes at IISCA. Previously he had been convicted of firearms and theft charges. He was believed to have been part of a scheme whereby stolen cars were purchased and stripped and the resulting parts sold to provide funds for the group. Joud was considered by Benbrika to be his deputy and took a leadership role in the group.[37]

Fadal Sayadi, age twenty-five at the time of his arrest, was born in Lebanon but immigrated to Australia at age three. According to court testimony, "Sayadi attended Northcote High School until the end of Year 10. Thereafter, he undertook an electrical apprenticeship and studied at the Northern Metropolitan College of TAFE but did not complete the course. He worked at Rydges Hotel for about 12 months as a room service attendant, and subsequently found sporadic employment as a concreter, a forklift driver and in a steelworks. He has experienced various periods of unemployment. He is married but has no children." In 1997, Sayadi had been convicted on minor charges relating to an attempted theft. He had reportedly attended sermons given by Sheikh Omran. His role in the group was that of a "security officer" and group elder.[38]

Ahmed Raad, age twenty-two at the time of his arrest, was born in Australia to Lebanese immigrants. He began to be a more observant Muslim after the death of his brother Mansour in 2003. He began attending the mosque regularly and seeking religious instruction, eventually from Benbrika. Ahmed had attended high school with his brother Ezzit Raad and Fadal Sayadi before dropping out in eleventh grade. When he left school in 1999 he attended classes for a spray painting apprenticeship but did not complete it. For a few months Ahmed Raad worked as a salesman and team leader for the EL Group, a mortgage business that makes unsolicited telephone calls to homeowners. Between 2002 and 2004, he undertook a plumbing apprenticeship and worked briefly with two plumbing firms. He eventually stopped working when he injured his elbow. After receiving WorkCover benefits for some time, he developed a business selling phone cards and then a business selling various products online. Neither venture was profitable. Ahmed was the cluster's treasurer.[39]

Followers (Melbourne)

Ezzit Raad, age twenty-three at the time of his arrest, was born in Australia to Lebanese immigrants. Like his brother Ahmed, he became a more observant Muslim after the death of his brother Mansour in 2003. He was married with two daughters. He was an electrician and was close to his brother, Ahmed. He was found guilty of "knowingly belonging to a terrorist organization."[40]

Abdullah Merhi, age twenty at the time of his arrest, was of Lebanese descent. He is one of the ten children of Lebanese immigrants who arrived in Australia in 1971. His father died suddenly in 2003 when Abdullah was eighteen years old. Merhi attended Princes Hill Secondary College until half way through Year 11. He began an electrical apprenticeship in 2002 and at the time of his arrest he was close to completing that apprenticeship. Merhi played football with the Fitzroy Junior Football Club and taught physical education classes at Eris Arabic School, a volunteer-run organization based in the Flemington Community Centre. Mehri reportedly attended sermons given by Sheikh Omran. He was married with one son.[41]

Izzydeen Atik, age twenty-five at the time of his arrest, had been previously arrested for minor crimes. He agreed to plead guilty and testify against his former associates at trial in return for a reduced sentence.[42]

Amer Haddara, age twenty-six at the time of his arrest, was the son of Lebanese immigrants. During two of his high school years he lived in Syria and studied Arabic. Haddara had earned a computer systems engineering degree from Victoria University in 2002. He was a volunteer computer technician at the Royal Institute for the Blind and was a committee member of the students' Islamic Society. Before his arrest, Haddara was running his own travel agency from home, offering pilgrimages to Mecca. Three weeks before his arrest, he had landed a job with a Prahran recruitment agency, Macro Recruitment, where he specialized in finding candidates for IT and engineering jobs. According to those who knew him, he made no secret of his business ambitions and liked to dress and act the part. He had reportedly attended sermons given by Sheikh Omran.[43]

Hany Taha, age thirty-one at the time of his arrest, was a father of three. Taha came from a large Lebanese migrant family and worked closely with his older brother Abdul and other relatives at the family panel-beating business. Police alleged Taha ran a vehicle rebirthing operation (rehabbing stolen cars) from the premises to help fund the terrorist cell's operations.

Taha is believed to have become fervent in his faith in 2000. Taha had been previously arrested for minor crimes.

Periphery (Melbourne)

Shane Kent, age twenty-eight at the time of his arrest, was an unemployed Muslim convert to Islam and had radicalized at the mosque and the Brunswick meeting hall of Sheikh Omran. Kent was married to a Turkish-born woman and had three children. He traveled to Pakistan in mid-2001, attending al Qaeda training camps with twenty-year-old Ahmed Kalek, who was born in Canberra but also converted to Islam. According to the Victoria Supreme Court prosecutor Mark Dean, Kent had received weapons and explosives training at the al Farouq camp in 2001 and pledged, in bin Laden's presence, to carry out jihad. He returned to Australia just before the September 11, 2001, attacks. Kent ultimately defected from Sheikh Omran and came under the wing of Abdul Nacer Benbrika.[45]

Bassam Raad, age twenty-three at the time of his arrest, was found not guilty on all counts.[46]

Majeed Raad, age twenty-one at the time of his arrest, was found not guilty on all counts.[47]

Shoue Hammoud, age twenty-five at the time of his arrest, was found not guilty on all counts.[48]

Overseas Travel and Link Up with Al Qaeda

Travel to Pakistan and Afghanistan provided opportunities for active core members of both of the Sydney and Melbourne clusters to link up with the transnational jihad, LeT, and al Qaeda itself. The ASJA connection to JI in Indonesia provided one network through which Australians would travel to training camps. Sheikh Omran was to some degree the conduit to JI in Indonesia and southwest Asia. In Sydney, Sheikh Zoud may have been the facilitator for individuals who wanted to travel to southwest Asia.[49]

Among the Sydney cluster, three individuals linked to Operation Pendennis attended a Lashkar-e-Taiba (LeT) training camp in Pakistan between

1999 and 2002: Khaled Cheikho and Abdul Rakib Hasan in 1999–2000 and Moustafa Cheikho in 2001.[50]

A member of the U.S.-based Northern Virginia Paintball group, Yong Ki Kwon, testified that he had prayed and shared meals with an Australian he knew as Abu Asad at the LeT camp in early November 2001. Abu Asad is believed to be Moustafa Cheikho. According to Kwon, "He [Abu Asad] said his uncle had gone to LeT camp and had gone back. Khalid was back about a year before Moustafa went to the camp.[51] Kwon also testified that he met and even shared a room with Willie Brigitte, who was in the company of "Abu Asad" at the very same camp.[52] All of this was corroborated, with the additional information that Abdul Rakib Hassan was in attendance at the same LeT camp, in the French court documents.[53]

Sheikh Zoud, the leader of the Haldon Street mosque, which the Cheikhos had been known to attend, may have facilitated their travel. In fact, according to Kwon, Moustafa Cheikho (Abu Asad) told Kwon that "to get to a LeT camp he had to get a reference letter from some sheikh in Australia." This was most likely Zoud in Sydney. In fact, former French terrorism magistrate Jean-Louis Bruguiere asserted in a dossier that Zoud was the chief recruiter of an informal terror network.[54]

Training and Skill Acquisition

The standard forty-five-day LeT training course, which Kwon and other foreigners had completed, included use of AK-47s, M16s, light machine guns, pistols, and rocket-propelled grenades. Kwon noted, "We learnt how to take them apart and put them back together and [then we'd] go out and shoot a couple of rounds." Trainees also learned reconnaissance, camouflage, escape tactics, cryptic talk, and target practice. "They'd make us hike up the mountains and spy on the other [LeT] camps, sometimes infiltrate them without being seen and report back," Kwon said.[55] He testified, "I remember seeing [Abu Asad/Mustafa Cheikho's] group doing combat maneuvers, crawling and rolling."[56]

Shane Kent, who was part of the Melbourne cluster, also traveled to southwest Asia for military training in 2001. He allegedly trained at a Jaish-e-Mohammed camp in Pakistan before proceeding to al Qaeda's al Farouq camp in Afghanistan, where it is believed he received weapons and explosives training. Kent was joined there by two other Australians he knew from the Ahlus Sunnah Michael Street Mosque in Melbourne—a twenty-year-old Canberra-born convert to Islam named Ahmad Kalek and another convert, Jack Thomas. Their travel had been arranged by a fellow Ahlus Sunnah follower at the mosque.[57] While Kent returned to Australia just before the September 11 attacks, Ahmad Kalek was later detained in Egypt and held in a Cairo prison for several months, before being sent home to Australia. He has not been charged but remains a person of interest to the Australian authorities.[58]

Al Qaeda Recruitment

Ahmed Kalek, Shane Kent's traveling companion to the al Qaeda camp, later told the Australian Federal Police (AFP) that he, Kent, and Jack Thomas had met bin Laden in Afghanistan. He noted, "Our group had a short conversation with Osama bin Laden during which he asked who we were and where we were from. He also asked how the Muslims in Australia were going." Although Kent, the only member of the Pendennis conspiracy to link up with al Qaeda, had pledged in bin Laden's presence to carry out jihad, he was barely involved on the periphery of the plot and no longer in any type of contact with al Qaeda by 2004–5 when the plot was going operational. As a result, although Shane Kent did get recruited to al Qaeda, it was immaterial to the Pendennis plot.[59]

Operational Cycle

In June 2004, an individual of Algerian descent entered a Melbourne police station to inform the officers at the station that he was in the inner circle of a group that was planning to commit acts of terror in Australia. This group would turn out to be the Melbourne cluster of Operation Pendennis. However, it was not until about a year later, on June 2, 2005, when the group made its first purchase of laboratory equipment, followed days later by an order for twenty-four bottles of hydrogen peroxide, hexamine tablets two and a half weeks later, and then another twenty-four bottles of hydrogen peroxide three weeks later. Although the precise catalyst is unclear, by June 2005 the Sydney cluster had entered the operational cycle.[60]

Local Skill Acquisition

Years before the chemical purchases began, members of both the Sydney and Melbourne clusters had traveled to southwest Asia for paramilitary training. However, a few months before the purchases began, both members of both clusters traveled to the Australian outback for outdoor group-based military training.

Six of the eight Sydney men attended "bush training camps" held in March and April 2005 at two western New South Wales properties. Local accounts recall that the members posed as recreational hunters. The LeT camp veterans, Khaled and Moustafa Cheikho along with Mohammed Elomar, likely ran the camps since the Cheikhos had already received training abroad. The groups left behind ammunition shell casings and unidentifiable burned and melted material.[61] The Melbourne suspects participated in outdoor bonding activities, including paramilitary-like training at a rural Kinglake property and at various commercial hunting properties.[62]

Target Selection

During the Pendennis trial in Melbourne in 2008, Izzydeen Atik, one of the members of the Melbourne cluster, asserted that the group planned to attack the Melbourne Cricket Ground stadium during the 2005 Australia Football League (AFL) Grand Final between the Sydney Swans and West Coast Eagles. The Melbourne Cricket Ground (MCG) is an Australian sports stadium located in Yarra Park in inner Melbourne. It is the largest stadium in Australia and has a capacity of 100,000. The MCG was the centerpiece stadium of the 1956 Melbourne Summer Olympics.[63] When ASIO and police raids forced the plotters to shelve the MCG plan, they switched targets to either the 2006 NAB Cup (a preseason Australian football tournament) or the Crown Casino Entertainment Complex. Atik noted, "The AFL Grand Final was the original target and because of the raids and because of security reasons and funding they were to be off until the following year."[64]

The NAB Cup is an AFL competition held before the beginning of the premiership season and the Crown Casino Entertainment Complex is a casino and entertainment center in Melbourne and attracts on average sixteen million visitors yearly. It incorporates several nightclubs, a Village

Cinema complex, and multiple restaurants, fast food outlets, food courts, and shops. The complex also houses Galactic Circus, an electronic games arcade, laser tag facility, and bowling alley. According to Atik, Abdul Nacer Benbrika (Abu Bakr), the cluster's leader, named the targets: "Abu Bakr told me of the targets that he intends to attack."[65] Atik's credibility, however, was called into question and the judge "warned the jury to be wary of basing any conviction solely on the evidence of Atik, whom he described as an admitted liar, con man and fraudster and a pretty unsafe witness."[66]

Although Atik's credibility was called into question and the judge "warned the jury to be wary of basing any conviction solely on the evidence of Atik, whom he described as an admitted liar, con man and fraudster and a pretty unsafe witness," in July 2009, Shane Kent plead guilty and confirmed that the locations listed by Atik had been the identified targets.[67]

Casing

Both the Sydney and Melbourne clusters conducted reconnaissance on a variety of potential targets. The Melbourne suspects filmed the Australian Stock Exchange and Flinders Street Station, Melbourne's landmark central train exchange, and had maps of Casselden Place, the Melbourne headquarters of both the Departments of Foreign Affairs and Trade and Immigration.[68] Members of the Sydney cluster (Mazen Touma, Mohammed Elomar, and Abdul Rakib Hasan) were arrested in 2004 surveilling the Lucas Heights nuclear power plant and were reported to have targeted the Sydney Opera House and the Sydney Harbour Bridge.[69]

Communications

Although the active core of each cluster met covertly every two to three weeks, the conspirators also used a number of conversational, security, and anti-surveillance tactics to try to conceal their activities. For example, Benbrika used at least ten different mobile phones, eight of which were registered under false names and addresses.[70] Aimen Joud had thirteen mobile phones, twelve of which were registered under false names and addresses. Individuals also communicated through PALTalk, transferred information on USB sticks, and utilized coded SMS messages.[71] There did not appear to be any ongoing communication between the Pendennis plotters and Pakistan.

Weaponization

The two clusters were on different trajectories with regard to weaponization. The Sydney cluster had rapidly advanced and was stockpiling material necessary for an attack. In fact, in conversations recorded just before the raids, the Melbourne cell members reportedly complained that the Sydney cell was ahead of them in planning an attack. As previously mentioned, the first purchases were made by the conspirators in the spring of 2005.[72]

In Sydney, the men had downloaded a list of ingredients needed to produce several types of IEDs including peroxide-based explosives in Arabic as well as a diagram of an electronic detonator that was marked non-functional. When the authorities searched the residences of the members of the Sydney cluster they found a USB stick containing instructions in Arabic for the manufacture of explosives—"The Illustrated Encyclopaedia"—as well as a CD entitled "Security and Intelligence" that included various topics related to the manufacture and detonation of different types of improvised explosives. The material found on the USB flash drive at Elomar's home contained recipes for making explosives using nitroglycerine, hexamine, hydrogen peroxide, acetone, and sulfuric acid (battery acid). There were also instructions for making a detonator from acetone and peroxide, as well as recipes for explosives made from fertilizer and mercuric fulminate. They included step-by-step instructions on how to manufacture explosives such as TATP and HMTD, with details and advice as to how to obtain the ingredients for the explosives and how to extract and prepare them for use.[73]

Although purchases began in June 2005, by the fall, the Sydney cluster was turning the Sydney house into a bomb-making factory, ordering the chemicals necessary for hydrogen peroxide explosive devices, including hydrogen peroxide, sulfuric acid, citric acid, glycerin, and acetone. Between September 28, 2005, and November 5, 2005, Hasan and, to a lesser extent, Jamal, were involved in ordering chemicals. For example, on September 28, 2005, Hasan and Jamal placed orders for battery acid and distilled water at Auto King. On the same day, Hasan ordered sixty liters of acetone at Peter's Hardware in Greenacre. Following the Operation Pendennis arrests, the

Sydney cluster was found to have been in possession of hundreds of liters of chemicals, including twenty-four 400-milliliter bottles of hydrogen, laboratory equipment, 165 detonators, 132 digital timers, batteries, firearms, and 7,500 rounds of ammunition.[74]

Although the men gave various explanations as to why they were purchasing these items, Australian chemical suppliers claimed they had tipped off the authorities about several attempts by this cluster to purchase large quantities of hydrogen peroxide, acetone, hydrochloric and/or sulfuric acid, and hexamine—all chemicals that can be used in explosives. Some of the Australian plotters used car thefts and credit card scams to finance the purchase of the materiel for conducting the attacks.[75]

While the plotters had not yet assembled a complete device, it appears they had acquired all the constituent parts for the three key components—the explosive, the detonator, and the triggers—as well as a backpack similar to that used by London's July 7 and July 21 bombers.

The Al Qaeda Factor

There was no outside command and control by al Qaeda or LeT. This plot was totally homegrown in terms of command and control. In fact, the head of the ASIO stated in March 2006, "There is no evidence . . . of any link so far to an outside controller or outside direction." Benbrika not only picked the targets but also determined the timing. During the 2008 Melbourne trial, Izzydeen Atik told the jury that group member Bassam Raad wanted to become a suicide bomber, but "he was waiting for Abu Bakr's command to send him off."[76] Shane Kent's 2001 training in the al Farouq camp and meeting with Osama bin Laden were the only Operation Pendennis connections to al Qaeda Core, but they were not relevant to the plot given his minor role and lack of ongoing communication. Al Qaeda training and al Qaeda inspiration were factors, but there were no links from an operational standpoint. This was an al Qaeda "inspired" plot.

Chapter 15

Operation Osage (Canada, 2006)

ON JUNE 2 AND 3, 2006, police and security agencies carried out a series of counterterrorism raids in the greater Toronto area that resulted in the arrest of seventeen individuals. One additional individual was arrested and charged in August. Canadian authorities believe that the men had been planning large-scale terrorist attacks, which included detonating truck bombs at least two locations in downtown Toronto (the Toronto Stock Exchange and CSIS Toronto headquarters) and at an undisclosed military base. Other attacks that the men considered included opening gunfire in a crowded public area, beheading Canadian prime minister Stephen Harper, and attacking various buildings such as the Canadian Broadcasting Center, the Canadian Parliament, and the CN Tower. The Toronto plotters consisted of eighteen people, almost all of whom were in their teens or early twenties. The group originated from two separate clusters: Mississauga, a suburb of Toronto, and Scarborough, a neighborhood in Toronto, both of which were relatively close together. The conspirators' goals were to conduct bombings that would be even bigger than the London 2005 bombings—to be called the "Battle of Toronto"—and to "pressure Canada into withdrawing troops from Afghanistan." Accounts from family and friends of the plotters suggest that most, if not all, were "well-integrated" into Canadian society.[1]

The Toronto Scene

For most of the 1990s, the combination of lax immigration laws and generous social benefits made Canada a safe haven for many with extremist ideas
who were seeking a sanctuary from persecution in the Middle East. Most
prominent and influential among these expatriates was Ahmed Khadr, a
well-known al Qaeda financier who was subsequently killed in a 2003 battle
with American forces in Afghanistan. Khadr, a naturalized Canadian citizen who had emigrated from Egypt to Toronto in the late 1970s, had claimed
that he feared persecution in his home country of Egypt. During the 1980s
and 1990s he and his family were able to travel to and from Canada to Afghanistan and Pakistan, all the while collecting millions of dollars in aid
that reportedly went to finance al Qaeda operations.[2]

In Toronto, the Khadr family attended and influenced the development
of an important local hub for reactionary Islam in Toronto—the Salaheddin
Islamic Center. This mosque and religious center promoted a Saudi/Wah-
habi interpretation of Islam. Moreover, free Korans, financed by the Saudi
government, were distributed at the center, which included essays on the
need and legitimacy of jihad. This ideology influenced a younger generation
of Muslims in the Toronto region, including two of Khadr's sons, who became mujahedeen and ended up in Guantanamo Bay as enemy combatants,
as well as other young men who did not have the same connections to southwest Asia and thus ultimately conspired to commit acts of terror at home.[3]

Gravitating to Reactionary Islam

Many of the cluster members were not brought up exposed to a fundamentalist interpretation of Islam. However, later in life, they were drawn to Salafism, which had proliferated in Canada.[4] In Mississauga, an identity crisis
among some high school–age members of the cluster may have caused them
to adopt this reactionary interpretation of Islam. Some members of the Scarborough cluster, led by Saad Khalid, a high school student at Meadowvale
Secondary School, formed the Religious Awareness Club. During lunchtime
he would preach Islam to other students, and he spent a good deal of time
with Fahim Ahmad and Zakaria Amara. The trio even created a chat group
called the Meadowvale Brothers. Schoolmates stated that the three began to
dress more traditionally and became more withdrawn.[5]

At least six members of the Mississauga cluster, including the three high schoolers, began to attend a storefront strip-mall mosque known as the Al Rahman Islamic Centre where forty-three-year-old Qayyum Abdul Jamal frequently spoke. He promoted views that were Wahhabi in nature and anti-Western. Fahim Ahmad and Zakaria Amara met Jamal at the center in 2005 after switching to mosques because theirs was not fundamentalist enough.[6] Two of the Scarborough cluster members, Steven Vikash Chand and Jahmaal James, attended the Salaheddin Islamic Center, a known extremist mosque. This location hosted both the al Qaeda–linked Khadrs and Imam Aly Hindy, who is notorious for inflammatory speeches and a radical interpretation of Islam. Hindy is known to have urged members of his congregation to avoid all cooperation with Canadian authorities.[7]

At Stephen Leacock Collegiate High School in Scarborough, Amin Mohammed Durrani had over a period of two years adopted a Salafi interpretation of Islam and presented himself as an example to others by wearing an ankle-length robe and a kufi skullcap and carrying the Koran. At lunchtime he gave informal sermons and proselytized about being a good Muslim to the other students. In 2005, he and his friends began to skip classes to attend Musalla-e-Namira, a private, informal prayer room on the top floor of two-story building near the high school.[8]

Politicization of Beliefs

Those who knew the suspects in the variety of communities from which they emerged noted that in the years leading up to 2006 they had became activists for Muslims worldwide and felt that Muslims were being treated unfairly in Canada.[9] At Al Rahman, Qayyum Abdul Jamal was known by the other congregants to have an "us-versus-them" view of the world in which Muslims were being oppressed by the West, and he often made provocative and unsubstantiated charges against the behavior of Canadian troops in Afghanistan. In addition, he often critiqued the wars in Iraq and Afghanistan, as well as the plight of Muslims abroad in general. According to one source, "He had no formal religious role in the mosque but his radical views were tolerated by the leadership because he cleaned the mosque for free."[10]

Fahim Ahmad, the leader of the Scarborough cluster, utilized emotional arguments about the oppression of Muslims to recruit individuals, including an individual who would become a primary CSIS/RCMP source to join his group. "Ahmed defined 'the enemy' as the Americans, and because of the 'close local connection between Canada and the United States, Canada was also the enemy.'"[11] According to a statement made to the police by Saad Gaya, a member of the Mississauga cluster, his goal in the attack was "religiously-inspired." In other words, Gaya wanted to coerce Canada into a political goal—withdrawing troops from Afghanistan—but used a religious justification to legitimize the means—to protect a Muslim country from attack.[12]

The Mississauga Cluster

Out of the eighteen individuals ultimately arrested, six had spent significant time in and had lived in and around Mississauga, a suburb of Toronto (Zakaria Amara, Saad Khalid, Qayyum Abdul Jamal, Ahmad Mustafa Ghany, Shareef Abdelhaleem, and Asad Ansari). The group ranged in age from nineteen to forty-three, with the bulk of the members in their early twenties. Some members of the group were born in Canada while others moved to Canada as children from Egypt and Pakistan. Fahim Ahmad, Zakaria Amara, and Saad Khalid were friends in Meadowvale Secondary School in Mississauga before Ahmad moved to Scarborough and became the leader of that cluster. The men were known to have become more strident in their faith as they grew older. Ultimately, the active core of the cluster that was responsible for the conspiracy and the plot consisted of four individuals (Zakaria Amara, Saad Khalid, Shareef Abdelhaleem, Saad Gaya, and two CSIS/RCMP informants, Mubin Sheikh and Shaher Elsohemy).[13]

Al Rahman was a central hub for the development of the Mississauga cluster. Fahim Ahmad and Zakaria Amara met Jamal at the center in 2005 after switching to mosques because theirs was not fundamentalist enough. They, and others, were drawn to the mosque for its literalist interpretation of Islam. The mosque had been associated with the Islamist south Asian movement Tanzeem-e-Islami originally but broke away in the wake of some differences with its North American arm, the Islamic Organization of North America (IONA).[14]

Qayyum Abdul Jamal, an older man who served as janitor and an ideologue to the young men of Mississauga, was part of the attraction to the location and was well-known in Mississauga. In fact, in the parking lot of Meadowvale Secondary School, students were quite familiar with him. Many had stories about the times he joined them for soccer games and cricket matches as well as the lessons on Islam that he gave at a nearby mosque. In addition, Qayyum Jamal hosted sessions at his home; neighbors noted the near continuous flow of young men filing in and out of his house at odd hours.[15]

Jamal, age forty-three at time of his arrest, had been a student and follower of the Tanzeem-e-Islami. This group seeks to install the Caliphate in Pakistan and has an anti-Western and anti-Semitic worldview. Qayyum Jamal was a naturalized Canadian citizen, was married to a convert, and had four children. He had been a factory worker and was an active member of the mosque who frequently led prayers. Qayyum Jamal had emigrated from Karachi at an unknown date. He had a reputation in the community for reaching out to young people, teaching them Islam, playing basketball with them, and taking them camping. In addition to preaching at the mosque, he cleaned the rugs and took out the trash. The men in the Mississauga cluster came to be influenced by his views and adopted them as their own.[16]

Khalid, Zakaria, and Fahim bonded over the Internet as well in an online chat room as the Meadowvale Brothers. While the young men's talk was primarily about movies and final exams, Zakaria Amara kept returning to the issue of sacrifice for Islam. "I love for the sake of Allah, and hate for his sake," he wrote, according to Canada's *Globe and Mail*.[17]

The three young men began discussing political issues and the permissibility of jihad online, and they watched jihadi videos online and communicated with like-minded individuals from around the world. This worldwide communication served as an "echo chamber" for their jihadist views, serving to only reinforce them. Similarly, the wives of Zakaria Amara, Fahim Ahmad, Qayyum Jamaal, and Ahmad Mustafa Ghany had a robust online community that discussed politics, social issues, and religion via personal blogs and a semi-private forum founded by Amara's wife. Their postings were often militant, intolerant, and extremist. Moreover, almost everything Canadian was rejected by these women. Advice was posted on issues ranging from "sisters-only" events to where to find halal Chinese food to videos of terrorist beheadings of Westerners.[18]

The Scarborough Cluster

Out of the eighteen individuals ultimately arrested, twelve had spent significant time in and had lived in and around Scarborough, a neighborhood in Toronto (Fahim Ahmad, Steven Vikash Chand, Jahmaal James, Mohammed

Dirie, Yasin Abdi Mohammed, Amin Mohammed Durrani, and five minors who went to high school with Durrani). The group ranged in age from sixteen to twenty-five. Some members of the group were born in Canada while others moved to Canada as children from Somalia and Pakistan. One was a Hindu convert to Islam. Fahim Ahmed, who was the link between the two clusters and was originally from Mississauga, ultimately moved to Scarborough and became the leader of the Scarborough cluster. Although it is unclear how they met, in 2005, Ahmad used his credit card to rent a car for two immigrants from Somalia, Mohammed Dirie and Yasin Abdi Mohammed, who were arrested attempting to bring firearms into Canada from the United States. Both Steven Vikash Chand and Jahmaal James attended the Salaheddin Islamic Center regularly. At the Stephen Leacock Collegiate Institute, a local high school, alumnus Mohammed Durrani and Steven Vikash Chand frequented the school grounds to recruit Muslim students to come to the Salaheddin Islamic Center.[19]

The Salaheddin Islamic Center was a central hub for the development of the Scarborough cluster. Steven Chand and Jahmaal James were regular congregants. The location was known among the community and to the Canadian intelligence agencies to be a hotbed of extremist rhetoric. Imam Aly Hindy was known to preach an intolerant and anti-Western version of Islam, and this location had been frequented by Canada's Khadr family, who was known to have close and ongoing links to al Qaeda and Osama bin Laden. This was also the location that minors recruited at Durrani's high school were encouraged to attend.[20]

By late March 2006, a falling-out had occurred between Zakaria Amara and Fahim Ahmad and, according to Canadian legal documents, "the 'group' finally split into two completely separate groups or factions headed by Ahmad and by Amara. Amara's group, largely based in Mississauga, decided to go its own way with Amara saying that he was finished with Ahmad as he wasn't moving things fast enough and not making concrete plans." Amara's Mississauga cluster became the active core of individuals who moved forward with the plot and the Scarborough group was marginalized.[21]

Anatomy of the Cluster

Active Core

Zakaria Amara, age twenty at the time of his arrest, was the leader of the Mississauga cluster and the actual plot. Known as Zak, he transferred out of

Meadowvale Secondary School in tenth grade. As a sixteen-year-old he began posting radical poetry online. Zak was attending Humber College and working part-time at a gas station when he was arrested. Zak had married right after high school and his wife attended Ryerson University.[22]

Saad Khalid, age nineteen at the time of his arrest, was born in Saudi Arabia and immigrated with his family to Canada at the age of eight. He was a naturalized Canadian citizen and was raised in a moderate Muslim household. Khalid was considered bright and outgoing in his early high school years. In 2003, his mother died in an accident. In the following years, he became more devout. At the Meadowvale Secondary School he created the Religious Awareness Club (RAC) and proselytized a fundamentalist form of Islam at lunchtime. When he was arrested, he was a first-year business student at the University of Toronto's Erindale campus in Mississauga.[23]

Shareef Abdelhaleem, age thirty at the time of his arrest, was born in Egypt and immigrated with his family to Canada at the age of ten. He worked as a computer programmer and was a regular attendee at Al Rahman.[24]

Saad Gaya, age eighteen at the time of his arrest, was born in Montreal and grew up in a middle-class family in an Oakville suburb. His parents, both immigrants from Pakistan, worked—the father as an engineer and the mother in a department store. Saad, the oldest of their three children, was a first-year student at McMaster University when he was arrested. He had achieved a high school average of 92 percent and won a scholarship to McMaster, where he made the dean's list in his first year. According to an interview he gave to the police, Saad "had been debating whether to become a teacher, a mathematician or a pharmacist." While at McMaster, he was simultaneously pursuing an Islamic degree from the online program at al Maghrib Institute. Saad had lived with his family in Pakistan for a period of time during 1995–98.[25]

Followers

Fahim Ahmad, age twenty-one at the time of his arrest, attended Meadowvale Secondary School with Zak Amara and Saad Khalid before transferring to another local school. When he moved to Scarborough, he became a regular at prayer services at the Islamic Foundation of Toronto. Fahim had met Qayyum Jamal in 2005 with Zak Amara and Saad Khalid.

Steven Vikash Chand, age twenty-five at the time of his arrest, was born in Canada to Hindu parents from Fiji. In some ways Chand was considered relatively well integrated, serving in the Canadian military from June 2000 until April 2004. It was at some point during this period that he converted to Islam. Chand was described as mild-mannered and easily influenced. Some speculate that his alienation from mainstream Canadian society and conversion to Islam was related to his parents' divorce, an event that further distanced him from his family. Chand began attending the Salaheddin Islamic Center, a known radical mosque led by fundamentalist imam Aly Hindy. He soon went from seeking answers to providing them. Chand began spending two or three days a week outside public schools handing out extremist literature and seeking converts among school-age children.

Ahmad Mustafa Ghany, age twenty-one at the time of his arrest, was born in Canada. His family had emigrated from Trinidad and Tobago to Canada and his father was a medical doctor. He was married to Zak Amara's sister and graduated from McMaster University with a degree in health sciences. All charges were dropped against Ghany after two years. He, too, had been a regular attendee at Al Rahman.[26]

Asad Ansari, age twenty-one at the time of his arrest, was a regular attendee at Al Rahman. He was described by the government as the group's "technical expert," adept at editing videos from the training camp and removing malicious software from Fahim Ahmad's computer.[27]

Ibrahim Alkhalel Mohammed Aboud, age nineteen at the time of his arrest, was not taken into custody or charged until early August 2006. He was arrested in connection with his attendance at a training camp in December 2005.

Jahmaal James, age twenty-three at the time of his arrest, was of West Indian extraction and regularly prayed at the Salaheddin Islamic Center. Unemployed, he too distributed material at local public schools. Jahmaal had recently been married to a woman in Pakistan and it is alleged that he received military training in Pakistan as part of that trip.

Amin Mohammed Durrani, age nineteen at the time of his arrest, was responsible, along with Steven Chand, for recruiting minors into the cluster as young as sixteen from the Scarborough high school he had attended.

Five Minors, age eighteen and under at the time of arrest, all attended the same high school as Durrani in Scarborough, where they were recruited.

Periphery

Mohammed Dirie, age twenty-two and already incarcerated at the time of the 2006 arrests, had immigrated to Canada from Somalia at age seven. He worked as a carpenter before being arrested in August 2005 with Yasin Abdi Mohammed for attempting to smuggle weapons and ammunition into Canada. He pleaded guilty and was given a two-year sentence.[28]

Yasin Abdi Mohammed, age twenty-four and already incarcerated at the time of the 2006 arrests, had immigrated to Canada from Somalia at age seven and was a naturalized Canadian citizen. He worked as a carpenter before being arrested in August 2005 with Mohammed Dirie for attempting to smuggle weapons and ammunition into Canada. He pleaded guilty and was given a two-year sentence.[29]

Mariya Ahmad, the wife of Fahim Ahmad, was nineteen years old at the time of her husband's arrest. Following the death of the Hamas spiritual leader Abdel-Aziz al Rantisi, she posted online, "May Allah crush these jews, bring them down to their knees, humiliate them. Ya Allah make their women widows and their children orphans."[30]

Nada Farooq, the wife of Zak Amara, was twenty years old at the time of her husband's arrest. They had married almost three years earlier and at the time she had posted that she wanted a prenuptial agreement that stated that if her husband refused an opportunity to participate in jihad, then she was entitled to a divorce. Nada was the daughter of a Canadian-based pharmacist but had been born in Karachi and had been raised in Saudi Arabia until the age of eleven. She had grown up significantly more religious than her parents.[31]

Cheryfa Mac Aulay Jamal, the wife of Qayyum Jamaal, was forty-four years old at the time of her husband's arrest. She was a Caucasian convert to Islam and had adopted a very literal and intolerant interpretation of Islam—one that forbid participation in Canadian democracy. She served as a leader among the Muslim women in the online and Mississauga communities.[32]

Rana Ghany, the wife of Ahmad Mustafa Ghany and sister of Nada Farooq, was nineteen years old at the time of her husband's arrest. She, too, had spent significant time in her preteen years in Saudi Arabia. Her online nickname was al Mujahidah—"the Jihadist." She often posted graphic photos of female militants and suicide bombers.[33]

Overseas Travel and Link Up with Al Qaeda

Only one member of the Toronto 18 is believed to have traveled to southwest Asia during the time that the clusters were forming. Jahmaal James, who visited Pakistan, is alleged to have received some training in an LeT camp in Balikot.[34] James traveled to Pakistan between November 5, 2005 and March 2006 via London and Dubai for the ostensible purpose of getting married to the niece of a Toronto Islamic bookstore owner, whom he knew from the Salaheddin Islamic Center in Toronto. Almost immediately upon his arrival in early November he consecrated the arranged marriage.[35] During this time, James also met up with Aabid Khan (aka Abu Umar), a twenty-year-old British Pakistani from Bradford, England, who was a regular and prolific contributor to a jihadist Internet forum called al Tibbyan and who, it is believed, facilitated James's participation in the LeT training camp (though James was only able to participate in the camp for one week due to illness).[36] Through interactions on al Tibbyan, Khan had befriended a number of the suspects in the Toronto terror case, including two Americans in Georgia who would later be arrested, and visited Toronto in 2005 to meet with them all. Khan attracted this following because as the Canadian journalist Stewart Bell notes, "Abu Umar was considered a 'go-to guy' who could help Western recruits gain access to Lashkar-e-Tayyiba's network of paramilitary training camps in Pakistan."[37] Khan was ultimately convicted in August 2008, in the U.K., of possessing material likely to be used in a terrorist attack and sentenced to twelve years in prison. At the time of his arrest, Khan had information on his laptop computer that suggested he was attempting to form an international terrorist cell to stage attacks in Britain, the United States, continental Europe, and Canada that would rival the impact of the September 11 attacks.[38]

As previously noted, Khan flew to Toronto in March 2005 to meet Fahim Ahmad and some other members of his cluster, as well as two men from the United States. According to British police evidence, Khan's plan was to rent basement apartments in Toronto where the group could spend a month or two bonding before flying to Pakistan for military training in camps. Once the training was completed, they would return to the basement apartments in Toronto and select their targets.[39]

According to records of his online chats, Khan contacted LeT to arrange military training for some of his contacts. In fact, Khan and two other U.K.-based individuals went to Pakistan to train, but the details of the nature and duration of their training are unclear. On June 6, 2006, four days after the arrests of the Toronto 18 in Canada, officers from the West Yorkshire Police arrested Aabid Khan at Manchester International Airport as he stepped off a flight from Pakistan.[40]

Two Americans, Syed Haris Ahmed, who was twenty-one at the time of his arrest, and Ehsanul Islam Sadequee, who was nineteen at the time of his arrest and from the greater Atlanta, Georgia, area, had also attended the meeting with Aabid Khan in Toronto during March 6–13, 2005. Syed Haris Ahmed, who was born in Pakistan and came to the United States at age twelve, was a naturalized citizen and a student at the Georgia Institute of Technology. Ehsanul Islam Sadequee was born in the United States but attended high school in Canada.[41]

According to interviews with U.S. federal agents, during these meetings in Toronto, the two Americans and Canadians discussed with Aabid Khan potential U.S. targets including military bases and oil refineries, as well as how to disrupt the Global Positioning System.[42] On or about April 10 and 11, 2005, just a few weeks after the trip to Toronto, both Ahmed and Sadequee conducted video surveillance of potential targets in Washington, D.C., including the Capitol, the headquarters of the World Bank, the Masonic Temple in Alexandria, Virginia, and a group of large fuel storage tanks near I-95 in northern Virginia. These short "casing" videos of symbolic and infrastructure targets for potential terrorist attacks were sent to Younis Tsouli (Irhabi007) and Aabid Hussein Khan.[43]

According to the FBI, between July and August 2005 Syed Haris Ahmed traveled to Pakistan for paramilitary training with LeT, which was facilitated by Khan. However, he was unable to obtain training. In August, Ehsanul Islam Sadequee departed for Bangladesh ostensibly to get married.[44] On March 23, 2006, Syed Haris Ahmed was arrested in Atlanta and charged with conspiring with and providing material support to terrorists. On April 2006, Ehsanul Islam Sadequee was arrested in Dhaka, Bangladesh, by government agents and returned to the United States. He was charged with the same terrorism offenses as Syed Haris Ahmed.

Al Qaeda Recruitment

There was no recruitment of any of the men by al Qaeda–linked individuals. Only Jahmaal James is alleged to have received some training in a

LeT camp in Balikot; he dropped out after a week and was not recruited by any terrorist organization.

Operational Cycle

A retreat to rural Ontario between December 2005 and January 2006 served as a paramilitary training camp for the majority of the men involved in the plot. The conclusion of this camp triggered the beginning of the operational cycle as the group named their plot Operation Badr and began to discuss strategies. At this early stage, the men discussed taking politicians hostage in the capital, demanding the removal of Canadian troops from Afghanistan and the release of Muslim prisoners, and executing the politicians "one by one" if the demands were not met. At one point, the two clusters disagreed on the means of the attack—Zakaria Amara (Mississauga) wanted to use truck bombs, while Fahim Ahmad (Scarborough) favored an attack with guns. Ultimately, Amara prevailed and Ahmad's cluster was shut out of the plot. Amara planned to depart Canada for Pakistan within hours of the non-suicidal attack.[45]

Training and Skill Acquisition

Soon after CSIS/RCMP informant Mubin Sheikh was able to make contact with leading members of the cluster in November 2005, he was recruited by Fahim Ahmad and tasked to take the lead in setting up an outdoor training camp for the men, at which he would serve as the primary trainer. The purpose of the camp was for training and for vetting of the individuals who participated. However, not all the participants knew the true purpose of the camp; some were told that the camp's purpose was religious and to learn outdoor survival skills.[46]

During December 18–30, 2005, at a location 150 kilometers north of Toronto, near the town of Washago, Ontario, for a period of twelve days during Christmas break, thirteen men and youths participated in the training camp, often in subzero (Fahrenheit) temperatures.[47] At the camp, run by both Zakaria Amara and Fahim Ahmad, Mubin Sheikh taught gun safety to the campers with a 9-mm handgun and ammunition that he had brought. Wearing camouflage, they participated in military marches, played paintball, did obstacle course runs, and received firearms training: "(The group) ventured into the deathly cold of winter without a proper tent, or in fact sufficient or proper supplies of any kind, was reduced to sleeping in the vehicles at night to prevent freezing to death, trooping off to Tim Hortons multiple times per day for coffee and use of the bathroom."[48]

Fahim Ahmad gave religious sermons at the camp to impart his ideological views to the participants. At the first *halaqa* (discussion circle), Ahmad played an audio disc entitled "The Constants of Jihad" by Anwar al Awlaki. Ahmad also held *halaqa*s comparing the Canadian countryside to Chechnya and called for victory over "Rome," which prosecutors have alleged was a reference to Canada. Around a campfire, Ahmad stated that "We're not officially al-Qaida but we share their principles and methods."[49] A subsequent camping trip was attended by ten individuals at the Rockwood Conservation Area in May 2006. However, a witness for the prosecution testified that the group slept in until noon, went swimming and hiking, and played with inflatable watercraft while discussing their plans for school and marriage.[50] Another individual's account differed, noting that a number of the accused individuals attended and the purpose of the camp was to "train." Moreover, there was a discussion circle inside a tent about military strategies.[51]

Target Selection/Casing

The group had planned three separate attacks in the greater Toronto area using three U-Haul vans that were to be packed with ammonium nitrate–based explosive devices. The vans were to be parked in three separate locations: the Toronto Stock Exchange and CSIS headquarters, both in downtown Toronto, as well as an unspecified military base. All three vans were to be triggered remotely. November 2006 was a potential target date.[52] Other plans such as opening fire on a crowd in a public place like the Toronto food courts or storming Parliament and beheading the Canadian prime minister were discussed but those plans were abandoned.[53] There seems to be minimal evidence of casing conducted on downtown Toronto targets. However, an external hard drive found in Zak Amara's home included satellite photos of Parliament buildings. Although surveillance and reconnaissance were done on Washington, D.C., targets by the two men from Atlanta, they were not part of the Toronto 18's target set.

Communication

The men met in person at cafés (Center de Khan, Second Cup), a Chinese restaurant, and Al Rahman Islamic Center, as well as the Canadian Tire Gas Bar (where Amara worked). They utilized cell phones, the Internet, and beepers and left messages in code for each other on USB memory sticks to stay in contact.[54]

Weaponization

Zak Amara searched the Internet, sometimes in the Meadowvale library, for information on how to build detonators and create a bomb, calculating the exact solutions of nitric acid and grams of mercury needed to detonate the bombs.[55] In February 2006, the CSIS informant Mubin Sheikh and Fahim Ahmad met Zakaria Amara in a park in Mississauga. He showed them a cell phone–activated detonator he was making. Government investigators who gained access to Zakaria Amara's apartment subsequently discovered that he was in the advanced stages of making his detonator with his cell phone.[56] They also found a handwritten binder titled "bomb manual," two circuit boards, and ammunition for a 9-mm pistol.[57]

By May 2006, Zak Amara and another accused individual from Mississauga, Shareef Abdelhaleem, sought to acquire three tons of ammonium nitrate and other chemical ingredients (nitric acid and mercury) used to make explosives. They had decided that they wanted to make a bomb bigger than the two-ton explosive that Timothy McVeigh used to shatter the federal building in Oklahoma City in 1995, killing 168 people. Amara gave Abdelhaleem $2,000 as a down payment to purchase ingredients (ammonium nitrate, nitric acid, and mercury) to make explosives. On May 18, 2006, Abdelhaleem gave his detailed order and the cash down payment to the second CSIS/RCMP informant.[58] On May 31, Saad Khalid gave a second payment of $2,600 to the second CSIS/RCMP informant to rent a facility in Newmarket, where the men would take delivery of the chemicals.[59]

The Al Qaeda Factor

At the December 2005 training camp north of Toronto, when the participants were sitting around a campfire, one of the leaders said, "We're not officially al Qaeda but we share their principles and methods."[60] In a recorded conversation one of the accused discusses the group's grand ambitions: "They're probably expecting what happened in London or something," he said. "Some bombing in a subway kills 10 people and everybody gets deported. We're not doing that. . . . So our thing it's, it's much, much greater on a scale . . . you do it once and you make sure they can never recover again."[61] In a statement that clearly shows the nature of the al Qaeda role in terms of inspiration, Shareef Abdelhaleem had suggested the group film a video that would make it look like "al Qaeda was the one who did it" and proposed they use the name "al Qaeda organization in Canada."[62] Clearly this was an al Qaeda "inspired" plot.

Chapter 16

The Al Qaeda Non-Plot: Lackawanna Cluster (2002)

IN SEPTEMBER 2002 seven men, all U.S. citizens of Yemeni descent who grew up in Lackawanna, New York, were charged with providing material support to al Qaeda. All seven had traveled to al Qaeda's al Farouq training camp in Afghanistan in the summer of 2001 and received paramilitary training there. One was arrested in Bahrain, five were arrested in Lackawanna, and one remains out of the reach of the United States. The trigger for the arrests was a series of e-mails sent in late summer 2002 by one of the men, Mukhtar al Bakri, to Lackawanna from Bahrain in which he described an upcoming "wedding" and another in which he mentioned a "big meal." In the past, the word "wedding" had been used as a code for a terrorist attack and "big meal" as code for an explosive.[1]

Six members of the alleged cell were subsequently arrested and pleaded guilty to aiding a terrorist organization. In December 2003, they received sentences of seven to ten years in prison. The seventh member, Jaber Elbaneh, is a fugitive believed to be in Yemen. In September 2003, the U.S. government announced a $5 million reward for his capture. After being arrested in Yemen in 2004, Elbaneh escaped in February 2006 from a Yemeni prison along with twenty-three other people, twelve of them al Qaeda members.[2] On May 20, 2007, Elbaneh turned himself in to Yemeni authorities. After an appeals court upheld his ten-year prison sentence for plotting to attack oil installments in Yemen, in May 2008, Elbaneh was returned to the same maximum-security prison in Sana from which he had escaped.[3] An eighth individual linked to the men of Lackawanna, Kamal

Derwish, was killed in Yemen on November 3, 2003, by a CIA Predator drone that was tracking al Qaeda operative Qaed Salim Sinan al Harethi, known as "Abu Ali" and believed to be one of the al Qaeda planners of the USS *Cole* bombing.[4]

The Lackawanna Scene

Yemenis first arrived in Lackawanna in the 1950s to work the unskilled jobs that Eastern Europeans and Irish, who immigrated before them, no longer desired. The first immigrants found jobs in the mills of Lackawanna Steel, partially because of the perception that they could better tolerate the extreme heat of the furnaces. By the 1960s, early Yemeni immigrants had brought their families to the United States and settled around the mills in the First Ward, which encompassed an area along Lake Erie separated from the rest of Lackawanna by a railroad bridge. This geographical separation was matched by the cultural isolation that many Yemenis in Lackawanna experienced. They created their own institutions, such as the Yemeni Benevolent Association, and slowly a small enclave of immigrants grew into the second largest Yemeni community in America after that in Detroit, numbering close to three thousand.[5]

When the mills faltered and began to close in the 1970s, unemployment rose and many returned to Yemen. When Kamal Derwish's father lost his job at the steel mill, the family moved to Yemen. Following his father's death, Kamal went to live with relatives in Saudi Arabia. There, Kamal adopted the country's official form of Islam, Wahhabism. Kamal, who subsequently developed links with al Qaeda, returned to Lackawanna in 2000 and helped encourage and radicalize the men who would become known as the Lackawanna Cluster.[6] The seven men from Lackawanna associated with this "plot" (Jaber Elbaneh, Mukhtar al Bakri, Sahim Alwan, Faysal Galab, Yahya Goba, Shafal Mosed, and Yasein Taher) emerged from a group of as many two dozen men from the community who would show up regularly at Kamal Derwish's apartment to discuss politics, current events, and religion over pizza. Most of the men knew each other from Lackawanna High School and from playing soccer together on the varsity team.[7]

Gravitating to Reactionary Islam

The primary Yemeni mosque in Lackawanna served as a community center as much as a house of worship for the local community. People would go there to socialize, attend prayers, and learn Arabic or study the Koran. Soon after his arrival in 2000, Kamal Derwish began to give sermons in the Yemeni mosque. His talks brought politics into the mosque as he called on the congregation and Muslims in general to come to the aid of their fellow Muslims around the world. The senior establishment was not pleased with the tone of his discussions and asked Derwish to take his talks somewhere else—which ended up being his apartment on Wilkesbarre Avenue, a short walk from the mosque.[8]

Derwish's *halaqa* was soon drawing more than twenty men. Pizza and religious conversation were the primary attractions, and the cluster of friends from Lackawanna High School soon became regulars.[9] Derwish, who had studied Islam in Saudi Arabia, was charismatic, well-spoken, and passionate and knowledgeable about Islam and thus appealed to the young men of Lackawanna. He had memorized sections of the Koran and the hadiths and had the legitimacy of having studied Islam where it had originated: in Arabia. Derwish served as "spiritual sanctioner," determining what was permissible and what was *haram* (forbidden).[10] In fact, according to some accounts, Derwish was able to explain Islam better than anyone the men had ever met. His answers to the men's questions were straightforward and logical. Derwish provided guidance on how to integrate faith into daily life and pushed the men toward a more devout and stricter form of Islam, more akin to the Wahhabi interpretation.[11] This was especially appealing to the Yemenis of Lackawanna, who were torn between their Muslim and American identities and whose knowledge of Islam in general was quite limited. Not only did Derwish seem to know more about Islam than the men's parents, but he had the ability to provide an Islamic framework through which international politics, global events, Islam, and the surrounding environment could be understood.

The young men of Lackawanna were captivated by Derwish's passionate rhetoric; one follower called him a "music man of religion." According to Sahim Alwan, who discussed Derwish's appeal as a spiritual leader, "Yes, very articulate, very impressive, very knowledgeable of the religion. . . . He was very likable. He joked a lot. You know what I mean? He was very social, I mean, very social. Young guys, older guys, his age guys, I mean, so yeah, he was a very likable guy."[12]

Politicization of New Beliefs

The conversations in the study sessions soon gravitated to political issues. Not only would the men study and analyze sections of the Koran, but they would also discuss issues of the day including the wars in Bosnia and Chechnya and the presence of U.S. troops in Saudi Arabia. Derwish talked about going to Palestine as a guerilla fighter and showed the men videotapes about the wars in Bosnia and Chechnya. In addition, Sayyid Qutb, as well as his political manifesto, *Milestones*, was also a topic of discussion. Even the attack on the USS Cole was framed not as a terrorist act but as Muslims fulfilling their obligation to defend Islam.[13]

Derwish was able to trigger an almost "vicarious suffering" among the men by continually raising issues that would highlight a moral outrage such as perceived injustices visited upon Palestinians by the Israelis (and American support for Israel), as well as Russian atrocities against the Muslim population in Chechnya and atrocities against Muslim women in Bosnia. Part of Derwish's means to trigger these powerful emotions was showing the men a videotape called *Five of the Russians*, which focused on the plight of Muslims in the Chechnya conflict in a very graphic way.[14] Derwish made a point to convey to the men that it was their religious obligation as Muslims to be prepared to help other Muslims in need. Part of that was the duty to train in preparation for military jihad.[15]

In the spring of 2001, Juma al Dosari, the newly hired imam for the Islamic Center of Bloomington, Illinois, came to Lackawanna upon Derwish's invitation. During his first talk at the center, al Dosari admonished the men for leaving their fellow Muslims to fight alone in Chechnya, Bosnia, and Kashmir. He triggered a sense of collective guilt and moral outrage, according to one congregant: "You need to wake up, people are dying and you are doing nothing to stop it," he reportedly said.[16] Al Dosari also railed against Arab governments that did nothing while Muslims died on a daily basis. According to people in the community, the leaders of the Lackawanna mosque were troubled by al Dosari's militant tone and he was not invited back.[17] In the study session that immediately followed the talk at the mosque, al Dosari, who was also presented as an expert on Islam, discussed his military exploits in Bosnia and Chechnya. More important, he told the men of the cluster that a pilgrimage to Mecca would not be enough to save their souls and that training for military jihad would be necessary.[18]

The Derwish Cluster

The cluster was made up of a subset of the men who attended the sessions at Derwish's apartment and ultimately traveled to Afghanistan for training. All seven were Yemeni Americans, both first and second generation. All were U.S. citizens and most of them were second-generation children of immigrants who had come to work at the Bethlehem Steel plant in the 1970s. None was particularly religious. The seven were graduates of Lackawanna High School. They were known by their peers and family as being more interested in playing soccer and hockey and partying than conducting jihad. They lived in a tight-knit Arab community, but most were all-American teenagers who played soccer together and enjoyed going to parties. The eighth individual, Kamal Derwish, was born in Buffalo but raised in Saudi Arabia.[19]

The Lackawanna group began as an autonomous cluster of young men whose motivations, cohesiveness, and adoption of a more reactionary interpretation of Islam all occurred in the context of the discussion group led by Derwish. It was underpinned by a localized, neighborhood phenomenon of primarily high school friends.[20]

Before Derwish had come back to Lackawanna, Yasein Taher and Mukhtar al Bakri had sought to promote their unique Muslim identity by establishing a local clique called the Arabian Knights. Not really a gang, the group made T-shirts and painted the name "Arabian Knights" on the back of their jackets as a cultural badge of honor. Unlike their parents, who as new immigrants sought to integrate almost completely into society and played down their heritage, the Arabian Knights promoted their ethnicity.[21]

However, the arrival of Kamal Derwish had a transformative effect on the trajectory of the seven men of Lackawanna. Derwish actually had al Qaeda "bona fides," and it was his informal social gatherings at his apartment, during which he played the role of the ideologue that attracted younger men from the community. This location became a place away from the community—almost a bachelor pad—where the men grew closer together as a group. A subset of these men would ultimately become his core group of followers who were willing to travel overseas.[22]

Derwish's family had left Buffalo to return to Yemen when he was five years old, but after his father was killed in a car accident, Derwish went to live with relatives in Saudi Arabia. Though he left the United States at an early age, he did return from time to time in the 1990s and even worked in a local plastics factory for a short while. In 2000, he returned to Lackawanna and after a short stint living with his uncle and cousin, he moved in with Yahya Goba, whom he had met at a pro-Palestinian rally in New York. During his time overseas, he had made some direct connections with al Qaeda Core. Derwish was twenty-nine at time of death in 2002.[23]

Anatomy of the Cluster

Followers

Jaber Elbaneh, age thirty-seven when the others were arrested, was born in Yemen and was married with seven children. Although his work history was uneven, he was employed at a cheese factory in South Buffalo when he began to become a regular at Derwish and Goba's apartment.[24]

Yasein Taher, age twenty-five at the time of his arrest, came from a moderately religious Yemeni family. Taher was the Lackawanna High School soccer team co-captain and a western New York soccer all-star. He was voted "friendliest" by his 1996 graduating class at Lackawanna High School and he married his high school sweetheart, a former cheerleader, who converted to Islam. Following high school, Taher attended the local community college and had odd jobs like pumping gas and working for a collection agency. He lived with his parents, in the back of their house, with his wife and young son.[25]

Sahim Alwan, age thirty at the time of his arrest, was a college-educated, married man with three children who worked as a counselor with the Iroquois Job Corps Center, a job-training facility located in Medina, New York. He was active in the Lackawanna Yemeni community and served as president of the mosque, often speaking on Friday nights to the congregants. As the son of a steelworker and a graduate of Lackawanna High School, he was considered a neighborhood success story.[26]

Yahya Goba, age twenty-six at the time of his arrest, did not grow up in Lackawanna. Born in Yonkers, New York, he spent two years in Yemen before moving to western New York in late 1996. Goba graduated from Lackawanna High School but did not go on to college. Instead, he worked odd jobs such as construction and pumping gas. Later, he moved in with Kamal Derwish.[27]

Faysal Galab, age twenty-seven at the time of his arrest, was born and raised in Lackawanna and was a star high school soccer player. In addition to soccer, Galab, like the others, seemed to be a typical American teenager, interested in clothes, partying, going to casinos, and the Buffalo Sabres. His father had been a steelworker at Bethlehem Steel. Galab was married to a local girl and had children. He was an underemployed car salesman and a part owner of a gas station in Lackawanna, where he spent much of his time.[28]

Shafal Mosed, age twenty-five at the time of his arrest, was born in Detroit and moved to Lackawanna his junior year in high school when his father, a Ford Motor Company autoworker, was transferred to the Buffalo stamping plant. Mosed had a great deal of responsibility at a young age as his father died soon after the move, his mother was ill, and he had three siblings to support. Mosed was enrolled in community college to study computers and worked as a telemarketer at the time of his arrest. He lived with his wife and two-year-old son. Like some of the others, Mosed was described as a "sports nut" and was a frequent gambler at the casinos across the border in Canada, according to members of the Lackawanna community. "He had his wild side," a friend remembers.[29]

Mukhtar al Bakri, age twenty-three at the time of his arrest, grew up in Lackawanna and attended Lackawanna High School. His father had worked for twenty-five years at the Sorrento Cheese Factory after arriving in western New York from Yemen. He and his twin brother had played on the high school soccer team. As teenagers, al Bakri and his brother were known to be wild, gambling across the border in Canada, smuggling cigarettes from Canada, smoking pot, drinking, and partying. Like most teenagers, they were known to wear baggy, hip-hop clothes and play music extremely loud. After their father decided the two sons would marry, they traveled to the Middle East and on September 9, 2002, his wedding night, Mukhtar al Bakri was detained by Bahraini police.[30]

Periphery

Juma al Dosari, age thirty at the time of his arrival in Lackawanna and originally from Saudi Arabia, was determined by the United States to be a member of al Qaeda. In 1989 he had traveled from his home in Saudi Arabia to Afghanistan using an Arab guest house in Pakistan. There he received instruction on the AK-47 and then subsequently traveled to Bosnia in 1995 to participate in the jihad in exchange for 710,000 Saudi riyals. In 1996, he traveled to Baku, Azerbaijan, to join other Arabs and to fight in Chechnya. Also in that year, he was arrested by Saudi authorities for questioning in the Khobar Towers bombing in 1996. After his Saudi passport was revoked, al Dosari obtained a passport from Bahrain and came to the United States where he worked as an imam in Bloomington, Indiana, before traveling to Lackawanna, New York. Al Dosari departed from the United States to Afghanistan via Bahrain and Iran in November 2001, was present at Tora Bora, and surrendered to Pakistani authorities when he crossed the Pakistani border in December 2001.[31]

Overseas Travel and Link Up with Al Qaeda

According to Sahim Alwan, the men heard about Afghanistan in the context of spirited religious discussions led by Kamal Derwish as well as Juma al Dosari. In an interview, Alwan noted, "Yeah, from, from Derwish mostly. He talked about it. He's mentioned Afghanistan. Scholars mention Afghanistan. Back in the time [during] the fight with the Taliban and the Northern Alliance and stuff like that." Derwish encouraged several members of the community to travel abroad as part of a pilgrimage to salvage and rectify their insufficiently devout Islamic lifestyle and not necessarily to participate in a military conflict.[32] Sahim Alwan recounted, "I was hungry for knowledge of the religion itself. It was a religious quest." Others came to believe that attacks on Muslims around the world had obligated them to train for military jihad to defend their Muslim brothers; the cluster was aware that military training would be part of the trip. Moreover, according to Alwan, "It was adventure. We were gonna go learn how to use weapons. That part of it was the exciting part. You're gonna be able to shoot and this and that."[33]

The catalytic event that spring that served as the tipping point for the men to travel abroad was the arrival of Juma al Dosari, a close friend of Kamal Derwish, whom he invited to Lackawanna. After al Dosari was essentially kicked out of the Islamic Center in Lackawanna for a speech in which he endorsed militant jihad, he became a fixture at the private sessions in Goba's apartment. His stories about the glory of soldiering for jihad in Bosnia and Chechnya energized and fascinated the men, and within days they began to mobilize for their trip abroad. According to some men in the Lackawanna cluster, al Dosari served as "the Closer."[34]

Ultimately, al Dosari's arrival, combined with Derwish's preaching and his manipulation of a combination of shame, peer pressure, lack of a strong identity, and a promise of adventure, were enough to convince the seven men from Lackawanna to leave for training in Afghanistan. The group kept the trip a secret and told others that they were going to Pakistan to study with the Islamic evangelical group Tablighi Jamaat as part of a search for their Islamic faith.[35] The men sold belongings, borrowed cash from relatives, and ran up their credit cards to raise enough funds for airline tickets, hiking boots, flashlights, and other supplies. According to one account, Jaber Elbaneh said he had no intention of returning home and ran up $145,000 in credit card debt.[36]

The men traveled in two groups to Afghanistan. Yasein Taher, Faysal Galab, and Shafal Mosed left on April 28 and arrived in Lahore, Pakistan, on April 29. They subsequently continued on to the al Farouq training camp, near Kandahar, Afghanistan, a few days later. The other group—Sahim Alwan, Jaber Elbaneh, Mukhtar al Bakri, and Yahya Goba—boarded a May 14 flight in Toronto and arrived in Karachi, Pakistan. In Pakistan they were met by Derwish, who led them to a variety of guesthouses and ultimately the al Farouq camp.[37]

Training and Skill Acquisition

According to Yasein Taher, the fact that they were going to be attending an al Qaeda training camp was a big surprise to the men and not what they had expected.[38]

The seven men from Lackawanna went through "basic training" at the al Farouq camp, while Kamal Derwish was placed in an advanced program. As part of their introductory course, the men fired Kalashnikovs and 9-mm handguns. They also learned the mechanics, ballistics, maintenance, and care of a variety of weapons including Kalashnikovs, PKs, M16s, RPG grenade launchers, and long rifles. Time was spent covering topography and navigation. One week was spent in explosives training and working with TNT and grenades. Instructors trained the men in utilizing C4 and plastic explosives as well as how to make Molotov cocktails. Construction and use of detonators and fuses were also covered.[39]

After only ten days of the six-week training, according to Sahim Alwan, he realized that was in over his head and faked an ankle injury to get out of the training. He subsequently asked Derwish to help him leave; Derwish agreed to help and facilitated a ride to Kandahar for him.[40]

Like Alwan, Taher, Mosed, and Galab all left before completing the six-week training course and all four men returned to the United States by late June. Goba and al Bakri finished the training and traveled in the Middle East before returning home in August. Derwish remained overseas, as did Elbaneh, who had told Alwan during the training that he was intent on becoming a martyr.[41]

Al Qaeda Recruitment

Before arriving at the al Farouq camp, Alwan, Derwish, and Elbaneh actually met Osama bin Laden when he arrived unexpectedly at the guesthouse that they were staying at in Kandahar.[42] At al Farouq in July 2001, bin Laden and Ayman al Zawahiri addressed the trainees at the camp, including the men from Lackawanna, discussing the alliance between their two organizations (Egyptian Islamic Jihad and al Qaeda) and their grievances against Israel, Saudi Arabia, and the United States.[43] They also discussed a "big" mission that would involve "40–50 brothers" whom all the trainees at the camp should pray for. However, no further detail was provided.[44] As he was preparing to leave Afghanistan and while waiting at a Kandahar guesthouse for a ride back to Pakistan, Alwan was summoned to a personal meeting with bin Laden. Bin Laden asked him why he was leaving and Alwan replied that he needed to get back to his family. Bin Laden also inquired about the status of Muslims in America and what they thought of martyrdom operations. Alwan says he changed the topic and asked about the rumors of conflict with the United States. One account says that bin Laden answered, "There's been threats back and forth," while another account says that bin Laden just smiled before blessing Alwan and bidding him farewell. Even though, from these accounts, there was clearly an opportunity for al Qaeda to recruit the men from Lackawanna (who were returning to the United States) to the organization, it did not happen.[45]

Operational Cycle

Travel to Pakistan appears to have to have scared the men rather than triggered the cluster's mobilization to action. During the year in between their return from Afghanistan in the summer of 2001 and their arrest in

September 2002, the men did not conduct any actions that could be judged to be part of any operational cycle.

Target Selection/Casing

There is no indication that the members of the Lackawanna cluster who returned to the United States had conducted any target selection or surveillance.

Logistics

There is no indication that the members of the Lackawanna cluster who returned to the United States had prepared logistically for any attack.

Communications

A series of e-mails from Mukhtar al Bakri, who had traveled back to the Middle East, to Yahya Goba in Lackawanna set off alarm bells in the U.S. intelligence community when in the summer of 2002 al Bakri discussed an upcoming "wedding," which was interpreted as possibly being a code for an attack. Another e-mail from al Bakri sounded equally suspicious to U.S. authorities. Entitled "Big Meal," the e-mail read: "How are you my beloved, God willing you are fine. I would like to remind you of obeying God and keeping him in your heart because the next meal will be very huge. No one will be able to withstand it except those with faith. There are people here who had visions and their visions were explained that this thing will be very strong. No one will be able to bear it."[46]

As far as Derwish's communications are concerned, U.S. intelligence determined that he used several aliases and realized that it had intercepted communications between him and two important al Qaeda figures: Osama bin Laden's son Saad and Tafiq bin Atash, known as "Khallad," who was a suspected intermediary between bin Laden and the USS *Cole* bombers. Bin Atash was believed to have attended a January 2000 al Qaeda meeting in Malaysia, which was also attended by two of the September 11 hijackers. Officials found the connection between bin Atash and Derwish particularly alarming.[47] Derwish was also still in contact with some of the men in Lacka-wanna—he had told Yahya Goba to destroy his passport and get a new one without incriminating stamps.[48]

Weaponization

The only weapon that the FBI searches of the men's homes found was an antique derringer firearm.[49]

The Al Qaeda Factor

Kamal Derwish clearly served as the human link between the seven men in Lackawanna and al Qaeda Core. He traveled ahead of the men to Pakistan, greeted them on their arrival, and within six to nine days of their arrival had arranged for several of the men to travel to Afghanistan and the al Farouq training camp. In addition, Derwish was in continual contact, until his death, with two important al Qaeda figures: Osama bin Laden's son Saad and Tafiq bin Atash. Moreover, he died in the same car with a Yemeni named Qaed Salim Sinan al Harethi, who was the top al Qaeda operative in that country and was a primary player in the 2000 attack on the USS *Cole*. He clearly could be considered an al Qaeda member.[50]

A few of the men met bin Laden in the guesthouse in Kandahar and all of the men were addressed by both bin Laden and Ayman al Zawahiri at the al Farouq training camp. Sahim Alwan had a personal meeting with bin Laden. However, to date, no evidence of recruitment by al Qaeda or movement in an operational direction by the men in Lackawanna has been produced. Although some of the men remained in contact with Derwish, no targets were selected, no casing of targets was done, and no effort was made by the men to weaponize. As a result, although the men trained in al Qaeda camps, met al Qaeda leadership, and remained in contact with al Qaeda-linked individuals, no al Qaeda plot can said to have been directed at the United States at the time of the arrests of the men from Lackawanna.

Conclusion

WHAT IS THE al Qaeda factor in al Qaeda plots? In order to make any informed judgment on this issue, we need to revisit the questions posed in the introduction.

Was there any al Qaeda role in the formation of the extremist Muslim social networks or "scenes" in Hamburg, Madrid, London, New York, Sydney, Toronto, and other cities that constituted the pool of future conspirators? To answer this question, we must acknowledge that al Qaeda could have influenced the development of these local extremist social networks in the West in two ways: either actively, through direct efforts like sending emissaries abroad, or more passively, through the spread of its ideology and the creation of a heroic narrative that inspires individuals.

Among the sixteen different plots examined in this book—plots that had origins in eleven different Western cities (New York, Montreal, Hamburg, London, Madrid, Amsterdam, Sydney/Melbourne, Toronto, Copenhagen, and Buffalo)—in only one case could al Qaeda be said to have played an active role in the generation of that scene: Madrid. Even there, the links are more coincidental than centrally planned.

The argument that al Qaeda created Madrid's scene hinges on the role of Imad Eddin Barakat Yarkas, also known as Abu Dahdah. During the 1990s, Abu Dahdah organized a militant Salafi support network for sending funds as well as volunteer jihadists from Spain to Bosnia and Afghanistan. He was arrested after 9/11, accused of setting up the July 2001 meeting between Mohammed Atta and Ramzi bin al Shibh in Spain based on analyses of phone calls made and received from the hijackers and others. Abu Dahdah's vocal support of these jihadist causes as well as his international links to al Qaeda–associated individuals made him a central figure among those recruiting and indoctrinating for al Qaeda in Spain. Moreover, he played a critical early role in the radicalization of the Madrid bombers. However, Abu Dahdah was originally a Syrian Muslim Brotherhood refugee in Spain, and the precise nature of his links to al Qaeda Core in Afghanistan remains murky at best. Under no circumstances was he taking direction from al Qaeda Core in Afghanistan in his efforts to create a Salafi scene in Madrid.

What Abu Dahdah definitely did, and what was replicated in many Western cities, was something that represented a much more passive role for al Qaeda and a much more organic effort by self-anointed "al Qaeda preachers" in the West. As noted in the Spanish indictment against him, Abu Dahdah distributed literature at the mosque about the activities of Muslim militants in Algeria, the Palestinian territories, Egypt, and Afghanistan, including communiqués issued by Osama bin Laden. Furthermore, Abu Dahdah began to indoctrinate young Muslims who expressed interest in the literature, recruiting several to fight in Bosnia against the Serbs.

London's Abu Qatada had a similar relationship with al Qaeda, serving as a fund-raiser, distributing materiel, and, most important, indoctrinating young men in Europe to aspire to the cause of al Qaeda and transnational jihad. In fact, videos of his sermons were found in the apartments of both the Hamburg 9/11 hijackers and the Madrid bombers.

It was the role of the "Blind Sheikh," Omar Abdel Rahman, in and around the al Farouq Mosque and the al Kifah Center in Brooklyn, New York, that would serve as the first example of a paradigm that would be repeated in many of other Western cities in future years. In the early 1990s Rahman, though not officially an al Qaeda member, served as the central node around which a local network of young men would gather, socialize, radicalize, and ultimately turn to violence.

These self-anointed "al Qaeda preachers" in the West, who often were Islamist-oriented political asylum seekers from the Middle East, provided a local context in which young men from varied demographic and economic strata, seeking political and religious answers, began to adopt al Qaeda's ideology and radicalize. The narrative of a war against Islam, the individual obligation to participate in militant jihad, and the rejection of Western democracy were doctrinal tenets of the worldview that was advocated. These men created an environment that fostered gravitation to reactionary Islam as well as politicization of these new beliefs. They brought politics into the mosque and called on members of the congregation and Muslims in general to mobilize and come to the aid of their fellow Muslims around the world. As a result, these "al Qaeda preachers" promoted travel overseas to fight in Bosnia, Chechnya, Afghanistan, and other "fields of jihad."

Not all al Qaeda preachers had the same standing. Some, like the "Blind Sheikh," Abu Qatada, and Abu Dahdah, were actual clerics or had some direct connection to the transnational jihadist networks tied to Afghanistan. Others, like Abu Hamza al Masri and Omar Bakri in London and Abdel Nacer Benbrika in Melbourne, Australia, were self-made al Qaeda preachers with little religious standing abroad but significant influence in the U.K. and Australia. As Abu Hamza al Masri famously said, "I am not a member of al-Qaeda or a puppet of Osama bin Laden, but that doesn't mean I don't share some of his views."[1]

In other cities, like Copenhagen and Montreal, there was no single individual who served as a beacon around which the scene developed but rather a group of individuals who were political asylum seekers from the Middle East (Egypt and Algeria) whose mosques served as the incubators for anti-Western and pro-jihadist ideology. In Amsterdam and Toronto, the underpinnings of the local scenes were much more organic, not based on or generated by political asylum seekers from the Middle East but rather fueled and enabled by the Saudi *dawah* mission, which spread reactionary Islam, hostile to the West, through local mosques and the Internet to young men looking for answers.

Was there any al Qaeda role in the formation of the breakaway clusters of men that in many cases formed the embryonic active core of conspirators?

Although the local al Qaeda preachers or ideologues had a role in fostering the breakaway clusters, in only one case was this "spinning-off" of a cluster from the scene directly catalyzed by someone with a direct al Qaeda link/ pedigree. Even then, the initiative was seemingly local and self-initiated rather than directed from Afghanistan.

In Lackawanna, New York, it was the return of Kamal Derwish, who had developed links with al Qaeda from his travel abroad and then returned to Lackawanna in 2000, who helped encourage, radicalize, and mobilize the men who would break away from the scene and become known as the Lackawanna Cluster. When the local mosque asked Derwish to take his talks somewhere else—which ended up being his apartment—he began to host *halaqas*, which were soon drawing more than twenty men. Pizza and religious conversation were the primary attractions and the cluster of friends from Lackawanna High School soon became regulars.[2]

Most important, according to some accounts, Derwish was able to explain Islam better than anyone the men had ever met—his answers to the men's questions were straightforward and logical. Derwish provided guidance on how to integrate faith into daily life and pushed the men toward a more devout and stricter form of Islam. He also discussed issues of the day, including the wars in Bosnia and Chechnya and the presence of U.S. troops in Saudi Arabia. Derwish emphasized to the men that it was their religious obligation, as Muslims, to be prepared to help other Muslims in need. Part of that was the duty to train in preparation for military jihad.[3]

Ultimately, the seven men from Lackawanna associated with this cluster emerged from a group of as many two dozen men from the community who showed up regularly at Derwish's apartment. Derwish would mobilize the men of this breakaway cluster to travel to Afghanistan and, through his al Qaeda contacts, get them into the al Farouq training camp.[4]

Was there any al Qaeda role in the allocation of responsibilities among the conspirators in the cluster?

Was it outside guidance from al Qaeda or organic development that determined who would be in the active core of the conspiracy, who would comprise the followers, and who would be on the periphery of the plot? What roles did people fall into?

Al Qaeda Core did direct and assign roles and responsibilities in at least four plots (9/11, Shoe Bombers, Operations Overt and Highrise) and potentially in three others (Operations Theseus, Vivace, and Dagger). In each of these seven plots, individuals living in the West traveled to Pakistan and/or Afghanistan with the intention to train and fight. In four of the plots and most likely in the three others, someone with direct al Qaeda Core linkages or standing redirected these individuals back to the West to carry out a plot on behalf of al Qaeda and assigned specific roles or responsibilities in the process.

In the 9/11 plot, the cluster of men from Hamburg traveled to Afghanistan in 1999 and met Osama bin Laden and Mohammed Atef, pledged their loyalty to al Qaeda, and volunteered for a "martyrdom operation." On their way back to Germany, they met Khalid Sheikh Mohammed in Karachi and ultimately returned to Hamburg in early 2000. Travel to Afghanistan and meeting al Qaeda Core personnel were clearly the catalysts for their mobilization to action. According to the 9/11 Commission, "Although Bin Laden, [Mohammed] Atef and [Khalid Sheikh Mohammed] initially contemplated using established al Qaeda to execute the planes operation, the late 1999 arrival in Kandahar of four aspiring jihadis from Germany suddenly presented a more attractive alternative . . . the enormous advantage of fluency in English and familiarity with life in the West. . . . Not surprisingly, Mohammed Atta, Ramzi bin al Shibh, Marwan al Shehi and Ziad Jarrah would all become key players in the 9/11 conspiracy." Almost immediately upon their return to Hamburg they began to research flight schools, since they clearly had been directed to gain the necessary skills to serve as pilots in the plot. Moreover, bin Laden and Atef had determined that Mohammed Atta's role would be that of operational leader.[5]

In the Shoe Bombers' plot, we know that "on or about November 20, 2001, the two potential bombers, Badat and Reid, traveled to Pakistan." In Karachi they stayed on the same street, though in different hotels.[6] It is most likely that on this trip they were given their mission, role, and responsibility. We know that at least Richard Reid met with al Qaeda because his most recent reconnaissance mission reports from Europe and the Middle East were discovered on Ayman al Zawahiri's computer in Afghanistan following the U.S. invasion.[7]

It seems that the final decision on targeting and roles/responsibilities was most likely made by Khalid Sheikh Mohammed. During a March 2007 hearing at Guantanamo Bay, Cuba, Khalid Sheikh Mohammed (KSM) confessed, "I was responsible for the Shoe Bomber Operation to down two American airplanes."[8] Furthermore, KSM's nephew, Ammar al Balucchi, was in contact with Badat and Reid (on behalf of KSM) to fine-tune their roles/responsibilities: "In late 2001 in Afghanistan, KSM directed Ammar to be the communications intermediary between al-Qa'ida and 'shoe bombers' Richard Reid and Saajid Badat."[9]

In Operation Overt, al Qaeda allocated roles and responsibilities when the men involved in the plot traveled to Pakistan in the spring of 2006. Abdulla Ahmed Ali traveled to Pakistan between April and June 2006, where he is understood to have been selected to head the suicide plot and received training on how to build the devices. Assad Sarwar traveled to Pakistan between June 18 and July 8.[10] Abdulla Ahmed Ali and Assad Sarwar testified that they were in touch with a Kashmiri militant who went alternately by the names "Yusuf" and "Jamil Shah." Sarwar told the court that he received explosives training from this man in Pakistan in the early summer of 2006.[11]

Al Qaeda closely managed roles and responsibilities from Pakistan in Operation Overt. At the trial sentencing hearing on September 14, 2009, the judge, in referring to the e-mails between the conspirators in the U.K. and Pakistan, said that "the e-mail correspondence demonstrates that this conspiracy was controlled, monitored carefully and funded by Pakistan, with the defendants Ali and Sarwar high level executives within this country [U.K.]."[12]

In Operation Highrise, Najibullah Zazi pleaded guilty to being assigned a role and responsibility by al Qaeda to serve as the leader of group to make improvised explosive devices and explode them in the New York City subway. Although Zazi and his associates initially intended to fight on behalf of the Taliban, they were recruited by al Qaeda shortly after arriving in Peshawar. Al Qaeda personnel transported Zazi and others to the Waziristan region of Pakistan and trained them to use several different kinds of weapons. During the training, al Qaeda leaders asked Zazi and others to return to the United States and conduct suicide operations. They agreed. Zazi later received additional training from al Qaeda on constructing the explosives for the planned attacks in the United States. Zazi had discussions with al Qaeda leaders about target locations, including subway trains in New York City.[13]

As previously mentioned, in three other plots (Operations Theseus, Vivace, and Dagger), al Qaeda's responsibility in assigning roles and responsibilities to the conspirators is not clear-cut but has been presumed by many analysts. In Operation Theseus, the intentions of plot leaders Mohammed Siddique Khan and Shehzad Tanweer certainly changed after their trip to Pakistan in late 2004–5. Like Zazi and his co-conspirators, what was planned as a mission to fight in Afghanistan as foreign fighters changed to that of a plot against their home country during their travels in Pakistan. Whom they met and what precise direction they may or may not have received in terms of roles and responsibilities may never be known, since Khan and Tanweer have taken this information with them to the grave. However, based on their change in plans, acts in furtherance of those plans, and the operational security they employed upon their return—along with their newfound capability to make hydrogen peroxide explosives—there is a high likelihood that they were trained and redirected to serve as the leaders of a plot against the London Metro by al Qaeda.

In Operation Vivace, a similar change in plans was observed by Muktar Ibrahim—from seeking to fight abroad to conspiring to attack London. In 2004, when he departed the U.K. for Pakistan, "MI5 judged they [Muktar Ibrahim and two associates] were going to take part in holy war activities in Pakistan. It was thought this might include going to terrorist training camps." According to Ibrahim's Saudi roommate, "actually they told me very clear[ly]: they are going go for Jihad and also Muktar [Ibrahim], he told me that maybe I'm not going to see him again, maybe we'll see each other in heaven."[14]

Though Muktar Ibrahim is still alive, he claimed his innocence at trial and has never clarified his links to al Qaeda. Nevertheless, like Mohammed Siddique Khan and Shehzad Tanweer, upon his return to London in the spring of 2005, he began acts in furtherance of the plot, recruited co-conspirators, and used his newfound capability to make hydrogen peroxide explosives. As a result, here, too, there is a high likelihood that Muktar Ibrahim was trained and redirected to serve as the leader of a plot against the London Metro by al Qaeda.

Finally, there is the 2007 Operation Dagger plot in Copenhagen. A clear link appears to exist between Hammid Khurshid and al Qaeda by way of Abu Nasir al Qahtani. According to the Danish Prosecutor's Office, the covert videotapings of Khurshid's apartment in Copenhagen revealed that, at one point, when watching videos of the 2005 escape from Bagram Prison and when al Qahtani's face appeared on the computer screen, Khurshid told his spouse about his acquaintance with al Qahtani. Khurshid noted, "He was my best friend, who was just under him."[15] Furthermore, the Danish Security and Intelligence Service (PET) and the Prosecutor's Office believe that Khurshid underwent military training at a camp in Pakistan, receiving training in reconnaissance, combat techniques, and the use of explosives in Pakistan or Afghanistan. PET has as many as fifty pictures of Khurshid allegedly taken in a training camp in Pakistan or Afghanistan.[16] It is highly likely that it was during a trip to southwest Asia that he became acquainted with al Qahtani.

It is still unclear whether al Qaeda allocated a role or responsibility to carry out a plot in Copenhagen. The journalist Sebastian Rotella has claimed that Khurshid met al Qaeda's then Chief of External Operations, Abu Ubaidah al Masri. Also, telephone monitoring revealed that Khurshid often spoke from Copenhagen with a person in Pakistan who was designated by the U.S. government as a terrorist recruiter.[17] Like both sets of London bombers, upon his return to the West, Khurshid began acts in furtherance of the plot and used his newly acquired capability to make hydrogen peroxide explosives. As a result, it is highly likely that Hammid Khurshid was trained and redirected to serve as the leader of a plot against Copenhagen by al Qaeda.

How did these individuals from the cluster link up with al Qaeda?

Did a worldwide network of al Qaeda recruiters spot promising individuals and direct them to al Qaeda camps in Afghanistan and Pakistan, or did individuals take the initiative, mobilize, and seek out al Qaeda in order to carry out their jihadist ambitions? Were there al Qaeda facilitators in certain cities? What was their role and who were they? What role did travel to a "zone of conflict" play?

From evidence surrounding the sixteen case studies presented here, it is apparent that in the cases when individuals were able to link up with al Qaeda, most often the initiative was "bottom-up," meaning that the individuals in the West sought out al Qaeda. In only one case, the Lackawanna cluster, did an al Qaeda individual—Derwish—show up in town and as a result deliver recruits to the central or core organization in Afghanistan.

In most cases, individuals in the West sought to carry out their general jihadist ambitions by traveling overseas to Pakistan and Afghanistan and ended up linking up with al Qaeda by coincidence—al Qaeda Core was not their destination. For example, and most tellingly, even the Bait al Ansar cluster from Hamburg originally planned to travel to Chechnya to fight jihad. A chance meeting on a train in Germany with Khalid al Masri in the fall of 1999 discouraged them from going to Grozny and instead put the men in touch with Mohamedou Ould Slahi, an al Qaeda operative who was based in Germany. Subsequently, Slahi explained that many aspiring jihadists were being arrested in Georgia and suggested they train in Afghanistan first before traveling onward to Chechnya to fight.[18]

Similarly, in the Shoe Bombers' plot, both Richard Reid and Saajid Badat ostensibly traveled to Pakistan (separately) in 1998 to further their Islamic education. However, there is speculation that this travel was facilitated by relationships at Finsbury Park Mosque and the real motive for the travel was to participate in some type of military jihad. While there is incomplete information on the exact whereabouts of both Reid and Badat during 1999–2001, it is fair to say that by 2001 both men had trained in al Qaeda camps.[19]

Even in Operation Theseus, Mohammed Siddique Khan and Shehzad Tanweer's final trip to Pakistan was self-initiated and planned as a martyrdom mission abroad. Al Qaeda was not initially part of the equation. From Khan's farewell speech to his wife and daughter, which was made just prior to his departure, "it was clear that Khan did not expect to see his daughter again. Put bluntly, he knew he was going to his death." Khan and Tanweer had planned for martyrdom abroad, but shortly after arriving in Pakistan to fight their plans changed and they chose to return to Britain to launch the first suicide attacks within the U.K.[20] If there was recruitment by al Qaeda, it was only once the men had arrived in Pakistan and made themselves available for a plot against the U.K.

Five years later, this scenario repeated itself when Najibullah Zazi and his two associates traveled to Pakistan to join the Taliban and fight coalition forces in Afghanistan. Circumstance intervened and, as noted in his guilty plea, "Although Zazi and others initially intended to fight on behalf of the Taliban, they were recruited by al Qaeda shortly after arriving in Peshawar. Al Qaeda personnel transported Zazi and others to the Waziristan region of Pakistan and trained them on several different kinds of weapons. During the training, al Qaeda leaders asked Zazi and others to return to the United States and conduct suicide operations. They agreed."[21] Once again, no al Qaeda recruiter sought these men out in the West. Rather, like the men from Hamburg in the 9/11 plot, they showed up in Afghanistan or Pakistan and then made themselves available to be utilized by al Qaeda.

In other plots, it wasn't al Qaeda recruiters but local facilitators who were able to connect aspiring local jihadists with al Qaeda–associated individuals in Afghanistan and Pakistan. In Montreal and London, the initiative was "bottom-up"; the facilitators were responding to the desire of these individuals when they put them in contact with people overseas—they were not "recruiting." For example, in Montreal in the summer of 1997, a member of the cluster, Abderrauf Hannachi, returned to Montreal from training at al Qaeda's Khalden Camp in Afghanistan. He told the other men of the Groupe Fateh Kamel Cluster about what he had learned at the camp and how it had transformed him into a mujahid or warrior. Reinforced by the positive feedback about training from other mujahedeen veterans, Ahmed Ressam and Mustapha Labsi began to develop an interest in receiving training.

Subsequently, Hannachi reached out to Abu Zubayda, the gatekeeper for al Qaeda's camps in Afghanistan, who secured spots for them in the camps.

Even in London in 2004, when the trip to Pakistan by Operation Vivace bomber Muktar Ibrahim was set up by a designated al Qaeda supporter and financier, the purpose of the trip was to fight—not to be recruited to join al Qaeda. Nevertheless, Mohammed al Ghabra, a known al Qaeda–linked individual who resides in the U.K. was likely the "fixer" for this trip.[22]

Clearly the case studies support a paradigm of al Qaeda plots versus the West that is underpinned by a "bottom-up" process, driven by individuals in the West who take the initiative to go overseas for training. Although there may be local "fixers" in Hamburg, London, or Sydney who have overseas links and can facilitate or enable an overseas connection, typically they are not recruiters in the traditional sense of the word—they are not soliciting individuals from the top down on behalf of an overseas terrorist organization. Instead, they are an important node in a facilitation network with links to terrorist groups overseas. A process including a local "fixer" enabling or linking individuals who mobilizing from the bottom up is a much more accurate description of the phenomenon of joining al Qaeda rather than that of a "recruiter" acting on behalf of al Qaeda from the top down. This pattern has persisted from 1999 in Montreal through Hamburg and London and Sydney and New York City in 2009.

In the U.K., "fixers" like Mohammed Qayyam Khan (Operation Crevice, Operation Theseus) and Mohammed al Ghabra (Operation Vivace) had the ability to get U.K. citizens to al Qaeda or al Qaeda–allied Kashmiri camps, regardless of the aspirants' ethnicity. Many of these networks were formed in the late 1980s and 1990s by political asylum seekers in Britain fleeing the security services of various Middle Eastern governments. Over the years, these networks developed links to terrorist groups overseas and existed primarily to support militant jihad overseas in places such as Bosnia, Kashmir, and Afghanistan. However, once al Qaeda broke the taboo of attacking the West with the 9/11 plot, these networks were in a prime position to assist U.K. citizens seeking to travel abroad, link up to al Qaeda or al Qaeda–allied groups, and return to the U.K. to launch attacks against London.

In sum, al Qaeda does not formally recruit in the West. This is a bottom-up process, not subject to an al Qaeda recruiter, driven by the desire of individuals raised in the West to train or fight jihad abroad.

If recruitment is not the dynamic that describes how individuals who are radicalized to violence in the West are able to link up with al Qaeda, what is it then? This analysis of case studies suggests that weak or peripheral connections, as well as random events, are often critical to making the connections with overseas terrorist groups and subsequently directly influencing how a plot develops.

Another part of the answer may lie in diaspora community links between the West and "zones of conflict" like Afghanistan and Pakistan. Sticking with the British example, a significant number of British Muslims are of Pakistani origin and came to the U.K. in search of work. The children of these immigrants still have relatives in Pakistan and, like any other diaspora community, travel back and forth to the country of their origin. For example, this travel has, on a number of occasions, enabled connections to be made to Pakistani terrorist groups (Rashid Rauf [Operation Overt], Omar Khyam [Operation Crevice], Mohammed Siddique [Operation Theseus]). These links, through al Qaeda–affiliated groups in Kashmir, the Federally Administered Tribal Areas (FATA), and North West Frontier Province (NWFP), have provided a mechanism for connecting to al Qaeda Core or another overseas terrorist group.

What was al Qaeda Core's role? Opportunistic recruiting. One hypothesis from this data is that al Qaeda Core and other groups have been opportunistic and relied on whatever batch of young Western volunteers was able to make it to southwest Asia and subsequently arrive at the doorstep of al Qaeda–linked training camps (whether enabled by a facilitation network or familial links). These would-be warriors were turned around and sent back to their country of origin to carry out terrorist operations. This could explain the operations represented by Operation Crevice, Operation Rhyme, Operation Theseus, Operation Vivace, Operation Overt, and Operation Highrise.

What happened to these individuals overseas?

What type of training did they receive? What skills were acquired overseas? Who provided the training—al Qaeda or another entity? How has this changed over time?

As noted in the 2007 New York City Police Department radicalization report,

Frequently, but not always, one or more members of a particular

Western-based cluster travels abroad. This travel often follows or con-
tributes to a member's decision to commit jihad. The travel is more often than not to a militant training camp—a camp usually in a country
or region that is regarded as a field of jihad. Pakistan, in particular, as
well as Iraq, Afghanistan, Kashmir, and Somalia are popular destinations. The "leaders" of these clusters are usually the ones who pursue
this travel—an experience that appears to be the final catalyst for group
action.[23]

As potential soldiers, they seek training and go to some length to join jihadi
training camps. They try to travel to zones of conflict for training or fighting—Afghanistan, Pakistan, Iraq, Somalia, Yemen—and travel through
Turkey, Syria, Egypt, and Iran to get there.

Essentially, conspirators from the sixteen case studies examined in this
book can be stratified among four different training camp experiences.

Pre-9/11 attendance at al Qaeda training camps. Conspirators from Operation Tradebom, the Millennium Plot, 9/11, the Shoe Bombers' plot, Operation Rhyme, Operation Pendennis, and the cluster from Lackawanna all
attended one or more al Qaeda facilities in Afghanistan. Until late 2001, al
Qaeda Core funded or controlled most of the training camps in Afghanistan, such as Khalden, al Farouq, and Darunta. These camps could accom-
modate hundreds of terrorist novices and had a formal curriculum with increased levels of sophistication, sometimes lasting up to a year for the select
few. Anyone who had traveled to Afghanistan for training before the fall
of the Taliban in 2001 was likely to have been trained in an al Qaeda Core
camp. However, those camps were subsequently destroyed.

While they were in existence, the range of training the camps provided
ranged from basic infantry training to more advanced military training
to improvised explosive device construction. For example, the fifteen 9/11
"muscle hijackers" underwent the basic training course, which included
firearms, heavy weapons, explosives, and topography: "At least seven of the
Saudi muscle hijackers took this basic training regime at the al Faruq camp
near Kandahar." Two others trained at Khalden Camp.[24] Similarly, the seven
men from Lackawanna went through "basic training" at the al Farouq camp
and, as part of their introductory course, fired Kalashnikovs and 9-mm
handguns. They also learned the mechanics, ballistics, maintenance, and
care of a variety of weapons including Kalashnikovs, PKs, M16s, RPG grenade launchers, and long rifles. One week was spent in explosives training

and working with TNT and grenades. Instructors trained the men on using C4 and plastic explosives as well as how to make Molotov cocktails. Construction and use of detonators and fuses was also covered.[25]

Once these more basic courses were mastered, individuals like Ahmed Ressam (Millennium Plot) advanced from bomb making with C4 and TNT to lessons on how to "blow up the infrastructure of a country," urban warfare, assassination techniques, and surveillance. Ressam ultimately moved from Khalden to the Darunta camp and received advanced training in detonator construction and chemical weapons and even experimented with cyanide and sulfuric acid.[26] Similarly, Ramzi Yousef and Ahmed Ajaj (Tradebom Plot) traveled to Afghanistan and attended Camp Khaldan and together they learned how to construct homemade explosive devices sometime between 1991 and 1992.[27]

Post-9/11 attendance at al Qaeda training camps. Ongoing intelligence gaps make these determinations difficult to make with 100 percent certitude, but there is a high degree of confidence that British conspirators from Operation Theseus, Operation Vivace, and Operation Overt all attended some type of al Qaeda–associated camps. After a series of truces were signed between FATA tribal leaders and the government of Pakistan between 2004 and 2006, more formal facilities were provided in Waziristan by al Qaeda, but they never reached the sophistication of instruction that prevailed before 2001.[28] More recently, al Qaeda camps have become melting plots of Afghan Taliban, al Qaeda, Pakistani Taliban, and Kashmiri groups, so clear delineations are hard to make.[29]

For example, the active core of Operation Theseus, Mohammed Siddique Khan and Shehzad Tanweer, told two of their associates who had also come for training, "We've already done what you've done, you can catch up to us in a bit, in about five/six weeks. So just ride it out here and we'll see you soon." After approximately three weeks during which Wahid Ali and Sadeer Saleem participated in weapons and physical training with "men from the tribal belt" at the compound to which they had brought by the Afghans, Khan and Tanweer returned. At that point Khan told the two late arrivals that plans had changed and that rather than stay in Pakistan, Khan and Tanweer were going back to the U.K. to "do something for the brothers." Ali and Saleem subsequently left the camp, toured around Pakistan, and returned to the U.K. on February 26, 2005.[30] It is unknown if either Mohammed Siddique Khan or Shehzad Tanweer received explosives training during this trip and whether it was al Qaeda training.

Similarly, in Operation Overt, the U.K. Crown Prosecutors asserted that some of the men convicted in this case traveled to the FATA region of Pakistan, where they received explosives training. U.S. officials allege that the training came "from al-Qaida specialists." Some U.K. officials have suggested to media outlets that al Qaeda's Chief of External Operations, Abu Ubaidah al Masri, may have even trained some of the individuals for the airline plot.[31] Abdulla Ahmed Ali and Assad Sarwar testified that they were in touch with a Kashmiri militant who went by the names "Yusuf" and "Jamil Shah." Sarwar told the court that he received explosives training from this man in Pakistan early in the summer of 2006.[32]

In Operation Highrise, Najibullah Zazi pleaded guilty to being assigned a role and responsibility by al Qaeda to serve as the leader of the group that would make improvised explosive devices and explode them in the New York City subway. Although Zazi and his associates initially intended to fight on behalf of the Taliban, they

> were recruited by al Qaeda shortly after arriving in Peshawar. Al Qaeda personnel transported Zazi and others to the Waziristan region of Pakistan and trained them on several different kinds of weapons. During the training, al Qaeda leaders asked Zazi and others to return to the United States and conduct suicide operations. They agreed. Zazi later received additional training from al Qaeda on constructing the explosives for the planned attacks in the United States. Zazi had discussions with al Qaeda leaders about target locations, including subway trains in New York City. Zazi took detailed notes during the training, and later emailed a summary of the notes to himself so that he could access them when he returned to the United States.[33]

Attended a training camp run by a jihadist group allied with al Qaeda and then attended an al Qaeda camp. For a few conspirators among the sixteen major operations covered in this book, there was an evolutionary process to their training. First they attended camps run by Kashmiri al Qaeda ally groups like Harkat ul Mujahedeen (Mohammed Siddique Khan [Operation Theseus]), Lashkar-e-Taiba (Dhiren Barot [Operation Rhyme]), and Jaish-e-Mohammed (Shane Kent [Operation Pendennis]) before they were able to be vetted or make the links necessary in order to attend an al Qaeda camp. Dhiren Barot was exposed to the transnational jihad through his interactions with militant groups such as Lashkar-e-Taiba and by receiving explosive and surveillance training at camps in Pakistan and in Kashmir's Kotti region. There he learned how to assemble bombs, work with poisons and chemicals, and prepare nitroglycerine. In fact, Barot's notebooks from this period contain information on assembling phosphorous and napalm explosives.[34]

Attended a training camp run by a jihadist group allied with al Qaeda. There were others who traveled to Pakistan and only received training at militant camps run by al Qaeda allies, such as Lashkar-e-Taiba (Operation Pendennis and Operation Osage) and Jaish-e-Mohammed (Hofstad Group). One group (Operation Crevice) set up and ran their own camp, hiring an instructor and an assistant who gave private lessons to at most a dozen students, who directly paid for their instruction. In this case, the duration of the training was as short as two days to as long as about three weeks.[35] Among the Hofstad Group conspirators, Jason Walters and Ismail Akhnikh traveled to Pakistan. While Akhnikh left after about three weeks, Walters stayed for about a month. According to Walters, he received basic training in Pakistan, learning how to use all types of weapons. He suggested that the training camp he attended belonged to the Kashmiri extremist movement Jaish-e-Mohammed, run by Maulana Masood Azhar.[36]

After Walters returned, he tried to convince his Internet friend, Galas03, that he had to go with him to a training camp in Pakistan and described his training. In an Internet chat, Walters said, "come to pakistan with me there they will train you, how to use guns, how to make weapons, just everything after that you can return." Walters boasted about his proficiency with weapons: "I can assemble and disassemble a kalashnikov blindfolded, also a seminov and all the other pistols and rifles." Walters also discussed the types of weapons he had trained on, which included "seminov, kalashnikov, MMG, zakayev, TT pistol, Makarov, hand grenades en rpg those I all learned." In December 2003, Jason Walters and Zakaria Taybi returned to Pakistan, but it was only for nine days.[37]

Among the Operation Crevice conspirators, Mohammed Junaid Babar and three associates traveled to Malakand in northern Pakistan to arrange with a local *maulana*, or religious teacher, to set up their own paramilitary training camp light weapons. They spent four to five days there preparing for it and came to an arrangement that Babar and his associates were to provide money and the *maulana* and his son would provide guns, food, tents, ammunition, and everything to train with.[38] In the interim, some members of the Operation Crevice cluster attended a training camp held in the Kohat region of Pakistan in May and June. Here the actual skills necessary to create an ammonium nitrate explosive device were learned by Khyam, Ayoub, and Amin from Dolat, whom they understood to be an al Qaeda instructor from Tajikistan. According to Babar, "The explosives training lasted two days during which they received theoretical training on devices and practical demonstrations." One of these demonstrations included exploding a device in a riverbed.[39]

Did al Qaeda's Chief of External Operations or an al Qaeda member of similar rank play a role in the plot?

For the plots that are either al Qaeda "command and control" or "suggested/endorsed," the fulcrum on which these plots, directed at the West, pivot is usually the individual commonly referred to as al Qaeda's Chief of External Operations. Considered the most important role in al Qaeda after Osama bin Laden and Ayman al Zawahiri, since 2001 as many as seven individuals have held this post in al Qaeda but subsequently have been caught, killed, or died of natural causes. They include the following: Mohammed Atef (killed in an airstrike, 2001), Khalid Sheikh Mohammed (caught 2003), Abu Faraj al Libi (caught 2005), Hamza Rabia (killed by a drone strike 2005), Muhsin Musa Matwali Atwa (aka Abu Abd al Rahman al Muhajir) (killed April 2006), Abu Ubaidah al Masri (died 2007 from Hepatitis C), Saleh al Somali (killed by drone strike December 2009), and Sheikh Sa'id al Masri (killed by drone strike May 2010). What role did this person, and thus al Qaeda, have, if any, in the plot?

There are three plots (9/11, Shoe Bombers, Operation Overt) where the Chief of External Operations or an al Qaeda member of similar rank clearly had a role in driving the plot forward in a command and control function; two plots (Operation Crevice and Operation Highrise) where an al Qaeda member of this rank "suggested/endorsed" a plot; and three plots (Operation Theseus, Operation Vivace, and Operation Dagger) where it is plausible, but unknown, if this occurred. In both the 9/11 plot and the Shoe Bombers' plot, Khalid Sheikh Mohammed has admitted to this role. He conceived of, directed, and funded the 9/11 plot from Afghanistan via Ramzi bin al Shibh and, as was noted earlier, confessed that he was "responsible for the Shoe Bomber Operation to down two American airplanes."[40] In Operation Overt, although his role was somewhat opaque, speculation is strong that Abu Ubaidah al Masri managed the plot from Pakistan via Rashid Rauf, his "link man" with the conspirators.

In one "suggested/endorsed" plot, Abdul Hadi al Iraqi, al Qaeda's military commander in Afghanistan, did precisely that for the Operation Crevice conspirators via Abu Munthir. According to one of the conspirators, "[Omar] Khyam had been told that, when he was in Pakistan, there was no room for him to fight in Afghanistan and that what he should do is to carry out operations in the UK." Ostensibly, it was al Qaeda–linked Abu Munthir who provided this "suggestion" to Khyam on behalf of Abdul Hadi al Iraqi.[41] Similarly, in Operation Highrise, the plot involving Zazi was, according to the indictment, court filings, and plea proceedings in the case, organized by Saleh al Somali, Rashid Rauf, and El Shukrijumah, who were then leaders of al Qaeda's "external operations" program dedicated to terrorist attacks in the United States and other Western countries.[42]

As for the London Metro attacks in the summer of 2005 (Operations Theseus and Vivace) and Operation Dagger in Copenhagen in 2007, we just don't know the role, if any, of al Qaeda's Chief of External Operations. Some British anti-terrorism officials have asserted that the conspirators in these plots were trained and directed by Abu Ubaidah al Masri, Chief of External Operations at that time. However, to date, there has been little information that can corroborate this hypothesis.[43]

Was there an al Qaeda "link man"? If so, what was his role?

For the plots that are al Qaeda "command and control" as well as some that were "suggested/endorsed," there often was a person who played the role of intermediary between the conspirators, once they returned to the West, and al Qaeda's Chief of External Operations. This individual, who was a relay station for communications, served as a layer of protection or buffer between the conspirators and the Chief of External Operations. This individual would also both issue orders to the operational team in the West and receive status reports from them to relay back to al Qaeda leadership. This "link man" can be thought of as somewhat of a "control officer" for the plot.

That said, only in al Qaeda "command and control" plots (9/11, Shoe Bombers, and Operation Overt) did this individual actually engage in sustained and ongoing communications and seek to exert control over the conspirators in the West. Individuals who have had this role include Ramzi bin al Shibh (9/11), Ammar al Baluchi (Shoe Bombers), and Rashid Rauf (Operation Overt). In other "suggested/endorsed" plots, like the Millennium Plot,

Operation Rhyme, Operation Crevice, and Operation Highrise, these "link men" served less as control officers and more as a relay station between plot leaders and al Qaeda. These included Abu Doha (Millennium Plot), Neem Noor Khan (Operation Rhyme), Abu Munthir (Operation Crevice), and "Ahmad" (last name unknown) (Operation Highrise). In other plots, like Operation Theseus and Operation Vivace, even the existence or identity of the "link men" for each plot is still unclear. In these cases, there was little if any control over the Western conspirators by al Qaeda Core.

A clear illustration of the operational relationship between an al Qaeda Chief of External Operations, the "link man," and the conspirators in the West is the 9/11 plot. After Ramzi bin al Shibh failed in his third attempt to get a visa to enter the United States, he assumed the role of coordinator (link man) between Khalid Sheikh Mohammed (KSM) and the men in the United States. In July 2001, Mohammed Atta (who led the conspirators in the West) met personally with Ramzi bin al Shibh outside Madrid in order to inform him of the timing of the attacks, the targets, and how the opera-tion would proceed. Following the meeting, Ramzi bin al Shibh purchased two phones—one for contact with Atta, the other for contact with KSM. In the following weeks, bin al Shibh would be in frequent contact with Atta via phone, e-mail, and instant messaging.[44] Similarly, as we have seen, KSM also played a role in the Shoe Bombers' plot. Moreover, KSM's nephew, Ammar al Balucchi, played the role of "link man": "In late 2001 in Afghanistan, KSM directed Ammar to be the communications intermediary between al-Qa'ida and 'shoe bombers' Richard Reid and Saajid Badat."[45]

What was al Qaeda's role in the operational cycle?

Did the group choose the target, direct casing of the target, provide the lo-gistics to deliver the attack, communicate with the conspirators, or assist in acquiring and/or building weapons to carry out their operation?

Target Selection

Iconic buildings, mass transit systems, airplanes, airports, military bases, nuclear power plants, civilian thoroughfares (e.g., malls, hotels), and par-ticular individuals have been among the set of targets that these conspiracies have sought to attack. When al Qaeda Core has commanded and controlled the plot (9/11, Shoe Bombers, and Operation Overt), the targets chosen for their operatives have been planned to be multiple and simultaneous, symbolic, potentially economically devastating, and spectacular in nature. When the plots involved conspirators only "suggested/endorsed" from overseas (Millennium Plot, Operation Rhyme, Operation Crevice, Operation Highrise, and possibly Operation Theseus, Operation Vivace, and Operation Dagger), more autonomy was provided to the actors—in fact, they chose the targets, which tended to be "targets of opportunity" that would still have significant impact. For the plots that were autonomous (Tradebom, Madrid, Hofstad, Operation Pendennis, and Operation Osage), targets of opportunity were also chosen, subject to change based on spontaneous discussions by the conspirators.

Casing

Meticulousness and advanced planning characterized the pre-9/11 ideal state of affairs for al Qaeda Core. The 9/11 plot was preceded by significant pre-operational reconnaissance—operatives were sent to New York City far in advance of the plot to case the Twin Towers of the World Trade Center and video was taken and brought back to Afghanistan. Moreover, although Dhiren Barot was arrested in 2004, his precise and detailed assessments of the New York Stock Exchange, Citicorp Building, World Bank, and Prudential Building, which were conducted pre-9/11 in 2000/2001, set off a wave of alarms in London, New York, and Washington, D.C., when they were discovered in 2004 in Pakistan.

The al Qaeda airplane plots (Shoe Bombers and Operation Overt) did not involve significant casing. Once the operatives were on the plane, they only had to explode their personal improvised explosive devices. Similarly, al Qaeda's mass transit plots (Operation Theseus, Operation Vivace, and Operation Highrise) did not involve rigorous pre-operational casing. The operatives were familiar with the metro or subway systems and did not necessarily need to conduct advance reconnaissance beyond a practice run in the weeks leading up to the attack. Similarly, for the purely autonomous clusters (Tradebom, Madrid, Operation Pendennis, and Operation Osage) casing was limited at best. The Australians did a drive-by of the nuclear power plant, but in the end, that was not even their final target.

Logistics

The primary element to examine in terms of logistics would be the provision of funds by the overseas terrorist organization. Once again, there is a disparity between pre-9/11 and post-9/11. In 1993 Khalid Sheikh Mohammed provided his nephew Ramzi Yousef with $660, Ahmed Ressam (Millennium Plot) was provided with funds and a laptop with instructions for explosives, Mohammed Atta and his conspirators (9/11) were provided with more than half a million dollars, and Richard Reid and Saajid Badat (Shoe Bombers) were believed to have been provided with funds for travel and certainly the explosive shoes for his plot. However, as the United States and its allies pressured al Qaeda in Afghanistan and the provision of funds became difficult, the only logistical assistance that al Qaeda Core could provide was instructions on how to create improvised explosive devices (Operation Crevice, Operation Theseus, Operation Vivace, Operation Overt, Operation Dagger, and Operation Highrise). Almost all of the conspirators in the other plots were on their own to not only fund but acquire material for their conspiracies and thus al Qaeda had a very limited role in those plots.

Communications

When analyzing communication among these plots, there are two issues to consider. First, to whom were the conspirators communicating—a terrorist organization overseas, or just among themselves in the West? Second, how did they communicate? In a number of the plots, ongoing or sporadic communications took place between the conspirators once they returned to the West and to Afghanistan or Pakistan. Not surprisingly, this issue is closely linked to the nature of the relationship between the conspirators and al Qaeda. If it was a command and control operation (9/11, Shoe Bombers, Operation Overt), communication was frequent, two-way, and usually involved the conspirators and their overseas "link man" discussing the timing and targets of the operation. For the plots that were only "suggested/endorsed" by al Qaeda, communication did occur between Pakistan and the West, but it was usually regarding a question about how to construct the device (Operation Crevice, Operation Highrise). For some plots (Operation Theseus and Operation Vivace), the nature and extent of communications between al Qaeda and the conspirators in the West is still unknown.

In terms of means of communications, whether it was between London and Waziristan or in and around Madrid, the conspirators communicated in several ways: cell phones, phone kiosks, Internet cafés, texting, pre-paid phone cards, e-mail, e-mails left in a draft folder, and USB drives.

Weaponization

With the exception of the shoe bombers in 2001 (explosive shoes), all of the conspirators in al Qaeda plots in the West have been responsible for acquiring and/or building their own weapons to carry out their operation. This was true for the vehicle-borne improvised explosive device used by Ramzi Yousef (Operation Tradebom) in 1993 against the World Trade Center, true of the improvised explosive devices made by Najibullah Zazi (Operation Highrise) in 2009, and true of almost everything in between. As time has gone on, Western police as well as security and intelligence services have learned what items are most likely to be used in these devices, such as ammonium nitrate or hydrogen peroxide, and have attempted to set up trip wires in their jurisdictions and beyond to raise the probability that these purchases will set off alarms. However, as Operation Highrise demonstrated, if you make purchases far enough from the target zone (Colorado), conspirators can clearly acquire some of these materials.

Given that most of the materials necessary for these devices have other benign uses, conspirators have sought to acquire them in the West at consumer electronics stores, beauty parlors, wholesale stores, and phone stores, and even directly from chemical and fertilizer companies. In only a few plots did conspirators seek to bring items necessary for weaponization from overseas. The few that stand out were: the Millennium Plot (hexamine booster); Operation Crevice (aluminum powder); and Operation Overt (Toshiba AA batteries). However, in general, weaponization was undertaken by Westerners, in the West, from items readily available in the West. Al Qaeda had a very limited role here. The only weapon-related assistance that al Qaeda Core could provide was instructions on how to create improvised explosive devices that the conspirators brought home with them or reached back to al Qaeda for (Operation Crevice, Operation Overt, Operation Dagger, and Operation Highrise).

What was al Qaeda's role in the launch of the plot?

Just because an individual attended a training camp run by al Qaeda or one of its jihadist allies, it does not mean that the operation that they subsequently were involved in was "commanded and controlled" by al Qaeda.

The degree and nature of the al Qaeda factor in al Qaeda plots against the West has varied over time. In fact, in some ways it has come full circle from 1993 to 2011 and back again. When the first attack against the World Trade Center was launched in 1993, al Qaeda was inchoate and one of a number of similarly aligned ideological groups or networks with a presence in Afghanistan and with a focus on jihad against the West. There was a minimal al Qaeda role in that plot, which was carried out by an autonomous cluster in the West, yet it was aligned with al Qaeda's long-term ideology and strategic goals.

During 1996–2001, al Qaeda was as close to an organized, centralized, hierarchical organization as it would ever be. It adopted a strategy that could be likened to that of a venture capitalist for terror, assessing different proposals (Millennium Plot, 9/11, Shoe Bombers) for plots and funding, staffing, and even commanding and controlling the conspirators in the West. When al Qaeda lost its sanctuary in Afghanistan after October 2001, the core had to scatter and began to deteriorate and lose power, influence, and much of its ability to project its power against the West. It had to decentralize and network with other groups in order to remain relevant. It evolved into an ideological movement with a limited role in providing strategic and tactical support to Western-based conspirators, mainly taking the shape of "suggestion/endorsement" coupled with providing legitimacy for the plotters. Other than the Operation Overt transatlantic airlines plot in 2006, the period from 2002 to 2009 did not see a plot that was under al Qaeda command and control. Rather, there was a profusion of plots that were "suggested/endorsed" by al Qaeda Core (Operations Crevice, Rhyme, Theseus, Vivace, Dagger, and Highrise), as well as a significant increase in the frequency of autonomous plots ideologically aligned with al Qaeda but without any operational link (Madrid, Hofstad, Operation Pendennis, and Operation Osage).

Although things have changed since 2001, much of the intelligence community, terrorism experts, and the press have continued to refer to the threat as one dominated and controlled by al Qaeda Core. A cognitive bias to "mirror image" and imagine that our adversaries were pursuing a coherent and coordinated worldwide strategy that was the result of centralized direction and planning provided a comfortable and ordered framework through which to imagine al Qaeda's efforts. The reality, as the case studies here illuminate, is that the al Qaeda threat was much more chaotic, uncoordinated, and fluid. Plots were often a function of fortuitous connections rather than thoughtful strategy. The journalist Jason Burke was close to the mark when he described al Qaeda as

> composed of individuals, small unknown groups and larger better known entities that constantly form, dissolve and reform. Some involve longstanding activists, some are nothing more than a couple of hot-headed youngsters; some militants have been in Afghanistan, some have been in Bosnia or Chechnya or both, some have never left their home countries. Some have contacts with bin Laden or people close to him, others get funding or orders from other activists, some get no funding at all. Some of them share aims, others disagree. Some are prepared to co-operate to achieve common aims, others are fiercely competitive. Their views and preferred tactics differ and change. Some militants become active late in life, others at an early age. Some are genuinely committed to a jihadi struggle, others are simply caught up in things beyond their understanding. This is not a structured coherent organisation taking orders from one man.[46]

Looking Forward

The death of Osama bin Laden in May 2011 was a sledgehammer blow to al Qaeda Core. Regardless of the nature of his precise operational role in the organization, in the ten years since 9/11, he had become a legendary and mythical source of inspiration to individuals in the West who aspired to join his movement, regardless of whether they were in London, New York, Toronto, or Madrid. His absence will further contribute to the degrading of the operational and inspirational role of al Qaeda Core.

Due to the rise of other important nodes in al Qaeda's worldwide network of allies and affiliates, the threat from al Qaeda–type terrorism has not ended. Rather, it has devolved into an expanded diffuse network of affiliates, allies, and ideological adherents. Since 2001, the Core networked laterally with other like-minded groups on the periphery who were aligned ideologically and formed a loose coalition of allies and affiliates to include al Qaeda of the Arabian Peninsula (AQAP), Teherek-e-Taliban (TTP), Lash-kar-e-Taiba (LeT), al Shabaab, and al Qaeda in the Islamic Maghreb (AQIM) among others. Each group served as a power center, node, or hub that had an informal and loose relationship to al Qaeda Core. If the Core continues to fade, other nodes in the network will seek to raise their profile and may even surpass the Core's ability to project a threat outward against the West. Since 2009, some of these affiliates and allies have already begun to attract "would-be warriors" radicalized in the West who otherwise might have attempted to join al Qaeda Core but chose alternatives and then were sent back in plots against the West.

There are several organizations that could seek to supplant al Qaeda Core and already have begun to serve as magnets for mobilized Westerners. The top tier include al Qaeda in the Arabian Peninsula, which has already attracted Anwar al Awlaki, Samir Khan, Umar Farouq Abdulmutallab, and Rajib Karim to its cause and launched two serious plots in 2010 and 2011 against Western-bound airliners (the deteriorating security situation in Yemen suggests more ungoverned spaces and a broader sanctuary for AQAP to plot, train, and operate in), as well as al Shabaab in Somalia, which has already attracted diaspora Somalis, converts, and other mobilized Westerners from Toronto, Minneapolis, Seattle, New Jersey, Chicago, London, and Melbourne to their cause. Although they have not launched attacks against the West as of publication, the attack in 2010 in Uganda served as proof that the group can and will act outside its primary theater of operations; it may also have been a preview of things to come. It, too, operates in a safe haven from which it can plot and train. The top tier also includes LeT, TTP, and the alphabet soup of other Pakistani-based jihadist groups including Harkat ul Mujahedeen (HuM), Jaish-e-Mohammed (JeM), and Harkat ul Mujahedeen Islami (HuJI). They operate in the same sanctuaries that al Qaeda survived in and have already attracted Westerners to train and plot with them including individuals discussed previously—Mohammed Siddique Khan, Jahmaal James, the Cheikhos, and Jason Walters, to name a few who ultimately were involved in other plots. How long will it be before other groups from Pakistan follow the lead of LeT with David Headley and TTP with Faisal Shehzad and target the West?

In the next tier of organizations, operating in the ungoverned spaces of the Sahel in Africa in between Mauritania, Mali, Algeria, and Niger is the loosely organized al Qaeda of the Islamic Maghreb. Not only does it have the appeal of a new frontier of jihad to a French-speaking diaspora community in Europe originally from North Africa, but its safe havens provide territory from which individuals can plot and train.

Although only preliminary data exist on the viability of these locations as radicalization incubators or logistical hubs, even the Caribbean and the South Africa, with their open borders and loosely governed spaces, deserve attention as they have begun to show evidence of both ideological affinity and loose logistical links to recent plots.

Clearly al Qaeda has become more of a movement than a structured organization with decentralized operational execution. Given that most of the operations against the West have been manned by inspired volunteers who join it from the "bottom-up" from the West and not as a result of the efforts of a recruiter, there is an obvious of reservoir of "would-be warriors" originating from the "scene" in the West. Thus it is not surprising that the trend of more recent plots in the West in the last two years in Portland (Oregon), Seattle, London, and Stockholm, among others, has been toward an ever-increasing number of self-initiated jihadist plots against the West in which the only al Qaeda factor is that of affinity and inspiration driven by al Qaeda's global jihadist ideology. Travel overseas and joining a group were not even necessary. Driven by the call to arms in English by ideologues like Anwar al Awlaki, this trend is likely to continue.

The reality that al Qaeda Core's role in "global jihadist plots" against the West has varied significantly over time and that al Qaeda Core's role in plots is in general decline is a critical finding. This greater and more nuanced understanding of the genesis and attempted execution of plots directed against the West should affect the counterterrorism strategies and resources that Western governments, intelligence agencies, and police forces use to thwart the jihadist threat directed toward cities such as London, New York, Madrid, and Toronto.

Though al Qaeda Core is still in existence in the borderlands of Afghanistan and Pakistan, its role should be neither overestimated nor ignored. Nevertheless, the findings that most of the "action" or "center of gravity" of the conspiracies of even these "al Qaeda plots" has been in the West—that radicalization, mobilization, and action has taken place in the West—should drive Western governments' efforts to focus more on local counterterrorism to identify and disrupt plots in the streets of London, New York, Hamburg, and Madrid than on large-scale military deployments abroad.

Afterword

AS POLICE COMMISSIONER, I lead an organization charged with the protection and defense of New York City. Ten years after the devastating attacks of September 11, 2001, New York City remains at the top of the terrorists' list of targets. It has been in their sights no fewer than thirteen times since 2001, at locations ranging from the World Trade Center, the Brooklyn Bridge, and synagogues to financial institutions like the New York Stock Exchange and Citigroup headquarters. They have also targeted the subway system, PATH tunnels, and the jet-fuel pipeline and supply tanks at John F. Kennedy Airport.

Given this unique history, the New York City Police Department has been a voracious consumer of intelligence related to al Qaeda. We have sought to stay on the cutting edge in analyzing the dynamics of this fast-changing threat. In fact, rigorous assessments of the anatomy of past plots have informed both our operations and our countermeasures.

In *The Al Qaeda Factor*, the NYPD's Director of Intelligence Analysis, Mitch Silber, has provided a critical new understanding of the al Qaeda–aligned threat. Since 2001, the broad risk of attack from this organization has evolved; it has decentralized and proliferated, potentially making it even more dangerous than before.

Not only is this work the definitive compendium of the most important al Qaeda plots against the West since 1993, but Director Silber's dissection of each plot provides a granular and high-resolution examination of the common dynamics that underpin each conspiracy. These analyses establish that al Qaeda's role in global jihadist plots has varied over time, and that in the vast majority of the plots, the radicalization and motivation of the conspirators has emanated from the bottom up and not the top down—a sobering conclusion.

Finally, as the law enforcement and intelligence community continues to assess the potential impact of Osama bin Laden's death, Director Silber's conclusion that al Qaeda Core does not dominate or control the current threat has important implications. The ongoing threat has not dissipated, remains serious, and will require continued vigilance, commitment of resources, and staying power.

Raymond W. Kelly
Police Commissioner of the City of New York

Notes

Chapter 1

1. Terry McDermott, *Perfect Soldiers* (New York: HarperCollins, 2005), p. 84.

2. Ibid., p. 37.

3. Ibid., p. 87.

4. Marc Sageman, *Understanding Terror Networks* (Philadelphia: University of Pennsylvania Press, 2004), p. 104.

5. Ibid.; *The 9/11 Commission Report: Final Report of the National Commission on Terrorist Attacks upon the United States* (New York: W. W. Norton, 2004), p. 164.

6. McDermott, *Perfect Soldiers*, p. 20.

7. Ibid., pp. 32–34.

8. *The 9/11 Commission Report*, p. 161; McDermott, *Perfect Soldiers*, p. 37.

9. *The 9/11 Commission Report*, p. 161.

10. McDermott, *Perfect Soldiers*, p. 52.

11. "*Frontline*: Inside the Terror Network," January 17, 2002, http://www.pbs.org /wgbh/pages/frontline/shows/network/etc/script.html.

12. *The 9/11 Commission Report*, p. 163.

13. McDermott, *Perfect Soldiers*, p. 56.

14. *The 9/11 Commission Report*, p. 162.

15. Ibid., pp. 164–65.

16. Ibid., p. 181.

17. McDermott, *Perfect Soldiers*, p. 66.

18. *The 9/11 Commission Report*, pp. 161–62.

19. Sageman, *Understanding Terror Networks*, p. 106; McDermott, *Perfect Soldiers*, p. 63.

20. Sageman, *Understanding Terror Networks*, p. 104.

21. Sageman, *Understanding Terror Networks*, pp. 56, 104–5; *The 9/11 Commission Report*, pp. 160–65.

22. Sageman, *Understanding Terror Networks*, pp. 104–5; *The 9/11 Commission Report*, pp. 164–65, 496; McDermott, *Perfect Soldiers*, pp. 63–65, 68–69.

23. McDermott, *Perfect Soldiers*, p. 37.

24. *The 9/11 Commission Report*, p. 162.

25. Ibid., p. 163.

26. Ibid., p. 161.

27. Ibid., p. 164; Sageman, *Understanding Terror Networks*, p. 104.

28. *The 9/11 Commission Report*, p. 181.

29. Ibid., p. 165.

30. Ibid.

31. Ibid.; McDermott, *Perfect Soldiers*, p. 72.

32. Ibid., p. 48.

33. *The 9/11 Commission Report*, p. 182.

34. McDermott, *Perfect Soldiers,* p. 89.

35. *The 9/11 Commission Report*, p. 167.

36. Sageman, *Understanding Terror Networks*, p. 107.

37. *The 9/11 Commission Report*, p. 234.

38. Ibid., pp. 234, 236.

39. Ibid., pp. 167–68.

40. Ibid., p. 215.

41. Ibid., pp. 223–24.

42. Ibid.

43. Ibid., pp. 237, 241, 248.

44. Ibid., p. 222.

45. Ibid., pp. 225, 244.

46. Ibid., pp. 248, 249.

47. Ibid., pp. 242, 248.

48. Ibid., pp. 224–25, 226.

49. Ibid., p. 249.

Chapter 2

1. Jenny Bofoth, "Gloucester Shoebomber Jailed for 13 Years," *The Times*, April 22, 2005.

2. Sean O'Neill and Daniel McGrory, *The Suicide Factory: Abu Hamza and the Finsbury Park Mosque* (London: Harper Perennial, 2006), pp. 28–30, 32.

3. Ibid., p. 43.

4. Chris Gray, "Richard Reid: How Eager Convert Was Turned into a Suspected Terrorist," *The Independent*, December 27, 2001.

5. Michael Elliott, "The Shoe Bomber's World," *Time*, February 16, 2002.

6. Gray, "Richard Reid"; O'Neill and McGrory, *The Suicide Factory*, p. 221.

7. Gray, "Richard Reid"; O'Neill and McGrory, *The Suicide Factory*, p. 221.

8. Ibid.; "KSM's Transatlantic Shoe Bomb Plot," *The NEFA Foundation*, Report #11 in a NEFA series, "Target America," September 2007.

9. Jason Bennetto, Matthew Beard, and Kim Sengupta, "Sajid Badat: 'I Believe He Is Innocent. He Is a Walking Angel," *The Independent*, November 29, 2003.

10. "Pakistan: British Investigators Search for Shoe Bomber's Accomplices in Karachi," *Karachi Jasarat* (Urdu), December 10, 2004; "KSM's Transatlantic Shoe Bomb Plot."

11. *U.S. v. Reid*, D.C. MA., 02-CR-10013-WGY, Government's Sentencing Memorandum, filed January 17, 2003.

12. "Reid: 'I Am at War with Your Country," CNN, January 31, 2003.

13. Elliott, "The Shoe Bomber's World"; "Pakistan: British Investigators Search for Shoe Bomber's Accomplices in Karachi."

14. O'Neill and McGrory, *The Suicide Factory*, pp. 224–25.

15. "At School with the Shoe Bomber," *The Guardian*, February 28, 2002; Olga Craig, "From Tearaway to Terrorist: The Story of Richard Reid," *Daily Telegraph*, December 30, 2001.

16. "At School with the Shoe Bomber"; Craig, "From Tearaway to Terrorist."

17. Elliott, "The Shoe Bomber's World."

18. Mark Honigsbaum and Vikram Dodd, "From Gloucester to Afghanistan: The Making of a Shoe Bomber," *The Guardian*, March 5, 2005.

19. Ibid.; O'Neill and McGrory, *The Suicide Factory*, p. 229.

20. O'Neill and McGrory, *The Suicide Factory*, p. 230.

21. Ibid.; Honigsbaum and Dodd, "From Gloucester to Afghanistan."

22. O'Neill and McGrory, *The Suicide Factory*, pp. 221–22.

23. Ibid., p. 226; "Belgium Frees Jailbreak Suspects," CNN.com, December 22, 2007, http://news.bbc.co.uk/2/hi/europe/7157235.stm.

24. O'Neill and McGrory, *The Suicide Factory*, p. 226; "Belgium Frees Jailbreak Suspects"; Honigsbaum and Dodd, "From Gloucester to Afghanistan."

25. "Guilty Plea in Shoe Bombing Case," CNN, February 28, 2005; Honigsbaum and Dodd, "From Gloucester to Afghanistan."

26. Honigsbaum and Dodd, "From Gloucester to Afghanistan."

27. Sources: "Reid Is Al Qaeda Operative," CNN, December 6, 2003, http://www.cnn.com/2003/WORLD/asiapcf/southeast/01/30/reid.alqaeda; Habibullah Khan and Brian Ross, "U.S. Strike Killed Al Qaeda Bomb Maker," ABC News, January 18, 2006.

28. *Republic of France v. Rama*, Magistrates' Court of Paris, file number 0413839059, Judgment, filed June 16, 2005.

29. Sources: "Reid Is Al Qaeda Operative."

30. "Pakistan: British Investigators Search for Shoe Bomber's Accomplices in Karachi."

31. *U.S. v. Badat*, D.C. MA., 04-10223-GAO, Superseding Indictment, filed October 4, 2004; Booth, "Gloucester Shoebomber Jailed for 13 Years," *Times Online*, April 22, 2005.

32. *U.S. v. Reid*; Alan Cullison, "Inside Al Qaeda's Hard Drive," *Atlantic Monthly*, September 2004.

33. Verbatim Transcript of Combatant Status Review Tribunal Hearing for ISN 10024, U.S. Department of Defense, revised as of March 15, 2007, http://www.nefa-foundation.org/miscellaneous/Barot/DOD_KSM.pdf

34. Richard Serrano, "Bombing Targets Pinpointed by Reid," *Los Angeles Times*, January 23, 2003.

35. Ibid.; *U.S. v. Reid.*

36. *Republic of France v. Rama.*

37. Ibid.; John Tagliabue, "France: Prison for Man Linked to 'Shoe Bomber,'" *New York Times*, June 17, 2005.

38. *U.S. v. Badat*; "Terror Suspect Admits Plane Plot," BBC News, February 28, 2005, http://news.bbc.co.uk/2/hi/uk_news/england/gloucestershire/4304223.stm.

39. "Terror Suspect Admits Plane Plot."

40. Booth, "Gloucester Shoebomber Jailed for 13 Years."

41. Ibid.; "Terror Suspect Admits Plane Plot."

42. Elliott, "The Shoe Bomber's World."

43. "Biographies of High Value Terrorist Detainees Transferred to the US Naval Base at Guantanamo Bay," Biography of 'Ali 'Abd al-'Aziz 'Ali (aka 'Ammar al-Baluchi), Office of the Director of National Intelligence, September 16, 2006, http://nefafoundation.org/web/miscellaneous/shoebomb/dni_bio.pdf.

44. Simon Reeve, "Shoe-Bomb Flight—A Trial Run?" *The Chronicle*, January 6, 2002.

45. Booth, "Gloucester Shoebomber Jailed for 13 Years"; "Terror Suspect Admits Plane Plot."

46. Serrano, "Bombing Targets Pinpointed by Reid."

47. *U.S. v. Badat*; Booth, "Gloucester Shoebomber Jailed for 13 Years"; O'Neill and McGrory, *The Suicide Factory*, p. 231.

48. *Republic of France v. Rama.*

49. Ibid.

50. Bennetto, Beard, and Sengupta, "Sajid Badat: I Believe He Is Innocent." Following his abandonment of the shoe bomber operation, Badat went to study at the College of Islamic Knowledge and Guidance in Blackburn, Lancashire. Badat, who was known as a bright but very quiet student, was enrolled in a five-year course of study but left during the summer of 2003 on his own accord and moved back to Gloucester until his arrest later that year.

Chapter 3

1. Woolwich Crown Court, *Regina v. Abdulla Ahmed Ali [aka Ahmed Ali Khan], Assad Sarwar, Tanvir Hussain, Ibrahim Savant, Arafat Waheed Khan, Waheed Zaman and Umar Islam [aka Brian Young]*, April 3–September 8, 2008.

2. Kenan Malik, "Born in Bradford," *Prospect Magazine*, October 2005.

3. Melanie Phillips, *Londonistan* (New York: Encounter Books, 2006), pp. 4, 14, 16, 40, 77; O'Neill and McGrory, *The Suicide Factory*, pp. i–xvii, 5, 34, 80, 272.

4. O'Neill and Boyes, "Islamic Missionary Group Links Alleged Plotters"; Kamran Siddique, "My Friend: The Football Fan Who Dreamed of Being a Doctor," *The Guardian*, August 16, 2006.

5. O'Neill and Boyes, "Islamic Missionary Group Links Alleged Plotters"; Siddique, "My Friend."

6. Woolwich Crown Court, *Regina v. Abdulla Ahmed Ali,* July 2, 2008; Dominic Kennedy and Hannah Devline, "Disbelief and Shame in a Community of Divided Faith," *The Times Online*, August 19, 2006.

7. "Profiles: Operation Overt," BBC News, September 8, 2008, http://news.bbc.co.uk/2/hi/uk_news/7604808.stm.

8. Woolwich Crown Court, *Regina v. Abdulla Ahmed Ali*, June 2, 2008.

9. Ibid., June 3, 2008.

10. Ibid., July 2, 2008; "Profiles: Operation Overt."

11. Serge F. Kovaleski, "Journeys to Realm of Militancy Began in Places Most Ordinary," *New York Times*, August 16, 2006.

12. Woolwich Crown Court, *Regina v. Abdulla Ahmed Ali*, June 2, 2008.

13. Author's copy of martyrdom videos; Cahal Milmo, "*You Will Be Destroyed*: Bombers Convicted of Heathrow Plot," *The Independent*, September 9, 2008.

14. Author's copy of martyrdom videos; Cahal Milmo, "*You Will Be Destroyed*."

15. Woolwich Crown Court, *Regina v. Abdulla Ahmed Ali*, April 22, 2008.

16. Ibid.

17. Ibid.; Jumana Farouky, "Profiling the Suspects: Converts to Islam," *Time*, August 11, 2006.

18. Woolwich Crown Court, *Regina v. Abdulla Ahmed Ali*, June 2, 2008; "Profiles: Operation Overt"; Milmo, "*You Will Be Destroyed*"; Cahal Milmo, "The Terrorists Who Changed Air Travel Forever," *The Independent*, September 9, 2008.

19. Woolwich Crown Court, *Regina v. Abdulla Ahmed Ali*, June 16 and 30, 2008; "Profiles: Operation Overt."

20. Woolwich Crown Court, *Regina v. Abdulla Ahmed Ali*, June 2, 2008; "Profiles: Operation Overt"; David Harrison and Adam Lusher, "Abdulla Ahmed Ali: A Terrorist in the Making at the Age of 14," *Daily Telegraph*, September 13, 2008.

21. Woolwich Crown Court, *Regina v. Abdulla Ahmed Ali*, June 2, 2008; "Profiles: Operation Overt"; Harrison and Lusher, "Abdulla Ahmed Ali"; Sean O'Neill and Michael Evans, "Analysis: How the Plan Was Put Together," *Times Online*, September 9, 2008, http://www.timesonline.co.uk/tol/news/uk/crime/article4708700.ece.

22. Woolwich Crown Court, *Regina v. Abdulla Ahmed Ali*, June 2, 2008; "Profiles: Operation Overt"; O'Neill and Boyes, "Islamic Missionary Group Links Alleged Plotters."

23. Richard Greenberg, Paul Cruickshank, and Chris Hansen, "Inside the

Terror Plot That Rivaled 9/11," *Dateline NBC*, September 16, 2008; "Profiles: Operation Overt"; Jason Burke, "Top British Terror Suspect Killed in US Missile Strike," *Observer*, November 23, 2008.

24. Woolwich Crown Court, *Regina v. Abdulla Ahmed Ali*, June 16, 2008; "Profiles: Operation Overt"; Milmo, "The Terrorists Who Changed Air Travel Forever."

25. Woolwich Crown Court, *Regina v. Abdulla Ahmed Ali*, June 17, 2008; "Profiles: Operation Overt"; Milmo, "The Terrorists Who Changed Air Travel Forever."

26. Woolwich Crown Court, *Regina v. Abdulla Ahmed Ali*, June 30, 2008; Siddique, "My Friend"; O'Neill and Boyes, "Islamic Missionary Group Links Alleged Plotters."

27. Steve Bird, "Men Had Converted to Devout Form of Islam, Residents Say," *Times Online*, August 11, 2006, http://www.timesonline.co.uk/tol/news/uk/article606322.ece; Farouky, "Profiling the Suspects."

28. Woolwich Crown Court, *Regina v. Abdulla Ahmed Ali*, July 2, 2008; "Profiles: Operation Overt."

29. Woolwich Crown Court, *Regina v. Abdulla Ahmed Ali*, June 2, 2008; "Man in Court Over 'Plot to Blow Up Aircraft,'" *The Independent*, October 26, 2009; Kovaleski, "Journeys to Realm of Militancy Began in Places Most Ordinary."

30. Woolwich Crown Court, *Regina v. Abdulla Ahmed Ali;* Janet Stobart and Sebastian Rotella, "Seven Britons Will Again Face Charges of Conspiring to Detonate Explosives Aboard U.S.-Bound Planes," *Los Angeles Times*, September 10, 2008.

31. Woolwich Crown Court, *Regina v. Abdulla Ahmed Ali*, June 4 and July 2, 2008; Adrian Morgan, "UK: Islamist 'Air Terror Plot' in Focus," September 12, 2008, http://www.westernresistance.com/blog/archives/004062.html.

32. Stobart and Rotella, "Seven Britons Will Again Face Charges."

33. Woolwich Crown Court, *Regina v. Abdulla Ahmed Ali*, April 3, 2008.

34. Ibid.; Milmo, "The Terrorists Who Changed Air Travel Forever."

35. Woolwich Crown Court, *Regina v. Abdulla Ahmed Ali,* July 7, 2008; Greenberg, Cruickshank, and Hansen, "Inside the Terror Plot That Rivaled 9/11."

36. Woolwich Crown Court, *Regina v. Abdulla Ahmed Ali*, June 3, 2008; Greenberg, Cruickshank, and Hansen, "Inside the Terror Plot That Rivaled 9/11."

37. Woolwich Crown Court, *Regina v. Abdulla Ahmed Ali,* June 10, 2008; "Profiles: Operation Overt," *BBC News*, September 8, 2008.

38. Greenberg, Cruickshank, and Hansen, "Inside the Terror Plot That Rivaled 9/11."

39. Milmo, "The Terrorists Who Changed Air Travel Forever."

40. Greenberg, Cruickshank, and Hansen, "Inside the Terror Plot That Rivaled 9/11."

41. Ibid.; Stobart and Rotella, "Seven Britons Will Again Face Charges."

42. Greenberg, Cruickshank, and Hansen, "Inside the Terror Plot That Rivaled 9/11."

43. Woolwich Crown Court, *Regina v. Abdulla Ahmed Ali,* July 19, 2007.

44. Woolwich Crown Court, *Regina v. Abdulla Ahmed Ali,* July 10, 2008.

45. Ibid., April 3, 2008.

46. Ibid., April 21, 2008; Milmo, "The Terrorists Who Changed Air Travel Forever."

47. Milmo, "The Terrorists Who Changed Air Travel Forever."

48. Woolwich Crown Court, *Regina v. Abdulla Ahmed Ali,* June 3, 2008; Milmo, "The Terrorists Who Changed Air Travel Forever."

49. Woolwich Crown Court, *Regina v. Abdulla Ahmed Ali,* June 3, 2008; Milmo, "The Terrorists Who Changed Air Travel Forever."

50. Woolwich Crown Court, *Regina v. Abdulla Ahmed Ali,* June 3, 2008; Milmo, "The Terrorists Who Changed Air Travel Forever."

51. Woolwich Crown Court, *Regina v. Abdulla Ahmed Ali,* June 4, 2008; Duncan Gardham and Gordon Rayner, "Airline Bomb Trial: Five Potential Suicide Bombers Still at Large," *The Telegraph,* September 9, 2008.

52. Milmo, "The Terrorists Who Changed Air Travel Forever."

53. Woolwich Crown Court, *Regina v. Abdulla Ahmed Ali*; Milmo, "The Terrorists Who Changed Air Travel Forever."

54. Woolwich Crown Court, *Regina v. Abdulla Ahmed Ali*; Milmo, "The Terrorists Who Changed Air Travel Forever."

55. Cahal Milmo, Ian Herbert, Jason Bennetto, and Justin Huggler, "From Birmingham Bakery to Pakistani Prison: The Mystery of Rashid Raud," *The Independent,* August 19, 2006.

56. Ian Cobain, "The Mysterious Disappearance of an Alleged Terror Mastermind," *The Guardian,* January 28, 2008; Asif Farooqi, Carol Grisanti, and Robert Windrem, "U.K. Plot Suspect Forced to Talk," NBC News, August 18, 2006.

57. Cobain, "The Mysterious Disappearance of an Alleged Terror Mastermind"; Farooqi, Grisanti, and Windrem, "U.K. Plot Suspect Forced to Talk."

58. Cobain, "The Mysterious Disappearance of an Alleged Terror Mastermind."

59. Woolwich Crown Court, *Regina v. Abdulla Ahmed Ali,* April 3, 2008.

60. Sentencing Hearing, Woolwich Crown Court, *Regina v. Abdulla Ahmed Ali,* September 14, 2009.

61. Ibid.

62. "Explosive Emails," BBC.com, 2009.

63. Woolwich Crown Court, *Regina v. Abdulla Ahmed Ali,* June 5, 2008.

64. Ibid.

65. Ibid., April 3, 2008.

66. Ibid.; Milmo, "The Terrorists Who Changed Air Travel Forever."

67. Woolwich Crown Court, *Regina v. Abdulla Ahmed Ali,* April 3, 2008; Milmo, "The Terrorists Who Changed Air Travel Forever."

68. Woolwich Crown Court, *Regina v. Abdulla Ahmed Ali,* April 3, 2008; Greenberg, Cruickshank, and Hansen, "Inside the Terror Plot That Rivaled 9/11."

69. Greenberg, Cruickshank, and Hansen, "Inside the Terror Plot That Rivaled 9/11."

70. Ibid.

71. *USA v. Adis Medujanin, Abid Naseer, Adnan el Shukrijumah, Tariq ur Rehman, FLU LNU and Name Redacted,* Eastern District of New York, 2010; Department of Justice Press Release, "Zarein Ahmedzay Pleads Guilty to Terror Violations in Connection with Al-Qaeda New York Subway Plot," April 23, 2010.

72. Sebastian Rotella, "Dangerous, Endangered: A Look Inside Al Qaeda," *Los Angeles Times,* April 2, 2008.

73. Sentencing Hearing, Woolwich Crown Court, *Regina v. Abdulla Ahmed Ali,* September 14, 2009.

Chapter 4

1. Sageman, *Understanding Terror Networks,* p. 100.

2. Stewart Bell, *Cold Terror: How Canada Nurtures and Exports Terror Around the World* (Toronto: John Wiley, 2005,), p. 156.

3. Fabrice de Pierrebourg, *Montréalistan: Enquête sur la mouvance islamiste?* (Montreal: Stankeï, 2007), p. 115; Bell, *Cold Terror,* p. 162.

4. Sageman, *Understanding Terror Networks,* p. 100.

5. Hal Bernton, Mike Carter, David Heath, and James Neff, "The Terrorist Within," *Seattle Times,* June 23–July 7, 2002.

6. Ibid.

7. Bell, *Cold Terror,* pp. 156–60; Sageman, *Understanding Terror Networks,* p. 101.

8. Bernton et al., "The Terrorist Within."

9. Sageman, *Understanding Terror Networks,* pp. 101–2.

10. *"Frontline*: Trail of a Terrorist—Ahmed Ressam's Millennium Plot," http://www.pbs.org/wgbh/pages/frontline/shows/trail/inside/cron.html; Sageman, *Understanding Terror Networks,* pp. 99–100.

11. *"Frontline*: Trail of a Terrorist"; Sageman, *Understanding Terror Networks,* pp. 99–100.

12. Sageman, *Understanding Terror Networks,* p. 100.

13. *"Frontline*: Trail of a Terrorist—Ahmed Ressam's Millennium Plot."

14. Bell, *Cold Terror,* pp. 148, 152–54, 156–57.

15. Sageman, *Understanding Terror Networks,* pp. 101–2.

16. Ibid.

17. *"Frontline*: Trail of a Terrorist—Ahmed Ressam's Millennium Plot"; Sageman, *Understanding Terror* Networks, pp. 101, 110.

18. Sageman, *Understanding Terror Networks,* pp. 102–3.

19. Ibid., pp. 102–3, 110.

20. De Pierrebourg, *Montréalistan,* p. 262.

21. Ibid., p. 252.

22. Sageman, *Understanding Terror Networks*, pp. 101–2.

23. De Pierrebourg, *Montréalistan*, p. 266; Bernton et al., "The Terrorist Within."

24. Sageman, *Understanding Terror Networks*, p. 102; Bell, *Cold Terror*, p. 162.

25. Bernton et al., "The Terrorist Within."

26. Bell, *Cold Terror*, pp. 164–65.

27. Sources: "Reid Is Al Qaeda Operative."

28. Combatant Status Review Tribunals Summaries, Abu Zubayda, http://projects.nytimes.com/guantanamo/detainees/10016/documents/11.

29. *USA vs. Abu Doha*, sealed complaint, U.S. Southern District Court, New York, July 2, 2001; testimony of Ahmed Ressam, *USA vs. Mokhtar Houari*, July 5, 2001; Sageman, *Understanding Terror Networks*, p. 102.

30. *USA vs. Abu Doha*.

31. Combatant Status Review Tribunals Summaries, Abu Zubayda.

32. Ibid.; testimony of Ahmed Ressam, *USA vs. Mokhtar Houari*; Sageman, *Understanding Terror Networks*, p. 102.

33. Sageman, *Understanding Terror Networks*, p. 102.

34. Bernton et al., "The Terrorist Within."

35. Sageman, *Understanding Terror Networks*, p. 102; Bell, *Cold Terror*, pp. 164–65.

36. Bernton et al., "The Terrorist Within."

37. Bell, *Cold Terror*, pp. 164–65.

38. Bernton et al., "The Terrorist Within."

39. De Pierrebourg, *Montréalistan*, p. 278.

40. Bernton et al., "The Terrorist Within."

41. John Kifner and William K. Rashbaum, "Brooklyn Man Is Charged with Aiding in Bomb Plot," *New York Times*, December 31, 1999.

42. De Pierrebourg, *Montréalistan*, p. 278.

43. *The 9/11 Commission Report*, p. 17.

Chapter 5

1. "Anti-Terror Investigation: The Full Charges," *The Guardian*, August 18, http://www.guardian.co.uk/uk/2004/aug/18/terrorism.world1.

2. O'Neill and McGrory, *The Suicide Factory*, pp. 28–30, 32.

3. Ibid., p. 43.

4. Duncan Gardham, "Average Student Who Met 9/11 Mastermind," *The Telegraph*, June 18, 2007.

5. Ibid.

6. "Muslim Convert Who Plotted Terror," BBC News, November 7, 2006.

7. O'Neill and McGrory, *The Suicide Factory*, p. 80.

8. David Carlisle, "Dhiren Barot: Was He an Al Qaeda Mastermind or Merely a Hapless Plotter?" *Studies in Conflict & Terrorism* 30, no. 12 (2007): 1057–71.

9. Isa Al Hindi, *The Army of Madinah in Kashmir* (Maktabah al Ansar, 2000).

10. Fact Sheet, Metropolitan Police and Duncan Gardham, "Telegraph Profiles: The Harrow Gang," *The Telegraph*, June 18, 2007.

11. Bhatti Fact Sheet, Metropolitan Police and Gardham, "Telegraph Profiles"; Gardham, "Average Student Who Met 9/11 Mastermind."

12. Bhatti Fact Sheet.

13. Tarmohammed Fact Sheet, Metropolitan Police and Gardham, "Telegraph Profiles."

14. Bhatti Fact Sheet.

15. Ibid.; Feroze Fact Sheet Metropolitan Police and Gardham, "Telegraph Profiles."

16. "Al Qaeda Bomb Plot Commander's Team Follow Him to Prison," *The Times*, June 16, 2007.

17. Carlisle, "Dhiren Barot."

18. Adam Fresco, "How Radical Islam Turned a Schoolboy into a Terrorist," *Times Online*, November 7, 2006.

19. Tarmohammed Fact Sheet.

20. Jalil Fact Sheet, Metropolitan Police and Gardham, "Telegraph Profiles."

21. Feroze Fact Sheet.

22. Shaffi Fact Sheet, Metropolitan Police and Gardham, "Telegraph Profiles"

23. Bhatti Fact Sheet.

24. Ul Haq Fact Sheet, Metropolitan Police and Gardham, "Telegraph Profiles."

25. Rehman Fact Sheet, Metropolitan Police and Gardham, "Telegraph Profiles."

26. Duncan Gardham, "Muslim Was Planning Dirty Bomb Attack in UK," *Daily Telegraph*, November 13, 2006.

27. "Muslim Convert Who Plotted Terror."

28. Fresco, "How Radical Islam Turned a Schoolboy into a Terrorist."

29. Jalil Fact Sheet.

30. Feroze Fact Sheet.

31. Ul Haq Fact Sheet.

32. Carlisle, "Dhiren Barot."

33. *U.S. v. Dhiren Barot*, http://www.justice.gov/criminal/press room/ press re-leases/2005 3952 2 pr-ChrgWponFMassDstrctConsp041305.pdf.

34. Carlisle, "Dhiren Barot."

35. Fresco, "How Radical Islam Turned a Schoolboy into a Terrorist."

36. Carlisle, "Dhiren Barot."

37. Isikoff and Hosenball, "Bin Laden's Mystery Man."

38. *The 9/11 Commission Report*, p. 150.

39. Carlisle, "Dhiren Barot."

40. *U.S. v. Dhiren Barot*.

41. *The 9/11 Commission Report*, p. 150.

42. Barot's Targeting Package on the New York Stock Exchange, http://www.nefafoundation.org/miscellaneous/Barot/NYSE.pdf.

43. Ibid.

44. Barot's Targeting Package on the Prudential Plaza, http://www.nefafoundation.org/miscellaneous/Barot/Prudential.pdf.

45. Carlisle, "Dhiren Barot."

46. Barot's Targeting Package on the International Monetary Fund and World Bank, http://www.nefafoundation.org/miscellaneous/Barot/IMF_WorldBank.pdf.

47. Duncan Gardham, "The British Fanatic Who Plotted to Kill Thousands," *The Telegraph*, November 7, 2006.

48. Carlisle, "Dhiren Barot."

49. Sean O'Neill and Adam Fresco, "The Video Made Five Months Before 9/11 Attacks," *Times Online*, November 7, 2006.

50. "In Pictures: Barot's Terror Plans," BBC News, 7 November 2006, http://news.bbc.co.uk/2/hi/in_pictures/6126018.stm.

51. "Final Presentation," http://nefafoundation.org/miscellaneous/Barot/Final-Presentation.pdf.

52. "Hazards," http://nefafoundation.org/miscellaneous/Barot/Hazards.pdf.

53. "Terrorist Jailed for Life for Conspiracy to Murder in the UK and US," Metropolitan Police Service Press Release, November 7, 2006, http://www.nefafoundation.org/miscellaneous/Barot/MPS_Barot_Sentenced.pdf.

54. Barot's "Rough Presentation for Gas Limos Project," http://www.nefafoundation.org/miscellaneous/Barot/GasLimos.pdf.

55. Ibid.

56. Ibid.

57. "The U.S. Targets," *The Telegraph*, November 7, 2006.

58. Carlisle, "Dhiren Barot."

59. "Operation Rhyme Terror Convictions," http://content.met.police.uk/News/Operation-Rhyme-terror-convictions/1260267585542/1257246745756.

Chapter 6

1. Central Criminal Court, Old Bailey, *Regina v. Omar Khyam, Anthony Garcia, Nabeel Hussain, Jawad Akbar, Waheed Mahmood, Shujah-Ud-Din Mahmood and Salahuddin Amin.*

2. Quintan Wiktorowicz, *Radical Islam Rising* (Lanham, MD: Rowman and Littlefield, 2005), pp. 185–88.

3. Central Criminal Court, Old Bailey, *Regina v. Omar Khyam et al.*, September 14, 2006.

4. Ibid., March 6, 2007.

5. "Profile: Waheed Mahmood," BBC News, http://news.bbc.co.uk/2/hi/uk_news/6149800.stm.

6. "Profile: Jawad Akbar," BBC News, http://news.bbc.co.uk/2/hi/uk_news/6149788.stm.

7. "Profile: Anthony Garcia," BBC News, http://news.bbc.co.uk/2/hi/uk_news/6149798.stm.

8. Central Criminal Court, Old Bailey, *Regina v. Omar Khyam et al.*, March 8, 2007.

9. Ibid., November 21, 2006.

10. Elaine Sciolino and Stephen Grey, "British Terror Trial Traces a Path to Militant Islam," *New York Times*, November 26, 2006; Central Criminal Court, Old Bailey, *Regina v. Omar Khyam et al.*, March 5, 2007.

11. Central Criminal Court, *Regina v. Omar Khyam et al.*, September 25, 2006.

12. Ontario Superior Court of Justice and "Her Majesty the Queen versus Mohammad Momin Khawaja," October 29, 2008, Court File No. 04-G30282.

13. Central Criminal Court, Old Bailey, *Regina v. Omar Khyam et al.*, April 27, 2006.

14. "U.K. Fertilizer Plot," BBC News, http://news.bbc.co.uk/2/shared/spl/hi/guides/457000/457032/html/nn1page9.stm.

15. Central Criminal Court, Old Bailey, *Regina v. Omar Khyam et al.*, April 27, 2006.

16. Ibid.; "The Home Counties Boys Who Planned Murder," *The Telegraph*, May 2, 2007; "U.K. Fertilizer Plot."

17. Central Criminal Court, Old Bailey, *Regina v. Omar Khyam et al.*, September 14, 2006; "Profile: Omar Khyam," BBC News, http://news.bbc.co.uk/2/hi/uk_news/6149794.stm.

18. Central Criminal Court, Old Bailey, *Regina v. Omar Khyam et al.*, September, 14, 2006.

19. Ibid.

20. Ibid.

21. Ibid., November 21, 2006; "Profile: Salahuddin Amin," BBC News, http://news.bbc.co.uk/2/hi/uk_news/6149790.stm.

22. Central Criminal Court, Old Bailey, *Regina v. Omar Khyam et al.*, November 21, 2006; "Profile: Salahuddin Amin."

23. Central Criminal Court, Old Bailey, *Regina v. Omar Khyam et al.*, November 21, 2006; "Profile: Salahuddin Amin."

24. "Profile: Waheed Mahmood."

25. Central Criminal Court, Old Bailey, *Regina v. Omar Khyam et al.*, October 4, 2006; "Profile: Jawad Akbar."

26. Central Criminal Court, Old Bailey, *Regina v. Omar Khyam et al.*, October 4, 2006; "Profile: Jawad Akbar."

27. Central Criminal Court, Old Bailey, *Regina v. Omar Khyam et al.*, March 19, 2007.

28. Central Criminal Court, Old Bailey, *Regina v. Omar Khyam et al.*, September 25, 2006; "Profile: Anthony Garcia."

29. Central Criminal Court, Old Bailey, *Regina v. Omar Khyam et al.*, September 25, 2006; "Profile: Anthony Garcia."

30. Ontario Superior Court of Justice and "Her Majesty the Queen versus Mohammad Momin Khawaja"; "Khawaja: The Canadian Connection," BBC News, http://news.bbc.co.uk/2/hi/uk_news/6152440.stm; "The Canadian: Chronology of Mohammed Momin Khawaja," *The Fifth Estate*, CBC-TV, 2006, http://www.cbc.ca/fifth/the-canadian.html.

31. Central Criminal Court, Old Bailey, *Regina v. Omar Khyam et al.*, March 23, 2006; "Supergrass Tells of Terror Fight," BBC.com, March 24, 2007, http://news.bbc.co.uk/2/hi/uk_news/4835666.stm.

32. Central Criminal Court, Old Bailey, *Regina v. Omar Khyam et al.*, March 23, 2006; "Supergrass Tells of Terror Fight."

33. Central Criminal Court, Old Bailey, *Regina v. Omar Khyam et al.*, March 23, 2006; "Supergrass Tells of Terror Fight."

34. Central Criminal Court, Old Bailey, *Regina v. Omar Khyam et al.*, September 25, 2006; "Profile: Nabeel Hussain," BBC News, http://news.bbc.co.uk/2/hi/uk_news/6149792.stm.

35. Central Criminal Court, Old Bailey, *Regina v. Omar Khyam et al.*, September 14, 2006; "Profile: Shujah Mahmood," BBC News, http://news.bbc.co.uk/2/hi/uk_news/6149796.stm.

36. Michael Elliot, May 27, 2007, http://archives.cnn.com/2002/ALLPOLITICS/05/27/time.alqaeda; "Fahad Hashmi, a Pakistani-American student, spoke at the meeting, praising the American Taliban, John Walker Lindh," *Village Voice*, November 5, 2008; United States Attorney Southern District of New York to United States District Judge Victor Marrero, *Re: United States v. Mohammed Junaid Babar*, November 23, 2010.

37. "Kazi Nurur Rahman," BBC.com, April 30, 2007, http://news.bbc.co.uk/2/hi/uk_news/6206886.stm.

38. Central Criminal Court, Old Bailey, *Regina v. Omar Khyam et al.*, March 18, 2007.

39. Ibid., March 27, 2006; "U.K. Fertilizer Plot."

40. Central Criminal Court, Old Bailey, *Regina v. Omar Khyam et al.*, March 23, 2006; "Supergrass Tells of Terror Fight."

41. Central Criminal Court, Old Bailey, *Regina v. Omar Khyam et al.*, March 13, 2007; "Timeline: Operation Crevice," http://news.bbc.co.uk/2/hi/uk_news/6207348.stm.

42. Central Criminal Court, Old Bailey, *Regina v. Omar Khyam et al.*, March 13, 2007; "Timeline: Operation Crevice."

43. Ontario Superior Court of Justice and "Her Majesty the Queen versus Mohammad Momin Khawaja."

44. Richard Brennan, "Accused Made Bomb Detonator, Crown Says," *The Star*, June 24, 2008.

45. "Timeline: Operation Crevice."

46. Ontario Superior Court of Justice and "Her Majesty the Queen versus Mohammad Momin Khawaja."

47. Central Criminal Court, Old Bailey, *Regina v. Omar Khyam et al.*, December 12, 2006.

48. Ibid.

49. Central Criminal Court, Old Bailey, *Regina v. Omar Khyam et al.*, March 15, 2007; "Timeline: Operation Crevice."

50. United States Attorney Southern District of New York to United States District Judge Victor Marrero, *Re: United States v. Mohammed Junaid Babar*, November 23, 2010.

51. Central Criminal Court, Old Bailey, *Regina v. Omar Khyam et al.*, March 24, 2006.

52. Ibid., March 15, 2007.

53. Ibid., March 5, 2007.

54. Ibid., March 6, 2007.

55. Ontario Superior Court of Justice and "Her Majesty the Queen versus Mohammad Momin Khawaja."

56. Central Criminal Court, Old Bailey, *Regina v. Omar Khyam et al.*, September 26, 2006.

57. Ibid., March 6, 2007.

58. "Traveling Pair Were Very Close Friends; Babar Claims About Khan and Shakil," *Huddersfield Daily Examiner*, April 18, 2008; "MI5 Followed UK Suicide Bomber," BBC.com, April 30, 2007, http://news.bbc.co.uk/2/hi/uk_news/6417353.stm.

59. Central Criminal Court, Old Bailey, *Regina v. Omar Khyam et al.*, March 13, 2007, September 15, 2006.

60. Central Criminal Court, Old Bailey, *Regina v. Omar Khyam et al.*, September 15, 2006.

61. Neil Atkinson, "Bomb Suspects Visited Terror Training Camps; Court Hears of Trips with July 7 Bombings Leader," *Huddersfield Daily Examiner*, April 11, 2008.

62. Ontario Superior Court of Justice and "Her Majesty the Queen versus Mohammad Momin Khawaja."

63. Central Criminal Court, *Regina v. Omar Khyam et al.*, March 29, 2006.

64. Ibid., March 5, 2007.

65. Mohammed Khan and Carolotta Gall, "Accounts After 2005 Bombings Point to Al Qaeda Role from Pakistan," *New York Times*, August 13, 2006.

66. Central Criminal Court, Old Bailey, *Regina v. Omar Khyam et al.*, March 9, 2007.

67. Ibid.

68. Ibid.

69. Ibid.

70. Duncan Gardham, "The Crawley Targets," *The Telegraph*, May 1, 2007

71. Shiv Malik, "The Jihadi House Parties of Hate," *The Times*, May 6, 2007.

72. Central Criminal Court, Old Bailey, *Regina v. Omar Khyam et al.*, March 28, 2006.

73. "Timeline: Operation Crevice."

74. Ibid.

75. Atkinson, "Bomb Suspects Visited Terror Training Camps."

76. Ontario Superior Court of Justice and "Her Majesty the Queen versus Mohammad Momin Khawaja."

77. Central Criminal Court, Old Bailey, *Regina v. Omar Khyam et al.*, November 30, 2006.

78. Ibid.

79. Ibid., March 28, 2006; "Timeline: Operation Crevice."

80. Central Criminal Court, Old Bailey, *Regina v. Omar Khyam et al.*, September 25, 2006; Ramaa Sharma, "Garcia's Neighbours Shocked," BBC News, April 30, 2007, http://www.bbc.co.uk/london/content/articles/2007/04/30/garcia_feature.shtml.

81. Ontario Superior Court of Justice and "Her Majesty the Queen versus Mohammad Momin Khawaja."

82. Ibid.

83. United States Attorney Southern District of New York to United States District Judge Victor Marrero, *Re: United States v. Mohammed Junaid Babar*, November 23, 2010.

84. Ontario Superior Court of Justice and "Her Majesty the Queen versus Mohammad Momin Khawaja."

85. Central Criminal Court, Old Bailey, *Regina v. Omar Khyam et al.*, March 15, 2007.

86. Ibid.; Jamie Doward and Andrew Wander, "The Network," *The Guardian*, May 6, 2007.

87. Central Criminal Court, Old Bailey, *Regina v. Omar Khyam et al.*, March 6, 2007.

88. Central Criminal Court, Old Bailey, *Regina v. Omar Khyam et al.*, March 31, 2006.

89. United States Attorney Southern District of New York to United States District Judge Victor Marrero, *Re: United States v. Mohammed Junaid Babar*, November 23, 2010.

90. Ibid.; Central Criminal Court, Old Bailey, *Regina v. Omar Khyam et al.*, March 31, 2006.

91. Ontario Superior Court of Justice and "Her Majesty the Queen versus Mohammad Momin Khawaja."

92. Central Criminal Court, Old Bailey, *Regina v. Omar Khyam et al.*, March 29, 2006.

93. Ibid., March 5, 2007.

94. Ibid., March 29, 2006.

Chapter 7

1. Crown Court at Kingston Upon Thames, *Regina v. Mohammed Shakil, Wahid Ali and Sadeer Saleem.*

2. Ibid.

3. Aidan Kirby, "The London Bombers as Self Starters," *Studies in Conflict and Terrorism* 30 (2007): 415–28.

4. "Biography of a Bomber," BBCRadio4, November 17, 2005, http://www.bbc .co.uk.

5. Neil Atkinson, "Accused Smoked with Bomb Gang Ringleader," *Huddersfield Daily Examiner*, May 9, 2008.

6. Russell Jenkins, "Killers May Have Been Recruited at Youth Centre," *The Times*, July 16, 2005.

7. O'Neill and McGrory, *The Suicide Factory*, pp. 271–72.

8. Shiv Malik, "My Brother the Bomber," *Prospect Magazine*, no. 135, June 2007.

9. Ibid.

10. "Undercover on Planet Beeston," *The Times*, July 2, 2006.

11. Amy Waldman, "Seething Unease Shaped British Bombers' Newfound Zeal," *New York Times*, July 31, 2005.

12. Ibid.

13. See "Profile: Mohammad Siddique Khan," BBC News, May 11, 2006; "Profile: Shezhad Tanweer," BBC News, July 6, 2006; "Profile: Hasib Mir Husain," BBC News, May 11, 2006.

14. "Bomber Influenced by Preacher," BBC News, May 11, 2006.

15. Crown Court at Kingston Upon Thames, *Regina v. Mohammed Shakil, Wahid Ali and Sadeer Saleem*, June 6, 2008; Olga Craig, "Bowling for Paradise," *Sunday Telegraph*, July 17, 2005.

16. Crown Court at Kingston Upon Thames, *Regina v. Mohammed Shakil, Wahid Ali and Sadeer Saleem*, May 20, 2008.

17. "Report of the Official Account of the Bombings in London on 7th July 2005," ordered by the House of Commons, May 11, 2006.

18. "Video of London Suicide Bomber Released," *Times Online*, July 6, 2006.

19. "Video of 7 July Bomber Released," BBC News, July 6, 2006.

20. Crown Court at Kingston Upon Thames, *Regina v. Mohammed Shakil, Wahid Ali and Sadeer Saleem*, June 6, 2008.

21. "Three Held Over July 7 Bombings," BBC.com, March 22, 2007, http://news.bbc.co.uk/2/hi/uk_news/6481495.stm.

22. Malik, "My Brother the Bomber."

23. Atkinson, "Accused Smoked with Bomb Gang Ringleader."

24. Crown Court at Kingston Upon Thames, *Regina v. Mohammed Shakil, Wahid Ali and Sadeer Saleem*, June 6, 2008.

25. Kevin Cullen, "Respected in Community, Bomb Suspect Hid Turmoil," *Boston Globe*, July 15, 2005.

26. Nasreen Suleaman, BBC interviews, in Tom Hundley, "Attacks Spur Identity Crisis for Britain," *Chicago Tribune*, December 16, 2005.

27. Ian Herbert, "Documentary Reveals London Bomber's Westernized Youth," *The Independent (London)*, November 18, 2005.

28. Ibid.

29. Ibid.

30. Malik, "My Brother the Bomber"; Herbert, "Documentary Reveals London Bomber's Westernized Youth"; Crown Court at Kingston Upon Thames, *Regina v. Mohammed Shakil, Wahid Ali and Sadeer Saleem*, June 6, 2008.

31. Kirby, "The London Bombers as Self Starters."

32. "Report of the Official Account of the Bombings in London on 7th July 2005."

33. Crown Court at Kingston Upon Thames, *Regina v. Mohammed Shakil, Wahid Ali and Sadeer Saleem*, May 20, 2008; Rachel Williams, "July 7 Plot Accused Tell of Times with Taliban," *The Guardian*, May 21, 2008.

34. Crown Court at Kingston Upon Thames, *Regina v. Mohammed Shakil, Wahid Ali and Sadeer Saleem*, June 6, 2008.

35. Jane Perlez, "U.K. Arrests of Islamists Fail to Solve Mysteries; Who Were Planners of London Attacks," *International Herald Tribune*, March 26, 2007; Crown Court at Kingston Upon Thames, *Regina v. Mohammed Shakil, Wahid Ali and Sadeer Saleem*, May 20 and June 6, 2008.

36. Cullen, "Respected in Community, Bomb Suspect Hid Turmoil."

37. Sam Greenhill, "My Baby Torment, by Wife of 7/7 Bomber," *The Mail Online*, July 27, 2007, http://www.dailymail.co.uk/news/article-471169/My-baby-torment-wife-7-7-bomber.html.

38. "Bomb-Plot Accused's Bid to Join Taliban," *Yorkshire Post*, May 21, 2008; Andrew Carey, "7/7 Accused: I Trained in Militant Camp," CNN, May 20, 2008, http://www.cnn.com/2008/WORLD/europe/05/20/uk.terrortrial/index.html; Crown Court at Kingston Upon Thames, *Regina v. Mohammed Shakil, Wahid Ali and Sadeer Saleem*, May 20 and June 6, 2008.

39. . "Bomb-Plot Accused's Bid to Join Taliban"; Carey, "7/7 Accused"; Crown Court at Kingston Upon Thames, *Regina v. Mohammed Shakil, Wahid Ali and Sadeer Saleem*, May 20 and June 6, 2008.

40. Malik, "My Brother the Bomber."

41. Crown Court at Kingston Upon Thames, *Regina v. Mohammed Shakil, Wahid Ali and Sadeer Saleem*, June 5, 2008; "MI5 Followed UK Suicide Bomber."

42. Central Criminal Court, Old Bailey, *Regina v. Omar Khyam et al.*, March 13, 2007.

43. Ibid., September, 15, 2006.

44. Ibid.

45. Atkinson, "Bomb Suspects Visited Terror Training Camps."

46. Richard Edwards and Duncan Gardham, "July 7 Bomber's Video Farewell to His Daughter," *The Telegraph*, April 11, 2008.

47. Ibid.

48. "Report of the Official Account of the Bombings in London on 7th July 2005."

49. Ibid.; Edwards, "July 7 Bomber's Video Farewell to His Daughter"; Crown Court at Kingston Upon Thames, *Regina v. Mohammed Shakil, Wahid Ali and Sadeer Saleem*, June 6, 2008.

50. Peter Walker, "Terror Trial Pair Flew to Pakistan After Alleged London Reconnaissance," *The Guardian*, April 14, 2008.

51. Crown Court at Kingston Upon Thames, *Regina v. Mohammed Shakil, Wahid Ali and Sadeer Saleem*, June 6, 2008.

52. Ibid.

53. Ibid.; David Brown, "7/7 'Conspirators' Visited London Landmarks," *The Times*, April 11, 2008.

54. Crown Court at Kingston Upon Thames, *Regina v. Mohammed Shakil, Wahid Ali and Sadeer Saleem*; Richard Edwards, "Trio Scouted Targets for July 7 Bombers," *The Daily Telegraph*, April 11, 2008.

55. "Report of the Official Account of the London Bombings in London on 7th July 2005."

56. Crown Court at Kingston Upon Thames, *Regina v. Mohammed Shakil, Wahid Ali and Sadeer Saleem*; Atkinson, "Bomb Suspects Visited Terror Training Camps."

57. "Revealed: Bomber Transcript," BBC News, May 1, 2007.

58. Ibid.

59. "7/7 Friends 'Made Tourism Calls,'" BBC News, April 14, 2008.

60. Roger Woods, David Leppard, and Michael Smith, "Tangled Web That Still Leaves Worrying Loose Ends," *Sunday Times*, July 13, 2005; Kurt Shillinger, "After London: Reassessing Africa's Role in the War on Terror," American Enterprise Institute: *National Security Outlook*, September 2005.

61. "Coroner's Inquest into the London Bombings of 7 July 2005," February 2, 2011, http://7julyinquests.independent.gov.uk/hearing_transcripts/02022011am.htm.

62. Gordon Rayner, "7/7 Inquest: Suicide Bombers Used Names of *A-Team* Characters in Text Messages," *The Telegraph*, October 19, 2010.

63. "Report of the Official Account of the London Bombings in London on 7th July 2005."

64. Ibid.

65. "Coroner's Inquest into the London Bombings of 7 July 2005."

66. "Report of the Official Account of the Bombings in London on 7th July 2005."

67. Central Criminal Court, Old Bailey, *Regina v. Omar Khyam et al.*

68. Ibid.

69. Ibid.; Doward and Wander, "The Network."

70. Greenberg, Cruickshank, and Hansen, "Inside the Terror Plot That Rivaled 9/11."

71. Sean O'Neill, Tim Reid, and Michael Evans, "7/7 Mastermind Is Seized in Iraq," *Daily Express*, May 2, 2007.

72. Stobart and Rotella, "Seven Britons Will Again Face Charges."

73. Woods, Leppard, and Smith, "Tangled Web That Still Leaves Worrying Loose Ends"; Shillinger, "After London."

74. Kirby, "The London Bombers as Self Starters."

75. Ibid.

76. "Report of the Official Account of the Bombings in London on 7th July 2005."

Chapter 8

1. Central Criminal Court, Old Bailey, *Regina v. Muktar Ibrahim, Manfo Asiedu, Hussein Osman, Yassin Omar, Ramzi Mohammed and Adel Yahya.*

2. Alison Pargeter, *The New Frontiers of Jihad: Radical Islam in Europe* (Philadelphia: University of Pennsylvania Press, 2008), p. 162.

3. O'Neill and McGrory, *The Suicide Factory*, pp. 221–22.

4. Central Criminal Court, Old Bailey, *Regina v. Muktar Ibrahim et al.*, January 15, 2007.

5. Ibid.

6. Central Criminal Court, Old Bailey, *Regina v. Mohammed Hamid et al.*, October 15, 2007; "Profile: Yassin Omar," BBC News, July 9, 2007, http://news.bbc.co.uk/go/pr/fr//2/hi/uk_news/6634917.stm.

7. "Profile: Yassin Omar," BBC News, July 9, 2007, http://news.bbc.co.uk/go/pr/fr//2/hi/uk_news/6634917.stm.

8. "Terror Training Camps: Key Quotes," BBC, February 26, 2008.

9. Central Criminal Court, Old Bailey, *Regina v. Muktar Ibrahim et al.*, February 7, 2007.

10. Sebastian Rotella and Jeffrey Fleishman, "London Bomb Suspects Stood Out as Radicals," *Los Angeles Times*, August 15, 2005; Souad Mekhennet and Dexter Filkins, "British Law Against Glorifying Terrorism Has Not Silenced Calls to Kill for Islam," *New York Times*, August 21, 2006; Central Criminal Court, Old Bailey, *Regina v. Mohammed Hamid et al.*, November 2, 2007.

11. Central Criminal Court, Old Bailey, *Regina v. Mohammed Hamid et al.*, October 15, 2007.

12. Pargeter, *The New Frontiers of Jihad*, p. 163; "Profile: Adel Yahya," BBC News, July 11, 2007, http://news.bbc.co.uk/2/hi/uk_news/6634965.stm; Central Criminal Court, Old Bailey, *Regina v. Muktar Ibrahim et al.*, May 18, 2007.

13. Central Criminal Court, Old Bailey, *Regina v. Muktar Ibrahim et al.*, February 7, 2007.

14. "Profiles: The Terror Gang Members," *The Independent*, February 26, 2008, http://www.independent.co.uk/news/uk/crime/profiles-the-terror-gang-members-787469.html.

15. Central Criminal Court, Old Bailey, *Regina v. Mohammed Hamid et al.*, October 15, 2007, November 21 and 22, 2007; Adrian Morgan, "Osama Bin London and British Terror Training Camps," Accuracy in Media, February 29, 2008, http://www.aim.org/aim-column/osama-bin-london-and-british-terror-tarining-camps.

16. "Profiles: The Terror Gang Members."

17. "The Attacks on London, Part 1: The Arrests," *The Independent*, July 31, 2005; Pargeter, *The New Frontiers of Jihad*, p. 159.

18. "Profile: Muktar Ibrahim," BBC News, July 11, 2007, http://news.bbc.co.uk/2/hi/email_news/6634901.stm.

19. Pargeter, *The New Frontiers of Jihad*, p. 159; "Profile: Yassin Omar," BBC News, July 11, 2007, http://news.bbc.co.uk/2/hi/uk_news/6634917.stm

20. Pargeter, *The New Frontiers of Jihad*, pp. 160–61; "Profile: Ramzi Mohammed," BBC News, July 11, 2007, http://news.bbc.co.uk/2/hi/uk_news/6634955.stm.

21. Pargeter, *The New Frontiers of Jihad*, pp. 160–61; "Profile: Ramzi Mohammed."

22. Pargeter, *The New Frontiers of Jihad*, p. 161; "Profile: Hussain Osman," BBC News, July 11, 2007, http://news.bbc.co.uk/2/hi/uk_news/6634923.stm.

23. Pargeter, *The New Frontiers of Jihad*, p. 161; "Profile: Monfo Kwaku Asiedu," BBC News, July 11, 2007, http://news.bbc.co.uk/2/hi/uk_news/6634923.stm.

24. Pargeter, *The New Frontiers of Jihad*, p. 162; "Profile: Adel Yahya," BBC News, July 11, 2007, http://news.bbc.co.uk/2/hi/uk_news/6634965.stm.

25. Central Criminal Court, Old Bailey, *Regina v. Mohammed Hamid et al.*, November 21, 2007, and January 16, 2008.

26. Ibid., May 31, 2007..

27. Central Criminal Court, Old Bailey, *Regina v. Abdul Sharif, Wahbi Mohammed, Ismail Abdulrahman, Sirah and Muhedin Ali*; "21 July Attack: Arrests and Charges," BBC News, January 27, 2006, http://news.bbc.co.uk/2/hi/uk_news/4732361.stm.

28. Central Criminal Court, Old Bailey, *Regina v. Abdul Sharif et al.*; "21 July Attack."

29. Central Criminal Court, Old Bailey, *Regina v. Abdul Sharif et al.*; "21 July Attack."

30. Central Criminal Court, Old Bailey, *Regina v. Abdul Sharif et al.*; "21 July Attack."

31. Central Criminal Court, Old Bailey, *Regina v. Abdul Sharif et al.*; "21 July Attack."

32. "21 July Attack."

33. Ibid.

34. Ibid.

35. Ibid.

36. Ibid.

37. Central Criminal Court, Old Bailey, *Regina v. Muktar Ibrahim et al.*, February 7–8, 2008.

38. Ibid.; Leppard, "Fixer for 21/7 Plot Free in London."

39. Leppard, "Fixer for 21/7 Plot Free in London."

40. Central Criminal Court, Old Bailey, *Regina v. Muktar Ibrahim et al.*, February 7–8, 2008.

41. Leppard, "Fixer for 21/7 Plot Free in London."

42. U.S. Treasury Department Press Release, "Treasury Designates Individual Supporting Al Qaida, Other Terrorist Organizations," December 19, 2006, http://www.ustreas.gov/press/releases/hp206.htm.

43. Leppard, "Fixer for 21/7 Plot Free in London."

44. Central Criminal Court, Old Bailey, *Regina v. Muktar Ibrahim et al.*, March 23, 2008; Leppard, "Fixer for 21/7 Plot Free in London."

45. Stobart and Rotella, "Seven Britons Will Again Face Charges."

46. Central Criminal Court, Old Bailey, *Regina v. Muktar Ibrahim et al.*, May 11, 2008.

47. Ibid., May 18, 2008, June 7, 2008.

48. "No Symbolism in 21/7 Stations," BBC, March 28, 2007.

49. Stobart and Rotella, "Seven Britons Will Again Face Charges"; Greenberg, Cruickshank, and Hansen, "Inside the Terror Plot That Rivaled 9/11."

50. "Links to Global Terror Network," *Manchester Evening News*, December 18, 2008.

51. Central Criminal Court, Old Bailey, *Regina v. Muktar Ibrahim et al.*, January 18, 2007; "Bomb Plotters Bought Chemicals," *The Daily Mail*, http://www.dailymail.co.uk/news/article-429802/Bomb-plotter-bought-chemicals.html/.

52. Central Criminal Court, Old Bailey, *Regina v. Muktar Ibrahim et al.*, April 17–18, 2007; "Bomb Plotters Bought Chemicals."

53. Ibid.

54. Central Criminal Court, Old Bailey, *Regina v. Muktar Ibrahim et al.*, April 25, 2007.

55. Duncan Gardham, "The Hydrogen Peroxide Bombs That Link 21/7 Terror Plot to 7/7 Suicide Bombers," *The Telegraph*, March 24, 2007.

Chapter 9

1. Julian Isherwood, "Guilty of Planning Terrorism," October 21, 2008, http://politiken.dk/newsinenglish/article585808.ece.

2. Michael Taarnby Jensen, "Jihad in Denmark," *Danish Institute for International Studies* (working paper, 2006), http://www.flw.ugent.be/cie/documenten/jihad-dk .pdf, pp. 8, 21, 56, 60; Pargeter, *The New Frontiers of Jihad*, p. 35.

3. Kasper Krogh, "The Network and Its Spiritual Leader," *Berlingske Tidende,* September 5, 2007.

4. Ibid.

5. Ibid.

6. Nicholas Kulish, "New Terrorism Case Confirms That Denmark Is a Target," *New York Times,* September 17, 2007.

7. Krogh, "The Network."

8. Ibid.

9. Kasper Krogh, Line Holm Nielsen, and Morten Frich, "Terrorism Arising from the Same Environment," *Berlingske Tidende,* September 6, 2007.

10. Krogh, "The Network."

11. "Moroccan-Born Dane Sentenced to Prison for Promoting Terrorism," Associated Press, April 11, 2007.

12. Krogh, "The Network"; "Danish Prosecutor Indicts Two on 'Terrorism' Charges," AFP, March 25, 2008.

13. Krogh, "The Network"; Morten Skjoldager and Claus Blok Thomsen, "Detainees Went to the Same Mosque," *Politiken,* September 5, 2007.

14. Skjoldager and Thomsen: "Detainees Went to the Same Mosque."

15. Krogh, "The Network."

16. Ibid.; Skjoldager and Thomsen, "Detainees Went to the Same Mosque."

17. Krogh, "The Network."

18. Ibid.

19. Soren Astrup and Morten Skjoldager, "Prosecutor: 22-Year-Old Knew Al-Qa'ida Leader," Politiken.dk, September 4, 2008.

20. Morten Skjoldager and Claus Blok Thomsen, "Photographs Incriminate Terror Suspect," Politiken.dk, January 18, 2008.

21. Rotella, "Dangerous, Endangered."

22. Elisabeth Arnsdorf Halsund, "This Small Amount Can Blow Up a Whole Hand," *Berlingske Tidende,* September 5, 2008.

23. Isherwood, "Guilty of Planning Terrorism."

24. Sorensen and Sparre "Glasvej."

25. Isherwood, "Guilty of Planning Terrorism."

26. Helle Harbo Sorensen and Sofie Sparre, "Glasvej: Convicted for Planning Terror," *TV2,* October 21, 2008.

27. Ibid.

28. Isherwood, "Guilty."

29. "Trial Opens in Denmark Against Pair Accused of Terrorism," AFP, August 11, 2008.

30. Halsund, "This Small Amount Can Blow Up a Whole Hand."

31. Isherwood "Guilty."

32. Ibid.

Chapter 10

1. The name of the investigation is provided by Judith Miller, "A Bullet Dodged," *New York Post*, September 26, 2009.

2. Karen Zraik and David Johnston, "Man in Queens Raids Denies Any Terrorist Link," *New York Times*, September 15, 2009; "2 Plead Not Guilty to More Charges in Alleged Plot to Bomb NYC Subway," February 25, 2010, http://edition.cnn.com/2010/CRIME/02/25/new.york.plot/. An audio recording of Afzali and Zazi's conversation clearly shows that Zazi had already purchased airline tickets to fly back to Denver before Afzali called to warn him that authorities were interested in Zazi. See A. G. Sulzberger, "Imam and Informant Tells Why He Lied," April 15, 2010, http://www.nytimes.com/2010/04/16/nyregion/16imam.html?ref=najibullahzazi.

3. Federal Bureau of Investigation, Document 103-1, Case 1:10-cr-00019-RJD, Date of Transcription, September 15, 2009, Date Filed, February 25, 2011. on www.pacer.gov, Database for public court filings.)

4. Ibid., Date of Transcription, January 13, 2010.

5. Samantha Gross, David Caruso, and Michael Rubinkam, "Radical Influences All Around NYC Terror Suspect," Associated Press, September 25, 2009.

6. David Von Drehle and Bobby Ghosh, "An Enemy Within: The Making of Najibullah Zazi," *Time*, October 1, 2009.

7. Federal Bureau of Investigation, Document 103-2, Case 1:10-cr-00019-RJD, Date of Transcription, September 18, 2009, Date Filed, February 25, 2011.

8. Federal Bureau of Investigation, Document 103-1, Case 1:10-cr-00019-RJD, Date of Transcription, September 15, 2009, Date Filed, February 25, 2011.

9. Federal Bureau of Investigation, Document 103-2, Case 1:10-cr-00019-RJD, Date of Transcription, September 18, 2009, Date Filed February 25, 2011.

10. Federal Bureau of Investigation, Document 103-1, Case 1:10-cr-00019-RJD, Date of Transcription, September 13, 2010, Date Filed, February 25, 2011.

11. Ibid.

12. Michael Wilson, "From Smiling Coffee Vendor to Terror Suspect," *New York Times*, September 25, 2009.

13. Ibid.; Von Drehle and Ghosh, "An Enemy Within."

14. William K. Rashbaum and David Johnston, "Officials Focus on New Suspects in Terror," *New York Times*, October 9, 2009.

15. Ibid.

16. Federal Bureau of Investigation, Document 103-1, Case 1:10-cr-00019-RJD, Date of Transcription, January 13, 2010, Date Filed, February 25, 2011; United States

District Court, Eastern District of New York, *USA v. Abdul Hameed Shehadeh*, October 2010.

17. Federal Bureau of Investigation, Document 103-1, Case 1:10-cr-00019-RJD, Date of Transcription, September 15, 2009, Date Filed, February 25, 2011; Federal Bureau of Investigation, Document 103-12, Case 1:10-cr-00019-RJD, Date of Transcription, September 22, 2010, Date Filed, February 25, 2011; "2 N.Y. Men Charged with Aiding al-Qaida," Associated Press, MSNBC.com, April 30, 2010, http://www.msnbc.msn.com/id/36873403/ns/us_news-security/.

18. Federal Bureau of Investigation, Document 103-1, Case 1:10-cr-00019-RJD, Date of Transcription, January 13, 2010, Date Filed, February 25, 2011.

19. Federal Bureau of Investigation, Document 103-2, Case 1:10-cr-00019-RJD, Date of Transcription, September 18, 2009, Date Filed, February 25, 2011.

20. Federal Bureau of Investigation, Document 103-1, Case 1:10-cr-00019-RJD, Date of Transcription, January 7, 2010, Date Filed, February 25, 2011.

21. Ibid.

22. Ibid.

23. Ibid.

24. Paula Newton, "Canadians Facing Terror Charges in 2009 N.Y. Subway Plot," March 15, 2011, http://articles.cnn.com/2011-03-15/world/canada.new.york.plot_1_zarein-ahmedzay-najibullah-zazi-terrorist-group?_s=PM:WORLD.

25. Department of Justice Press Release, "Charges Unsealed Against Five Alleged Members of Al Qaeda Plot to Attack the United States and United Kingdom," July 7, 2010.

26. Federal Bureau of Investigation, Document 103-1, Case 1:10-cr-00019-RJD, Date of Transcription, January 7, 2010, Date Filed, February 25, 2011.

27. Ibid.

28. *USA v. Adis Medujanin et al.*; Department of Justice Press Release, "Najibullah Zazi Pleads Guilty."

29. *USA v. Adis Medujanin et al.*; Department of Justice Press Release, "Zarein Ahmedzay Pleads Guilty."

30. *USA v. Adis Medujanin et al.*; "Memorandum of Law in Opposition to the Defendant's Motion to Suppress His Post-Arrest Statements," Federal Bureau of Investigation, Document 103, Case 1:10-cr-00019-RJD, Date Filed, February 25, 2011.

31. *USA v. Adis Medujanin et al.*; Department of Justice Press Release, "Zarein Ahmedzay Pleads Guilty."

32. Department of Justice Press Release, "Najibullah Zazi Pleads Guilty."

33. *USA v. Adis Medujanin et al.*; "Memorandum of Law in Opposition to the Defendant's Motion to Suppress His Post-Arrest Statements," Federal Bureau of Investigation, Document 103, Case 1:10-cr-00019-RJD, Date Filed, February 25, 2011.

34. Department of Justice Press Release, "Najibullah Zazi Pleads Guilty"; Department of Justice Press Release, "Charges Unsealed Against Five Alleged Members of Al Qaeda Plot."

35. Department of Justice Press Release, "Charges Unsealed Against Five Alleged Members of Al Qaeda Plot."

36. Department of Justice Press Release, "Najibullah Zazi Pleads Guilty."

37. *USA v. Adis Medujanin et al.*; Department of Justice Press Release, "Zarein Ahmedzay Pleads Guilty."

38. *USA v. Adis Medujanin et al.*; Department of Justice Press Release, "Zarein Ahmedzay Pleads Guilty."

39. Department of Justice Press Release, "Charges Unsealed Against Five Alleged Members of Al Qaeda Plot"; *USA v. Najibullah Zazi*, Eastern District of New York, 2009.

Chapter 11

1. *USA, Appellee, v. Mohammed A. Salameh, Nidal Ayyad, Mahmoud Abouhalima, also known as Mahmoud Abu Halima, Ahmad Mohammed Ajaj, also known as Khurram Khan, Defendants-Appellants, Ramzi Ahmed Yo, Bilal Alkaisai, also known as Bilal Elqisi, Abdul Rahman Yasin, also known as Aboud, Defendants*, Docket Nos. 94-1312, 94-1313, 94-1314, 94-1315, U.S. Court of Appeals for the Second Circuit.

2. Craig Pyes, Judith Miller, and Stephen Engelberg, "One Man and a Global Web of Violence," *New York Times*, January 14, 2001; Mary B.W. Tabor, "Slaying in Brooklyn Linked to Militants," *New York Times*, April 11, 1993.

3. Benjamin Weiser, Susan Sachs, and David Kocieniewski, "U.S. Sees Brooklyn Link to World Terror Network," *New York Times*, October 22, 1998.

4. Ibid.

5. *The 9/11 Commission Report*, p. 72.

6. *USA, Appellee, v. Omar Ahmad Ali Abdel Rahman, Ibrahim A. El-Gabrowny, El Sayyid Nosair, Tarig Elhassan, Hampton-El, Amir Abdelgani, Fadil Abdelgani, Victor Alvarez, Mohammed Sale and Fares Khallafalla, Defendants-Appellants*, Docket Nos. 96-1044L, 96-1045, 96-1060, 96-1061, 96-1062, 96-1063, 96-1064, 96-1065, 96-1079, 96-1080, U.S. Court of Appeals for the Second Circuit.

7. Richard Behar, "The Secret Life of Mahmud the Red," *Time*, October 4, 1993; Rex Hudson, "The Sociology of Terrorism: Who Becomes a Terrorist and Why?" Federal Research Division, Library of Congress, September 1999.

8. John Miller, Michael Stone, and Chris Mitchell, *The Cell* (New York: Hyperion, 2002), p. 53.

9. Behar, "The Secret Life of Mahmud the Red."

10. Miller, Stone, and Mitchell, *The Cell*, pp. 50, 77; Peter Lance, *1000 Years for Revenge* (New York: Regan Books, 2003), p. 30

11. Miller, Stone, and Mitchell, *The Cell*, pp. 43, 50, 55.

12. *USA, Appellee, v. Omar Ahmad Ali Abdel Rahman et al.*

13. Behar, "The Secret Life of Mahmud the Red."

14. Miller, Stone, and Mitchell, *The Cell*, p. 85.

15. *USA, Appellee, v. Mohammed A. Salameh et al.*

16. Hudson, "The Sociology of Terrorism."

17. Ibid.

18. *USA, Appellee, v. Omar Ahmad Ali Abdel Rahman et al.*

19. Miller, Stone, and Mitchell, *The Cell*, p. 78.

20. Ibid.; Lance, *1000 Years for Revenge*, pp. 23–24.

21. *USA, Appellee, v. Mohammed A. Salameh et al.*; *The 9/11 Commission Report*, p. 73; Miller, Stone, and Mitchell, *The Cell*, pp. 43, 50, 55, 77.

22. Ibid., p. 82.

23. Hudson, "The Sociology of Terrorism."

24. Behar, "The Secret Life of Mahmud the Red."

25. Ibid.

26. Ibid.

27. Ibid.

28. "Nidal Ayyad," Global Jihad, http://www.globaljihad.net/view_page.asp?id=97.

29. Ibid.

30. "Bloomington Native Linked to '93 Bombing," *Indianapolis Star*, October 11, 2001; Miller, Stone, and Mitchell, *The Cell*, p. 85.

31. *United States v. Salameh*, Docket Nos. 98-1041, 98-1197, 98-1355, 99-1544, 99-1554, U.S. Court of Appeals for the Second Circuit April 4, 2005; "Last World Trade Center Bombing Conspirator Sentenced—Eyad Ismoil Gets 240 Years, $10 Million Fine," CNN, April 3, 1998; Jayne Noble Suhle and Ed Timms, "Cases Highlight Flaws in Federal Visa System," *Dallas Morning News*, November 8, 1998.

32. *USA, Appellee, v. Mohammed A. Salameh et al.*

33. Lance, *1000 Years for Revenge*, p. 30; Miller, Stone, and Mitchell, *The Cell*, pp. 47–48.

34. Miller, Stone, and Mitchell, *The Cell*, pp. 48–49.

35. Ibid., pp. 66, 83, 86, 104; Joseph Fried, "Sheikh Sentenced to Life in Prison in Bombing Plot," *New York Times*, January 19, 1996.

36. Ibid.

37. Miller, Stone, and Mitchell, *The Cell*, pp. 140–44.

38. Ibid.

39. Ibid., pp. 38, 39 76.

40. Miller, Stone, and Mitchell, *The Cell*, p. 54.

41. Behar, "The Secret Life of Mahmud the Red."

42. *USA, Appellee, v. Mohammed A. Salameh et al.*; *The 9/11 Commission Report*, p. 73.

43. Miller, Stone, and Mitchell, *The Cell*, pp. 43, 50, 55, 77.

44. *The 9/11 Commission Report*, p. 147.

45. Pyes, Miller, and Engelberg, "One Man and a Global Web of Violence."

46. *The 9/11 Commission Report*, p. 147.

47. *USA, Appellee, v. Mohammed A. Salameh et al.*; Miller, Stone, and Mitchell, *The Cell*, pp. 66, 83, 86, 104.

48. *USA v. Mohammad A. Salameh, Nidal Ayyad, Mahmud Abouhalima, Ahmad Mohammad Ajaj, Ramzi Yousef and Abdul Rahman Yasin*, United States District Court, Southern District of New York, October 4, 1993; *USA, Appellee, v. Mohammed A. Salameh et al.*

49. *The 9/11 Commission Report*, p. 164.

50. Pyes, Miller, and Engelberg, "One Man and a Global Web of Violence."

51. Miller, Stone, and Mitchell, *The Cell*, p. 79.

52. *The 9/11 Commission Report*, p. 147.

53. *USA, Appellee, v. Mohammed A. Salameh et al.*

54. Ibid.; *USA, Appellee, v. Omar Ahmad Ali Abdel Rahman.*

55. Miller, Stone, and Mitchell, *The Cell*, p. 93.

56. *USA, Appellee, v. Mohammed A. Salameh et al.*

57. Ibid.

58. Miller, Stone, and Mitchell, *The Cell*, pp. 85, 91.

59. *USA, Appellee, v. Mohammed A. Salameh et al.*; Miller, Stone, and Mitchell, *The Cell*, p. 92.

60. *USA, Appellee, v. Mohammed A. Salameh et al.*; Miller, Stone, and Mitchell, *The Cell*, p. 92.

61. Miller, Stone, and Mitchell, *The Cell*, p. 92.

62. *The 9/11 Commission Report*, p. 73.

63. *United States v. Salameh*, 152F.3d at 107–8.

64. *The 9/11 Commission Report*, p. 164.

65. Ibid.

66. Pyes, Miller, and Engelberg, "One Man and a Global Web of Violence."

67. Miller, Stone, and Mitchell, *The Cell*, p. 79.

Chapter 12

1. Indictment of Imad Eddin Barakat Yarkas, *El Mundo*, October 15, 2005.

2. Lorenzo Vidino, *Al Qaeda in Europe* (New York: Prometheus Books, 2006), p. 308.

3. Main Court de Instrucción no. 6, *Indictment N° 20/2004*, Proceedings, April

10, 2006, pp. 1341–55 (translation of court-related documents provided to the author); Scott Atran, *Talking to the Enemy* (New York: HarperCollins Publishers, 2010), p. 179.

4. Atran, *Talking to the Enemy*, pp. 181–82.

5. Casimiro Garcia-Abadillo, *11–M* (La Venganza, Madrid: La Esfera de los Libros, 2005), pp. 115–19; Fernando Reinares, "Jihadist Radicalization and the 2004 Madrid Bombing Network," *CTC Sentinel* 2, no. 11 (November 2009): 16–19.

6. Testimony of a protected witness during the Madrid bombing trials at Spain's National Court, *Sumario 20/2004*, vol. 114, p. 39514, and vol. 163, pp. 61,923–24; Main Court de Instrucción no. 6, *Indictment N° 20/2004*, Proceedings, April 10, 2006, pp. 1341–55.

7. Lawrence Wright, "The Terror Web: Were The Madrid Bombings Part of a New, Far-Reaching Jihad Being Plotted on the Internet?" *The New Yorker*, August 2, 2004; Vidino, *Al Qaeda in Europe*, p. 308.

8. Main Court de Instrucción no. 6, *Indictment N° 20/2004*, Proceedings, April 10, 2006, p. 1226.

9. Tim Golden, Desmond Butler, and Don Van Natta Jr., "Suspect in Madrid Was Under Scrutiny in 3 Countries," *New York Times*, March 17, 2004; Keith Johnson, John Carreyrou, David Crawford, and Karby Legett, "Islamist's Odyssey: Morocco to Madrid, a Bomb Suspect Grew Radicalized," *Wall Street Journal*, March 19, 2004.

10. Main Court de Instrucción no. 6, *Indictment N° 20/2004*, Proceedings, April 10, 2006, pp. 1341–55.

11. Jose Maria Irujo, *El Agujero: Espana Invadida por la Yihad* (Madrid: Aguilar, 2005), pp. 84–86.

12. Ibid.

13. Main Court de Instrucción no. 6, *Indictment N° 20/2004*, Proceedings, April 10, 2006, pp. 1212–21.

14. Sebastian Rotella, "Jihad's Unlikely Alliance," *Los Angeles Times*, May 23, 2005.

15. "La Célula del 11–M Recopiló Información, Para la Matanza, en Internet Entre Febrero y Julio de 2003," *Belt Iberica*, March 8, 2005.

16. Main Court de Instrucción no. 6, *Indictment N° 20/2004*, Proceedings, April 10, 2006, pp. 1212–21.

17. Ibid., pp. 1341–55.

18. Manuel Marlasca and Luis Rendueles, *Una Historia del 11–M, Que No Va a Gustar a Nadie* (Madrid: Temasde Hoy, 2007); Wright, "The Terror Web"; Vidino, *Al Qaeda in Europe*, p. 308.

19. Main Court de Instrucción no. 6, *Indictment N° 20/2004*, Proceedings, April 10, 2006, pp. 1356–68.

20. Tribunal of Milan, Indictment of Rabei Osman el Sayed Ahmed and others, June 5, 2004.

21. Main Court de Instrucción no. 6, *Indictment N° 20/2004*, Proceedings, April 10, 2006, pp. 1341–55.

22. Ibid., pp. 1212–21.

23. Javier Jordán, "The Madrid Attacks: Results of Investigations Two Years Later," *Terrorism Monitor* 4, no. 5 (March 9, 2006).

24. Irujo, *El Agujero,* pp. 84–86; Tribunal of Milan, Indictment of Rabei Osman el Sayed Ahmed and others, June 5, 2004; Craig Whitlock, "A Radical Who Remained Just Out of Reach; Suspect in the Madrid Attacks Moved Freely in Europe," *Washington Post,* March 14, 2004.

25. "Piecing Together Madrid Bombers' Past," BBC, April 14, 2006.

26. Wright, "The Terror Web."

27. Reinares, "Jihadist Radicalization and the 2004 Madrid Bombing Network."

28. "Piecing Together Madrid Bombers' Past."

29. Atran, *Talking to the Enemy,* pp. 185–86.

30. Ibid., p. 187; James Graff, "Morocco: The New Face of Terror?" *Time,* March 21, 2005.

31. "Piecing Together Madrid Bombers' Past"; Garcia-Abadillo, *11-M,* pp. 115–19.

32. Irujo, *El Agujero,* pp. 77–79; Golden, Butler, and Van Natta, "Suspect in Madrid Was Under Scrutiny in 3 Countries"; Johnson et al., "Islamist's Odyssey."

33. Peter Ford, "Terrorism Web Emerges from Madrid Bombing," *Christian Science Monitor,* March 22, 2004.

34. Declassified Report from the National Intelligence Council—Information note: SUBJECT: Terrorist Attacks in Madrid. Allekema Lamari NIE X-1397192B, in Main Court de Instrucción no. 6, *Indictment Nº 20/2004,* Proceedings, April 10, 2006, pp. 1341–55; Reinares, "Jihadist Radicalization and the 2004 Madrid Bombing Network."

35. Global Jihad, http://www.globaljihad.net/view_page.asp?id=120.

36. Garcia-Abadillo, *11-M,* pp. 115–19; Casmiro Garcia-Abadillo, "34 de los 40 que el juez implica en el 11-M estaban bajo control policial," *El Mundo,* April 24, 2006; Global Jihad, http://www.globaljihad.net/view_page.asp?id=120.

37. Owen Bowcott, "In Morocco's Gateway to Europe, Disbelief Greets Arrests over Madrid Bombings," *The Guardian,* March 19, 2004.

38. Indictment of Imad Eddin Barakat Yarkas, *El Mundo,* October 15, 2005; Global Jihad, http://www.globaljihad.net/view_page.asp?id=91.

39. James Sturcke, "Madrid Bombings: The Defendants," *The Guardian,* October 31, 2007.

40. Jordán, "The Madrid Attacks."

41. "Principales procesados por los atentados del 11-M Major processed by the 11-M," *El Mundo,* April 11, 2006.

42. Renwick McLean, "Madrid Suspects Tied to E-mail Ruse," *New York Times,* April 27, 2006; Reinares, "Jihadist Radicalization and the 2004 Madrid Bombing Network."

43. "Principales procesados por los atentados del 11-M Major processed by the 11-M."

44. Global Jihad, http://www.globaljihad.net/view_page.asp?id=87.

45. Reinares, "Jihadist Radicalization and the 2004 Madrid Bombing Network."

46. Ibid.

47. Vidino, *Al Qaeda in Europe*, p. 324.

48. Atran, *Talking to the Enemy*, pp. 185–86.

49. Ibid.

50. Atran, *Talking to the Enemy*, 189–90.

51. "Piecing Together Madrid Bombers' Past."

52. Reinares, "Jihadist Radicalization and the 2004 Madrid Bombing Network"; Atran, *Talking to the Enemy*, pp. 185–86.

53. Reinares, "Jihadist Radicalization and the 2004 Madrid Bombing Network"; James Sturcke, "Madrid Bombings: The Defendants," *The Guardian*, October 31, 2007.

54. Sturcke, "Madrid Bombings."

55. Reinares, "Jihadist Radicalization and the 2004 Madrid Bombing Network"; "Principales procesados por los atentados del 11–M Major processed by the 11–M"; Atran, *Talking to the Enemy*, 191.

56. Sturcke, "Madrid Bombings."

57. Ibid.

58. Ibid.

59. Ibid.

60. Atran, *Talking to the Enemy*, pp. 185–86.

61. Declassified Report from the National Intelligence Council in the Main Court de Instrucción no. 6, *Indictment N° 20/2004*, Proceedings, April 10, 2006, pp. 1212–21; "Pakistan Finds Passport of a Spaniard Married to One of the March 11 Plot in Spain," *El Mundo*, October 30, 2009.

62. "'El Tunecino' Empezo A Pensar En La Guerra Santa Ante De Los Atentados Del 11–S," EFE, January 24, 2005.

63. Sebastian Rotella, "Al Qaeda Fugitive Sought in Bombings," *Los Angeles Times*, April 14, 2004.

64. "Report: FBI Finds Link Between 9/11, Madrid Bombers," Reuters, November 11, 2004.

65. Fernando Reinares, "The Madrid Bombings and Global Jihadism," *Survival* 52, no. 2 (April–May 2010): 83–104.

66. "FFI Explains al-Qaida Document," Norwegian Defence Research Establishment, March 19, 2004.

67. Ibid.

68. Ibid.

69. Main Court de Instrucción no. 6, *Indictment N° 20/2004*, Proceedings, April 10, 2006; Atran, *Talking to the Enemy*, p. 192.

70. Atran, *Talking to the Enemy*, p. 195.

71. "Investigation Report on the Origin of the Explosives Used in the Terrorist

Attacks of March 11," July 14, 2005, completed by the U.C.E. 2, Police Headquarters of the Information Service of the Civil Guard.

72. Ibid.

73. Garcia-Abadillo, "34 de los 40 que el juez implica en el 11–M estaban bajo control policial."

74. Main Court de Instrucción no. 6, *Indictment* N° *20/2004*, Proceedings, April 10, 2006.

75. Ibid.

76. Ibid., pp. 1212–21.

77. Ibid.

78. McLean, "Madrid Suspects Tied to E-mail Ruse."

79. Main Court de Instrucción no. 6, *Indictment* N° *20/2004*, Proceedings, April 10, 2006.

80. Ibid.

81. Tribunal of Milan, Indictment of Rabei Osman el Sayed Ahmed and others, June 5, 2004.

82. Ibid.

83. Main Court de Instrucción no. 6, *Indictment* N° *20/2004*, Proceedings, April 10, 2006.

84. Elizabeth Nash, "Madrid Bombers 'Were Inspired By Bin Laden Address'," *The Independent*, November 7, 2006; "El auto de procesamiento por el 11–M," *El Mundo.*

85. "Quien os Protegera des Nosostros?" *El Mundo*, March 12, 2004.

86. Abdel Bari Atwan, *The Secret History of Al-Qa'ida* (London: Abacus, 2007), p. 116; Reinares, "The Madrid Bombings and Global Jihadism."

87. Wright, "The Terror Web."

88. Ibid.

89. "El Tunecino' Empezo A Pensar En La Guerra Santa Ante De Los Atentados Del 11–S."

90. "Report: FBI Finds Link Between 9/11, Madrid Bombers."

91. Reinares, "The Madrid Bombings and Global Jihadism."

92. Manuel R. Torres, "Spain as an Object of Jihadist Propaganda," *Studies in Conflict and Terrorism* 32, no. 11 (November 2009): 940–41. A translation of the audio recording is available at http://www.memri.org/ bin/articles.cgi?Area=sd&ID=SP69504 and http://news.bbc.co.uk/2/hi/middle_east/4443364.stm.

93. Atran, *Talking to the Enemy*, p. 180.

94. Wright, "The Terror Web."

95. Declassified Report from the National Intelligence Council in the Main Court de Instrucción no. 6, *Indictment* N° *20/2004*, Proceedings, April 10, 2006, pp. 1341–55.

96. Tim Golden, Desmond Butler, and Don Van Natta Jr., "Suspect in Madrid Carnage Not an Unknown," *New York Times*, March 22, 2004.

97. Elaine Sciolino, "Spain Continues to Uncover Terrorist Plots, Officials Say," *New York Times*, March 13, 2005.

Chapter 13

1. Author's conversation with Dutch National Police, May 2005.

2. *Saudi Influences in the Netherlands—Links Between the Salafist Mission, Radicalisation Processes and Islamic Terrorism*, AIVD report, January 6, 2005.

3. Andrew Higgins, "A Brutal Killing Opens Dutch Eyes to Threat of Terror," *Wall Street Journal*, November 22, 2004; *Report by the Dutch Ministry of Justice on the van Gogh Assassination*, November 10, 2004.

4. Glenn Frankel, "From Civic Activist to Alleged Murderer," *Washington Post*, November 28, 2004.

5. *Report by the Dutch Ministry of Justice on the van Gogh Assassination*.

6. Dr. Albert Benschop, "Chronicle of a Political Murder Foretold—Jihad in the Netherlands," University of Amsterdam, http://www.sociosite.org/jihad_nl_en.php#jason_w.

7. Ibid.

8. Emerson Vermaat, "Wrong Decision by Dutch Appeals Court in Hofstad Group Terror Case," PipeLineNews.Org., January 31, 2008, http://www.investigative-project.org/595/wrong-decision-by-dutch-appeals-court-in-hofstad-group.

9. Emerson Vermaat, "The Hofstadgroup Terror Trial," *FrontPageMagazine.com*, January 10, 2006.

10. "Hollandse Martine actief voor jihad," Volkskrant, July 6, 2005, http://www.volkskrant.nl/binnenland/article140887.ece/Hollandse_Martine_actief_voor_jihad.

11. Frankel, "From Civic Activist to Alleged Murderer"; Toby Sterling, "Changes Sway Holland Slaying Suspect," Associated Press, November 8, 2004.

12. Petter Nesser, "The Slaying of the Dutch Filmmaker," FFI, Norwegian Defense Research Establishment, February 2, 2005.

13. Benschop, "Chronicle of a Political Murder Foretold."

14. Nesser, "The Slaying of the Dutch Filmmaker."

15. "Chatting with Terrorists," January 28, 2005, http://dutchreport.blogspot.com/2005/01/chatting-with-terrorists.html.

16. Jaco Alberts and Stephen Derix, "Hoe georganiseerd wren Samri A. en zign vrienden?" *NRC Handelsblad*, April 9, 2005.

17. Craig S. Smith, "Dutch Look for Qaeda Link After Killing of Filmmaker," *New York Times*, November 6, 2004; Lorenzo Vidino, "The Hofstad Group: The New Face of Terrorist Networks in Europe," *Studies in Conflict and Terrorism* 30, no. 7 (July 2007): 579–92; *Report by the Dutch Ministry of Justice on the van Gogh Assassination*; Benschop, "Chronicle of a Political Murder Foretold."

18. Vermaat, "The Hofstadgroup Terror Trial"; Smith, "Dutch Look for Qaeda

Link After Killing of Filmmaker"; Vidino, *Al Qaeda in Europe*, p. 308; Vidino, "The Hofstad Group."

19. Higgins, "A Brutal Killing Opens Dutch Eyes to Threat of Terror"; Nesser, "The Slaying of the Dutch Filmmaker"; Ferry Biederman, "Syrian Mystery Man Sought in Van Gogh Case," Radio Holland, December 3, 2004.

20. Vidino, "The Hofstad Group."

21. Higgins, "A Brutal Killing Opens Dutch Eyes to Threat of Terror."

22. Frankel, "From Civic Activist to Alleged Murderer"; Higgins, "A Brutal Killing Opens Dutch Eyes to Threat of Terror."

23. Frankel, "From Civic Activist to Alleged Murderer"; Higgins, "A Brutal Killing Opens Dutch Eyes to Threat of Terror"; Benschop, "Chronicle of a Political Murder Foretold."

24. Emerson Vermaat, "Samir Azzouz—A Terrorist in the Making or a Real Terrorist?" November 23, 2005, http://www.militantislammonitor.org/article/id/1307.

25. Higgins, "A Brutal Killing Opens Dutch Eyes to Threat of Terror"; Smith, "Dutch Look for Qaeda Link After Killing of Filmmaker."

26. Alberts and Derix, "Hoe georganiseerd wren Samri A. en zign vrienden?"; Janny Groen and Annieke Kranenberg, *Women Warriors for Allah* (Philadelphia: University of Pennsylvania Press, 2010), appendix.

27. Alberts and Derix, "Hoe georganiseerd wren Samri A. en zign vrienden?"; Groen and Kranenberg, *Women Warriors for Allah*; Vidino, *Al Qaeda in Europe*, p. 308.

28. Emerson Vermaat, "Nouredine el Fatmi—A Terrorist and a Seducer of Teenage Girls," January 15, 2006, http://www.militantislammonitor.org/article/id/1547; Benschop, "Chronicle of a Political Murder Foretold."

29. Vermaat, "The Hofstadgroup Terror Trial."

30. Ibid.

31. Groen and Kranenberg, *Women Warriors for Allah*, appendix; Global Jihad, http://www.globaljihad.net/view_page.asp?id=964.

32. Groen and Kranenberg, *Women Warriors for Allah*, appendix; Global Jihad, http://www.globaljihad.net/view_page.asp?id=964.

33. "Jihad Is Forever: Wife of Terrorist Samir Azzouz Tells How They Fell in Love at Hamas Demo and Planned 'Honeymoon' in Chechnya," October 27, 2006, http://www.uitkijk.net/islam.php?subaction=showfull&id=1161151500&archive=&start_from=&ucat=3.

34. "Moroccan-Dutch Youth Riot in Amsterdam Following Fatal Incident," October 16, 2007, http://www.digitaljournal.com/article/240329/Moroccan_Dutch _youth_riot_in_Amsterdam_following_fatal_incident.

35. Ibid.

36. Benschop, "Chronicle of a Political Murder Foretold."

37. Ibid.

38. Vermaat, "The Hofstadgroup Terror Trial."

39. Benschop, "Chronicle of a Political Murder Foretold."

40. Ibid.

41. Ibid.; Groen and Kranenberg, *Women Warriors for Allah*, appendix.

42. Hans de Vreij, "The 'Hofstad' Trial—Developments," January 27, 2006, http://static.rnw.nl/migratie/www.radionetherlands.nl/currentaffairs/hof051205–redirected.

43. Benschop, "Chronicle of a Political Murder Foretold"; Groen and Kranenberg, *Women Warriors for Allah*, appendix.

44. Benschop, "Chronicle of a Political Murder Foretold"; Groen and Kranenberg, *Women Warriors for Allah*, appendix.

45. Benschop, "Chronicle of a Political Murder Foretold"; Groen and Kranenberg, *Women Warriors for Allah*, appendix

46. Benschop, "Chronicle of a Political Murder Foretold"; Groen and Kranenberg, *Women Warriors for Allah*, appendix.

47. Emerson Vermaat, "Emerson Vermaat: Trial of Terror—Hofstadgroup Trial to Determine if Van Gogh Killer Acted Alone," *FrontPage Magazine*, January 20, 2006; Groen and Kranenberg, *Women Warriors for Allah*, appendix.

48. "Three Years in Jail for Preparing Terrorist Attacks on MPs," NIS News Bulletin, http://www.nisnews.nl/public/260308_1.htm.

49. Vermaat, "Wrong Decision by Dutch Appeals Court in Hofstad Group Terror Case."

50. "Hollandse Martine actief voor jihad."

51. Benschop, "Chronicle of a Political Murder Foretold."

52. Ibid.

53. Vermaat, "The Hofstadgroup Terror Trial."

54. Author's conversation with Dutch police, May 2005; Vermaat, "Wrong Decision by Dutch Appeals Court in Hofstad Group Terror Case."

55. Vermaat, "Wrong Decision by Dutch Appeals Court in Hofstad Group Terror Case."

56. "Hofstadkopstukken wilden in voetsporen Mohammed B. Treden," Operation Ministerie, The Hague, November 7, 2005; Vidino, "The Hofstad Group."

57. Ibid.

58. Adrian Morgan, "Dutch Islamist Gets Eight Years Jail Sentence," December 4, 2006, http://www.dailyestimate.com/article.asp?idCategory=35&idarticle=6902.

59. Nesser, "The Slaying of the Dutch Filmmaker."

60. Elaine Sciolino, "Dutch Struggle to Prevent Terror and Protect Rights," *New York Times*, November 7, 2005; Vidino, "The Hofstad Group."

61. Vermaat, "The Hofstadgroup Terror Trial"; Benschop, "Chronicle of a Political Murder Foretold."

62. De Vreij, "The 'Hofstad' Trial—Developments."

63. Open letter to Hirshi Ali in Nesser, "The Slaying of the Dutch Filmmaker."

Chapter 14

1. Trevor Stanley, "Australian Anti-Terror Raids: A Serious Plot Thwarted," *The Jamestown Foundation* 3, no. 23 (December 2, 2005).

2. *Regina v. Abdul Nacer Benbrika, Aimen Joud, Shane Kent, Fadl Sayadi, Hany Taha, Abdullah Merhi, Bassam Raad, Ahmed Raad, Shoue Hammoud, Ezzit Raad, Majed Raad, and Amer Haddara,* February 3, 2009, Supreme Court of Victoria, http://www.austlii.edu.au/au/cases/vic/VICSC/2009/21.html.

3. Sally Neighbour, "Militant Networks," *The Australian*, November 18, 2006.

4. Stanley, "Australian Anti-Terror Raids."

5. Neighbour, "Militant Networks."

6. "Lies, Bombs, and Jihad," *The Australian*, September 16, 2008, http://www.theaustralian.news.com.au/story/0,25197,24350617–5001561,00.html.

7. Neighbour, "Militant Networks."

8. Ibid.

9. Ibid.

10. *Regina v. Benbrika et al.*, February 3, 2009.

11. Stanley, "Australian Anti-Terror Raids."

12. *Regina v. Benbrika et al.*, February 13, 2008; Alison Caldwell, "Terrorism Suspects Part of Al Qaeda Inspired Group, Court Told," The World Today, July 24, 2006, http://www.abc.net.au/worldtoday/content/2006/s1694910.htm.

13. *Regina v. Benbrika et al.*, February 13, 2008; Nick McKenzie, "Suspect Claims ASIO Surveillance Unjust," *The 7:30 Report*, August 4, 2005.

14. Martin Chulov, "Accused 'Trained in Pakistani Camp,'" *The Australian*, November 9, 2005; Peter Faris, "Mohammad Omran," *The Age*, May 5, 2004, Radical Islam in Australia, http://www.farisqc.observationdeck.org/?p=376; Mark Coultan and Ellen Connolly, "The Baggage of Bilal Khazal," *Sydney Morning Herald*, June 4, 2004.

15. Neighbour, "Militant Networks."

16. Michael Pelly, "Terrorist Met Australian at Boot Camp," *The Australian*, January 13, 2009; Stanley, "Australian Anti-Terror Raids."

17. *Regina v. Mohamed Ali Elomar et al.*, February 15, 2010, New South Wales Supreme Court.

18. Ian Munro with Barney Zwartz, "Arrested: A Man Apart Who Fought to Stay in Australia," *Sydney Morning Herald*, November 9, 2005.

19. *Regina v. Benbrika et al.*, February 13, 2008; Stanley, "Australian Anti-Terror Raids."

20. *Regina v. Benbrika et al.*, February 13, 2008; Stanley, "Australian Anti-Terror Raids"; Neighbour, "Militant Networks."

21. "The Melbourne Suspects," *Sydney Morning Herald*, November 12, 2005.

22. *Regina v. Benbrika et al.*, February 13, 2008; "Abdul Nàcer Benbrika," http://www.nationmaster.com/encyclopedia/Abdul-Nacer-Benbrika

23. *Regina v. Benbrika et al.*, February 13, 2008; "Abdul Nacer Benbrika."

24. "Abdul Nacer Benbrika."

25. *Regina v. Benbrika et al.*, February 13; Munro with Zwartz, "Arrested: A Man Apart Who Fought to Stay in Australia."

26. *Regina v. Mohamed Ali Elomar et al.*, February 15, 2010,.

27. Ibid.; Nick Leys, "Butcher Is Not a Stranger to ASIO," *The Australian*, November 9, 2005.

28. *Regina v. Mohamed Ali Elomar and Others*, February 15, 2010; Pelly, "Terrorist Met Australian at Boot Camp"; http://www.dailytelegraph.news.com.au /stor...5001022,00.html.

29. *Regina v. Mohamed Ali Elomar et al.*, February 15, 2010; Stanley, "Australian Anti-Terror Raids"; "Terror Suspect Admits Training with Brigitte," *The Age*, May 4, 2005.

30. *Regina v. Mohamed Ali Elomar et al.*, February 15, 2010.

31. Stanley, "Australian Anti-Terror Raids."

32. Coultan and Connolly, "The Baggage of Bilal Khazal."

33. Ibid.

34. Ibid.

35. Ibid.

36. Ibid.

37. "The Melbourne Suspects"; *Regina v. Benbrika et al.*, February 3, 2009.

38. "The Melbourne Suspects"; *Regina v. Benbrika et al.*, February 3, 2009.

39. "The Melbourne Suspects"; *Regina v. Benbrika et al.*, February 3, 2009.

40. "The Melbourne Suspects"; *Regina v. Benbrika et al.*, February 3, 2009.

41. "The Melbourne Suspects"; *Regina v. Benbrika et al.*, February 3, 2009.

42. Gary Hughes, "Terror Lurking Within," *The Australian*, February 5, 2009.

43. "The Melbourne Suspects."

44. Ibid.

45. Natasha Robinson, "Rocker Rolled to Jihad," *TheWest.com.au*, November 10, 2005; "Terror Accused to Stand Trial on 'Jihad Promise,'" September 22, 2006, http:// old.cageprisoners.com/articles.php?id=16610.

46. Gary Hughes, "Lies, Bombs and Jihad," *The Australian*, September 16, 2008.

47. Ibid.

48. Ibid.

49. Martin Chulov, "Australian Terror in Our Midst, "*The Australian*, March 23, 2004; Neighbour, "Militant Networks."

50. Chulov, "Accused 'Trained in Pakistani Camp'"; "Le process 'Willie Brigitte,'" Tribunal Correctional de Paris, verdict of March 13, 2007.

51. Ibid.; Pelly, "Terrorist Met Australian at Boot Camp."

52. "Terror Suspect Admits Training with Brigitte."

53. Ibid.; "Le process 'Willie Brigitte,'" Tribunal Correctional de Paris, verdict of March 13, 2007.

54. Ibid.

55. "Terror Suspect Admits Training with Brigitte."

56. "Terror Accused to Stand Trial on 'Jihad Promise'"; Chulov, "Australian Terror in Our Midst."

57. Neighbour, "Militant Networks."

58. Ibid.

59. "Terror Suspect Admits Training with Brigitte"; Robinson, "Rocker Rolled to Jihad"; "Terror Accused to Stand Trial on 'Jihad Promise.'"

60. *Regina v. Mohamed Ali Elomar et al.*, February 15, 2010.

61. Ibid.; Jordan Baker, Ben Cubby, and Aaron Timms, "Remote Sites Used for Jihad Training," *The Age*, November 15, 2005.

62. Ibid.

63. Katie Bice, "AFL Grand Final Terror Plot," *The Herald-Sun*, April 16, 2008.

64. Ibid.

65. Ibid.

66. Hughes, "Lies, Bombs and Jihad."

67. Ibid.; "Australian Admits Plotting to Kill Thousands," AFP, July 28, 2009, http://www.google.com/hostednews/afp/article/ALeqM5iy7ec1S6djxSTgb7e7eFRSsswreA.

68. Stanley, "Australian Anti-Terror Raids."

69. Ibid.

70. *Regina v. Benbrika et al.*, February 13, 2008; Norrie Ross, "Terror Plot to Kill 1000, Court Told," *Herald Sun*, February 13, 2008.

71. Ross, "Terror Plot to Kill 1000, Court Told."

72. Cameron Stewart and Natalie O'Brien, "Blizzard of Chatter Set Alarms Ringing," *The Australian*, November 9, 2005.

73. *Regina v. Mohamed Ali Elomar et al.*, December 14–19, 2009; Simon Kearney and Natalie O'Brien, "Chemical Supplier in Tip-Off to Hotline," *The Australian*, November 10, 2005.

74. *Regina v. Mohamed Ali Elomar et al.*, December 14–19, 2009; Kearney and O'Brien, "Chemical Supplier in Tip-Off to Hotline."

75. *Regina v. Mohamed Ali Elomar et al.*, December 14–19, 2009; Kearney and O'Brien, "Chemical Supplier in Tip-Off to Hotline."

76. Bice, "AFL Grand Final Terror Plot."

Chapter 15

1. *Regina v. Zakaria Amara*, Agreed Statement of Facts.

2. Bell, *Cold Terror*, pp. 2, 16–17, 185, 223, 246.

3. Ibid.; "Teacher Witnessed Transformation of Bomb-Plot Suspects," CBC News, June 8, 2006, http://www.cbc.ca/story/canada/national/2006/06/08/amiruddin02062006.html.

4. Michelle Shephard and Isabel Teotonio, "Schoolkids to Terror Suspects," *Toronto Star*, June 5, 2006.

5. Ibid.

6. Isabel Teotonio and Jessica Leeder, "Jihadist Generation," *Toronto Star*, June 10, 2006.

7. Andrew Mcgregor, "The Dangerous Dreams of Toronto's Terrorists," *The Jamestown Foundation* 3, no. 2 (June 13, 2006).

8. Teotonio and Leeder, "Jihadist Generation."

9. Shephard and Teotonio, "Schoolkids to Terror Suspects."

10. Teotonio and Leeder, "Jihadist Generation"; Mcgregor, "The Dangerous Dreams of Toronto's Terrorists."

11. *Regina v. Zakaria Amara*, Agreed Statement of Facts.

12. *Regina v. Saad Gaya*, Agreed Statement of Facts.

13. Shephard and Teotonio, "Schoolkids to Terror Suspects"; *R. v. Zakaria Amara*, Agreed Statement of Facts.

14. Stewart Bell, "A Terror Suspect's Mentor," *National Post*, September 7, 2006; Teotonio and Leeder, "Jihadist Generation."

15. Greg McArthur, Omar El Akkad, and Joe Friesen, "The Friendly Zealot," *Globe and Mail*, June 6, 2006.

16. McArthur, El Akkad, and Friesen, "The Friendly Zealot."

17. Colin Freeze, "Terror Plot Finds Its End—Not with a Bang But a Whimper," *Globe and Mail*, November, 9, 2009.

18. Omar El Akkad and Greg McArthur, "Hateful Chatter Behind the Veil," *Globe and Mail*, June 29, 2006.

19. Doug Struck, "School Ties Link Alleged Plotters," *Washington Post*, June 11, 2006.

20. Stewart Bell, "The Path to Terror in Canada," *National Post*, September 2, 2006; Bell, *Cold Terror*, pp. 2, 16–17, 185, 223, 246.

21. *Regina v. Zakaria Amara*, Agreed Statement of Facts; Ontario Superior Court of Justice, Between Her Majesty the Queen—and—Saad Gaya, heard April 22 –25 and May 1, 2008.

22. Stewart Bell, "Anti-Terror Sweep: The Accused," *National Post*, September 5, 2006.

23. Shephard and Teotonio, "Schoolkids to Terror Suspects."

24. Bell, "Anti-Terror Sweep: The Accused."

25. Thomas Walkom, "Average Suburban Terrorist," *Toronto Star*, September 30, 2009; Ontario Superior Court of Justice, Between Her Majesty the Queen—and—Saad Gaya, heard April 22 –25 and May 1, 2008.

26. Bell, "Anti-Terror Sweep: The Accused."

27. Ibid; Megan O'Toole, "Toronto 18's Asad Ansari Sentenced to 6 Years and 5 Months . . . Goes Free," *National Post*, October 4, 2010, http://news.nationalpost.com/2010/10/04/toronto-18s-asad-ansari-sentenced-to-6-5-years-goes-free/.

28. Michelle Shephard, "How Internet Monitoring Sparked a CSIS Probe," *Toronto Star*, June 3, 2006.

29. Ibid.

30. El Akkad and McArthur, "Hateful Chatter Behind the Veil."

31. Ibid.

32. Ibid.

33. Ibid.

34. Bell, "The Path to Terror in Canada."

35. Ibid.

36. Ibid.

37. Ibid.

38. Bill Gillespie, "Convicted British Terrorist Had Links to Accused in Toronto 18 Case: U.K. Court Documents," CBC News, October 22, 2008.

39. Ibid.

40. Ibid.

41. Affidavit of FBI Special Agent Michael Scherck, United States District Court, Eastern District of New York, *U.S.A. v. Ehsanul Islam Sadequee*, March 28, 2006, http://nefafoundation.org/.

42. Ibid.

43. United States District Court for the Northern District of Georgia Atlanta Division, *U.S.A. v. Syed Haris Ahmed and Ehsanul Islam Sadequee*, July 19, 2006, http://nefafoundation.org/.

44. Ibid.

45. Struck, "School Ties Link Alleged Plotters"; *R. v. Saad Khalid*, Agreed Statement of Facts.

46. Isabel Teotonio, "Attack Was to Be Bigger than London Bombings, Expected Evidence Shows," *Toronto Star*, March 26, 2008; *Regina v. Zakaria Amara*, Agreed Statement of Facts.

47. *Regina v. Zakaria Amara*, Agreed Statement of Facts.

48. Ibid.

49. Joseph Brean, "We Weren't Just Out There Picking Daisies," *The National Post*, June 10, 2008; Melissa Leong, "Ontario Man Guilty of Taking Part in Terror Plot," Canwest News Service, September 25, 2008; *Regina v. Zakaria Amara*, Agreed Statement of Facts.

50. Thomas Walkom, "Crown's Linchpin Shakes Case," *Toronto Star*, June 25, 2008.

51. Teotonio, "Attack Was to Be Bigger than London Bombings."

52. *Regina v. Zakaria Amara*, Agreed Statement of Facts.

53. Struck, "School Ties Link Alleged Plotters."

54. *Regina v. Zakaria Amara*, Agreed Statement of Facts.

55. Struck, "School Ties Link Alleged Plotters."

56. "Among the Believers: Cracking the Toronto Cell," CBC, *The Fifth Estate*, http://www.cbc.ca/fifth/torontoterror/timeline.html.

57. *Regina v. Zakaria Amara*, Agreed Statement of Facts.

58. Ibid.; "Among the Believers."

59. Ibid.

60. Leong, "Ontario Man Guilty of Taking Part in Terror Plot."

61. Teotonio, "Attack Was to Be Bigger than London Bombings, Expected Evidence Shows."

62. *Regina v. Zakaria Amara*, Agreed Statement of Facts.

Chapter 16

1. "*Frontline*: Chasing the Sleeper Cell," PBS, http://www.pbs.org/wgbh/pages/frontline/shows/sleeper/inside/cron.html.

2. Dina Temple-Raston, *The Jihad Next Door* (New York: Perseus Books Group, 2007), pp. 195, 208–10.

3. "Yemen Puts Qaeda Operative Back in Jail," *International Herald Tribune*, May 19, 2008.

4. Temple-Raston, *The Jihad Next Door*, pp. 195, 208–10.

5. Ibid., pp. 14–17.

6. Ibid.; Matthew Purdy and Lowell Bergman, "Where the Trail Led: Between Evidence and Suspicion; Unclear Danger: Inside the Lackawanna Terror Case," *New York Times*, October 12, 2003; "*Frontline*: Chronology: The Lackawanna Investigation," PBS, October 16, 2003, http://www.pbs.org/wgbh/pages/frontline/shows/sleeper.inside.cron.html.

7. Temple-Raston, *The Jihad Next Door*, p. 44.

8. Ibid., pp. 31, 44.

9. Ibid., p. 44.

10. Ibid., pp. 31, 32, 36, 52.

11. Ibid., p. 44.

12. "*Frontline*: Chasing the Sleeper Cell."

13. Temple-Raston, *The Jihad Next Door*, pp. 32, 54–59.

14. Ibid., p. 32.

15. Ibid., pp. 32, 55.

16. Ibid., p. 87.

17. "*Frontline*: Chasing the Sleeper Cell."

18. Temple-Raston, *The Jihad Next Door*, p. 88.

19. "Buffalo Terror Suspect Admits al Qaeda Training," CNN.com, May 20, 2003; "*Frontline*: Chasing the Sleeper Cell."

20. "*Frontline*: Chasing the Sleeper Cell."

21. Temple-Raston, *The Jihad Next Door*, p. 43.

22. Ibid., p. 31.

23. "*Frontline*: Chasing the Sleeper Cell"; Temple-Raston, *The Jihad Next Door*, pp. 31–32, 36–37.

24. Temple-Raston, *The Jihad Next Door*, p. 46.

25. "*Frontline*: Chasing the Sleeper Cell"; Temple-Raston, *The Jihad Next Door*, pp. 27–29.

26. Temple-Raston, *The Jihad Next Door*, p. 45.

27. Ibid., p. 38.

28. Ibid., pp. 45–46.

29. Ibid., p. 45.

30. Ibid., pp. 4, 5, 6.

31. Combatant Status Review Board TO: Tribunal Member, Juma al Dosari, http://projects.nytimes.com/guantanamo/detainees/261-juma-mohammed-abdul-latif-al-dosari/documents/5.

32. "*Frontline*: Chasing the Sleeper Cell."

33. Ibid.

34. Temple-Raston, *The Jihad Next Door*, pp. 81–87.

35. "*Frontline*: Chasing the Sleeper Cell"; Temple-Raston, *The Jihad Next Door*, pp. 81–91.

36. Temple-Raston, *The Jihad Next Door*, p. 91.

37. "*Frontline*: Chasing the Sleeper Cell."

38. Conversation with author, October 13, 2010.

39. "*Frontline*: Chasing the Sleeper Cell"; Temple-Raston, *The Jihad Next Door*, pp. 110–11, 114–15.

40. "*Frontline*: Chasing the Sleeper Cell."

41. Ibid.

42. Temple-Raston, *The Jihad Next Door*, pp. 107–8.

43. Ibid., pp. 117–18.

44. Yasein Taher, New York State Intelligence Conference, October 13, 2010.

45. Ibid.; Temple-Raston, *The Jihad Next Door*, p. 122.

46. "*Frontline*: Chasing the Sleeper Cell."

47. Ibid.

48. Temple-Raston, *The Jihad Next Door*, p. 153.

49. Ibid., p. 187.

50. John J. Lumpkin, "CIA Can Kill Citizens Who Aid al-Qaida," Associated Press, December 4, 2002.

Conclusion

1. "Free Radical," *Time*, May 6, 2002, http://www.time.com/time/magazine/article/0,9171,221114,00.html#ixzz1CYtjA5HL.

2. Temple-Raston, *The Jihad Next Door*, pp. 31, 44.

3. Ibid., pp. 32, 55.

4. Ibid., p. 44.

5. *The 9/11 Commission Report*, pp. 160, 167–68.

6. *U.S. v. Badat*; Booth, "Gloucester Shoebomber Jailed for 13 Years."

7. *U.S. v. Reid*; Cullison, "Inside Al Qaeda's Hard Drive."

8. Verbatim Transcript of Combatant Status Review Tribunal Hearing for ISN 10024.

9. "Biographies of High Value Terrorist Detainees Transferred to the US Naval Base at Guantanamo Bay."

10. Woolwich Crown Court, *Regina v. Abdulla Ahmed Ali*, April 3, 2008; Milmo, "The Terrorists Who Changed Air Travel Forever."

11. Woolwich Crown Court, *Regina v. Abdulla Ahmed Ali*, June 3, 2008; Greenberg, Cruickshank, and Hansen, "Inside the Terror Plot That Rivaled 9/11."

12. Sentencing Hearing, Woolwich Crown Court, *Regina v. Abdulla Ahmed Ali*, September 14, 2009.

13. Department of Justice Press Release, "Najibullah Zazi Pleads Guilty."

14. Ibid.; Leppard, "Fixer for 21/7 Plot Free in London."

15. Astrup and Skjoldager: "Prosecutor: 22-Year-Old Knew Al-Qa'ida Leader."

16. Skjoldager and Thomsen: "Photographs Incriminate Terror Suspect."

17. Isherwood, "Guilty of Planning Terrorism."

18. *The 9/11 Commission Report*, pp. 165–66.

19. O'Neill and McGrory, *The Suicide Factory*, pp. 221–22; Honigsbaum and Dodd, "From Gloucester to Afghanistan."

20. Crown Court at Kingston Upon Thames, *Regina v. Mohammed Shakil, Wahid Ali and Sadeer Saleem*; Edwards, "July 7 Bomber's Video Farewell to His Daughter."

21. Department of Justice Press Release, "Najibullah Zazi Pleads Guilty."

22. Leppard, "Fixer for 21/7 Plot Free in London."

23. Mitchell Silber and Bhatt, *Radicalization in the West: The Homegrown Threat* (New York: New York City Police Department, 2007).

24. *The 9/11 Commission Report*, p. 234.

25. Temple-Raston, *The Jihad Next Door*, pp. 110–11, 114–15.

26. Bell, *Cold Terror*, pp. 164–65.

27. *USA, Appellee, v. Mohammed A. Salameh et al.*; *The 9/11 Commission Report*, p. 73.

28. Sageman, "Testimony Before Senate Foreign Relations Committee," Fall 2009.

29. "The 2008 Belgium Cell and FATA's Terrorist Pipeline," *CTC Sentinel*, April 2008.

30. Crown Court at Kingston Upon Thames, *Regina v. Mohammed Shakil, Wahid Ali and Sadeer Saleem*.

31. Woolwich Crown Court, *Regina v. Abdulla Ahmed Ali*, July 15, 2008; Greenberg, Cruickshank, and Hansen, "Inside the Terror Plot That Rivaled 9/11."

32. Woolwich Crown Court, *Regina v. Abdulla Ahmed Ali*, June 3, 2008; Greenberg, Cruickshank, and Hansen, "Inside the Terror Plot That Rivaled 9/11."

33. Department of Justice Press Release, "Najibullah Zazi Pleads Guilty."

34. "Muslim Convert Who Plotted Terror."

35. Central Criminal Court, Old Bailey, *Regina v. Omar Khyam et al.*, March 24, 2006.

36. Benschop, "Chronicle of a Political Murder Foretold."

37. Ibid.

38. Central Criminal Court, Old Bailey, *Regina v. Omar Khyam et al.*, March 24, 2006.

39. Ibid., March 15, 2007.

40. Verbatim Transcript of Combatant Status Review Tribunal Hearing for ISN 10024.

41. Central Criminal Court, Old Bailey, *Regina v. Omar Khyam et al.*, March 5, 2007.

42. Department of Justice Press Release, "Charges Unsealed Against Five Alleged Members of Al Qaeda Plot."

43. Stobart and Rotella, "Seven Britons Will Again Face Charges."

44. *The 9/11 Commission Report*, pp. 225, 244, 248, 249.

45. "Biographies of High Value Terrorist Detainees Transferred to the US Naval Base at Guantanamo Bay."

46. Jason Burke, "*Talking to the Enemy* by Scott Atran—Review," *The Observer*, October 24, 2010, http://www.guardian.co.uk/books/2010/oct/24/scott-atran-talking-to-the-enemy-review.

Index

Acknowledgments

THERE ARE A number of individuals and institutions that I feel it is important to acknowledge, who inspired, facilitated, and supported this project.

First, there are my current and former students from my Modern Urban Terrorism course at Columbia's School of International and Public Affairs whose enthusiasm, questions, and interest in this subject inspired me to take on this project. Through their inquiry I came to realize that there was no compendium of all of the most important al Qaeda plots, that analyzed them critically.

I need to acknowledge the institution of the New York City Police Department and Police Commissioner Kelly in particular. Without the unique creative and innovative environment of the NYPD, I would never have had the opportunity to grow professionally and reach the point where I could even consider and complete a work like this. Moreover, working this issue from the trenches has provided me with fantastic and unique insight that could not be obtained anywhere else. This platform is the product of Police Commissioner Kelly, who created the department's counterterrorism and intelligence programs and sent me to various locations around the world to learn about past plots, get the ground truth, and bring those findings back to New York in order to better inform our efforts to protect the city from another terrorist attack.

The findings from those trips informed the NYPD's 2007 report, "Radicalization in the West: The Homegrown Threat," and in many ways this project builds from the research that my colleagues and I conducted for that monograph. Issues and findings that were considered and concluded in that report have a direct linear relationship to the genesis of *The Al Qaeda Factor.* However, I should state clearly that the findings in this independent project are my own and do not represent the opinions of the New York City Police Department.

Dr. Marc Sageman has had a fundamental influence on my work ever since I read his groundbreaking work *Understanding Terror Networks.* He has been someone I have considered one of the pre-eminent experts on al Qaeda associated terrorism and its genesis. Over the years, Marc has been a mentor to me, as well as a coworker (serving as the NYPD's Scholar in Residence), a coprofessor at Columbia's School for International and Public Affairs, and, probably most importantly, my toughest critic, challenging and pushing me to search more deeply and evolve my thinking on this subject. Marc has also become a friend in the process.

I am also indebted to Brian Michael Jenkins, a true luminary in the world of terrorism analysis. Based on his relationship with the NYPD, Brian has served as a mentor, guide, and sounding board for me since 2006 and helped evolve and broaden my thinking on this subject through his review and discussion of emerging issues in the field.

Another individual consistently encouraging my efforts has been Alain Bauer, Criminologist at the Sorbonne University in Paris.

Lastly, and probably most importantly, I need to acknowledge my wife Beth because without her support this project would have been impossible. She encouraged my work on this project when I was not at my day job—on weekends, on vacation, and while I sat on the floor in the kids' bedrooms as they went to sleep most nights. I am totally indebted to her for her support and wise counsel along the way.

Finally, as I have mentioned, although I am employed at the NYPD, writing this book was an extracurricular activity. I take complete responsibility for this project and its findings.